Building Online Communities with phpBB 2

Stoyan Stefanov

Jeremy Rogers

Mike Lothar

PACKT PUBLISHING

BIRMINGHAM MUMBAI

Building Online Communities with phpBB 2

First edition: May 2005

Published by Packt Publishing Ltd.
32 Lincoln Road
Olton
Birmingham, B27 6PA, UK.

ISBN 1-904811-13-2

www.packtpub.com

Cover Design by www.visionwt.com

Credits

Author
Stoyan Stefanov
Jeremy Rogers
Mike Lothar

Technical Reviewers
Stefan Koopmanschap
Patrick O'Keefe

Layout
Niranjan Jahagirdar

Indexer
Niranjan Jahagirdar

Commissioning Editor
Douglas Paterson

Technical Editors
Paramita Chakrabarti
Niranjan Jahagirdar

Proofreader
Chris Smith

Cover Designer
Helen Wood

Foreword

phpBB is probably the most widely used Internet community software in the world. Some reasons are obvious, some not so. It's free and very flexible. It has a solid community filled with dedicated individuals behind it. It has a dedicated development team, with constant development of new versions, patches for existing versions, and more. It is also a quality script—a good product. These things, and more, have made phpBB the immensely popular script that it is.

If you invest the time, this book can be your guide to making phpBB do what you want it to. You will learn how to install and configure the script, use all of the standard features and functions, customize the look and feel, install hacks, create hacks, program in phpBB, and much more. This is accomplished through detailed explanations, step-by-step guides, and visual examples.

With it's good and it's bad, the phpBB community is, overall, a good place. It is very large and very international. There are not many people that have had as much first-hand experience with the phpBB community as I have. I started phpBBHacks.com in early April of 2001. Since then, we've grown to become a major part of the phpBB community—the largest source of phpBB-related downloads, with a friendly and thriving support community and the constant goal of being the ultimate phpBB resource.

Given my position, I have had the opportunity to interact with many individuals within the community from all parts of the world, including phpBB developers, prominent hack and template authors, and phpBB users just looking for some quick help.

What is the number one reason that the community is as good as I say it is? For me, it is because of the selfless individuals who exist within it. One of those, Jeremy Rogers, is a co-author of this book. Besides being a good friend of mine, Jeremy is on my Support Team at phpBBHacks.com and has helped literally tens of thousands of users through his work at the site.

This book goes hand in hand with the community. There is only so much that it can help you with. It is a plentiful resource, but there is a limit to any book as your problems become more individual and personal and less generic in nature—so it wisely references the phpBB community throughout. If you take a serious interest in phpBB and use phpBB, you are a member of the phpBB community, too.

Welcome.

Patrick O'Keefe
Administrator/Webmaster—phpBBHacks.com

About the Authors

Stoyan Stefanov is a web developer and a project manager from Montreal, Canada. He has studied in the Technical University of Sofia, Bulgaria, and McGill University, Montreal. He is a Zend Certified Engineer, with more than five years of professional web-development experience and has worked on award-winning websites for companies of all sizes—from multinational corporations to two-man startups.

He volunteers his spare time administering and programming a Bulgarian-speaking phpBB-powered online community, and contributing to the PHP community through code and articles.

Jeremy Rogers has been developing web-based applications in PHP and other languages for a little more than six years. Shortly after discovering phpBB in early 2002 and deploying it on a video-game website, he began tinkering with and learning about the internal workings of the software. Since then, he has authored dozens of expansions and tutorials related to phpBB. Jeremy currently serves the phpBB community as a phpBBHacks.com Support Team member, a capacity in which he has answered thousands of questions regarding the software, its applications, and related topics.

I would like to thank Patrick O'Keefe, for opening the doors to a wide world that led me here.

Mike Lothar has been around as a web designer for several years, both as a freelance artist working for some of the major Danish advertising companies, and as a co-founder of an independent web company. His interest in phpBB and its templates came fairly late. At the time of this book's release, his templates had gained a wide recognition, used by a variety of sites ranging from those of US presidential candidates to those of artists and bands. Mike supports modification and personalization of phpBB skins at his community forum, `http://www.mikelothar.com`.

Table of Contents

Introduction

phpBB is a free, open-source Internet community application, with outstanding discussion forums and membership management. Written in the PHP scripting language, and making use of the popular MySQL database, phpBB is a standard among web-hosting companies throughout the world, and is one of the most widely used bulletin-board packages in the world. phpBB short-circuits the need for you to be a web development master in order to create and manage massive online communities.

This book takes you through setting up and running your own phpBB-powered online community. In easy to follow language and with clear instructions, you will learn how to install your own system, tackle basic forum administration tasks, and customize the forum. After that, you will learn advanced administration and customization techniques, followed by information for extending phpBB programmatically.

What This Book Covers

The book starts with an overview of phpBB and online communities. *Chapter 1* also gives some background information to phpBB, and gives you an idea of what you can achieve with phpBB with some real-life examples of phpBB-powered communities.

Chapter 2 walks you through a full installation of phpBB, including the necessary preparation work and post-installation tasks. It also looks at configuring the installation, and troubleshooting tips to get you started with your new forum and online community as quickly as possible.

After you are set up and running, *Chapter 3* dives straight into the phpBB environment, familiarizing you with the basics of configuring your site, creating forums and users, and introducing you to the basics of phpBB administration. In order to fully understand the different features and their administration, the chapter starts with a tour of phpBB from the user and administrator points of view.

Chapter 4 looks at some more ways to customize your forum's appearance and features. Making these customizations is essential to giving your community a unique identity that makes it stand out among other online forums. The appearance of a forum is mainly controlled by phpBB's styling system, which manages the colors, images, and visual layout of the forum. In this chapter, you will learn about the basics of a phpBB 2.0 style, adding and removing styles, fixing common style installation problems, customizing styles, and adding new features, including "modifications", to the forum.

Chapter 5 completes your mastery of phpBB administration. You will learn about making your board multi-lingual, configuring avatars, managing smilies, forum, user, and group permissions, as well as the human side of forum administration—moderation, flamewars, and banning.

To give your forum a truly unique look, you will probably want to create your own template. Creating your own template can be a very interesting process, but can also be quite time consuming. *Chapter 6* takes you through this process, from designing a new template to realizing that design to create a new look for a forum. Starting with a rough sketch on paper, we move through all the steps until we have a finished template.

As your community grows, you may find that you need to expand the capabilities of your forum. Eventually you may need a feature and find yourself unable to locate an existing modification for it! *Chapter 7* shows you how to create a new modification (also known as a hack) for yourself, to help you get that extra feature you are so missing. In this chapter, you will start off by learning what modifications are, and the skills and tools needed to create a modification. After that, we create a simple modification, and show you how to make the modification available to other phpBB users.

Chapter 8 rounds things off with a look at what you need to know in order to program new, custom phpBB features. The chapter starts with a simple phpBB script, before moving on to working with the phpBB database, using phpBB messages and multiple languages, working with the template engine and authenticating users. We build a new phpBB extension at the end of the chapter, consolidating your phpBB programming knowledge.

There are also four appendices, covering the phpBB file and directory structure, phpBB resources, permission cheatsheets, and a guide to the phpBB database structure.

What You Need for Using This Book

To get the most from this book you will need administrative access to a working installation of phpBB—*Chapter 2* takes you through this.

Conventions

In this book, you will find a number of styles of text that distinguish between different kinds of information. Here are some examples of these styles, and an explanation of their meaning.

There are three styles for code. Code words in text are shown as follows: "To illustrate the difference, you can `print_r()` the results of both functions".

A block of code will be set as follows:

```
define('IN_PHPBB', true);
$phpbb_root_path = './';
include($phpbb_root_path . 'extension.inc');
include($phpbb_root_path . 'common.'.$phpEx);
```

When we wish to draw your attention to a particular part of a code block, the relevant lines or items will be made bold:

```
define('IN_PHPBB', true);
$phpbb_root_path = './';
include($phpbb_root_path . 'extension.inc');
include($phpbb_root_path . 'common.'.$phpEx);
```

New terms and **important words** are introduced in a bold-type font. Words that you see on the screen, in menus or dialog boxes for example, appear in our text like this: "clicking the Next button moves you to the next screen".

> Tips, suggestions, or important notes appear in a box like this.

Any command-line input and output is written as follows:

```
>\. mydump.sql
   Query OK, 1 row affected (0.00 sec)
```

Reader Feedback

Feedback from our readers is always welcome. Let us know what you think about this book, what you liked or may have disliked. Reader feedback is important for us to develop titles that you really get the most out of.

To send us general feedback, simply drop an e-mail to `feedback@packtpub.com`, making sure to mention the book title in the subject of your message.

If there is a book that you need and would like to see us publish, please send us a note in the SUGGEST A TITLE form on `www.packtpub.com` or e-mail `suggest@packtpub.com`.

If there is a topic that you have expertise in and you are interested in either writing or contributing to a book, see our author guide on `www.packtpub.com/authors`.

Customer Support

Now that you are the proud owner of a Packt book, we have a number of things to help you to get the most from your purchase.

Downloading the Example Code for the Book

Visit `http://www.packtpub.com/support`, and select this book from the list of titles to download any example code or extra resources for this book. The files available for download will then be displayed.

> The downloadable files contain instructions on how to use them.

Errata

Although we have taken every care to ensure the accuracy of our contents, mistakes do happen. If you find a mistake in one of our books—maybe a mistake in text or code—we would be grateful if you would report this to us. By doing this you can save other readers from frustration, and also help to improve subsequent versions of this book.

If you find any errata, report them by visiting `http://www.packtpub.com/support`, selecting your book, clicking on the **Submit Errata** link, and entering the details of your errata. Once your errata have been verified, your submission will be accepted and the errata added to the list of existing errata. The existing errata can be viewed by selecting your title from `http://www.packtpub.com/support`.

Questions

You can contact us at `questions@packtpub.com` if you are having a problem with some aspect of the book, and we will do our best to address it.

1

Introduction to phpBB

An online bulletin board in essence is an Internet-enabled version of the bulletin boards found in stores and other public areas. It's basically just a place where people leave messages for others to read. Well, the online bulletin board applications have become much more powerful and sophisticated than that, but the general principle is the same. phpBB is one of the most popular free software that implement the bulletin board idea on the Web today.

In the first chapter of this phpBB book, you will learn about:

- Online communities
- phpBB history
- phpBB development and where it's heading
- What can be achieved with phpBB, and examples of existing phpBB sites

Online Communities

An online community is a group of people that gather together on a website for some reason. This reason can be any subject of interest common to the group, like occupation, hobby, passion, or location. Such online communities are very popular, and their popularity is growing as more and more people start surfing the Web. Think about it—everyone has something he or she is passionate about. And everybody likes meeting people who share their interests. Historically, such computer-based communities existed even before the Internet; using, for example, the modem-to-modem based bulletin board systems (BBS).

An essential part of being in a community is sharing and contributing (for example, commenting on a subject or pointing out topics of interest for the group). This way the site visitors are no longer just looking at a website that is set in stone. They are changing its face by contributing content. Today, the ability to post comments on the websites we visit has become so common that we almost expect it to be there.

Static, brochure-like sites are becoming outdated. Communities rule the Web. This is good news for both site owners and site visitors. Sites are built to be visited and used by people and at the same time, the people are taking part in building the sites they visit. Site owners can get immediate feedback on what their visitors like or dislike, and visitors get new and fresh content on every visit. It's quite common these days that the community would not just *influence* a site owner's decisions, but even *make* the decisions through polls or open discussions. So it's not an exaggeration to say that more often than not, the success or the failure of a website is determined by the success or the failure in building an online community around the website. At the end of the day, a site is build to be used by the people and the people have the final say if this site is worth something or not.

Building the Community—The Tools

In order to set up the place where your online community will meet, you need tools. You can invest your efforts into creating the tools yourself—assuming of course that you have expertise in web programming, server administration, and so on—or you can decide not to reinvent the wheel and can adopt a solution. That's where phpBB comes in.

There are different sorts of community-building tools out there. They can be as simple as a guestbook, or more complicated like chat systems, web logs (blogs), or mailing lists. Or they can be forums, also known as bulletin boards. The forum systems inherited and extended the bulletin board systems (BBS) from the dark pre-Internet ages, adding a web browser interface to them. phpBB belongs to the family of forum tools for building an online community.

The Name

The name consists of two parts—"PHP" and "BB". PHP is the programming language in which the software is written, and "BB" stands for "bulletin board"; it's a bulletin board tool written in the PHP programming language.

PHP is also an abbreviation and it stands, or at least used to stand, for Personal Home Page. PHP is no longer just a set of personal home page tools as it was in the beginning, but has grown to become a true programming language. Its abbreviation has gone one level deeper, and now recursively stands for "PHP Hypertext Preprocessor". But it's really known simply as PHP.

The Environment

In technical terms, here's what you need in order to use phpBB:

- The programming code to be executed
- A database to store information
- Web-server software, since this is a web application
- A computer to run all this!

As you already know, phpBB is coded using the **PHP** server-side programming language. Additionally in order to run, phpBB needs a database. That's where all discussions' data is stored. There are different database systems out there that phpBB can work with, but the most popular and most commonly used in today's PHP applications is **MySQL**. Finally, phpBB needs a web server and a computer running an operating system. phpBB can run on different operating systems and web servers, but it's mostly used on a **Linux** platform with the **Apache** web server.

Using the web developers' lingo, you might say that phpBB is mostly used in LAMP environments, where LAMP is an abbreviation for Linux, Apache, MySQL, and PHP. One important thing about the LAMP environment is that its components are free and open source. In practice "free and open-source" means:

- You can use the software without paying for software licenses.
- The programming code of the software is available to you if you want to modify it to better suit your needs.

Another good thing about phpBB is that it has very low requirements for the hosting server. Due to the fact that the phpBB environment consists of free software products, you can find a good and quite inexpensive hosting provider very easily. Just searching Google for "phpbb hosting" yields about a million results.

Why phpBB?

Why should you pick phpBB from all the options you have to choose from? Well, since you're reading this book, chances are you've already made up your mind, so let me just give you a few hints about how to deal with this fellow webmaster friend of yours that's running vBulletin, Phorum, or another type of system.

- phpBB is free. And it seems like it's going to stay this way. There have already been offers from companies to buy phpBB, but those were refused.

- phpBB is one of the most popular forum software. All those webmasters out there cannot be wrong. Continued usage of phpBB to power their web communities is their best testimonial.
- People know phpBB. Being so popular, it's very likely that your visitors have seen and used it already. They don't have to learn an entirely new system, and can start posting at once, feeling comfortable in a known environment.
- phpBB is mature. It has been around for more than four years of active and heavy use, which in Internet terms is a pretty long period.
- phpBB is feature rich and is open for custom feature additions. You can code your own custom features or you can use one or more of the numerous phpBB add-ons, also known as MODs or hacks, contributed by the community of phpBB users.
- phpBB's looks are customizable. You can easily change fonts and colors. You can even change the layout or use an existing layout contributed by other phpBB users.

History

James Atkinson is the creator of the software. He's the first developer and now the project manager of the phpBB project. Like a lot of other open-source projects, phpBB started as a personal project. James wanted to set up a discussion forum on his wife's site. At this time, he had two options: using a commercial package like the pioneer UBB (Ultimate Bulletin Board, written in Perl) or using the free solution named Phorum, which was written in PHP, but had a thread style James didn't like very much. So he decided to go on his own and create a UBB-like PHP-based bulletin board system.

phpBB was "born" on July 1st, 2000, at 06:45 PM. We know the exact date and time, because that's when James posted a message on an Internet forum saying that he had created a bulletin board and would like some help with the testing. A few weeks later he opened up the source code for the project, making it free and available for everyone who wanted to join in and contribute to the development.

Other enthusiasts joined, and on December 16th, 2000, the first official phpBB was released—phpBB version 1.0. After this, the release-feature requests-development-testing-release wheel started spinning for the phpBB team.

phpBB became really popular after version 2.0 was released on April 4th, 2002. This version was a complete rewrite of the source code, because the software had become much more feature rich than originally expected, and the old codebase just couldn't accommodate the new development. The interface was also completely revamped.

Development

phpBB is an open-source project and has some specifics as such:

- The developers are **volunteers** from around the world. phpBB is an example of a successful open-source project. It has an impressive team list of about 50 people, when most open-source projects have two or three.
- There's a **community** of users who often convert into collaborators.

You might be wondering how the community and the open-source nature of phpBB can help its development. There are a lot of ways, but just to name the major ones:

- Using and thus testing the software
- Reporting bugs so they can be fixed by the developers
- Contributing new features through MODs and hacks, and in this way extending the functionality
- Contributing new templates for the other phpBB admins to use
- Supporting other phpBB users with tips and advice
- Advocating and promoting phpBB, in this way increasing the size of the community

phpBB is under constant development. The work for the next version 3 is well underway, and in the spirit of this open-source project, the work in progress is available for preview and comments as it's developed.

Example phpBB Sites

One of the great things about phpBB is that it's highly customizable and extendable both in terms of functionality and looks. This means that:

- You can use your preferred color scheme, fonts, and overall layout.
- You can modify phpBB and develop your own feature extensions, or you can use existing modifications.

In this section, you will find a few real-life examples of how phpBB is used to power online community sites.

A Standard phpBB Layout

Let's start with an example of an out-of-the-box solution that uses the default phpBB style and the default set of features. On this example site, even the phpBB logo is left intact. This is the site of Distributed Proofreaders (`http://www.pgdp.net/phpBB2/`), a site that uses phpBB to provide a web-based method of easing the proofreading work associated with the digitization of public-domain books into Project Gutenberg e-books. By breaking the work into individual pages, many proofreaders can be working on the same book at the same time.

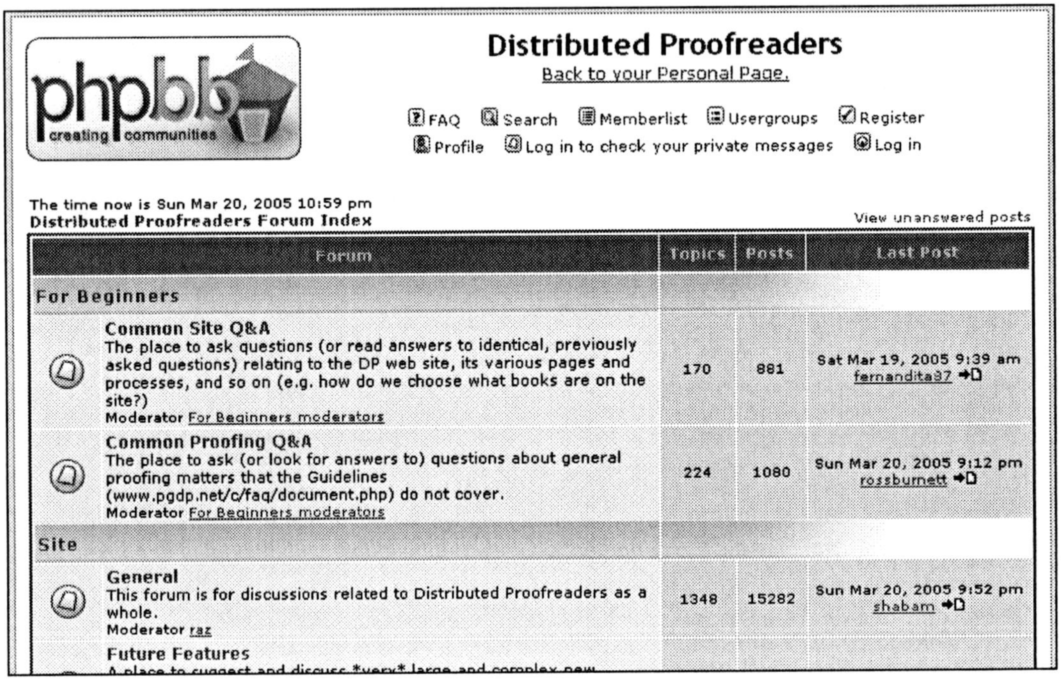

Standard Sites with Different Templates

The next examples are phpBB installations with the default feature set, but with different styles. You have a lot of options when it comes to the presentation of your board.

Instead of going with the default phpBB looks, you can find a pre-made template that better suits your needs and layout/color preferences. Or, if you can't find a template you'd like to use and you know some HTML, you can even create your own custom templates. Here are some sites that use templates different than the default one.

Mike Lothar: The personal site of one of the authors of this book (`http://community.mikelothar.com/`). His chapter (Chapter 6) guides you through the process of creating your own custom templates:

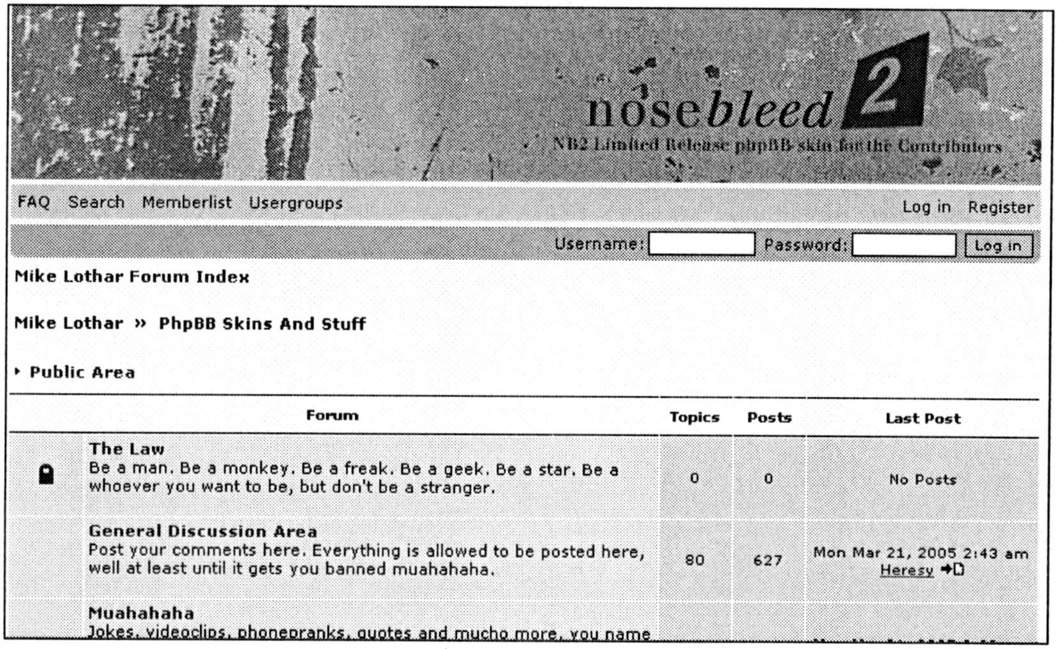

Keenspot: A bulletin board for discussing comic books (`http://forums.keenspot.com/`):

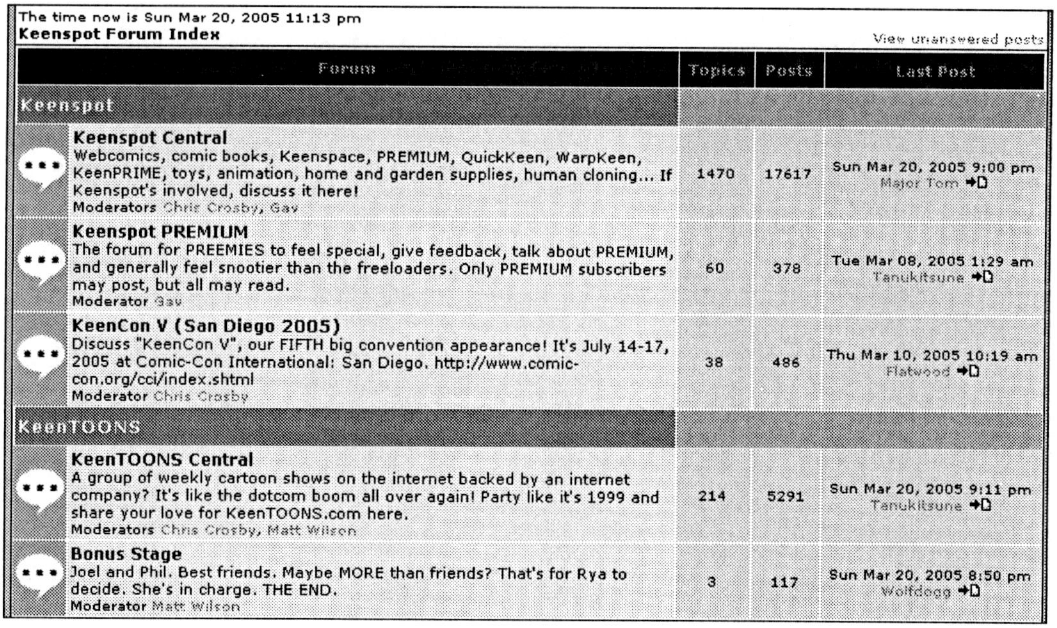

ForumPlasma: A gaming community (`http://www.forumplasma.com/`):

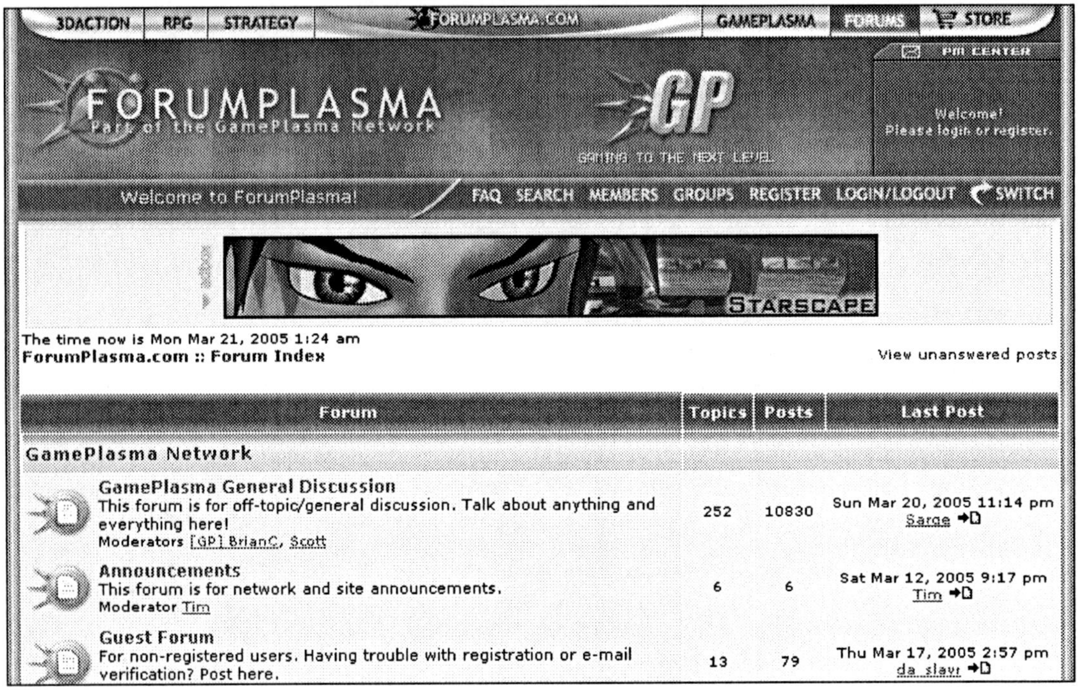

Sites with Standard Style and Modified Features

Some sites opt in for the default phpBB style, but introduce new features. These new features are often called modifications (MODs) or hacks.

You can find lots of pre-made MODs available for free download, and you can use them to enhance your board.

Dogomania forums: A community of dog owners. The site differs from the standard phpBB installation with its custom header, footer, and navigation (`http://forum.dogomania.com/`):

Chinese language and culture forums: Header and footer are modified to place advertising; a number of other modifications are introduced. The site also features RSS feeds and WAP and PDA views to the forums (`http://www.chinese-forums.com/`):

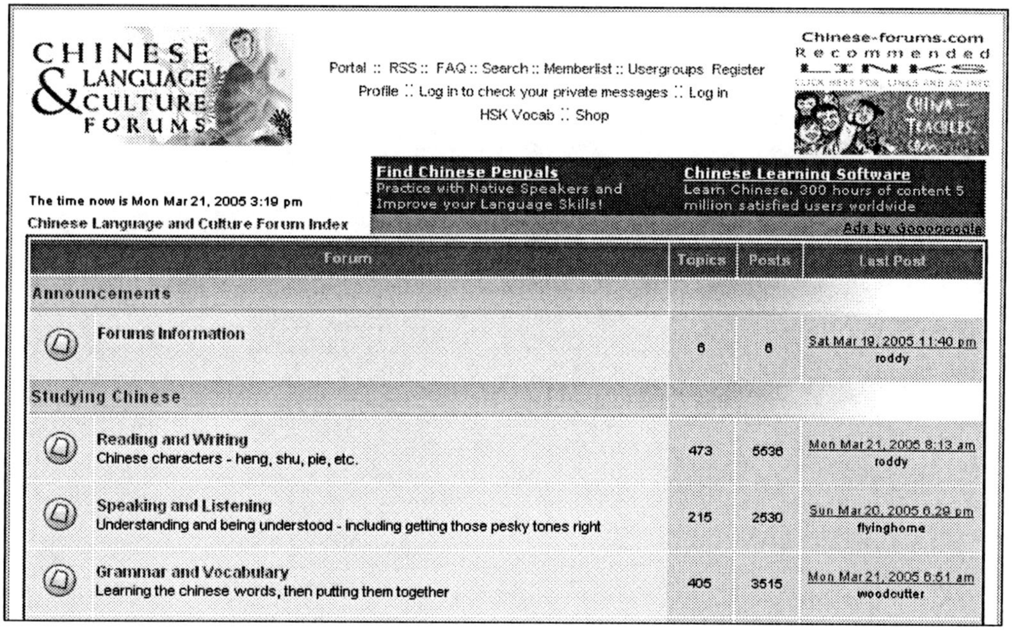

Modified phpBB Installations with Custom Templates

Designers Realm: A community of designers of all flavors—web, graphic, print, etc. The site has a custom layout and is heavily modified from the base phpBB installation (`http://www.designersrealm.com/`):

Jaredwsmith's forum: A very nice custom layout, custom header, footer, navigation, and a number of modifications installed (`http://www.jaredwsmith.com/forums`):

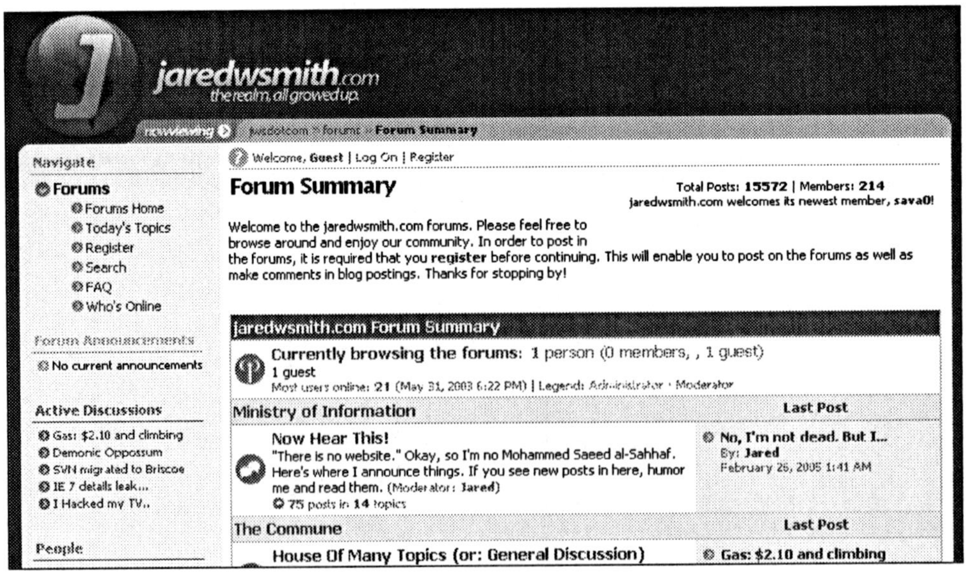

GaiaOnline

GaiaOnline is the ultimate phpBB bulletin board. The template for this site is custom, and quite a few features, customizations, and optimizations are introduced. With about 200 million posts and 1.5 million registered users, this is the biggest bulletin board on the Internet (`http://www.gaiaonline.com`):

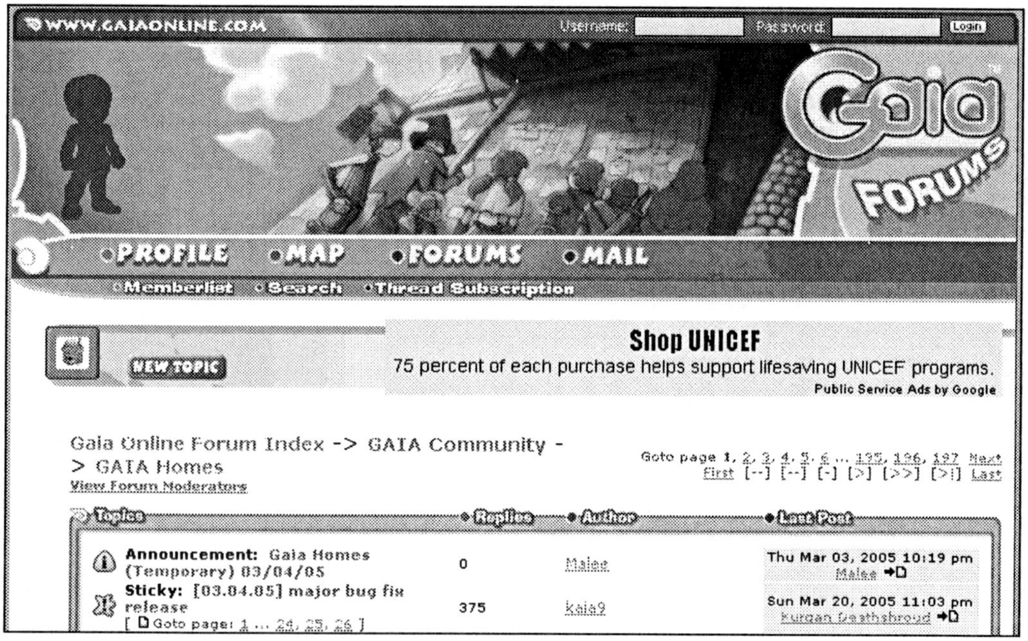

Summary

This chapter familiarized you with the phpBB solution and the problem it solves. You've learned about its history and development. You also saw a number of existing phpBB-powered community websites that can give you a hint about what you could achieve with the software. You're now ready to learn about the installation, configuration, and customization of a phpBB board. Very soon, as soon as the end of the next chapter, you'll be able to start your own community site. Let's take the trip to the world of phpBB.

2

Installing and Configuring phpBB

Now that you have a general idea of what phpBB is, it is time to install it on your server or your personal computer and to start using it. The installation process is generally not hard—phpBB has a built-in browser-based installer that makes the job much easier—but there are some pre-requisites and some details you need to be aware of before you begin. There are also some post-installation tasks that you need to perform once phpBB is installed on your system. In this second chapter of the book you will learn:

- What are the pre-requisites before you install phpBB
- How to download and install phpBB
- The basic post-installation tasks, along with some security tips
- Where and how to look for help when in trouble

Pre-Installation

In this section you'll find out about the phpBB server requirements, which are on the lower end (price-wise) of the server configurations offered by hosting providers. Then the section discusses some database-related topics and ends with a checklist you can use to make sure you have everything you need to start the installation process.

Requirements

phpBB is very flexible in terms of server requirements and you have a lot of options. But let's concentrate on the configuration that is most widely used, consisting of:

- Any major operating system
- Apache web server

- MySQL database system, version 3.22 or higher
- PHP version 4. PHP3 will also do, but it's recommended that you use the latest stable 4.3 version

phpBB was designed with portability in mind, so all of the requirements listed above are very flexible. Let's look at them in more detail and also see what options do you have.

- **The operating system (OS)**: phpBB is OS independent. That means it can run on all sorts of operating systems—Windows, Linux, MacOS. You should not have any problem meeting this requirement and can enjoy running your forums in your preferred or most affordable environment.
- **The web server**: phpBB can run on various web servers, including the most popular Apache and Microsoft's Internet Information Systems (IIS). If you're using a hosting service, the web server requirement won't be in the way. But if you want to install phpBB on your computer, you'll have to take care of this detail. Although describing how to install a web server is not within the scope of this book, you'll find some useful information further down.
- **The database system**: Currently supported by phpBB are MySQL 3.22 or higher (including MySQL 4.x), PostgreSQL 7.0.3, MS SQL Server (7 or 2000, directly or via ODBC) and MS Access (2000 or XP) via ODBC. Again, depending if you're installing phpBB locally or on a remote server, you'll need to either install a supported database system on your computer or simply ask you service provider what database you have access to.
- **PHP**: In general, all PHP applications consist of files containing programming instructions that are executed by what is called a PHP interpreter. The PHP interpreter is a piece of software that you'll need to have running on the system where you want to install phpBB. If you go with a hosting service, the good news is that PHP is so popular that it would be actually harder to find a host that doesn't support it.

  PHP 4.x is the most widely used PHP version and also the most widely used for phpBB installations. As already mentioned, PHP 3.x will be sufficient to have your board running, but it's not recommended. PHP 5 is also not recommended (yet), because phpBB is not thoroughly tested on this platform, due to the fact that phpBB was developed prior to the release of PHP 5.

> phpBB will run on PHP versions 3.x and 4.x, but if you have a choice, you should aim at the latest stable PHP 4.3.x version.

The Attack Plan

Now that you're clear on the requirements, let's explore the options for the system to install phpBB to:

- **You have an existing web hosting service**: In this case all you need to do is contact your hosting provider and ask them if they support PHP and any of the databases listed above, preferably MySQL. If they don't, find out if they can install/enable these for you. If they still can't help you, you'll need to pick one of the remaining options.
- **You're shopping around for a good hosting provider**: The good news is that even the most inexpensive hosting packages often include PHP and MySQL support. There are lots of points to consider when choosing a hosting provider, but at the very least, browse for some independent reviews on the Web. Don't just rush into the cheapest package with huge or even unlimited bandwidth and disk space. Ask your host-to-be a question or two (for example concerning the requirements above) and judge the speed and the quality of their response. You'd want a reliable support when in need.
- **You want to install phpBB on your own computer**: Sometimes, even if you go with one of the first two options, you might still want to test your board locally. For example, if later on you want to experiment with installing or creating new styles or modifications, it would probably be easier (and definitely safer) to develop and test on your own computer before going live.

If you want to set up the environment on your computer, you have two options: to install all the necessary components one by one, configure them, and make them work together, or to use one of the all-in-one installations (bundles) you can find on the Internet. They usually include one downloadable installer program that takes care of installing and configuring all you need—Apache, PHP, MySQL—and often more. Such all-in-one bundles are XAMPP (`http://www.apachefriends.org/en/`) and others that are listed at HotScripts, for example (`http://www.hotscripts.com/PHP/Software_and_Servers/Installation_Kits/`).

If you want to set up your environment yourself and not make use of the bundles available out there, here's what you need to do.

Time For Action - Setting Up the Environment on Your Local Computer

1. Install the Apache web server.

> Go to `http://httpd.apache.org/download.cgi`. Download the latest stable 1.3.x version of the server for your operating system from the mirror closest to you. Install it, and if in doubt, refer to the documentation at `http://httpd.apache.org/docs/`.

2. Install PHP.

> Download the latest stable 4.3.x. release for your operating system from `http://www.php.net/downloads.php`. Install, referring to the documentation (`http://www.php.net/manual/en/install.php`) as necessary.

3. Install MySQL.

> Download the latest recommended version from `http://dev.mysql.com/downloads/`. The documentation is just a click away at `http://dev.mysql.com/doc/mysql/en/Installing.html`.

4. Install phpMyAdmin (optional).

> phpMyAdmin is a free and a very popular web application for managing MySQL databases through a simple and intuitive browser interface. You don't need it absolutely, but it can make your life a whole lot easier when it comes to database operations. It requires PHP but you've already installed it anyway, so you're all set. The latest stable version can be downloaded from `http://www.phpmyadmin.net/`.

While you were downloading, you've probably noticed the suggestions to download "source" or "binaries". Download the binaries, but if you're really curious about what the behind-the-scenes code looks like, download the source files, play around with them and try compiling them yourself. This, of course, will require some knowledge in C programming. All this source code is free for use, learning, and modifications. Welcome to the wonderful world of open-source software!

Now with a web server running PHP and MySQL (or another database system), let's take a look at some database preparation work.

Finishing Pre-Install Touch—The Database

phpBB will need access to a database, so you'll have to use an existing database or create a new one. Depending on whether you'll be installing on your local computer or on a remote server, you'll have different options for setting up the database required by phpBB; we'll take a look at those options. If you have a choice, use a new empty database for phpBB; it makes maintenance easier.

Setting Up the Database for Local Installations

If you're installing phpBB on your personal computer, you should have no restrictions creating a new database to use with phpBB. You can do that by using phpMyAdmin or using the console (the command prompt). With phpMyAdmin, creating a new database is really easy; this is one of the first options you're presented with when you load the application. If you don't have phpMyAdmin installed, you can use the command prompt to create a new database. Let's see how to do it both ways. For the purposes the examples in this chapter, let's say your new database is named "forums".

Time For Action—Creating the Forum Database with phpMyAdmin

1. Go to your main phpMyAdmin page.
2. Enter the text forums into the Create new database field.
3. Click the Create button.

What Just Happened

You've created a new database. In the database dropdown that you see in your phpMyAdmin on the left, you will now find a new option—the "forums" database that you've just created.

Time For Action—Creating the Forum Database Using the Command Prompt

1. Access your command prompt. (Windows users, click Start, then Run, and then type cmd).
2. In the command prompt (console window), follow the path to where MySQL is installed using `cd directory_name` to enter a directory (`cd` as in "change directory") and `cd ..` to go back (one level up), if you've mistakenly entered a wrong directory.
3. Once you are in the directory where MySQL is installed, go to the `bin` directory where you'll find several MySQL executables.
4. Type `mysql -u root -p`.

> This instruction means "connect to MySQL using the username `root` and ask me for a password". `root` is the default username when MySQL is installed. If you have created other MySQL user accounts, you can use one of them.

5. When prompted to provide a password, hit *Enter* (*Return* on Macs). What this means is you give a blank password. Username `root` with a blank password is the default MySQL account. If you have changed this password, type it in.

6. You'll see a welcome message and the `mysql` prompt if you've successfully connected. Type `CREATE DATABASE forums;` and hit *Enter*. Do *not* forget the semicolon at the end.
7. If you want to verify that the database has been created, type `SHOW DATABASES;` and hit *Enter*. You should see your newly created database in the list.
8. That's it. Type `exit`, hit *Enter* and MySQL will politely say `Bye` to you.
9. Type `exit` again to close your command prompt.

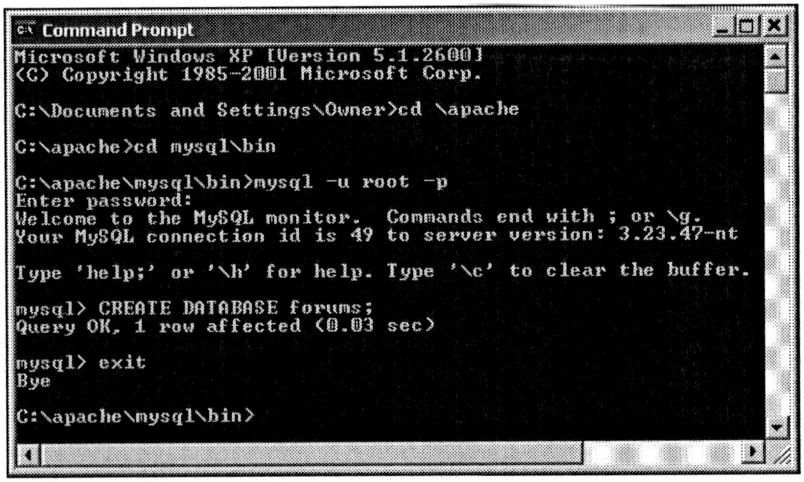

Setting Up the Database for Remote Installations

In this case the process may vary considerably depending on your specific hosting package and its limitations. Some possible scenarios include:

- Some hosts give you one database only with a predefined name. Find out what that name is; this is the database you'll be using.
- Some hosts let you create your database(s) with phpMyAdmin installed on their server.
- Some give you a different web interface for creating a database as part of the hosting package's control panel.
- Some can give you shell access to their server. Shell access means you'll be able to use a command prompt and execute instructions (commands) on the remote server. In this case, find out from your hosting provider how to establish a shell connection to your server. After you're connected, repeat the steps for creating a database using the command prompt as previously described. This time you'll be using the database username and password given to you by your host.

In order to establish a shell connection you'll need a program, called a **shell client**. A popular choice is the free PuTTY telnet and SSH client (`http://www.chiark.greenend.org.uk/~sgtatham/putty/`).

Security tip: If at all possible on your host, create a new MySQL user account, give it only privileges to the new database you've just created and use it for the phpBB installation. This may seem a bit too paranoid, but the reason is that usually hosts give you one username and password only and it's good for everything—FTP, MySQL, control panel, and shell access. So the reason behind creating a new MySQL username/password combo is that if it gets revealed for some reason, the villain who has it can do only limited damage. This password is good for one database only and not FTP, shell, or control panel access.

When creating this new database user account, it's a good idea to assign only "select", "insert", "update", and "delete" privileges; the other possible privileges are not needed for the normal functioning of phpBB. The phpBB installation though will also require a "create" privilege and some modification installations might need "alter" or "drop" privileges. So the most security-oriented option would be to assign "select", "insert", "update", "delete", and "create" privileges to the new database user, and once the installation is completed, remove the "create" privilege.

The actual process of creating the new database user may vary, depending on your hosting provider's policies. Some might not allow it, some might give you a special interface for it, and some might give you access to phpMyAdmin. Creating a new MySQL user account using phpMyAdmin is pretty straightforward; just click the Users link on the phpMyAdmin main page and then fill out the Add form.

If you're using the command prompt for creating a new user, use the following query:

```
GRANT SELECT,INSERT,UPDATE,DELETE,CREATE
 ON forums.*
 TO 'mysecretusername'@'localhost'
 IDENTIFIED BY 'mysecretpassword';
```

In this example, `forums` is the database name, `localhost` is the database host name, `mysecretusername` is the username to be assigned to this database user, and `mysecretpassword` is the password.

phpBB Pre-Installation Checklist

At this point you're now ready to install phpBB. But take a minute to answer the following questions before you go on; it's just to double-check that you have everything you need (Chapter 7, which discusses modifications and hacks, discusses a few skillsets and tools that you might find helpful):

- Do I have a web server running?
- Is my web server running PHP?

- Is my web server running MySQL or PostgreSQL or MSSQL or MS Access?
- Do I know my FTP hostname, username, and password? (This step is for remote servers only, see the note after the checklist.)
- What's my username to access the database?
- What host is this database running on? (Ask your hosting provider; it's often `localhost` or `127.0.0.1`. In the case of ODBC, a DSN is needed instead.)
- What is the name of my database (e.g. `forums`)?

A note about FTP: You'll need an FTP program, also known as an *FTP client*, in order to transfer files from your computer to a remote server. There are a lot of free/trial FTP programs you can use. Just a simple Google search will yield a lot of results. Generally, using an FTP program is not much different than copying files to different locations on your local computer. The difference is that you need to establish a connection to the remote computer first. In order to do that, you need an FTP hostname, a username and a password, which you probably already have, supplied by your hosting provider.

Installation

Now that all the prerequisites have been met, let's start the installation process:

1. **Download**: Download the compressed phpBB files from `http://www.phpbb.com/downloads.php` selecting a compression format that you know how to decompress.
2. **Decompress**: Unzip the files to a selected directory, using your preferred compression utility (WinZip for example). If you're installing locally, unzip to a directory within your web root. The top-level directory of the phpBB directory tree will be called `phpBB2`.
3. **FTP**: If you're installing locally, skip this step. If you're installing on a remote server, copy the whole `phpBB2` directory as-is to the remote server. You can do this easily using an FTP program to connect to your server and transfer the files.
4. **Select you phpBB root**. This step is the time when you need to make an important decision—where on your server you are installing phpBB and how you are naming it. The reason why this is important is because this will determine how your users will see your board. Let's say your domain is `http://www.yourdomain.com`. You have the following options:
    - If you copy the `phpBB2` directory and its contents to your web root and install without any modifications, your forums will be available at `http://www.yourdomain.com/phpBB2`.

  - You can simply rename the phpBB2 directory to something you like, say forum. In this case, your community will be located at http://www.yourdomain.com/forum.
  - You have the option of hosting the board in your web root so that it's accessible directly at http://www.yourdomain.com/ or, if you use a sub-domain, something like http://forum.yourdomain.com/. If you decide to go this way, than you need to copy the *contents* of the phpBB2 directory in your (sub)domain's web root, which is not the phpBB2 directory itself, but the files and directories that are contained within it.

For the purposes of this chapter, we'll go with the second option, http://www.yourdomain.com/forum, as it is probably the most common one.

5. config.php: You need to change the permissions for this file, so that it's writable by phpBB during the installation. Go to the main directory where phpBB is installed and find the file called config.php. Change the file permissions so that it's writable by the phpBB installer scripts, or in other words, on Linux systems, chmod it to 666 (or -rw-rw-rw-). On Linux/Unix systems, chmod is a command that means "change mode", and is used to adjust file permissions. File permissions specify who can do what to a particular file. Your options to change a file's mode include:
   - If you have shell access to your Linux server, go to your phpBB directory and type chmod 666 config.php. This will do.
   - If you have FTP-only access, chances are your FTP client (the program you use for copying files to the remote server) will give you the option of chmod-ing, only you have to find it. In some FTP clients, this option is simply called chmod, in others it's under file properties or permissions.
   - If you canot change the file permissions, don't worry. If the phpBB installer cannot write this file during the installation, you'll be given the option of downloading the config.php file on your system and then FTP-ing the file, overwriting the one already in the phpBB root.
6. **Start the phpBB installer**: Point your browser to the phpBB directory, which in our case is http://www.yourdomain.com/forum/. You'll be redirected automatically to the installation script, which is located at http://www.yourdomain.com/forum/install/install.php.

You should see a screen like the one shown overleaf.

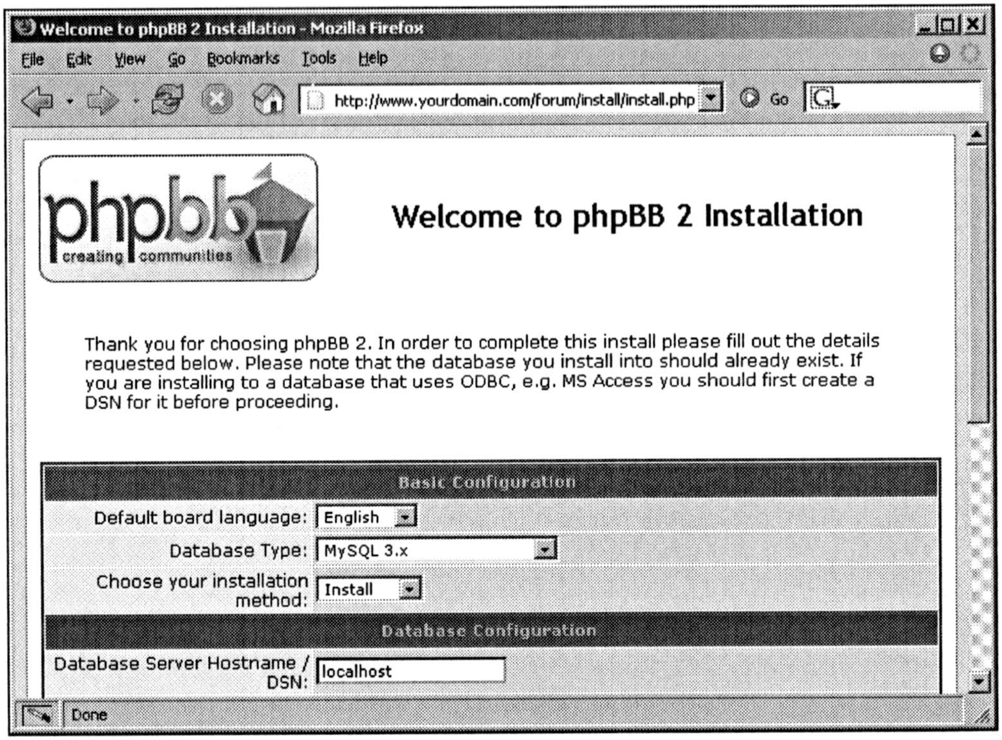

7. **Installer data form**: Complete the form that is presented on the installation screen. That's where your checklist from the previous section comes in handy. A description of the fields in this form follows, as some might not be so self-explanatory. In brief, most of the fields in this form are pre-filled by the phpBB installer; the ones you need to worry about are basically just the database name, username, password, and the administrator username, password, and e-mail address.

Option	Setting
Default board language	Since you haven't installed additional languages yet, English is the only option. Later on if you decide to use other languages, you can always change this setting.
Database Type	The database system you'll be using, most likely MySQL 4.x or MySQL 3.x
Choose your installation method	Install or Upgrade. You go with Install, since you have no previous phpBB installation.

Option	Setting
Database Server Hostname / DSN	Usually localhost; refer to your checklist.
Your Database Name	Refer to your checklist.
Database Username	Refer to your checklist.
Database Password	Refer to your checklist again.
Prefix for tables in database	phpbb_ is the default value. After the installation, all tables in the database to do with phpBB will have this prefix in their name, such as phpbb_users, and phpbb_posts. It's not compulsory to use a prefix, but it's a nice way to tell your phpBB tables from all the rest, in case you have other non-phpBB related tables in the same database. This also allows you, for example, to have two or more distinct phpBB installations that share the same database; you just need to use a different prefix for each installation. Don't use spaces in this prefix, otherwise the installer will return an error. It's a good idea to leave the default phpbb_ value for the prefix, if you don't have a reason to change it. Most of the phpBB modifications that you may want to install later on will assume this prefix.
Admin Email Address	Your e-mail address. It will be used, for example, as a sender e-mail address when phpBB notifies a user about a new private message. So a good idea is to supply a working e-mail address that you check often. An e-mail that represents your board, like `admin@yourdomain.com` would be a good choice.
Domain Name	Your domain's name. The phpBB installation will probably figure it out, otherwise type it in yourself.
Server Port	The default is 80. Normally you don't need to change this value.
Script path	The relative path to your installation. Normally the phpBB installer will guess it properly and you don't have to change it.

Option	Setting
Administrator Username	The administrator username is an important one. There is no default, but using Administrator is a common choice.
Administrator Password	Choose it wisely and make it difficult to guess. This option cannot be left blank.

8. **Finish installation**: Click the Install button. If everything so far was fine, you've filled out all the required data in the install form, and there were no error messages, phpBB will install successfully. Congratulations! Click Finish installation and move on to the post-installation tasks.

Troubleshooting the Installation

This troubleshooting guide is not a comprehensive list; it just contains some common problems that phpBB users have. If your problem is not listed here, see the last section of this chapter for guidelines on how to look for help.

Symptom

Error message: Your config file is un-writeable at present.

Reason

For some reason, step 5 of the install steps listed above was not completed. Read the description of step 5 again, but only if you need more background information on the nature of the error. Otherwise just see the solution that follows.

Solution

The phpBB installer itself will recover from this situation. Just follow the instructions on the screen.

You are given the option of downloading the `config.php` file the installer tried to write. Download the file, then copy/FTP it, overwriting the `config.php` file that is already in the phpBB root directory.

Alternatively, you are also given the option of using the installer to FTP the file for you, provided that your version of PHP supports FTP-ing (most likely). If you want to use this option, you'll have to enter the data you normally use to connect to the server with your desktop FTP client (CuteFTP, SmartFTP, etc.). Be sure to enter the full path to where the phpBB installer can copy the `config.php` file. The full path is the same as that visible in your FTP client. In other words, the phpBB installer is trying to act as an FTP client for you.

Symptom

Error message: Could not connect to the database.

Reason

There can be several reasons for this message:

- You don't have a database system installed.
- The database system is installed, but it's not running.
- You didn't select the correct database type from the dropdown described in step 7.
- The database hostname/DSN is incorrect.
- The database name you provided refers to a non-existing database.
- Your username to access the database is incorrect or this database user has insufficient privileges.
- Your password to access the database is incorrect.

Solution

Read the pre-installation section again. Be sure to complete the checklist at the end with the correct data. If you're still having problems, consult the last section at the end of this chapter for an idea where you can look for help.

Symptom

Error message: The passwords you entered did not match.

Reason

This refers to the administrator password and the password confirmation you've entered at the very end of the installer form, under Admin configuration.

Solution

Be sure to enter the same password in both fields. The password cannot be blank.

Symptom

Error message: The PHP configuration on your server doesn't support the database type that you chose.

Reason 1

PHP actually supports the database system you want to use, but you didn't select it from the installer form's database type field.

Solution

Click your browser's Back button and select the appropriate database type.

Reason 2

Exactly as the message says, your PHP installation doesn't support the selected database system.

Solution

Talk to your hosting provider, or, if you're installing locally, read the PHP documentation on how to enable support for your selected database type.

Symptom

Error message: An error occurred trying to update the database
Table 'phpbb_auth_access' already exists.

Here phpbb_ is the table prefix you've typed in the installer form.

Reason 1

Although very unlikely, it may happen that in your database you have a table totally unrelated to phpBB, having the same name as a phpBB table.

Solution

This is a naming conflict. To get around this, go back and choose a different table prefix.

Reason 2

You're trying to install using a database that already contains a phpBB installation.

Solution

If you want to keep the existing installation, go back to the installer form and simply choose a different prefix. This way you're resolving the naming conflict and you'll have two phpBB installations, which use the same database.

If you don't want to keep the existing installation, for example it was a failed installation, you have to remove all database tables created by the previous installation. Which tables to remove? You can tell by their prefix. Use the friendly phpMyAdmin to remove those tables or if you can't use it, connect to MySQL on the command prompt, as described earlier in this chapter, and delete the tables manually. To do so, you need to use the `DROP TABLE` syntax, which is actually very simple but also a bit dangerous because it deletes a whole database table and its contents permanently.

Time For Action—Deleting phpBB Tables using phpMyAdmin

1. Load the phpMyAdmin main page.
2. Select forums from the dropdown on the left-hand side. forums is the database name; use your database name if different.
3. On the right, where all the tables are displayed, check the box next to each table you want to delete. You can also use the Check All link to select all the tables in this database.

4. Select Drop from the action options.

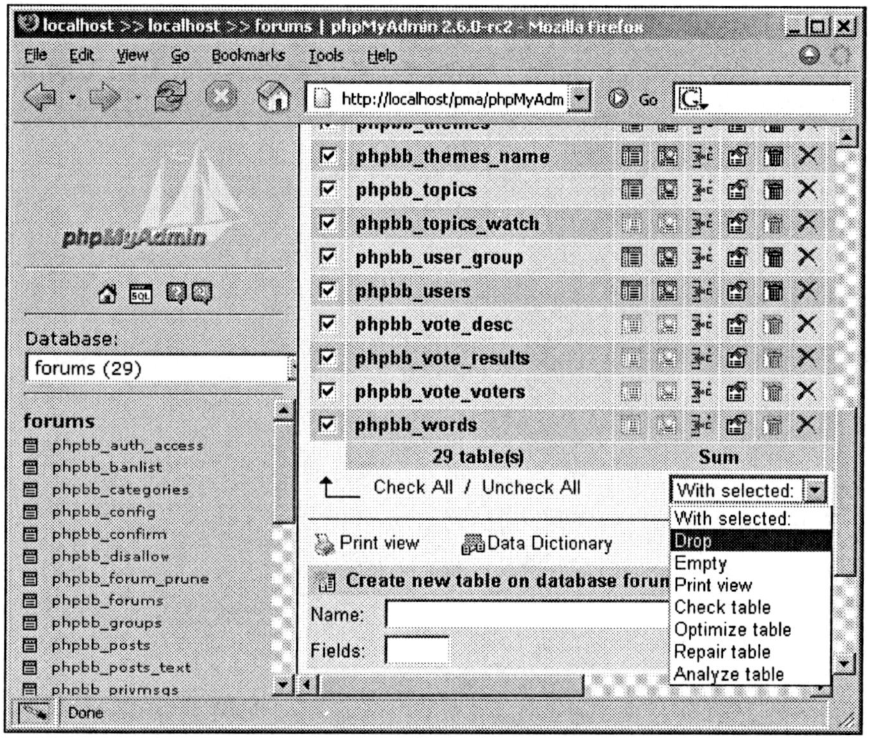

Time For Action—Deleting phpBB Tables Using the Command Prompt

1. Connect to MySQL using the console as described in the pre-install section.
2. Once you're connected to MySQL, change the database in use, by using `\u forums`, where `forums` is the name of your database.
3. List all tables with `SHOW TABLES;` and then delete them one by one using `DROP TABLE table_name_here;`.

Alternatively if you're sure there are no tables that you need in this database— that is there's nothing but some no-good phpBB tables from a failed installation—you can do it in one shot: after connecting to MySQL, type `DROP DATABASE forums;`.

This will delete the whole database. Permanently! So be careful. You need to recreate it again for the next installation.

> Deleting tables and databases is a one-way process, meaning you can't go back. So think twice before you delete anything. Think about making backups when you're in doubt before destroying some tables.

Quick tip: Here's a MySQL query that allows you to quickly back up a table:

```
CREATE TABLE 'new_table_name'
SELECT * FROM 'table_to_back_up';
```

This will create a new table, called `new_table_name` in the same current database, and the new table will have the same structure and content as the table named `table_to_back_up`.

If you want to back up a table in a different database, you can use:

```
CREATE TABLE 'new_database'.'new_table_name'
SELECT * FROM 'source_database'.'table_to_back_up';
```

Post-Installation Tasks

After you've installed phpBB, you need to perform a few post-install operations, namely to delete unneeded directories and to set some basic configuration options.

Time For Action—Deleting Unneeded Directories

1. Connect to your server via FTP (skip this step for local installations).
2. Go to the directory where phpBB is installed.
3. Delete the `install` and `contrib` directories.
4. (Optionally) delete the `docs` directory as well.

What Just Happened?

After a successful installation, when you visit your new phpBB forum's homepage you'll get a hint about your post-install tasks. You're advised to delete the `install` and `contrib` directories, because leaving them on the server is considered a security risk, so big that phpBB won't even run if it detects their presence.

The doc directory can be deleted as well if you like; it's not a security threat, but can save some disk space.

Basic Configuration

After the unneeded directories are deleted, you can access your new and shiny bulletin board that you just installed. Great! It works!

Now it's a good idea to familiarize yourself a bit with the administration panel. And you can do this right away by editing some general configuration variables.

Time For Action—Initial Configuration Using the Administration Panel

1. Load your bulletin board in the browser, i.e. visit `http://www.yourdomain.com/forum`. It looks like the following screenshot.

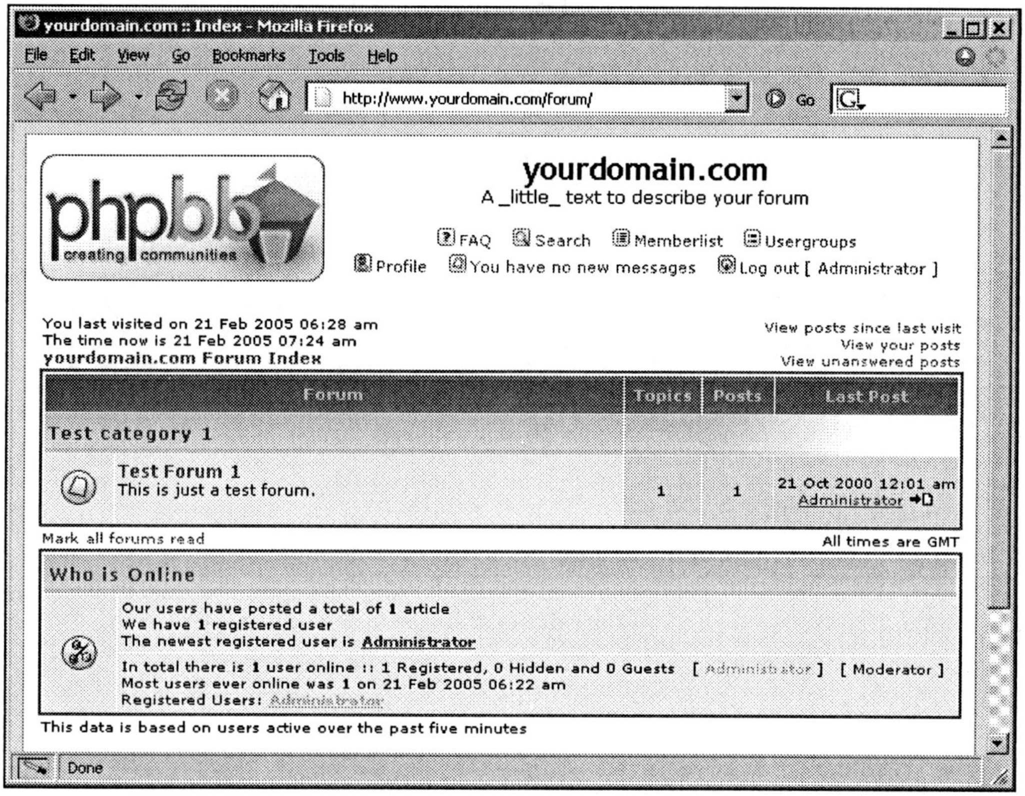

2. Log in using the form at the bottom of the page. Depending on how the installation ended, you may be logged in already. If you're not, use the administrator username and password that you selected during the installation.
3. Click the Go to Administration Panel link; it is located at the bottom of every page.
4. Click the Configuration link found under the General Admin section in the left-hand menu.
5. Edit the fields as needed (discussed shortly).
6. Click Submit when done.

What Just Happened?

You successfully logged in to your Administration Panel, the place for managing your phpBB-powered bulletin board. You loaded the general configuration settings form and saved the settings.

Most of the fields in this form are pre-filled with values that are just fine as the phpBB installer set them, but some are better if edited. What follows is a list of fields of interest:

General Board Settings

Site name: A friendly name for your site: often, the domain name. It will appear at the top of every page. The default is `yourdomain.com`, and you can see it in action in the previous screenshot.

Site description: A brief description of what the site is about, preferably not more than six to seven words. It will appear at the top of every page and is not required. Again, look at the previous screenshot to see the default value A _little_ text to describe your forum.

Enable account activation: This refers to the way new users are accepted. There are three options:

- The users are accepted right away, as soon as they sign up (this is the default option).
- They have to confirm their subscription by clicking a link received by e-mail. This way they confirm their wish to become members and also authenticate that they are the owners of the e-mail address supplied during registration. This is probably the most used option.
- The members' sign-up applications need to be reviewed and approved by an administrator.

System Timezone: The time zone where your community is mainly located. It's a default value that every member can overwrite.

Enable GZip Compression: Enabling this option will cause all pages to be compressed when sent from the server and decompressed after they are received by the user's computer if the user's browser supports compression. If it doesn't, the page won't be compressed by the server. This results in a faster working site and uses less bandwidth, but increases the server load because of the overhead of compressing every page that is served.

Cookie settings

Cookie name: Normally you don't change this. You might need to alter this value only if you host more than one forum under the same domain name. If this is the case, you can use a different cookie name for each installation.

Cookie secure: Enable this option if your site runs on Secure Socket Layer (SSL); in other words if your pages are displayed using the secure HTTPS protocol, instead of just HTTP.

Session length [seconds]: Determines how long the user session "lives" before it's deleted. It's a security-related setting, which determines how many seconds users can stay inactive (not visiting any board page) before they are logged out by phpBB.

Avatar Settings

"Avatar" refers to those little member-specific graphics that appear in the posts below a member's username. You have three ways to provide this functionality.

- Enable gallery avatars: Users can select from a number of predefined graphics that you upload to a specified directory.
- Enable remote avatars: Users can put links to graphics that they find on the Internet, stored on other servers.
- Enable avatar uploading: Users can upload graphics to your server.

Avatar Storage Path: Where the uploaded avatars are stored; the default is images/avatars, which translates to `http://www.yourdomain.com/forum/images/avatars/`.

Avatar Gallery Path: Where the pre-defined graphics are stored; the default is images/avatars/gallery, which translates to `http://www.yourdomain.com /forum/images/avatars/gallery/`.

COPPA Settings

COPPA stands for Children's Online Privacy Protection Act. Basically it requires parents' written consent if their children are to become members of your forums. For more information, see phpBB user guide and `http://www.coppa.org`.

E-mail Settings

Admin Email Address: The e-mail address that you provided during the installation.

Email Signature: This will be appended to every e-mail phpBB sends on your behalf, such as private message notifications, topic-watch notifications, etc. Use your imagination to come up with friendly message footers to your members.

Use SMTP Server for email: You have the option of using an SMTP server to send mail, instead of the native PHP mail function. Some hosts disable the PHP mail function because of the danger of unethical clients misusing it (to send spam). If this is the case, you need to use an SMTP server to send the mails. Your Internet service provider (ISP, the one you use to connect to the Internet) has most likely given you access to an SMTP server to send e-mails (with Microsoft Outlook, for example). You can use this SMTP server for your bulletin board. You can also use this option if you install phpBB on your own PC and don't have a mail server set up.

Setting Up the avatars Directory

If you're allowing members to upload avatars to your server, you have to make the directory that stores them writable. The file permissions (on a Linux machine) need to be 777. Using the same methods for changing the file permissions as we used for `config.php` in the pre-install section, change the permissions to 777 for the `image/avatars` directory or wherever you decided to store members' avatars.

Security Tips

Making sure that your board is as secure as possible should always be a concern. Here are some tips that can help you get started.

Administrator Password

Make your administrator password difficult to guess. It's a very important password, so you wouldn't want other people to guess it and play around with your board. This is also true for any moderators you decide to assign later on. Remind them to change their passwords to something really hard to guess. For example using the same password as the username is definitely not advisable. Be creative and go with something like y0u11n3v3rgue$$ (read "you'll never guess") and wh00p3375 (read "whoopee 75"). It's also a good idea to change this password regularly and to use it only for this board (not for other services like Hotmail and the like).

Disallow Remote Connections to the Database

Remote connections allow you to access your database from a remote location. For instance, from your local machine you can query the database that is running on the remote hosting server. This definitely has benefits—for example for making local backups of the data in the remote database—but it can be a security risk. If the username and password to access the database are somehow revealed, then if the remote connection is enabled, an intruder can access your data from his or her computer. If the remote connection is disabled, the hacker will have to have access to the remote server in order to be able to connect to your database. Additionally with remote connection enabled, the potential hacker can try to guess what your password is by trying different combinations until he or she is connected.

Some hosting providers let you enable/disable remote connections, while some don't allow remote connections at all. Check what your situation is and (unless you have a very good reason) make sure the remote connection is disabled.

MySQL Account

Use a new MySQL account (or a new account for any other database you might be using for that matter) for the bulletin board. This was described in more detail in the pre-install section of this chapter.

config.php

After you change the permissions of the `config.php` file (described in the pre-installation section) so that it's writable by all, and you install phpBB, it's time to revert back. Using the exact same methodology as described before, change the permissions to 664.

Here is a more visual description of the config file after the `chmod 664 config.php` command. This is a screenshot from an FTP client for Windows.

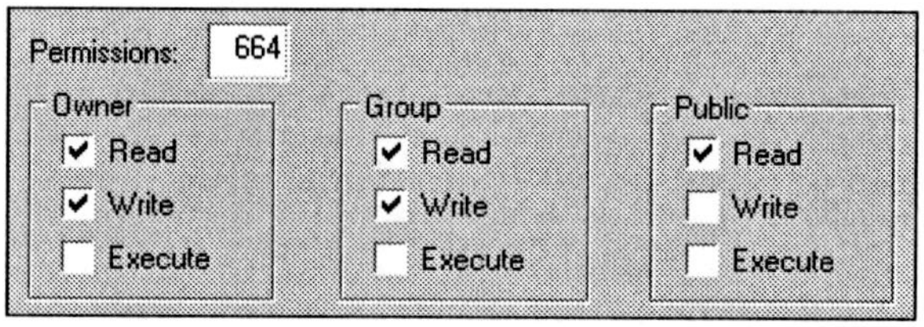

.htaccess Protection for the Administration Panel

A little extra layer of protection for the admin panel can be the setting of an `.htaccess` directory protection. `.htaccess` is a file that can contain a number of instructions for the Apache web server that are applicable for the directory where the `.htaccess` file is and to all sub-directories. Setting up `.htaccess` protection will result in an additional username/password window that will be displayed when you enter the admin panel. Setting up the protection may not be a trivial task, and there are quite a few tutorials available on the Web that can help you with this. `.htaccess` documentation can be found on the Apache website at `http://httpd.apache.org/docs/howto/htaccess.html`.

It's possible that your hosting provider gives you access to an easier interface (a control panel) that can help you setting up the protection.

So using `.htaccess` directly or through a friendlier interface you can protect the `admin` sub-directory within the root phpBB directory using a username and password different than the "normal" administration password. This way you're making it harder for potential intruders as they have two different username/password pair to deal with.

Finding Help

Remember how we spoke about the huge community of phpBB users? Well, these are the people that can help you out if you have a problem that you cannot figure out. On phpBB.com, there is a support section that contains "static" articles such as the user guide, the knowledge base, and the FAQ, and there's also the community section (that is not surprisingly powered by phpBB) where phpBB users from around the globe share their experience. The same sort of community of users you can find on phpBBHacks.com.

When you encounter a problem, don't panic; you're not alone, and chances are someone has had and resolved the exact same problem, and this individual is most likely to share the resolution. So it's very probable that the question you have has already been asked and answered. All you need to do is find it. If you can't find the resolution you need, post your question on the bulletin board, but make sure you search first.

Then even though you've found your answer, don't leave right away. You could dawdle for a while and help others with problems that you know how to fix.

Summary

We've walked a long way in this chapter: setting up the different components required to have phpBB running, doing some database preparation work, downloading phpBB, and installing it. You also have an idea now of the essential phpBB configuration options and how to make your board more secure.

At this point you have the knowledge and know-how to start up your community website. Today!

3
A Quick Tour of phpBB

In the previous chapters you learned about what phpBB is and how to install it. It is time now to take a closer look at how it actually works and the kind of features it offers to users, moderators, and administrators.

In this chapter you will learn:

- How phpBB works from a visitor's perspective
- What the moderator's capabilities are
- How the most popular administration features work

Visitor Experience

As more and more people join your online community, chances are that they'll start asking questions about some of the board features. You should be able to guide them and respond to their concerns if you want to be a good, understanding, and helpful host to the community. That's why it's a good idea to know in detail how your phpBB-powered forum works.

If you've just jumped from the previous chapter, you may be still logged in as an administrator. Log out and let's get started with the tour of the new forum walking in visitor's shoes.

Overview

If somebody hits the forum you've just created following the steps from the previous chapter, they are very likely to see something like the following:

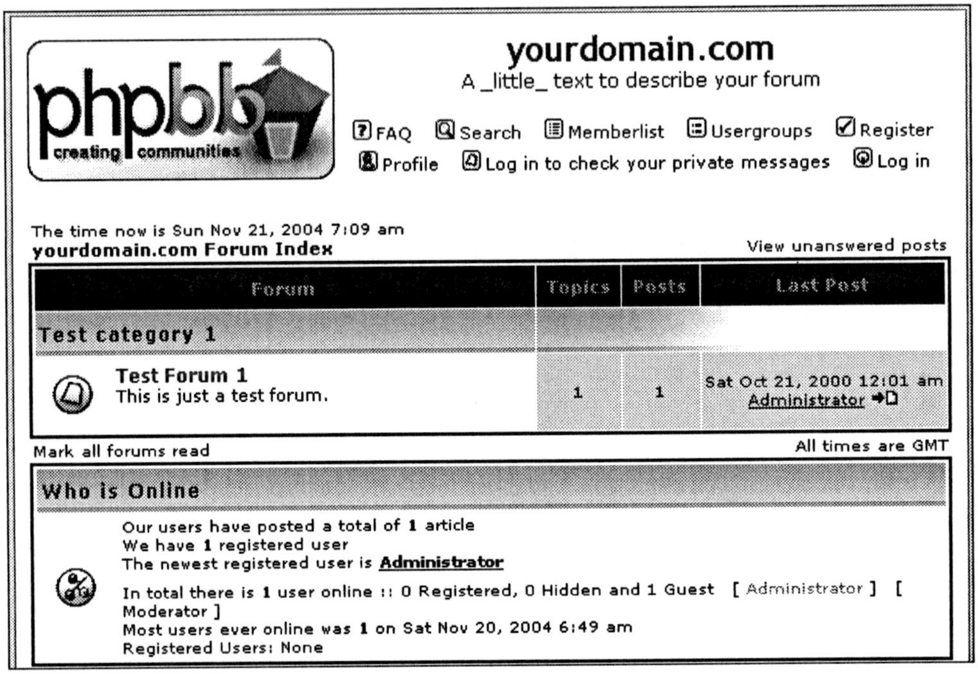

This screenshot shows how phpBB gets shipped, with all defaults and a test posting in a test forum. The only registered user of the board is the admin user that you created while installing. At the top of the screen, next to the phpBB logo, there's a set of links that go together with some small icon images. These links represent the main navigation of the forum. One of the links is the link to register and become a member of the community. Off we go!

Registration

There are three steps to the registration procedure—reading and accepting the registration terms, filling out the user profile form, and (optionally) a registration confirmation by e-mail.

Step 1

When the visitors select the Register link from the top menu, they are presented with the "Registration Agreement Terms". There are three options they can choose from:

- Accept the terms and be 13 years old or older: This option triggers the standard registration procedure.
- Accept the terms and be younger than 13 years: This option is the same as the one above with one more addition. In compliance with COPPA (Children's Online Privacy Protection Act of 1998) regulations, a parent

or guardian needs to send a standard form to you, the forum administrator, by mail or e-mail. This form grants permission for the child to participate in the forums. A blank COPPA form is sent by phpBB to the e-mail address supplied during the registration.

- Don't agree to the terms: Choosing this option aborts the registration process and the visitor is redirected to the main forum page.

Step 2

When the visitor accepts the phpBB terms, the registration form is displayed. The exact meaning of each of the fields in this registration/profile forms will be described shortly. For now let's concentrate on the absolutely required fields:

- Username
- Valid e-mail address
- Password and password confirmation

Step 3

After all the information is filled out, the user clicks Submit. If there are validation errors, like incorrect syntax for e-mail address or password mismatch, information about the error will be displayed at the top of the form. On an error-free and successful registration, a "thank-you" screen is displayed. Depending on how the board is configured (see the Email Address field's explanation in the table shown in the *Editing Your Profile* section that follows), the thank-you screen might advise the users to check their e-mail for a confirmation message in order to complete the registration.

Logging In

After successful registration, the user can log in using the form at the bottom of the forum's front page.

There's a checkbox next to the password field that says Log me on automatically each visit. Users should be careful when using this convenience, especially on shared computers. You as an administrator should be even more careful on using this option, as terrible things can happen if "The Bad Guy" takes over your account. Think about who else might be using your computer—family, visiting friends, etc.

Editing Your Profile

Logged-in users can edit their original profile created during registration. If they click the Profile link in the top navigation menu, they are presented with a profile form that is actually the same as the registration form, except for two things:

- The username is not editable. The Administration Panel allows for a configuration where the users *can* change their usernames, but this is not the default option, and for a good reason. Giving users the opportunity to change their identity means that it will become difficult for people to tell who's who in your community.
- There are now three password fields: one for the old password, one for the new password, and one for confirming the new password. These are fields are normally left blank, and are used only if the user wants to change the password.

OK, let's revise what we've learned so far about user profiles with a simple exercise.

Time For Action—Creating and Editing "The Dude" Profile

1. Go to the homepage of your forum and select Register from the top navigation menu.
2. On the Accept terms page, select I am over 13...
3. Fill out the form using username The Dude, password test and an e-mail address of yours. Leave everything else as it is.
4. Click the Submit button.
5. So far the registration is successful. Visit the homepage again. You will see The Dude under Who is Online, shown as The newest registered user.

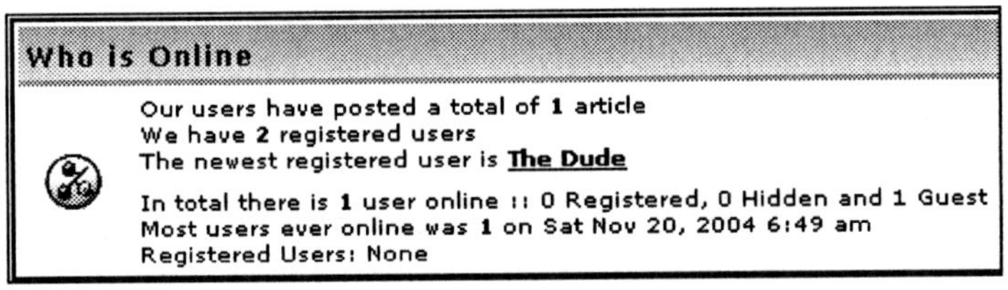

6. Now go to your e-mail inbox and check your e-mail. You should see a Welcome to yourdomain.com Forums message. This message, depending on the board configuration discussed earlier, will either advise you that you're now a member, or will provide you with a link to activate and finalize your membership application. Welcome aboard!
7. Go back to the board homepage. Scroll down to the login form. Enter The Dude as a username and the test passwords and press Log in. After a successful login, you'll see The Dude in the list of registered users online.

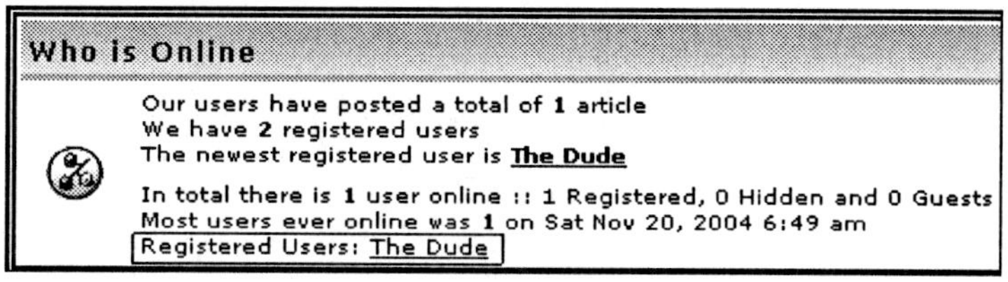

8. Look at the main navigation links at the top and select Profile. The profile form is displayed.
9. In the blank signature field, type in the following: Humans are not proud of their ancestors, and rarely invite them round to dinner. - Douglas Adams. Leave everything else as is.
10. Click Submit to save your amended profile.

What Just Happened?

You have successfully registered a new profile, logged in, and edited this profile. This user is now ready to post.

Understanding the meaning behind the user profile fields is a key to many phpBB features, so here's a detailed description. Take your time to learn about those fields; you're going to see them time and time again in different areas of your forum.

Field name	Description
Registration Information	
Username*	Selected username. Spaces and special symbols are allowed with the exception of the quotation mark ("). Maximum 25 characters are allowed.
E-mail address*	User's e-mail address. The forum can be configured to request a registration confirmation by e-mail in order to activate a user account. If such confirmation is required, an e-mail is sent to the address provided in this field. Many phpBB administrators opt for e-mail confirmation just to make sure that users enter valid e-mail addresses. This has a very good reason—if you don't require the e-mail confirmation and users register with fake e-mail addresses, you'll start receiving lots of bounced messages to your admin e-mail address. Why these bouncing messages? Well, phpBB will send e-mails on your account (you'll be the sender), for private-message notifications, topics-watch notifications, and so on, and on mail-delivery failures due to wrong recipient addresses, these mails bounce back to the sender.

<table>
<tr><th>Field name</th><th>Description</th></tr>
<tr><td>Password*</td><td>Anything is acceptable as a password, including single letters, although such simple passwords are really not recommended.</td></tr>
<tr><td>Confirm password*</td><td>phpBB requests the password to be confirmed just for the users to verify that they've entered their intended password correctly. A note about the passwords: they are encrypted before they are saved to the database using the MD5 one-way encryption algorithm. In plain English: there's no way for a saved password to be retrieved; at least the modern computer algorithms are not capable of doing it. This means that only the users know their passwords. If a user forgets a password, there's a procedure to create a new password, but none to restore the old one.</td></tr>
<tr><td colspan="2">Profile Information
As the form says, this section of the registration contains information that is publicly viewable by all community members, even those that are not registered. Part of it accompanies every post the user writes, part of it is only displayed when somebody accesses the user profile page. This section contains, for example, user data about their ICQ, AOL, MSN, and Yahoo! Messenger services and some other personal data.
There is a special field called signature. The text in this field is appended to the bottom of every post made by the user. It can contain links, URLs, and formatting, and is often used to add a touch of personality. People use it for various reasons like favorite wisdom quotes, funny quotes, or self-advertising. The way people use it can sometimes vary depending on what the community is about. In some rare occasions, it can actually be used for its original purpose—to contain the name of the poster or anything that looks like a real signature. The way to format a signature is the same as that to format a normal posting, which will be discussed a bit further.</td></tr>
<tr><td colspan="2">Preferences</td></tr>
<tr><td>Always show my e-mail address</td><td>Selecting "Yes" will reveal the user's e-mail address in the posts and in the profile. Selecting "No" would still allow other members to send e-mail to this user, but without knowing the exact e-mail address. They can do so by using a specially designed phpBB e-mail interface.</td></tr>
<tr><td>Hide your online status</td><td>If "Yes" is selected, when this user is logged in, the username will not be listed in the "Who is Online" area on the front page of the forum. Many people go with this option for privacy reasons. Hidden users are displayed when logged in as an admin though.</td></tr>
</table>

Field name	Description
Always notify me of replies	On selecting "Yes", phpBB will send an e-mail to the user every time somebody replies to a topic created by this user or a topic where the user has posted. This can be unselected on a per-posting basis.
Notify on new Private Message	On selecting "Yes", phpBB will send an e-mail when the user receives a private message.
Pop up window on new Private Message	On selecting "Yes", when the user is currently logged in and receives a private message, a new browser window will pop up to the user, notifying of the new message.
Always attach my signature Always allow BBCode Always allow HTML Always enable Smilies	These four "Always" fields refer to corresponding checkboxes when the user writes a posting. If they are checked, the corresponding checkboxes will be checked by default, but still can be changed on a per-posting basis.
Board Language	The language for the forum. English is the only language that is shipped with the default installation, but the good news is that there are more than 50 other translations that are available. Chapter 5 explains how you can add new languages to your board.
Board Style	Here the user selects how the board will look like for them. "subSilver" is the default and only board style, but shortly you'll find about how to add more styles or customize them or even create your very own!
Timezone	The users can select the time zone they are in, so that all date/time data displayed on the board is converted to their local time.
Date format	Users can configure the way the date/time data is presented to them, using the formatting options of the `date()` PHP function. There are quite a few options: details can be found in the PHP manual entry located at `http://www.php.net/date`. By default, the dates will be displayed like "Sat Nov 21, 2004 1:01 pm", but this can be changed to something like "2004-11-21 13:01" or "21st of November, 2004 at 01:01 pm" or whatever the user is most comfortable with.

Posting

Posting messages is the main activity in a bulletin board; everything else is a more or less just additional features. So it's a good idea to know all the details about posting.

Anatomy of a Posting

Let's see what a posting looks like, and what different elements it is composed of:

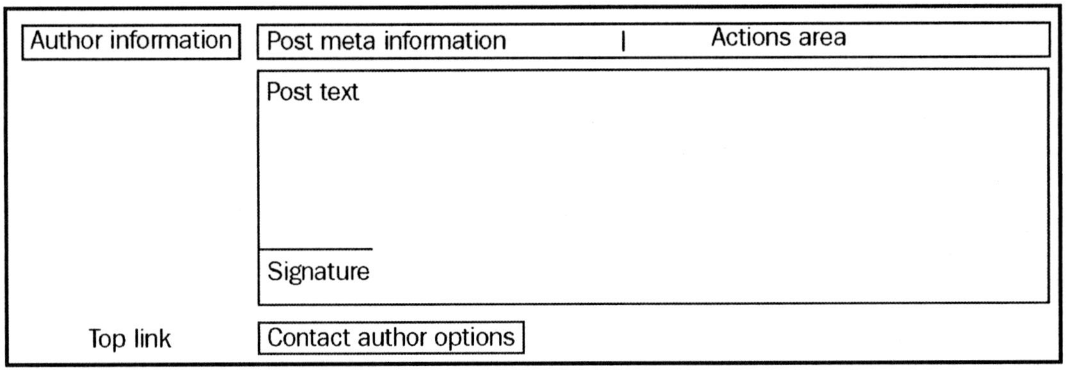

The *Author information* box consists of author's nickname, joined-in date, number of posts, and location. It can also contain the avatar image, rank, and rank image, but these are not enabled by default. Ranks and avatars are discussed a bit later.

Post meta information consists of one tiny post graphic, date/time stamp, and post subject. This teeny tiny graphic () is so small that most people won't even notice it, and even if they do, they would think it's just an ornament. But it's in fact a functional graphic; it's an exact link to this post. It's not very likely that someone would want to go to the post they are reading at the moment, but this can be very useful when you want to give a link to a specific post, as opposed to a link to the topic in general. To get the exact URL of a posting, right-click this miniature graphic and copy the URL that it links to. The graphic can also be different in color, which has a meaning. In the default phpBB template, an orange-colored box denotes that it's an unread post, whereas a white-gray box means that user has already read this post.

The *Actions area* contains buttons for the actions available to the user for this posting. The quote button is always there, and it looks like this: . Another action button that can be available is the edit button, which looks like this: . Whether the edit button is available depends on the user privileges, but in the default phpBB forum configuration, an author can edit his or her postings and a moderator can edit everybody's postings. The author can also have a delete action, depending on the privileges and the specific posting. The default phpBB configuration allows the author of the post to delete it only if there are no more posts after that. Moderators have access to all action buttons—quote, edit, delete, and the button to view the poster's IP address.

The *Post text* area contains the actual text of the message and the *signature* area contains the user's signature in his/her profile.

The *Top link* is just a "Back to the top" link leading to the beginning of the current page.

The *Contact author options* area at the very least contains a button to access the author's profile and a button to send the author a **private message (PM)**. This area can also contain other information as entered in the profile: the e-mail address, ICQ number, MSN messenger ID, web address, and so on. The nice thing about the ICQ button is that it will show the ICQ status of the author (online or offline) provided of course that the author is allowing the status to be viewed in the ICQ settings.

Replying

A reply is a new posting in an existing discussion topic. It's initiated by clicking the post reply () button located at the top and the bottom of a topic listing. A reply can also be initiated by clicking the Quote action button, mentioned earlier, located in a post's actions area. In this case, the post body will be pre-filled with the quoted posting.

Here's the interface for posting a reply:

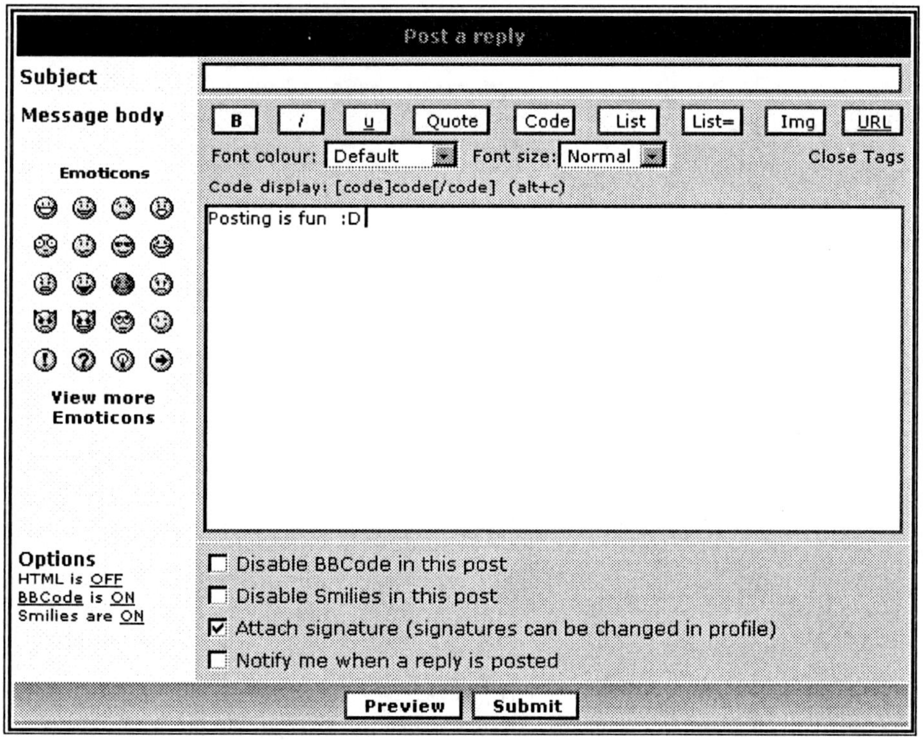

The only thing the user really needs to worry about on this form is the message body. Everything else is optional. Here are some more details about the posting interface:

- The subject (if entered) will appear in the post's meta information box (see the *Anatomy of a Posting* section)
- There are formatting options that use the so-called **BB Code (BB tags)**, where BB stands for **bulletin board**. The formatting options empower the users to improve the looks of a posting (or sometimes even ruin it).
- Emoticons (mostly known as smilies) are those cute little images that help the users add a touch of personal and informal look to their postings. Clicking one of these graphics on the left will insert its textual representation in the message-body field. For example, if you click , you'll see :D inserted in the textbox, as shown in the preceding screenshot.
- The blue text View more Emoticons is actually a link to a new window popup with more smilies to choose from. This link is something people often miss and then start asking you why on earth would you hide from them this Mr. Green icon that everybody else seems to be using all the time. The explanation is that it's there, but is only accessible through the View more Emoticons popup.
- The options section, located below the message body, contains the checkboxes we mentioned a bit earlier; their default values are defined in the user's profile.
- Clicking on the Preview button will show the message body exactly the way it'll look when posted. It's always a good idea to use this feature.
- If the board configuration allows unregistered visitors to post, they'll see an additional field above all the rest, and this will be a required field to enter a username.
- Below the posting form, there is a listing of the latest previous postings (not displayed in the previous screenshot). This makes it easier for the post's author to recall what others have said before.

Starting a New Topic

Starting a new topic is very similar to posting a reply in an existing one. It's initiated by clicking the new topic button. The form is very similar to the one we just saw, except that Subject is a required field, and there are fields to include a poll that will go together with the topic.

Some more topics of interest about the polls:

- When starting a new topic, uses can set a poll question, multiple answers (at least two), and the number of days before the poll expires.

- Once the poll expires, visitors can still see the results of the poll, but can no longer vote.
- Setting the number of expiration days to `0` (or leaving it blank) will cause the poll to be always accessible for voting (an **eternal poll**).
- Creating a poll requires a separate privilege that can be restricted from the admin panel, but it's allowed by default.

Formatting a Posting

Users can format postings by using a small set of instructions (BB tags). When posting, you insert these tags here and there in the post body, and when you view a post, the tags are processed to produce the desired formatting. If you know some basic HTML tags, chances are you'll have a pretty good idea of how the BB tags work and you can start typing them almost right away.

If you don't know either HTML or BB tags (and most of your visitors won't know them), don't worry; you don't have to learn this whole new secret code by heart. phpBB has an intuitive interface to guide you through this almost as easily as using a word-processing software. Just looking at the formatting toolbar should make most of the options clear.

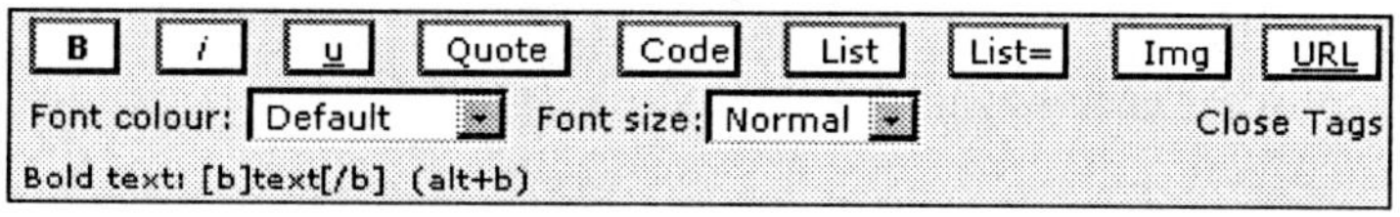

There are two ways to apply a formatting: you can either type the tags out, or you can select the word or phrase you want to format and then click the appropriate button from the toolbar. Unfortunately, due to different JavaScript support in the different browsers, the second option is not available in some browsers or platforms. But the good news is that about 95% of all Internet users will have access to this feature, because they'll be using a browser that supports it.

There is always an **opening BB tag** that shows where to start the formatting and a **closing BB tag** that shows where the formatting should end. The opening tag is of the form `[tag]` and the closing of the form `[/tag]`. Let's take a look at the bold tag, as it's probably the tag that's used the most. If you want to bold the word "fun" in the sentence "Posting is fun", you type (or use the toolbar to produce the same result) "`Posting is [b]fun[/b]`". These tags might look scary if this is your first acquaintance with them, but are really easy once you get used to them.

You know that you can apply this formatting by typing the sentence, selecting the word "fun", and then clicking the B icon. There is another way of using the toolbar to do this:

1. Type Posting is.

2. Click the B icon (this will insert the opening `[b]`).
3. Type fun.
4. Click the B icon again (this will insert the closing `[/b]`).

Unlike the selection method for formatting (described previously), the scenario above will work in almost any browser that knows at least something about JavaScript. After step 2 above, the B icon will get an asterisk, indicating that there is an opened `[b]` tag that's not yet closed. On completion of step 4, the asterisk will disappear.

Images can be inserted into your postings by using the `[img]` tag, assuming that the image is available on the Internet, i.e. you know its web address that starts with something like `http://`. You can also put web links into the postings, using the `[url]` tag, although phpBB is smart enough to guess when you have a web link in your posting and will automatically display it as a clickable link.

You can consult the phpBB user guide for more detailed information on the BB tags, but let's first see an example to get a pretty good idea of how the tags work.

If you look at the screenshot earlier, which shows the formatting toolbar, you'll notice that it looks like three distinct lines (or rows), containing respectively:

- Formatting command buttons, like B for bold, I for italics, etc.
- Two dropdowns containing font formatting and a Close Tags link. This link will close all currently opened tags (assuming they were opened from the toolbar, not typed). For example, if you type Posting is, click the B button followed by the I button, type fun, and finally click Close Tags, you'll get the result: Posting is [b][i]fun[/i][/b]. Clicking Close Tags has given the same results as clicking I and then B to close the tags you've already opened.
- The third line in the toolbar contains tips on how to use the BB tags. If you place your mouse over a toolbar icon, you'll see that the contents of the tips line change to reflect the button's function. The preceding illustration had the mouse cursor hovering over the B button. In brackets, a tip shows a keyboard combination that can be used for formatting. This combination has the same effect as clicking a toolbar button, and can help you post faster using just the keyboard and not even worrying about moving your hand from the keyboard to the mouse, and then moving the mouse to the desired icon.

  The result from the example can even be achieved using just the keyboard: type Posting is, hold the *ALT* key (the Apple key for Mac users), press *B*, press *I*, release *ALT*, type fun, hold *ALT*, press *I*, and then press *B*.

Time For Action—Formatting a Post

1. You already know how to use the bold and italics formatting tags, but this time let's also add **underlining**. Use your preferred method (the toolbar or the keyboard or simply type the tags yourself) in order to produce the following BB code: Posting is [b][i][u]fun[/u][/i][/b]!.
2. The next thing is the **quoting**. Normally you would use the Quote action button when replying, but it doesn't hurt to know how to do it manually:

```
I can quote other posters like this:
[quote="The Dude"]For my name is The Dude...[/quote]
```

3. Now we take a look at the `[code]` tag, which is mostly used when people **paste programming code** into their postings, but can be used for other purposes like better aligning in a table-like manner, because it uses a fixed-width font. Type:

```
I can write "phpBB" using binary:
[code]01110000 01101000 01110000 01000010 01000010[/code]
```

4. Next, the **listings**. Listings use the `[list]` tag to mark the beginning and the end of a listing, and use the asterisk `[*]` for a listing item. The listing start tag can take parameters like `1` or `A`. Try this:

```
And I can list stuff like this:
[list][*]one[*]two[/list]
or even enumerate, like this
[list=1][*]first[*]second[/list]
```

5. Then add an **image** using the `[img]` tag and the web address of a known image, as follows:

```
I can use images:
[img]http://www.packtpub.com/images/Packt.png[/img]
```

6. Now **links**. Links are inserted using the `[url]` tag, where there are two possible scenarios. Try them both as shown here:

```
Links: [url]http://www.packtpub.com[/url], fancy links:
[url=http://www.packtpub.com]Packt Publishing[/url]
```

7. And finally, the `[color]` and the `[size]` tags. Their start tags take parameters like `[color=black]`, `[color=blue]`, `[size=7]`, etc. Try the following to get a better idea:

```
and [color=red]different [/color][color=green]colors [/color]and
[size=18]font [/size][size=9]sizes[/size]!
```

What Just Happened

Click the Preview or Submit button, and you'll see what you just did. It should look like the following screenshot.

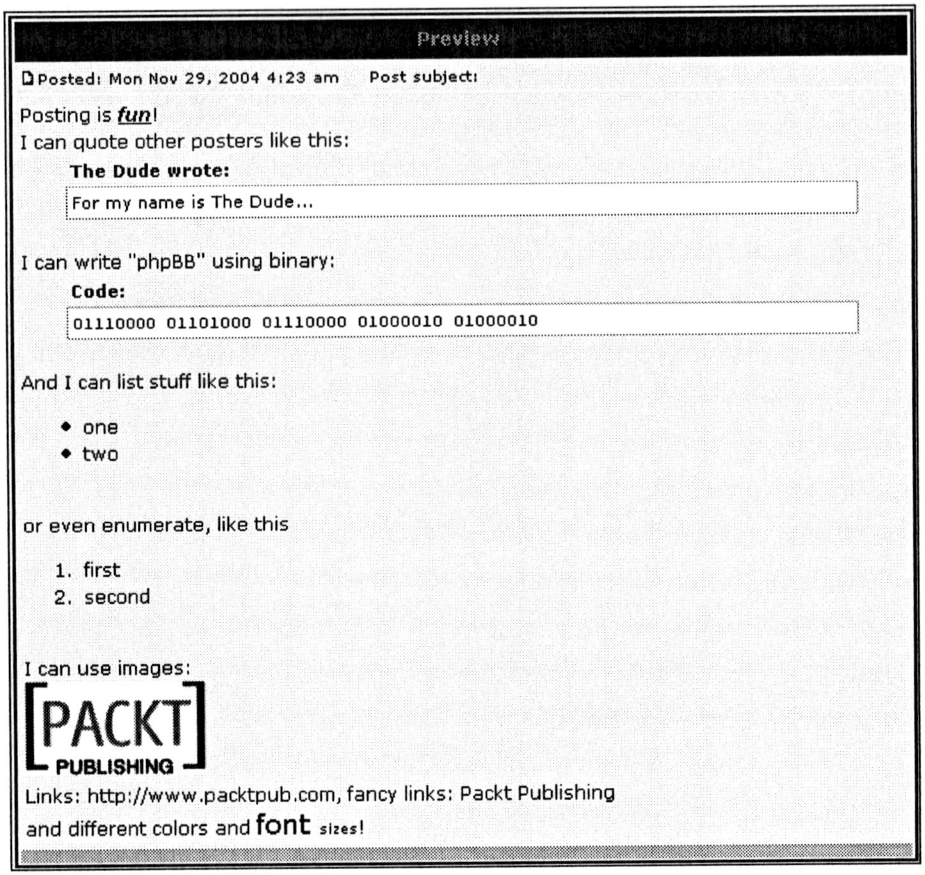

Congratulations! You've just formatted a posting using almost all of phpBB's formatting capabilities!

Editing a Posting

Users are allowed to edit their own postings. Again this is the default phpBB configuration and can be changed from the Administration Panel. Users edit their postings by using the Edit link located in the actions area.

After a posting has been edited, a small print message appears at the bottom of the posting, advising other users that this posting has been altered. The message goes like:

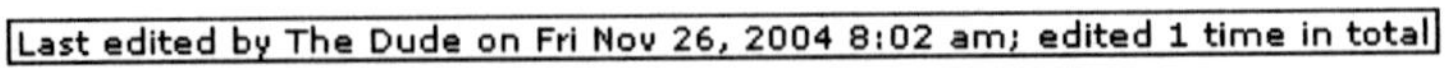

This message always appears, with only one exception. It will not appear if the posting was edited *before* another user has posted in the same topic.

Deleting a Posting

Users are allowed to delete their own postings but only if it's the last posting in the discussion topic. As soon as a reply is posted (even by the same user) the deletion of a posting is no longer possible.

Postings are deleted by using the delete action icon (☒) located in the post's actions area.

Searching

Pretty soon your forums will be full of topics that will span more than one topics-listing page. This will make it a bit difficult to locate a specific older topic. phpBB's search feature comes to the rescue here. It's accessible through the Search top-navigation link. The search form gives you many options to find your topic of interest, such as which forum to search, how to display the results, and so on.

Chances are you and your members will ignore most of the search options in your searches. After all, we are so used to simple search boxes like Google's, for example, that we rarely look for other options. But here is one simple option that can help you a lot. This option is Search for all terms. It helps when you search using more than one word. Unlike Google, where the results will be narrowed when you add more words, phpBB will search for each individual word and return more results (broadening the search as opposed to narrowing it).

For example, if you search for milk chocolate, you'll get all results for milk and chocolate, which is probably not what you want. Checking the Search for all terms option will return only those posts where both words can be found.

You can also use the wildcard (*) for searching a part of a word. For example *late will return postings containing the words chocolate and late.

Sending and Receiving Private Messages (PM)

One neat phpBB feature is that users can communicate privately with each other *outside* the public board area, through private messages (PM). (PM is also used as a verb, as in "Please PM me".) PMs work very similarly to the normal e-mail we're all used to. The interface for writing a PM is the same as for writing a posting, only there is a field for the recipient's username at the top. Also, you can look up a username if you're not sure about the spelling.

There are the following private message boxes:

- **Inbox**: Stores all incoming messages, just like in a normal e-mail mailbox.
- **Sentbox**: Contains all messages that you've sent to other members.
- **Outbox**: Temporarily contains those messages that you've sent but which have not yet been read by the recipient. You can edit or delete messages in

the outbox. As soon as the recipient reads the message, the sender can no longer amend it. At this point it's final. Sometimes it can so happen that a user receives an e-mail and a popup window notification about a new PM and when this user goes to the inbox, there are no new messages. This does not happen very often, because the ability to edit or delete messages in the outbox is a somewhat hidden feature that most people are not aware of. But in any event, be prepared to answer the users' queries as to why they receive notifications but no messages.

- **Savebox**: Stores sent or received messages. You can move messages to this box from the other boxes. This is useful as storage for keeping some important messages that you want to have separated from the others so that you don't accidentally delete them. The savebox can also be used to offload the other boxes when they are reaching their storage limits.

When viewing a message listing, you can click the checkbox located next to each message and then move the checked messages to the savebox or delete them by using the appropriate action button at the bottom of the listing. Be careful not to confuse the Delete All button with the Delete Marked one; even though they both look the same (even the Are you sure... confirmation message), but Delete All clears all the contents of a PM box.

Time For Action—The Dude PMs the Administrator

1. You're logged in as The Dude. Click the You have no new messages 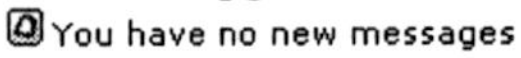 link at the top navigation menu. You're now in your empty and lonely inbox.
2. Click New Post. You're presented with the interface for writing a PM; this interface is similar to the one for writing a posting.
3. You want to PM the Administrator user, the user you created during installation as described in Chapter 2. Suppose you're not sure if it was called Administrator or simply Admin. Click the Find a username button next to the text field for the username of the recipient. A new window shows up.
4. Type Admin* (note the asterisk) and click Search (* is a wildcard, which means *any username* starting with "Admin" should be matched.
5. A dropdown with the matches appears; in our case, there's only one match. Click Select.

6. Now the username field is pre-filled. Enter test #1 in the subject line and the same in the message body. Add :) to make it friendlier.
7. Click Preview. Looks good?
8. Click Submit to send the message.
9. Repeat the steps with test #2 as a subject line and a message body.
10. Go to your sentbox. It's empty.
11. Go to your outbox. You see the two messages that you've just sent. Check the box next to test #1.
12. Click Delete Marked and confirm the deletion.
13. Logout and log back in as Administrator. Go to your inbox by using the You have 1 new message link.
14. You see that you have a new PM from The Dude with the subject test #2. Click the subject line to read the message.
15. Click Save Message to move the message to the savebox.

What Just Happened?

You've successfully created, sent, altered, received, and saved a PM. If you now log back in as The Dude, you'll see that your outbox is empty, but the sentbox now contains the test #2 message.

Voting in Polls

You already know that polls can be created when posting a new topic. Here are some notes about voting in these polls:

- Only registered users can vote.
- Non-registered users only see the poll results.
- The votes are kept confidential; there's no way to tell how a particular user has voted.
- You can view the results without voting by selecting View Results.
- Don't forget that the poll results are not 100% reliable, because an existing user can register as a new member only to vote a second time.

Staying Current with the Topics

As you know already, you can get a notification if someone posts a reply to a topic that you created or posted in. You **subscribe** to this topic by making sure Notify me when a reply is posted is checked when you write your posting. In addition to that, you can start watching a topic even if you don't post in it.

You can do so by using the Watch this topic for replies link located at the bottom of the topic. You can stop receiving notifications on a topic's update at any time, by using the Stop watching this topic link at the bottom of every page of the topic you're watching.

Viewing Information about Other Users

There are a few ways to find about the other members of the community. The memberlist feature and the usergroups provide different sorts of user listings, while the "Who's online" feature provides information about who is currently logged in and what are they currently doing.

Memberlist

If users want to know more about the other members of the community, they can obtain a member listing. Clicking the Memberlist top navigation link will bring up a list of all registered users. There are sorting options at the top of this listing. If, for example, you want to get a spicier listing like "Hmm, who's posting the most?", you can sort on the basis of the number of posts. You can select Total posts as Select sort method and Descending as your Order. This will show you the top posting members.

Well, in our example board, there's nothing spicy in the list of just the Administrator and The Dude, but it can get much more interesting as your community grows. Here's how this type of Memberlist report looks like when executed on phpBB.com's community.

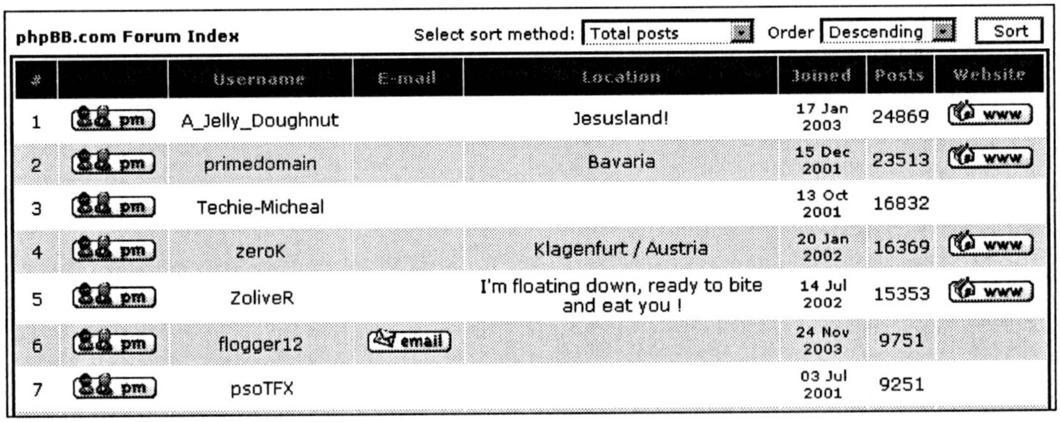

phpBB.com Forum Index — Select sort method: Total posts — Order: Descending — Sort

#		Username	E-mail	Location	Joined	Posts	Website
1	pm	A_Jelly_Doughnut		Jesusland!	17 Jan 2003	24869	www
2	pm	primedomain		Bavaria	15 Dec 2001	23513	www
3	pm	Techie-Micheal			13 Oct 2001	16832	
4	pm	zeroK		Klagenfurt / Austria	20 Jan 2002	16369	www
5	pm	ZoliveR		I'm floating down, ready to bite and eat you !	14 Jul 2002	15353	www
6	pm	flogger12	email		24 Nov 2003	9751	
7	pm	psoTFX			03 Jul 2001	9251	

Usergroups

This is an advanced phpBB feature that allows the creation of groups of users based on some criteria. Groups are defined by an administrator and are assigned a group moderator. By default, no groups exist. Users can apply to join a usergroup and, depending on the configuration (there might or might not be a need for the group moderator to approve the users), are approved.

Who Is Online

This section of the board homepage was already mentioned. Interestingly, there is a sort of a hidden feature here—something that is not obvious enough for most people to notice. It's the fact that the Who is Online heading is actually a link. (The same is true for the title of a forum category.)

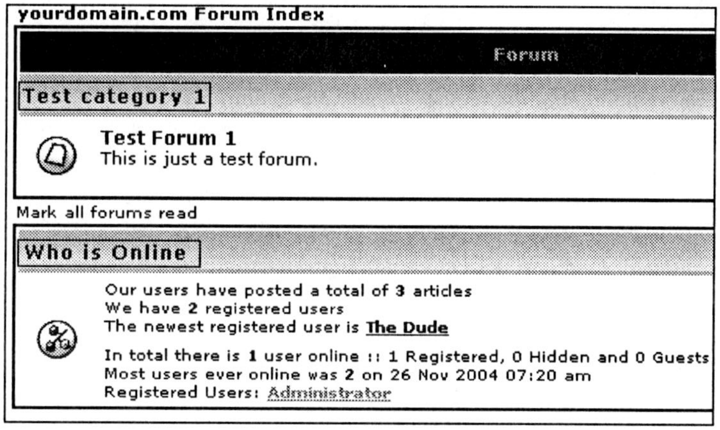

Clicking Who is Online will bring a special "spy" screen, which is publicly available. This sneaky feature allows everybody to see what others are doing at the moment.

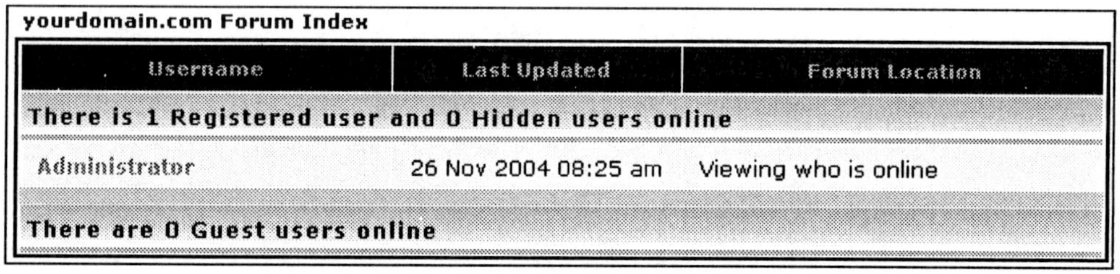

This can potentially become a long list of all currently logged-in users as well as the guests currently browsing the site.

Moderator Experience

At this point you have a pretty good idea about the regular members' perspective of your board. Now let's look at how a moderator works with phpBB. To begin with, what *is* a moderator? All dictionary definitions aside, a moderator is a community member who has some more privileges over the postings and the topics than those that the regular users have. Moderators are usually respected veteran members who are volunteering their time and energy to make the forum a better place for discussions in line with the administrator's vision for the community.

Moderators are your best helpers in managing your site, so you should make sure you make their tasks clear to them and educate them so that they don't have any technical difficulties on the way.

In order to visualize better what's discussed in the chapter, you need a moderator account. You can make our The Dude user a moderator, or you can create a new user and assign moderator privileges to it. Let's take The Dude as an example.

Time For Action—Assigning Moderator Privileges to a User

1. Log in as an administrator.
2. Go to the Administration Panel.
3. In the left-hand menu, under User Admin click on the Permissions link.

4. You are now in the User Permissions Control section.
5. In the textbox, type in The Dude and click Look Up User.

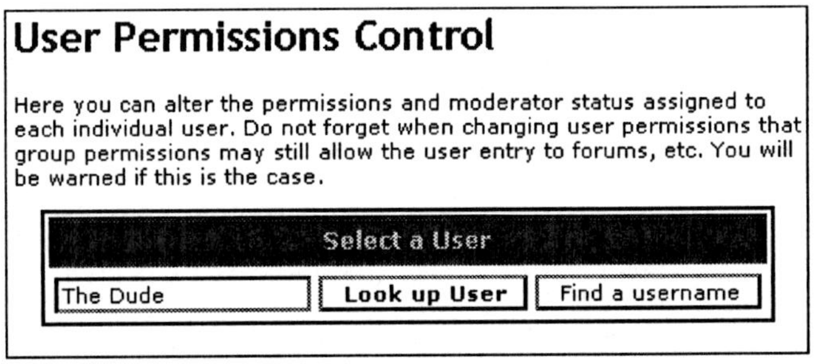

6. Now you see a form to set the permissions for The Dude.
7. Select Is Moderator as shown in the illustration and click Submit:

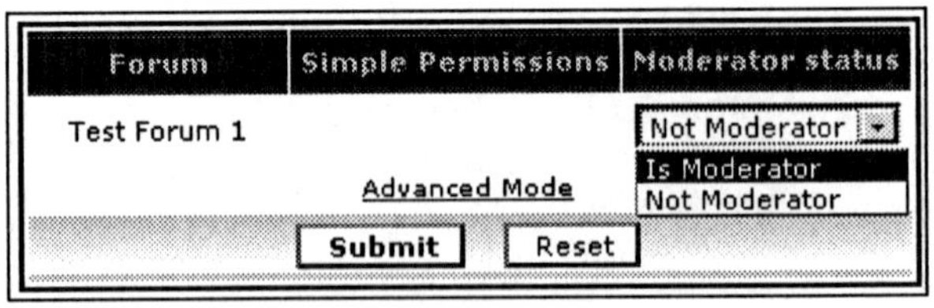

What Just Happened?

You've successfully changed The Dude's authorization level; this user is now a moderator for Test Forum 1. Logout from your administrator account and log back in as The Dude, and you're ready to start exploring what a moderator can do.

A moderator can take up two groups of tasks; these are related to *managing postings* and *managing topics.*

Managing Postings

Now that you're logged in as The Dude, the moderator, if you go to any posting and look at the actions area for the posting, you'll see the buttons for all actions a moderator can perform on a posting.

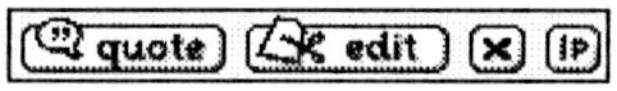

Editing and Deleting

Editing posts and deleting them from the users' perspective was already discussed earlier in this chapter. It's the same thing for moderators with only one simple but quite significant difference: in the default phpBB configuration, moderators can edit and delete *any* posting for the topic, and not just *their* postings.

Editing the First Posting in a Topic

When a moderator edits the first posting in a discussion, there are some more options, because the first post contains some topic-related information. For example, changing the post's subject changes the topic's subject.

There are also options for changing the type of the posting/topic. The possible options for the topic type are as shown:

If you post a topic as Announcement or Sticky, it will stay on the top of the topic listings. One difference between the two types is in the icon that will be displayed next to the topic title. Another (more important) difference is that sticky topics are displayed on the top of the first page of topic listings, while the announcements are on the top of all listing pages. What this means is that if there are so many topics in your forum that they span several pages (a page has 25 topics by default), a topic marked Announcement will be on top of *all the pages*, whereas the Stickys will be on the top of the *first page only.* Here's an example of what a sticky topic and an announcement look like.

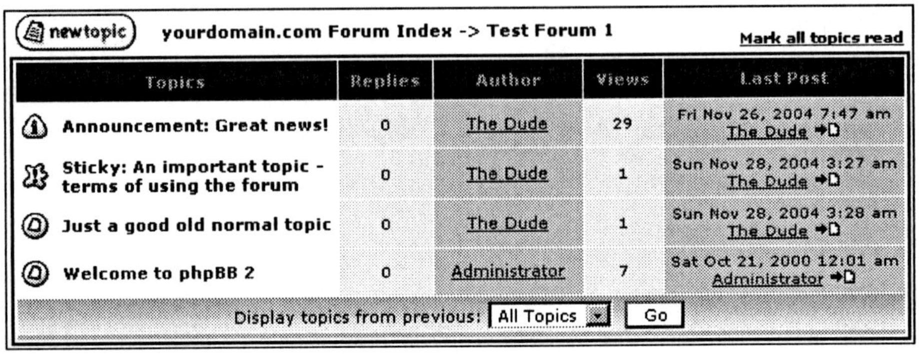

Another specific thing about editing the first posting in a topic is that you have the option of deleting it in the edit interface.

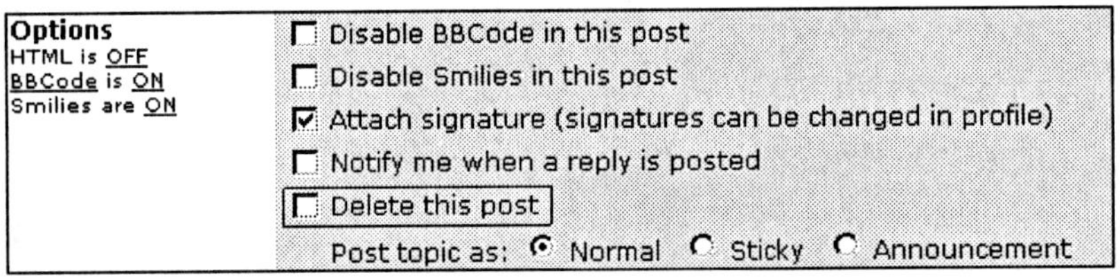

If a posting contains a poll, the poll can also be edited or deleted.

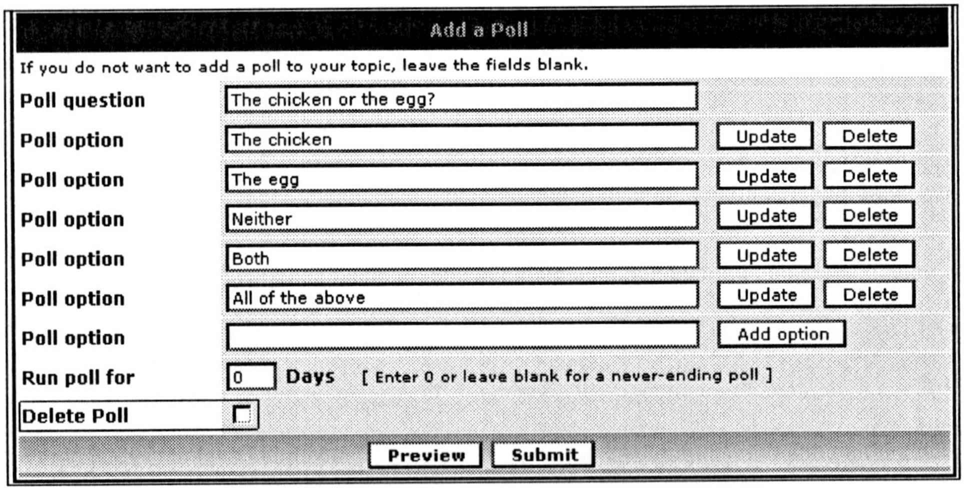

Here are some other specifics about editing the first post in a topic. It's a good idea to try the listed scenarios yourself, just to make sure you feel comfortable doing it.

- If it's the only posting in the topic and you delete it, the topic is deleted.
- If the first posting contains a poll and you delete the posting, the poll stays.

- If there are other postings after the first when you delete it, the topic stays. The title of the topic is kept from the deleted post subject.
- A poll can be safely removed from a topic, keeping everything else as is.

Viewing Poster's IP Address

If you click the IP action icon, you are presented with the IP information screen.

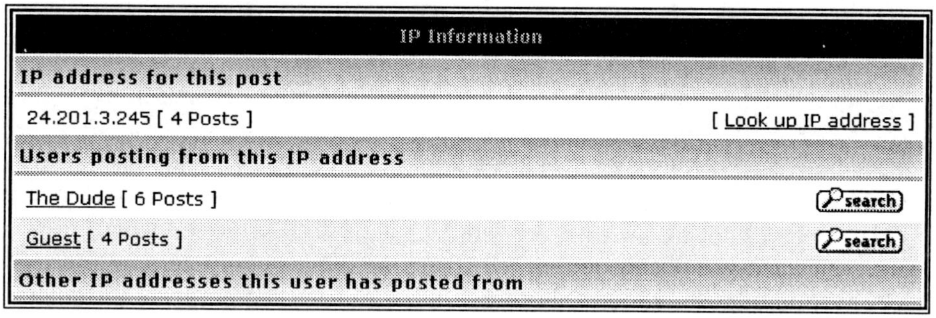

What you see on this screen is the IP address of the user, a list of users that have posted using this IP address, and finally a list of other IP addresses (if any) that were used by this user to post other messages. Here is some information that you might find useful:

- An IP address is a numeric identifier, unique for every computer connected to the Internet. IP stands for Internet Protocol. Internet Service Providers (ISP) all over the world assign IP addresses to their clients every time an Internet connection is requested. This means that if you connect to the Internet, disconnect, and reconnect, the IP address assigned to you the second time may be different from that assigned the first time.
- If you click the Look up IP address link shown in the above screenshot, phpBB will try to resolve (give a friendlier representation of) the IP address. This feature may not always work, because not all IP addresses can be resolved. In the example above, the numeric IP address will be resolved as shown in the image below:

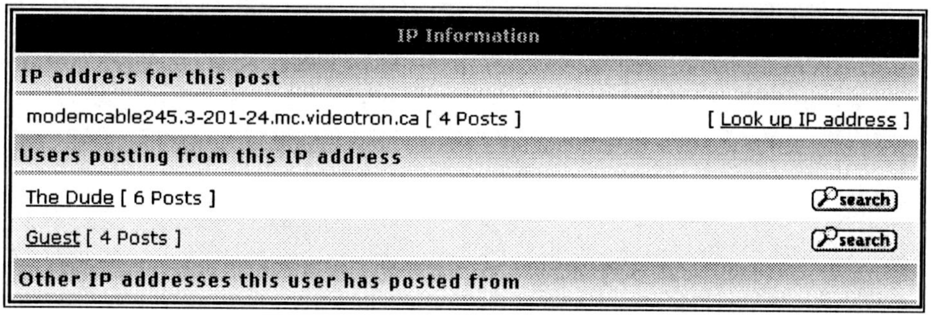

The last part of the IP address (`videotron.ca`) gives information about the Internet Service Provider (ISP). Some companies have their own IP addresses and they act as if they were their own ISP. Resolving a poster's IP address can at times give you information about the poster's employer or the poster's ISP, or no information if it cannot be resolved. Keep in mind:

- One user can be listed with several IP addresses, and this can happen quite often, because ISPs change the IP addresses assigned to their clients. Also, a member can use more than one computer and Internet connection to post (for example, home and office computers).
- Several users may use the same IP address. Maybe the first possibility you think of is that a person has registered a new username and is posting from both usernames. Although it's a probable scenario, it's not necessarily always the case. Two users may have the same ISP (or may be employed at the same company) and thus may have the same IP address. Another explanation is that two users are friends and one is using the other's computer and Internet connection to post. And yet another—two users are posting from the same Internet club (game club, Internet café, etc.).
- In the IP information interface, clicking on the username brings up the user's profile page.
- In the same interface, clicking on the **Search** button will list all posts by a particular user.

Managing Topics

Managing topics is the second group of options that a moderator has that the regular users don't. One way to manage a topic is by altering the first posting in this topic. This was discussed in the *Managing Postings* section earlier in this chapter (you might want to go back and take a look; the other options discussed here are strictly topics-related).

At the bottom of every topic, a moderator has access to four action icons, as shown:

In the order that they appear, they mean:

- **Delete a topic**: Remove the topic permanently from the database.
- **Move a topic**: Move the topic from its present forum to another forum. Another forum refers to a forum in the same bulletin board.
- **Lock a topic**: Users (except moderators and administrators) can no longer post in this topic.
- **Split a topic**: Divide a topic into two.

Deleting, Locking, and Unlocking Topics

All these options are actually simple to use. You just need to list a topic and then select the appropriate action icon. phpBB then asks you to confirm the chosen action. That's it! The unlock icon is displayed only in locked topics.

Moving Topics

In order to test this functionality you need at least two forums. So before you continue, let's first create a new forum.

Time For Action—Creating a Forum

1. Log in as Administrator (the user account you created when installing), and then click the Go to Administration Panel link.
2. On the left-hand menu, under Forum Admin, click Management.

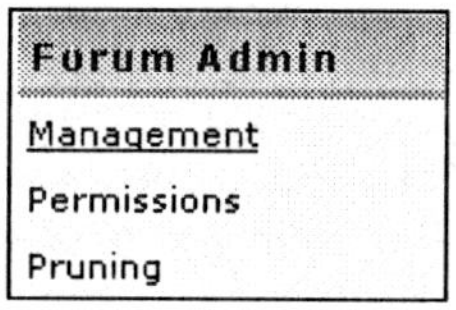

3. Type New Forum in the first field, and click on Create new forum.

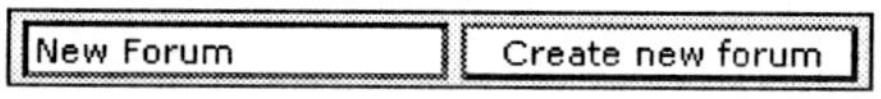

4. You see a new form; leave it as is and click Create new forum.
5. Go back to the forum, clicking the phpBB icon on the top left.

What Just Happened?

You've created a new forum. Don't worry about the details; they will be discussed in more detail later in this chapter. OK, back to moving topics. This simply involves displacing a topic to another forum, and is often needed when somebody posts a topic in not-the-best-place on the bulletin board. Log out now and log back in as The Dude.

A moderator moves a topic by selecting the action icon. The following confirmation screen is displayed:

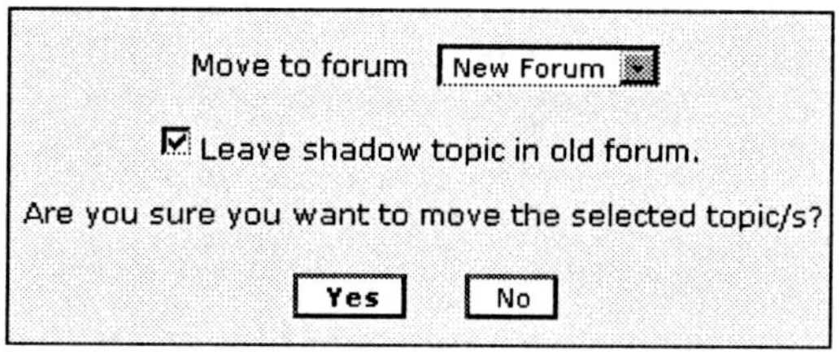

This screen lets the moderator select the forum to which the topic is to be moved. There is also a Leave shadow topic in old forum checkbox (checked by default). Select this option to leave in the old forum a link to the new location. The link looks exactly like a normal topic, except that it has Moved before the title, as shown here:

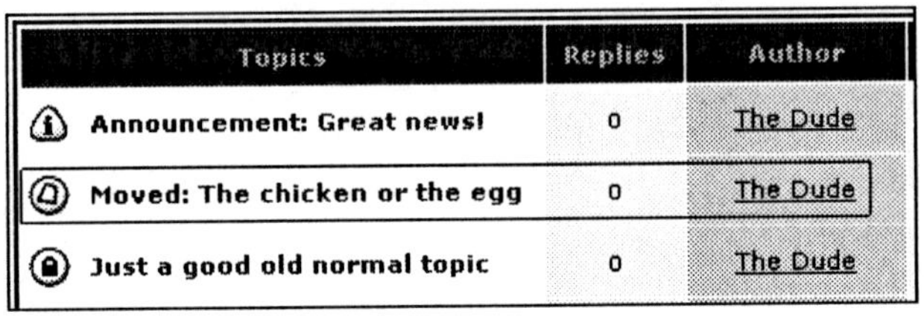

Splitting Topics

Sometimes a discussion digresses from the original topic; at other times, people discuss two different questions in the same topic—postings start overlapping, and it's difficult to follow the discussion. To avoid confusion caused by such a situation, a moderator can split the discussion into two topics. To do so, the moderator clicks the split icon. The following special interface for splitting topics is presented:

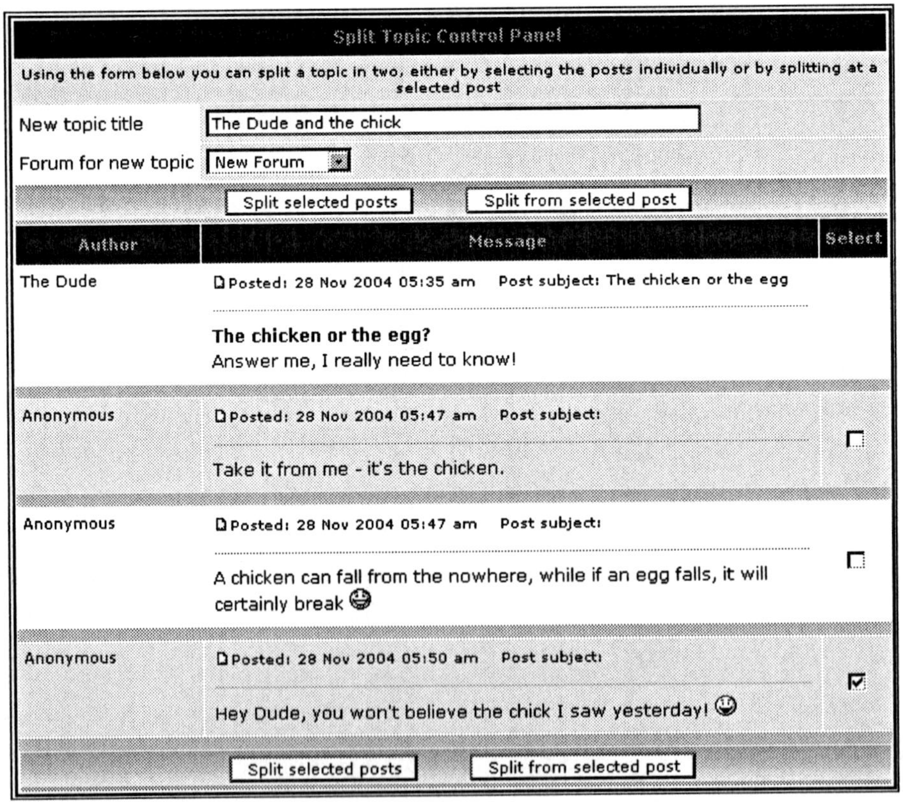

Essentially, splitting a topic involves creating a new topic to accommodate some already existing messages, while removing them from the topic under which they were originally posted. Thus said, a new topic needs a title, a forum to reside in, and at least one posting.

The Split Topic Control Panel, shows a text field for the title and a dropdown to choose an existing forum. There is a checkbox next to each posting. There are two splitting options:

- To select each posting individually. It's time-consuming to check each individual posting, but this is an option when two separate questions are discussed in a total overlap.
- To select one posting and then split the complete discussion. This is applicable when at some point a discussion takes a totally different direction. In this case, the checked posting is the beginning of the *new* topic.

Two tips:

- Especially on heavily loaded boards, it's a good idea to temporarily lock a topic before splitting. This gives enough time for the moderator to rethink the details, while preventing other users from posting at the same time and adding to the confusion.
- Have in mind that the author of the first message in the newly created topic becomes the author of the new topic.

Doing It All Together—The Moderator Control Panel

phpBB has a feature called the Moderator Control Panel, which gives access to all the actions discussed above for managing topics. To access this interface, click the moderate this forum link, located at the bottom right corner of every forum page.

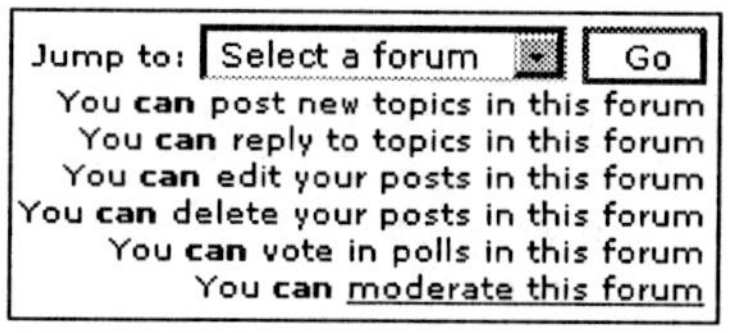

This brings up the Moderator Control Panel interface (screenshot overleaf):

- This interface has a Select checkbox next to each topic, and a number of action buttons at the bottom. It allows you to check several topics and perform an action on them all at once.
- Clicking a topic title brings up the Split Topic interface.
- All actions (deleting, locking, unlocking, moving, and splitting) work in the exact same way as already discussed earlier in this chapter, only the interface is different so as to allow altering multiple topics at once.

The following screenshot shows the Moderator Control Panel:

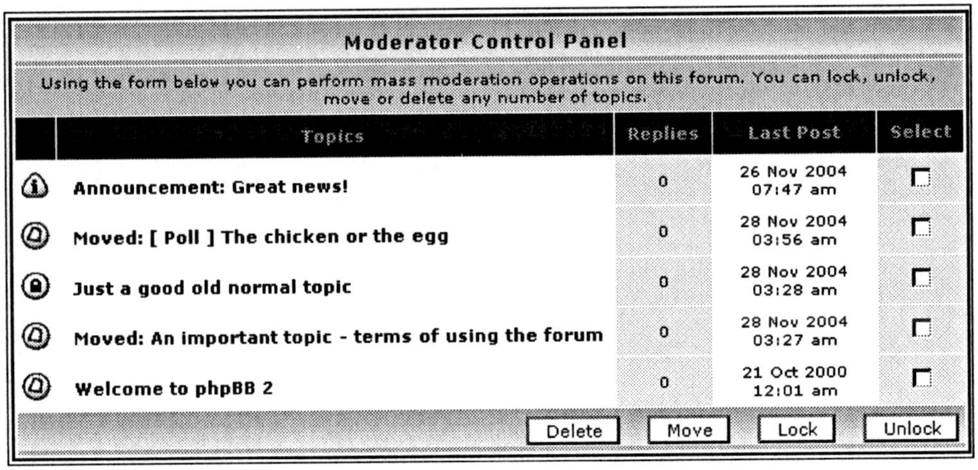

Administrator Experience

This is it. You've come to the most important part—administering your board. You've already seen some of the features described previously in this chapter as well as in Chapter 2, but it's now time to take a more organized approach and make sure you understand what your administrative options are and how to use them.

This section will later describe some basic phpBB admin features that you're likely to use more frequently than others. For more advanced and exotic options, make sure you read Chapter 5, which goes into details about security-related questions, smilies, usergroups, and other issues.

In order to test what's being described further on, you need to log in as a user with administrative privileges. There can be multiple administrators to your board, but in any event, at least one administrative user account exists—the account created while installing phpBB. We'll log in with this account, use the Go to Administration Panel link, and let's start exploring administrative options.

Administration Panel Overview

The Administration Panel has two main areas (referred to as **frames** in HTML terms):

- The left-hand navigation area, which contains links to all your administrative options. It's divided into groups of similar options like Forum Admin, User Admin, etc.

- The right-hand content area, where the appropriate content is loaded when you click a link from the navigation area.

Your Administration Panel front page looks as shown on the following screenshot:

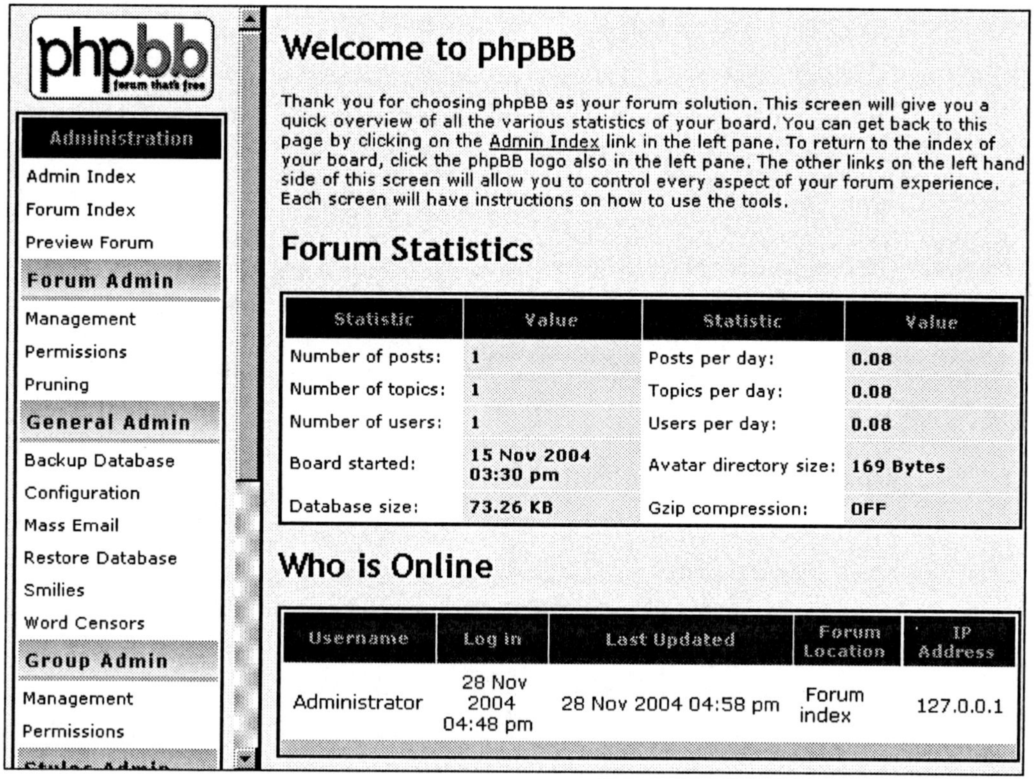

The Administration Panel front page also has some general statistics about the forum usage and a Who is Online section that works in a similar way to the one that visitors can access on the forum homepage (see the *Visitor Experience* section earlier in the chapter), except that this one has an IP address column as well. Clicking on an IP address redirects you to a third-party site that provides some IP-related tools that you may find useful.

The first three options of the navigation menu are pretty straightforward and you may want to give them a try just to get a more comfortable feeling browsing the Administration Panel. They are not actually administrative options but simply links to the board's front page and the Administration Panel. The phpBB logo in the top-left corner is also a link to the homepage of the board.

Now let's take a closer look into the other groups of options on the navigation menu.

Forum Admin

As the title says, this is a group of options for you to administer your forums, to create, edit, delete, or rearrange forums and their categories, as well as to set their options and rules of use (referred to as **permissions**).

Forum Management

Clicking the Management link in the Forum Admin options group brings up the Forum Administration interface. This interface allows you to create, edit, and delete forums and to organize them into categories.

Creating New Forums and Categories

The simplest way to create a new forum was already briefly discussed in the *Moderator Experience* section. Now let's take a more detailed approach. The following screenshot shows how the interface looks after we've added the new forum in the previous section. If you haven't done what was described in the *Moderator Experience* section, you'll have the default phpBB look, which is same as shown below minus the New Forum row:

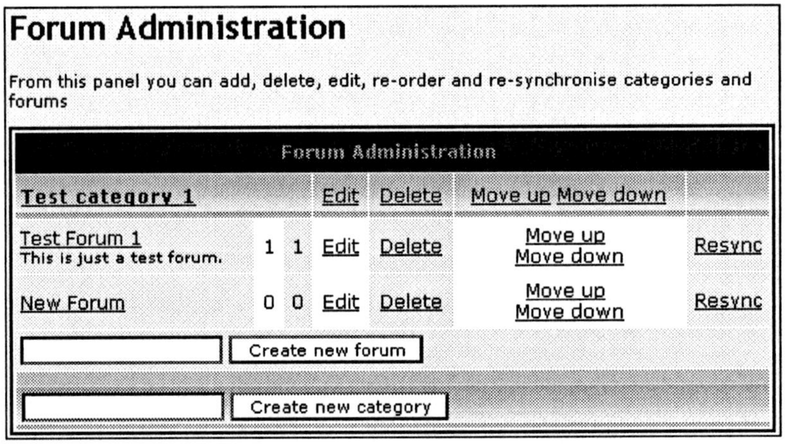

Time For Action—Creating a New Category

1. Type Fun in the second text field of the Forum Administration interface.
2. Click Create new category.
3. Click the link in the Click Here to return to Forum Administration line once the category is created.

What Just Happened

You've created a new blank category (blank because it doesn't contain any forums yet). Here's how the Forum Administration screen will look after you complete the above steps:

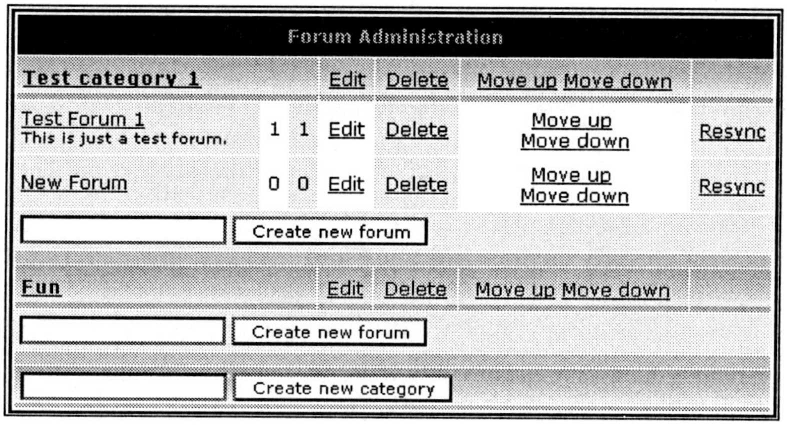

At this point, because the new category is still empty, visitors see no changes made to the board's homepage.

Now let's add some forums to the new category.

Time For Action—Creating a New Forum

1. Type Funny pics in the textbox after the Fun category you've just added in the Forum Administration interface.
2. Click Create new forum. You are now presented with the following form:

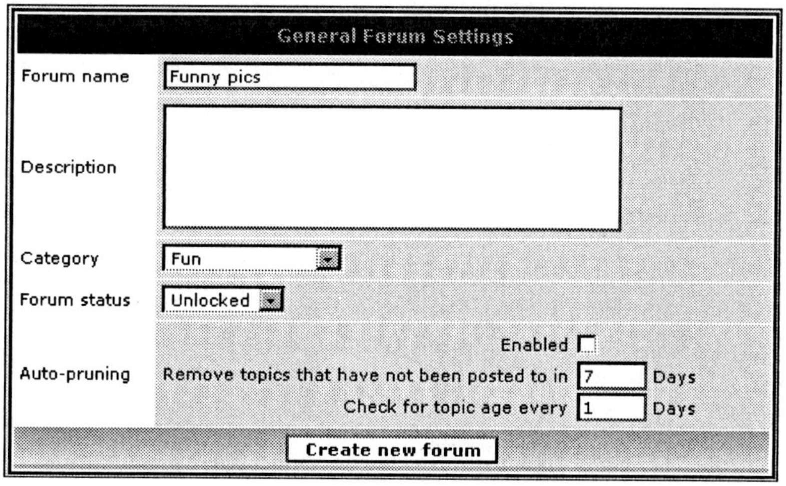

3. In the Description field, type Collection of links to funny images found on the web.
4. Leave Category dropdown as is.
5. Leave the Forum status dropdown as is.

6. In the Auto-pruning section leave the defaults.
7. Click the Create new forum button.
8. Click the link Click Here to return to Forum Administration. At this point we are repeating the exercise, but with a few modifications.
9. To start creating another new forum, type Funny quotes, but this time do it in the *first* text field.
10. In the Description field, type Here you'll find links to funny quote web sites the admin finds amusing.
11. Change the value in the Category dropdown from Test category 1 to Fun.
12. Change the value in the Forum status dropdown from Unlocked to Locked.
13. In the Auto-pruning section, select Enabled.
14. In the Auto-pruning section, change the first text value from 7 to 30.
15. In the Auto-pruning section, change the second text value from 1 to 7.
16. Click the Create new forum button.
17. Click the link in the Click Here to return to Forum Administration.

What Just Happened

Here's the result of what you've just done as shown in the Administration Panel:

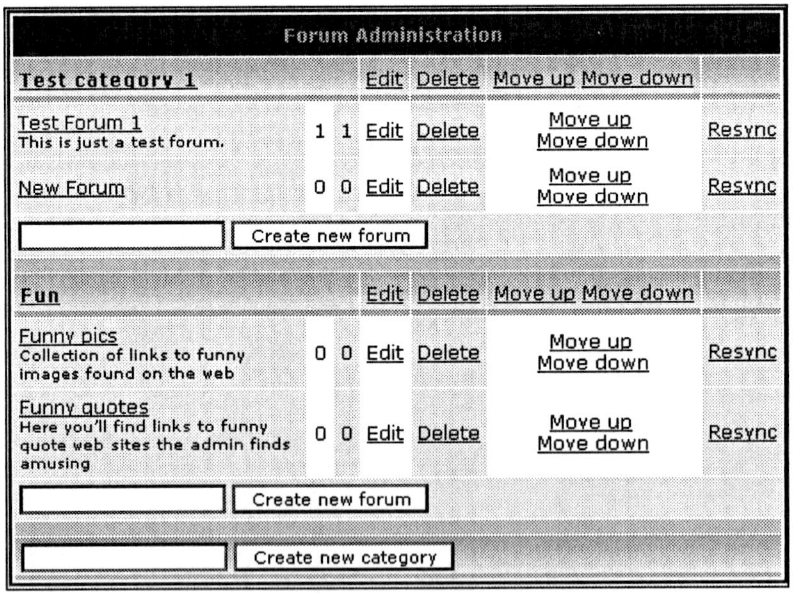

And here's what your users will see—the changed board on the home page:

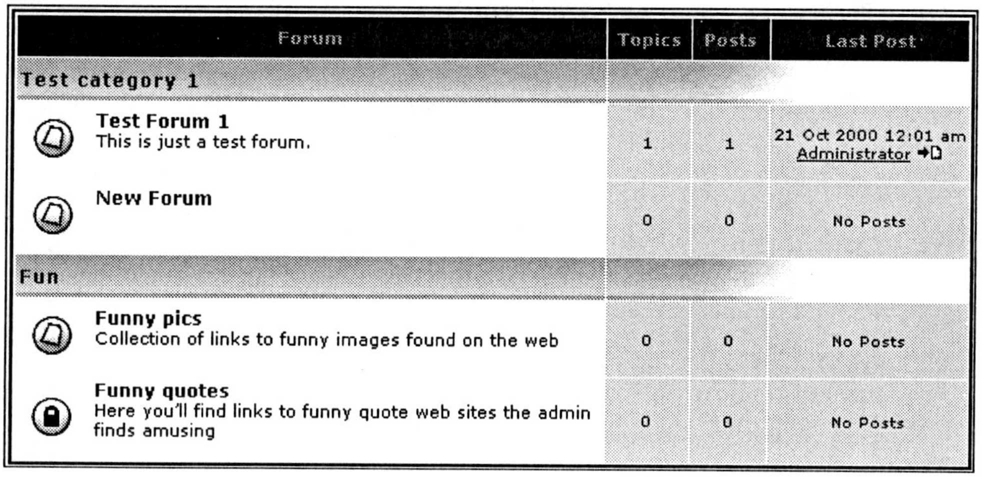

Now let's take a step back and see exactly what happened, using the same numbers as in the preceding *Time For Action* section:

1. You gave a name to your new forum.
2. You initiated the creation of the new forum.
3. You gave a description to your forum.
4. You used the phpBB-proposed value for a category.
5. You used the phpBB-proposed value for the Locked/Unlocked forum status (in this case, Unlocked). What this means is that users can post in this forum. Locked, as you know, would mean that users cannot post in the forum, but administrators and moderators still can.
6. You used the phpBB default value for the Auto-pruning option, which is not to use this option. If you enable the auto-pruning feature, phpBB will delete all topics that were inactive for a specified period of time. The Inactivity of a topic is counted from the time of the last posting to it.
7. You finalized the creation of the new forum.
8. You went back to the Forums Administration interface.
9. You started the process of creating a new forum again and set the title.
10. You specified the forum description.
11. This time you didn't use the proposed value, but changed the forum category. This category was proposed by phpBB, because you typed the forum name under Test category 1 and not under Fun on step 9.
12. You decided to have this forum locked so that users would not able to post, but you still could.
13. You turned on the auto-pruning option.

14. You set that phpBB should delete all topics older than 30 days, counted from the date of the last posting in this topic.
15. You set phpBB to check topics for auto-deletion every seven days.
16. You finalized the creation of the new forum.
17. You went back to the Forums Administration interface.

Fine Tuning Existing Forums and Categories

After a forum is created, it can be managed further—edited, deleted, or positioned in relation to the other forums in the board.

Editing

You can edit an existing category or a forum by clicking the Edit link located next to the title of the category/forum. The edit forms look exactly the same as the Create new forum one and work the same way.

Deleting

You can delete categories and forums by using the Delete links next to their titles. One specific point here: when you delete a forum or a category that has been around for some time and people have been posting in it, you might not want to delete *all* the postings. To simplify this, phpBB allows you to move the existing topics into another forum or a category before deleting the selected topic.

When you delete a category, you can pick a new category to move all forums to, as shown below (this interface shows Delete Forum and Forum name, but actually refers to deleting categories; you'll spot the difference with the actual deleting-a-forum interface):

When you want to delete a forum, you are given the option of moving all the topics to another forum. Unlike with category deletion, when you delete a forum you can even choose to delete the topics and the postings as well. Think again before using this option though. Deleting your community's postings may not be such a good idea.

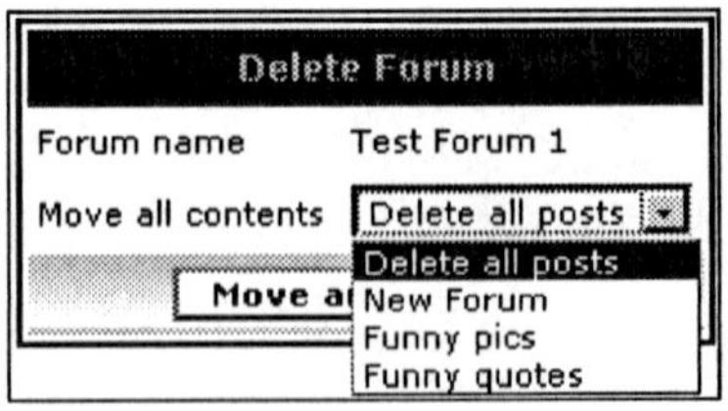

Changing Display Order

You can change the order of displaying categories and forums on the board's home page, by using the Move up and Move down links, next to each forum or a category.

Time For Action – Tweaking display order

1. Click the Move down link next to the Test category 1 category.
2. Click the Move up link next to the New Forum forum.

What Just Happened

The Fun category is now the first one that the users will see. Also, within Test Category 1, you've switched the forums' order so that New Forum is displayed before Test Forum 1. Here's how users will see your board after the tweaks.

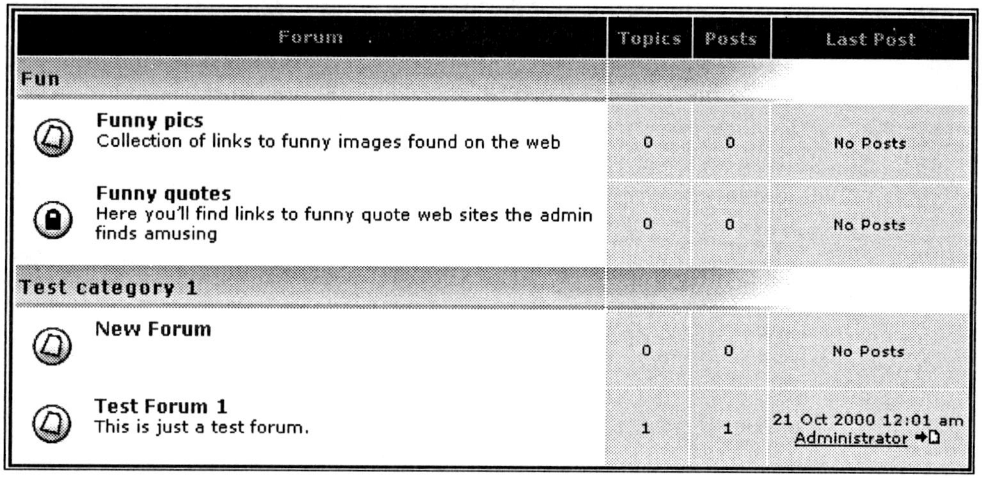

Using the Resync Options

If you spot some weird things happening on you board, use the Resync option as a first attempt to recovery. If there are some data inconsistencies for whatever reasons, Resync will try to bring the data into a consistent state.

Resync can do no harm to the board data. So don't worry, you can't break anything. (Well, don't take that last sentence as a challenge.) If ever in doubt about whether you should be using this option, just use it. On the other hand, if you find yourself using it too often, there might be other problems; isolate the symptoms and seek a cure on the phpBB community forums.

Who Can Do What—Setting Up Forum Permissions

phpBB takes the security aspects of running a bulletin board really seriously. That's why there is a powerful and options-rich system of permissions and user privileges.

You'll find some more detailed information about the permissions system in Chapter 5, which contains details on some advanced phpBB features. You'll also find more information in the phpBB user guide. So before you start playing around with the permissions, make sure you know what you're doing. For now, we'll just take a quick look into the permissions that are used most often, and leave the details for later.

There are two modes of setting a forum's permissions: **simple** and **advanced**. Using the simple mode, you can pick permission patterns (a set of advanced permissions grouped together to be easier to use) from a list of preset values. Example options for simple mode are "Public" forum, "Registered" forum, and "Hidden" forum.

These simple options are carefully analyzed and selected by the phpBB team, so using them instead of the advanced options is probably the safest thing to do until you are comfortable managing forum and user permissions. Let this be your rule of thumb: use the simple mode unless you have a good reason not to and you know what you're doing.

The two simple mode options used the most frequently are "Registered" and "Public". To get a rough idea, in a "Public" forum, a visitor doesn't have to be a registered user in order to post. In a "Registered" forum, only registered users can post. In both cases, only moderators and administrators can use more advanced features like specifying topic-type (sticky and announcement) or editing and deleting other people's posts.

By default, all the forums that phpBB creates are public. A good (and common) practice is to change a forum's permissions to "Registered" after you create it.

Time For Action—Setting Forum Permissions in Simple Mode

1. Select Permissions from the Forum Admin options in the left navigation:

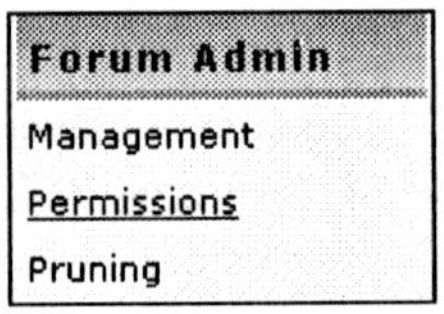

2. Select the Funny pics forum and click on the Look up Forum button.
3. Select Registered from the Simple Mode options dropdown and click Submit.

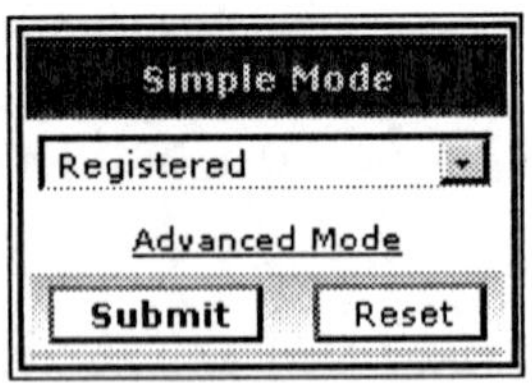

What Just Happened?

Only registered users are now allowed to post in the "Funny pics" forum. You did this by setting phpBB permissions in simple mode.

Pruning

Pruning is a feature that allows you to clean up old inactive topics to free up database space. You already saw how the auto-pruning feature works. The only way pruning is different from auto-pruning is that it's initiated by you, and not done automatically.

Think twice before you use this feature—deleting topics is irreversible! Are you sure you don't need these topics anymore? Remember that your community members have spent quite some time writing all these postings. Do you want to throw their postings away? Consider buying more database space if you're short, before deleting people's topics. If you're still positive you want to prune postings, here's how.

Time For Action—Pruning a Forum

1. Select Pruning from the Forum Admin options from the left navigation menu.

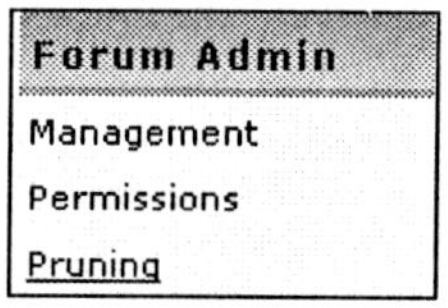

2. Pick All forums if you want to clean them all. You also have the option of pruning individual forums.
3. Type 30 as the number of days.
4. Click Do Prune.

What Just Happened?

You've just deleted all topics in all forums that were inactive for more than 30 days. Here's a sample outcome of this action, this is a report of how many topics and postings were deleted.

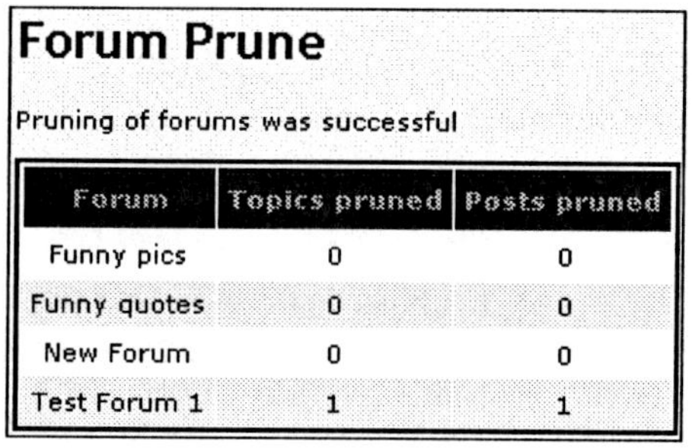

Forum Prune

Pruning of forums was successful

Forum	Topics pruned	Posts pruned
Funny pics	0	0
Funny quotes	0	0
New Forum	0	0
Test Forum 1	1	1

Systems Administration Using General Admin Options

Now let's move to the General Admin group of options, which allow you to do the basic system administration tasks.

Configuration

You can access the general configuration options by clicking the Configuration link from the General Admin options on the left navigation menu. (Don't worry about skipping Backup Database; a description of this option follows in a bit.)

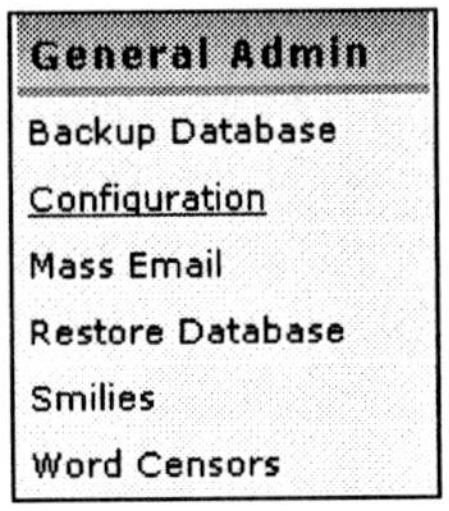

This brings the "General Configuration" form that contains the very root board settings, such as domain name, enabling private messages, and so on. You already know about these settings from Chapter 2.

Database Backup and Restore

It's a good idea to make backup copies of your data, just in case something happens. Your hosting provider is likely to make such backup copies; you can also make backups using phpMyAdmin or using MySQL command-line utilities. If you're using a different database system, you may have other options. If you have access to phpMyAdmin, use it. If your hosting provider is making copies, find out about their frequency and the level of effort required to restore the database. It's your responsibility not to allow data to be lost, and it should be taken seriously.

Scared ya, huh? Good. Now for the good news: if you're worried you don't have access to tools to back up your data, rest assured, phpBB provides you with a database backup utility. Sometimes it can be your only option, so let's look into it.

Time For Action—Backing Up Your Board Data

1. Click Backup Database from the navigation menu.
2. In the Backup Options form that you see, click Start Backup, leaving all values at default. You get a Please wait message.
3. A file dialog window asks you what to do with the `phpbb_db_backup.sql` file that was requested for download. Save this file into a selected folder on your computer.

What Just Happened

You've just created a backup file containing the SQL instructions for your database and saved it on your computer. It's a good idea to store these backup files carefully, keeping them organized by using appropriate filenames and directories. For example, filenames can contain the date the backup was created. Every once in a while, burn those files on a CD; you never know when your PC will crash and cause you to lose your data backups.

Time For Action—Restoring Your Database from a Backup Copy

1. Click Restore Database from the left navigation menu in the Administration Panel.
2. Locate an existing backup copy file (you can use the `phpbb_db_backup.sql` file you created in the previous exercise).
3. Click Start Restore.
4. If everything is OK, you'll get a message that the restore was successful.

What Just Happened

You restored your board database from a backup copy saved on your computer, containing all configuration, forums, topics, users: to put it simply—all the data your board needs in order to run.

Depending on the size of the database, the time taken to execute backup and restore operations may vary. For very large databases, these operations may even fail because of some server restrictions imposed by your hosting provider. If you're experiencing problems, be sure to read Chapter 5 for more information on database backup and restore options, and feel free to seek advice on phpBB.com or phpBBHacks.com forums.

Mass E-Mail

You can use phpBB to send an e-mail to all your users, or to just one usergroup. This feature is really easy to use: you just select the Mass Email link from the menu on the left, select the recipients, type in the subject and the message body, and click the E-mail button. This hopefully will fire an e-mail to all users.

"Hopefully", because there is a chance that this feature will not work for you. Because of all these people that send unsolicited mail (read **spam**), Internet providers and hosting companies are taking measures against everything that looks like a mass mail. So if you have a lot of users in your database or your host has strict mail-usage rules, you may not be able to mass-mail your users.

You can try using the SMTP server of your ISP if the attempt to send without any configuration changes fails. The mail settings are located under the Configuration link in the General Admin section.

The way phpBB mailer works is it adds all recipients to the BCC. Imagine you're sending a normal e-mail in your favorite e-mail environment. Now imagine you add all users in the BCC (Blind Carbon Copy) field. The result: the e-mail is sent to all recipients, and they cannot see who else is on the BCC list.

Smilies

You know smilies, those cute little icons (also known as emoticons) that you can use to lighten up your postings and show some emotion, as well as to give the reader a cue as to how to react to your text. Well, good news: phpBB comes with a package of smilies by default and is also flexible enough to allow you to add, edit, and delete the smilies that your members can use in their postings.

Clicking Smilies in the General Admin option group brings the Smiles Editing Utility.

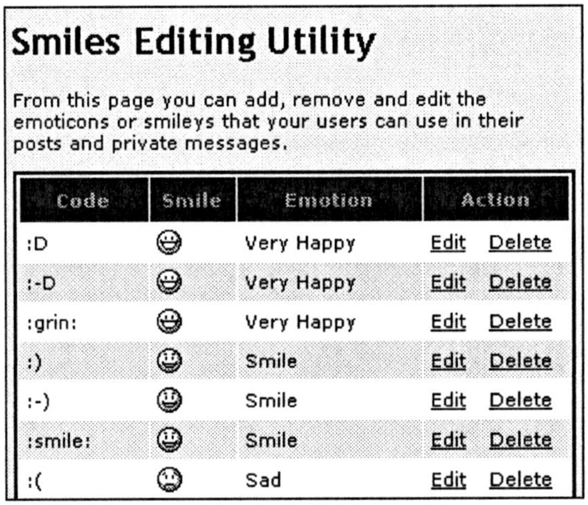

It's pretty easy to edit or delete smilies. Just use the corresponding link located next to each smilie. You can also add new icons and even add batches of new icons, packaged in special files (`.pak`). There's more information on this in Chapter 5.

Filtering Words Using Word Censors

phpBB allows you to censor words that your members use in their postings. Censoring means replacing a bad word with another (not as bad) one. It actually doesn't need to be a word per se; it can be a part of a word or a phrase.

Time For Action—Creating a Word Filter

1. Click on the Word Censors link on the navigation menu.
2. In the new screen, click Add new word. A new form appears:

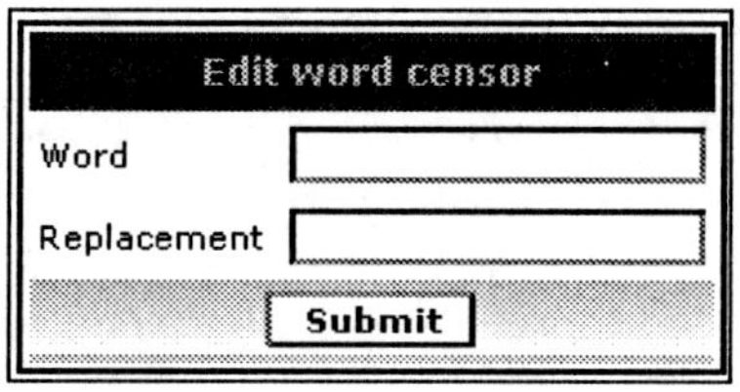

3. Type The Dude Sucks in the Word field.
4. Type The Dude Rocks! in the Replacement field.
5. Click Submit.

What Just Happened

You introduced a new word replacement filter for posting texts. You can now go to the board's front end and test how this feature works.

Some additional information:

- The words you choose to censor will be censored not only in posting texts but also in post/topic subjects, PM, usernames, polls answers, and poll questions.
- The words are replaced only when displaying. In the database, phpBB stores the original texts. So if you decide to remove a Word Censor, the original text will start showing up.
- You can use the * wildcard to match a partial word. In the previous example, if you go with matching and replacing The Dude su*, this will also match all alternative phrases like The Dude sukz, The Dude sux, etc., and all of them will be replaced.

Introduction to User Management

Managing users is an activity that you might do quite often. Sometimes users have problems with their profiles, forget passwords, no longer have access to old e-mail accounts, and so on. This is when you step in to help your users.

This section, as the title says, is an introduction and contains only the features you are likely to use more or less frequently. More advanced and less used features will be discussed in Chapter 5.

Editing User Profiles

To edit a user profile, click on the Management link of the User Admin options.

You are already familiar with the screen for selecting a user based on the username. If you're not sure about a username spelling, use the Find a username feature.

After you type (or find) a username, clicking the Look up user button brings up the user profile. The form for editing the profile is the same as the one the users see on the board front end with one addition: the Special admin-only fields section:

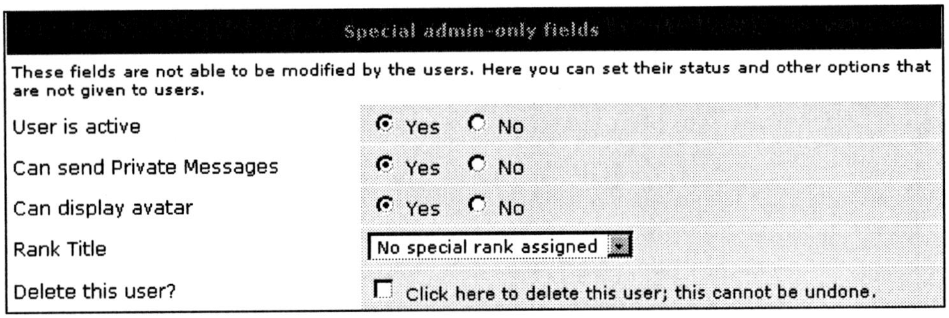

The options are quite self-explanatory:

- You can deactivate the user, so the user can no longer log in.
- You can disallow the use of private messaging or avatars for this user. Disallowing PM means that the user cannot send a PM, but can receive PMs from other users.
- You can assign a rank (ranks and avatars are discussed further).
- You can delete this user.

Deleting Users

To delete a user, do as described above, and then check the Delete this user? checkbox at the bottom of the edit form and click Submit. Deleting a user is permanent; you cannot revert. However, deleting a user doesn't mean deleting all the postings made by the user. When a user is deleted, all the postings by this user become "guest" postings. At this point, the username is recycled and becomes available for a new registration.

Permissions

The interface for setting user permissions can be accessed using the Permissions link in the User Admin navigation group:

Again you are presented with the familiar Select a User form. After choosing the user to edit, you see the User Permissions Control screen:

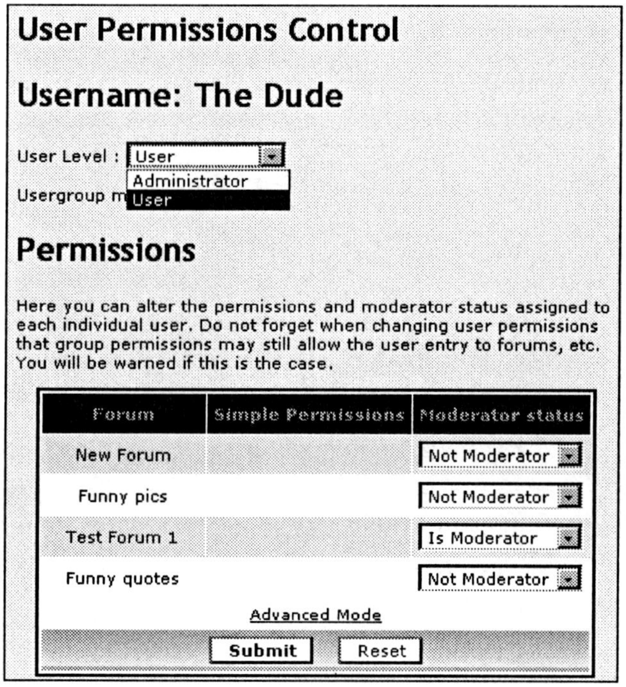

Here, you have the option of making this user an administrator, which will automatically give the user access to the Administration Panel and will make the user a moderator of all the forums. In short, this means that the user will have exactly the same privileges as you.

The other option is to selectively make the user a moderator on per-forum basis. You've already done this; remember how you made The Dude a moderator at the beginning of the *Moderator Experience* section?

Here the Simple Permissions column is empty. The same is true for the detailed permissions of you click on Advanced mode. This is because these options are applicable and can be set for private forums only, and there's no private forum among those listed. Private forums and detailed permissions are described further in the book.

Banning Users

Yes, it's not a pleasant task, throwing out users. But what can you do? C'est la vie, it happens. There are all kinds of people out there and sometimes hidden behind the anonymity of the Web, some folks start doing things that they wouldn't normally do. Like using bad grammar. Or forgetting to post on Thursdays. Just joking, of course.

Anyway, the idea is that it's up to you to define unwanted behavior for your specific community, but when it comes to the worst, you'd better know what your options are.

To access the ban control interface, use the Ban Control link under User Admin from the navigation menu on the left-hand side.

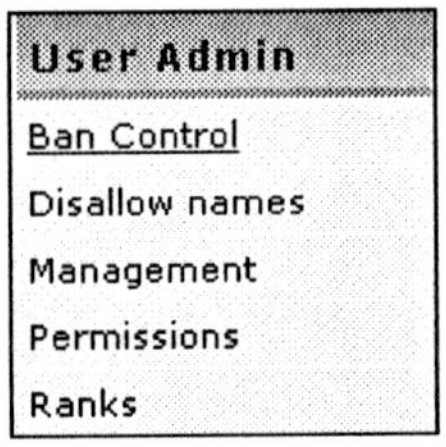

The interface for banning users may seem a bit confusing at first, but it's actually good for providing an at-a-glance overview of what sort of bans are currently defined. The form consists of three groups of two form fields each. These three groups represent the three ways to ban a user, and the two fields are for adding and removing bans respectively. The form itself contains some help on the available options.

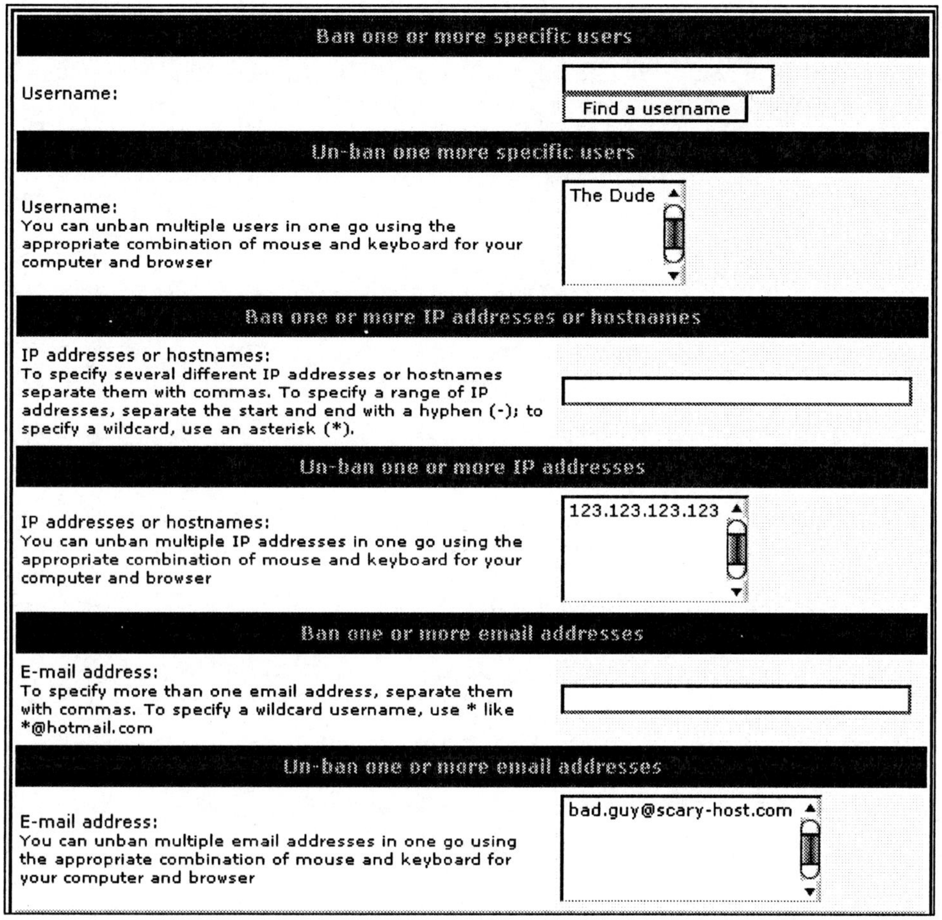

When you ban a user using any of the three methods and the user tries to access the forum, they'll see a message as follows:

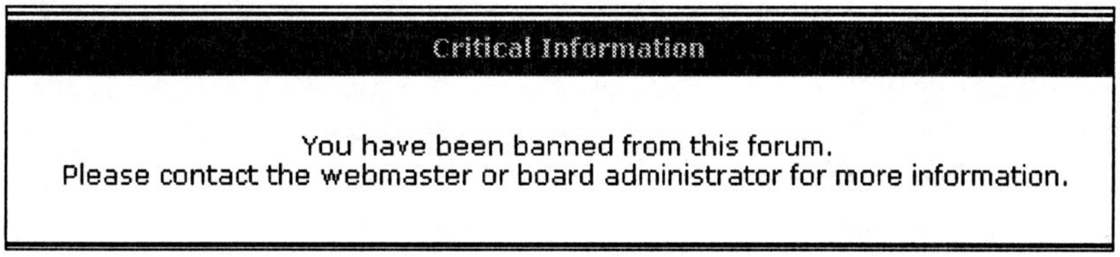

Disallowing Users

While you can ban users after the damage is done, disallowing certain usernames is a preventative act. When a username (or a part of it) is disallowed, it cannot be used for registrations. So this feature is used before a username is taken, to prevent it from being taken. The form for disallowing usernames contains an interface for both adding and removing rules. The form is accessible through the Disallow names link on the left.

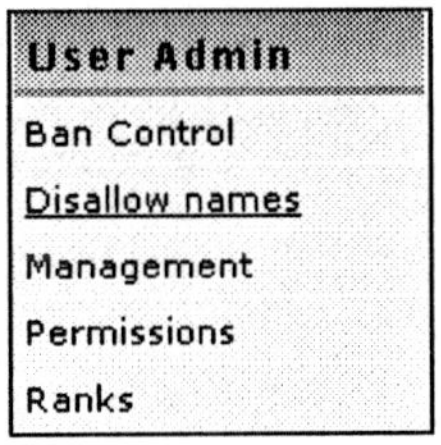

The following example shows how everything starting with Mod (as in Moderator) or Admin is disallowed to prevent imposters from using usernames suggesting that they are not just regular users, but have special community powers.

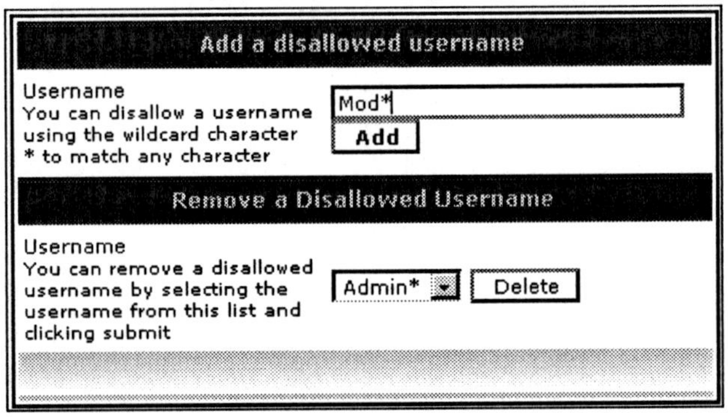

Summary

Running through the phpBB's basic features was a long way to go. This is true, because phpBB is a feature-rich bulletin-board system that provides a lot of flexibility to all user types—regular members, moderators, and administrators. To get philosophical, in theory and practice, it is known that greater flexibility often comes at the price of increased complexity. But this is not necessarily the case for most of the phpBB features as they are really intuitive and easy to use.

If you did the *Time For Action* sections in this chapter, you should now have a pretty good idea how things are working around your new BB. If you didn't do the practice parts, now is the time to go back and do them or just to set the book aside and jump into experimenting with phpBB, you favorite bulletin-board system.

4
Customizing Your Forum

Now that you have installed phpBB and gained some experience with the Administration Control Panel, you are ready to begin altering some more advanced aspects of the forum's appearance and features. Changing these areas of phpBB will be essential for giving your forum a unique identity that stands out among online forums. The appearance of a forum is mainly controlled by phpBB's styling system, which manages the colors, images, and visual layout of the forum. Features can be added, removed, or altered by installing modification scripts downloaded from phpBB-related websites.

By the end of this chapter, you will have learned about:

- The basics of a phpBB 2.0 style
- Correct methods of editing phpBB files
- How to add and remove styles
- Common style installation problems
- Ways to customize a style
- The benefits of creating and altering styles
- Methods of changing forum images
- How to add new forum features

phpBB Styles

If you look at several different phpBB forums, you may notice several differences in each forum. They may use different colors and images, display features in a different order, or omit some features entirely. This multitude of effects can be accomplished by using different phpBB styles. A phpBB **style** is the appearance of a forum, created by a combination of a layout, colors, and images. When you installed phpBB, the default style, called subSilver, was also installed. subSilver is the most commonly used style on phpBB forums, but there are well over two hundred different styles that have been publicly released. It is common for forums to have multiple styles available for user selection.

> When dealing with phpBB, you will sometimes see the terms style, theme, and template used interchangeably. In this chapter, themes and templates are defined as two smaller aspects of the overall style to reduce confusion. This is the way the terms are used most often in phpBB's code and Administration Control Panel. Even the latter sometimes uses theme in place of style, however.

Structure of a Style

In order to effectively customize a style, you must first understand the parts that compose the design of that style. Styles, like houses, are built from smaller components that work together to create a frame. That frame, like the walls of the house, provides a structure for displaying the internal contents of a forum. These frames can be very complex creations so let us look at how the basic pieces are put together and stored, before we get into the actual customization of a style.

Style Elements

Styles are composed of three primary **style elements**, or smaller portions that work together to create the overall visual appearance of the style. These are the template, theme, and image set elements. Each style is self-contained and includes all the style elements needed to operate correctly.

The first and most important part of a style is the template element. The **template element** is a set of text files containing the entire markup that is used to generate the visual layout of a forum. The **markup** consists mainly of a markup language such as **Hypertext Markup Language** (**HTML**) and phpBB's own special template features, but can also include client-side scripting languages such as JavaScript. Template files are used to arrange most of the information displayed by your forum. You can identify template files by looking at the name of a file; all template files have names ending with `tpl`. Some examples are `index_body.tpl`, `viewtopic_body.tpl`, and `message_body.tpl`. Although this is rare, it is possible for multiple styles to use one set of template files with different themes and/or image sets.

The **theme** element of a forum style is a grouping of formatting rules used to define the visual decoration of a forum. The most common uses of the theme are specifying the font face, colors, background colors, and borders of page elements. Theme elements can be difficult to locate because they can be stored in three different locations. Most styles store theme data in one or more **Cascading Style Sheet** (**CSS**) files, such as `subSilver.css` and `formIE.css`. The name of the CSS files will vary with each forum style, but many times, there will be at least one CSS file named after the forum style. Some styles will place their CSS formatting rules in the `overall_header.tpl` template file instead of a separate CSS file. Others may use a combination of the `overall_header.tpl` technique and database storage of some values. The subSilver style uses the combination method, but also includes a CSS file that can be used after a manual change.

An **image set** element includes all the images that are part of a style. Some examples are the folder images, voting result bar graphics, and language-specific buttons such as "Reply" and "New Topic." There are also images that may be used mainly for decorative purposes, such as background or header images. Decorative images are sometimes considered part of the theme, instead of the image set.

In addition to the template files already discussed, the template element can also contain two special configuration files related to the theme and image set elements. The theme configuration file, `theme_info.cfg`, is used for saving theme database data associated with a template. The saved data can then be imported into another forum's database later. For the most part, you will only rarely need to edit this file. It is usually automatically generated or provided as needed. The second configuration file holds template configuration data. In most cases, that will merely be a list of graphic files in the image set of a style. These template configuration files have a name based on their matching template, such as `subSilver.cfg`.

Style Storage

Details of all of the styles available on a forum are stored in the forum's SQL database. The database only holds a list of installed styles, the name of an associated template element for each style, and some limited theme data. No image set data is stored in your database.

On the other hand, style elements are stored in the `templates` directory of the forum file system. The `templates` directory contains subdirectories that are named uniquely and after each individual set of template files. Each subdirectory of `templates` will contain template, theme, image set, and configuration files for one or more styles. Until new styles are installed or created, the only subdirectory in `templates` will be `subSilver`.

In most cases, a `templates` directory will contain two other subdirectories: `admin` and `images`. The `admin` subdirectory will contain template files used to display the Administration Control Panel. The `images` subdirectory will hold the image set used in the style, and may have language-named subdirectories, such as `lang_english` or `lang_dutch`, for images that display typed text in different languages. Some more advanced styles may include directories other than `admin` and `images`.

Editing phpBB Files

Throughout this chapter, you will be learning about and using a new skill that will be very useful to you as the administrator of a phpBB forum. You have already learned about some of the powerful configurations and features available through the Administration Control Panel, but there are many more that are not found there. These features can only be accessed (or in some cases, added) by editing phpBB's files yourself.

You must be careful to follow proper procedures when altering the files because phpBB is a delicate and complicated set of scripts. Doing so can save you a lot of headaches later, as many have learned first hand.

> You will be reminded of these procedures at several later points in the book. Try to follow them before manually editing any files, even if you are not reminded. This cannot be stressed enough, because these procedures can save you a lot of time when dealing with problems.

Before editing any file, the most important thing you should do is create a backup of that file. This simply means creating a copy of the file in its current condition. If you encounter problems due to your editing later, you can replace the edited file with the backup. That will effectively revert your forum to the pre-edited state of the file. At some point in your phpBB experience, you will definitely need to use a backup of a file. Everyone makes mistakes at some point, and it is nothing to be ashamed about. At other times, things simply do not work. Regardless of the cause, very few mistakes can be permanently fatal to a phpBB forum if you make backups before doing anything.

When you do edit a phpBB file, it is important to use the correct type of program. phpBB uses three types of files: graphics, text files containing program code, and text files containing display code. **Graphics** are standard image files you would see on any website and should be edited in programs such as Jasc Paint Shop Pro, Adobe Photoshop, or any other program capable of handling them. The text files, however, are special. Making a mistake in a graphic file will not damage your forum, but making one in a display code file or program code can easily cripple your forum.

All of phpBB's **program code files** contain the essential scripting needed to operate and display all aspects of a phpBB-powered forum and website. They are the backbone of phpBB. These files may have filename extensions of `.php`, `.inc`, or `.cfg`, and are plain text files created in a Unix text file format. This mainly means that when editing the files, you need to use a program capable of understanding the Unix text format. The majority of simple text-editing software will have no problems with this. Microsoft Notepad, perhaps the most commonly used text editor of the Microsoft Windows operating system, cannot understand the Unix format fully. It displays all the contents of a Unix text file on one long line, so Notepad is not the best choice for phpBB administrators. WordPad editor, also included with Microsoft Windows, is able to read Unix files without any problems. Most dedicated phpBB coders use more advanced text-editing programs with special features related to the PHP programming language. Some popular examples are EditPlus, TextPad, and PHPEdit, but there are many more available. You should, however, not need anything more complex than WordPad for the examples here.

The **display code files** are the `.tpl` files of the template element and the `.css` files of the theme element we learned about earlier. Like the program code files, these are plain text files saved in a Unix text file format. WordPad will again be our choice for editing these files for the examples in this chapter. There are special HTML editing programs, such as Dreamweaver MX, that can be used to edit template files. Those programs tend to cause as many problems as they solve, so you may want to avoid them for now unless you are very familiar with the program you choose.

Finally, there is one more note about editing both program and display code files. When saving these files, you need to make certain to save them in the proper file format. These are supposed to be plain text files, so you must save them as that. To save an edited phpBB file in WordPad, just click the Save toolbar icon or select Save from the File menu. WordPad should automatically save the file correctly. If you must select Save As, make certain to choose Text Document in the Saves as type selection list.

> Microsoft WordPad may be able to read Unix file formats, but it does not save files in that format. Instead, it saves files in a **personal computer (PC)** format.

Installing a New Style

One of the easiest ways to customize the appearance of your forum is to download and install a new phpBB style. Hundreds of different styles have been created based on topics like color schemes, popular movies, television shows, hobbies, sports, etc. The majority of these styles are free to download and use, although there are also some commercial styles and style designers available. Some websites that offer style downloads also provide demonstration forums in which you can preview any of the styles without downloading anything. Two of the best websites for downloading phpBB styles are:

- The phpBB Styles Database:
  `http://www.phpbb.com/styles/`.
- The phpBBHacks Templates Database:
  `http://www.phpbbhacks.com/templates.php`.

> Remember, some online communities use the terms template or theme when referring to a complete style, rather than names of style elements. `phpBBHacks.com` tends to use template in this manner.

Be certain to select a style that is compatible with the version of phpBB that you are using. The two sites above will list the compatible phpBB versions for each style, but other sites may not. Also keep in mind that some other sites carry styles for special ported versions of phpBB that are used with content management systems like PHP-Nuke. Those styles will *not* be compatible with an original flavor phpBB forum and vice versa.

Once you have selected and downloaded a new style, you will need to install the style to your forum. The installation is not a hard process if everything is prepared properly.

You will however find it a bit daunting if the process or the creation of the style has been handled incorrectly.

Most downloads will come in a ZIP file format. Before you can install a downloaded style, you need to decompress the ZIP file. There are various software programs you can use to accomplish this task. If you downloaded phpBB in a ZIP file, you are most probably already familiar with decompressing a file. Even if you are not, there are many decompression software programs you can download. Some of the more famous names include WinZip, WinAce, and WinRAR. Some, like ZipGenius (`http://www.zipgenius.it/`) or XAce, are free. WinZip has a Wizard mode that is very easy to use, so we will not look at decompression in great detail here.

Creating a Copy Style

For the purposes of illustration, this chapter will discuss the usage of a sample style called subBook. Instead of downloading and uncompressing this style, it was created as a quickly renamed copy of the subSilver style. If you would like to create your own subBook style so you can follow along, follow these simple instructions.

Time For Action—Creating a Copy Style

1. Make a copy of the `templates/subSilver` directory. The copy should contain all the same files found under `subSilver`.
2. Change the name of the copy directory to `subBook`.
3. Rename the `subSilver.cfg` and `subSilver.css` files to `subBook.cfg` and `subBook.css`, respectively.
4. Open the `theme_info.cfg` file for editing. In this file, you will see `subSilver` used several times. Change each of these instances to `subBook`. Take care that you do not delete or change anything else in the file. Remember to follow the proper editing procedures you learned earlier.
5. The name of the subSilver style is referenced in around forty to fifty lines inside template files in your `subBook` directory. The exact files and number of times vary depending on the version of phpBB 2.0 you are using. When creating a new style from subSilver as we are doing, you need to change all these references to the name of the new style (subBook in our case). Clearly, this step will take some time. This will not affect our installation or uninstallation examples, so you may skip most of this for now. Some advanced text editors have special search and replace features that can help you do this more quickly. At the very least, do these steps on the `overall_header.tpl` file.
6. Save and close all open files.

What Just Happened?

Every style available for phpBB is based around a set of files stored in the `templates` directory. The easiest way to create a new style is to copy the files of another and make a few changes to some of the copied files. These files are the configuration files, such as `subSilver.cfg` and `theme_info.cfg`, which phpBB uses for installing and managing styles. The Cascading Style Sheet file, `subSilver.css` in this case, was also renamed. As a result, references to `subSilver.css` in `overall_header.tpl` also had to be changed to the new name of that file. Completing these steps gives you a new style, which you can edit as much as you like without affecting your forums' other styles.

Installing One Element at a Time

Once you have a new style to install, either from downloading or copying `subSilver`, you need to place that style's directories and files into the `templates` directory of your forum. phpBB's Administration Control Panel can automatically detect all styles placed into this directory. If your forum is on a remote server, as most forums and websites tend to be, then you will have to upload the directories and files to that server via one of the methods supported by your web hosting company. This is usually through **File Transfer Protocol (FTP)**, SSH, or some other setup. Once you have copied or placed the files into `templates`, you have completed two thirds of the style installation already:

With the new style's files placed in your forum file system, you are now ready to install the style through phpBB's Administration Control Panel. Log in to your forum using an administrator account and enter the Control Panel. In the navigation menu frame, scroll down to the Styles Admin section. There are several options here; we are only interested in the Add link for the moment. Click this link to enter the Styles Administration page.

The Styles Administration page lists all the uninstalled styles phpBB has detected in your `templates` directory. You may notice that this page uses both **theme** and **style** to refer to the styles. This confusion stems from the fact that we have already installed the image set and template style elements simply by placing them into the `templates` directory. All that remains is to install the theme element, and thereby complete the style's installation. To install a theme, just click the Install link next to the entry in the list. phpBB will now show the style in the drop-down selection list found in user profiles and the phpBB configuration page:

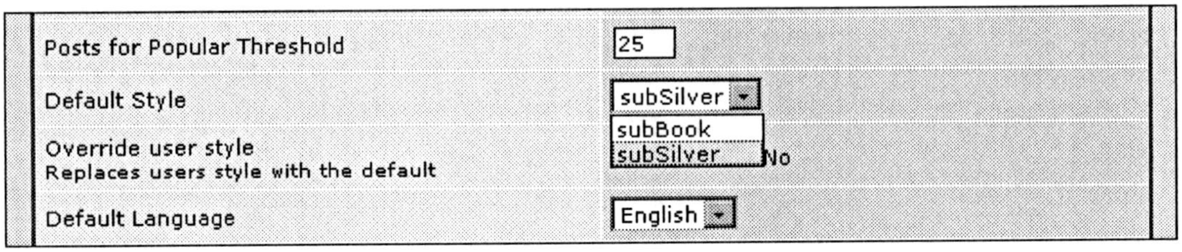

Troubleshooting

phpBB is a complicated set of scripts, so even something that should be simple, like installing a style, can cause you problems. There are many causes of these problems, ranging from designer mistakes to errors in the copying of the files, but all of them are easy to fix. Let us examine some of the more common troubles encountered by forum administrators in the past.

Style Does Not Appear in Administration

If a style does not appear in the Styles Administration page after you have copied it to the `templates` directory, there is usually a problem with the `theme_info.cfg` file that should be in the style's directory. Make sure this file has been copied and that the name of the file has not been changed. If the file is present and named correctly, then there is a problem inside the file itself. Some styles have been distributed with errors in this file.

Open `theme_info.cfg` for editing. It should resemble the subSilver file shown in the figure that follows. Note that each line begins with `$subSilver[0]`, followed by other characters. The `subSilver` part is extremely important, and must be spelled in exactly the same manner as the name of the style's `templates` directory and cannot contain any spaces. The name will be different for each template, of course. phpBB will consider all of these to be completely different things:

- `subSilver`
- `sub Silver`
- `Subsilver`
- `SubSilver`
- `subsilver`

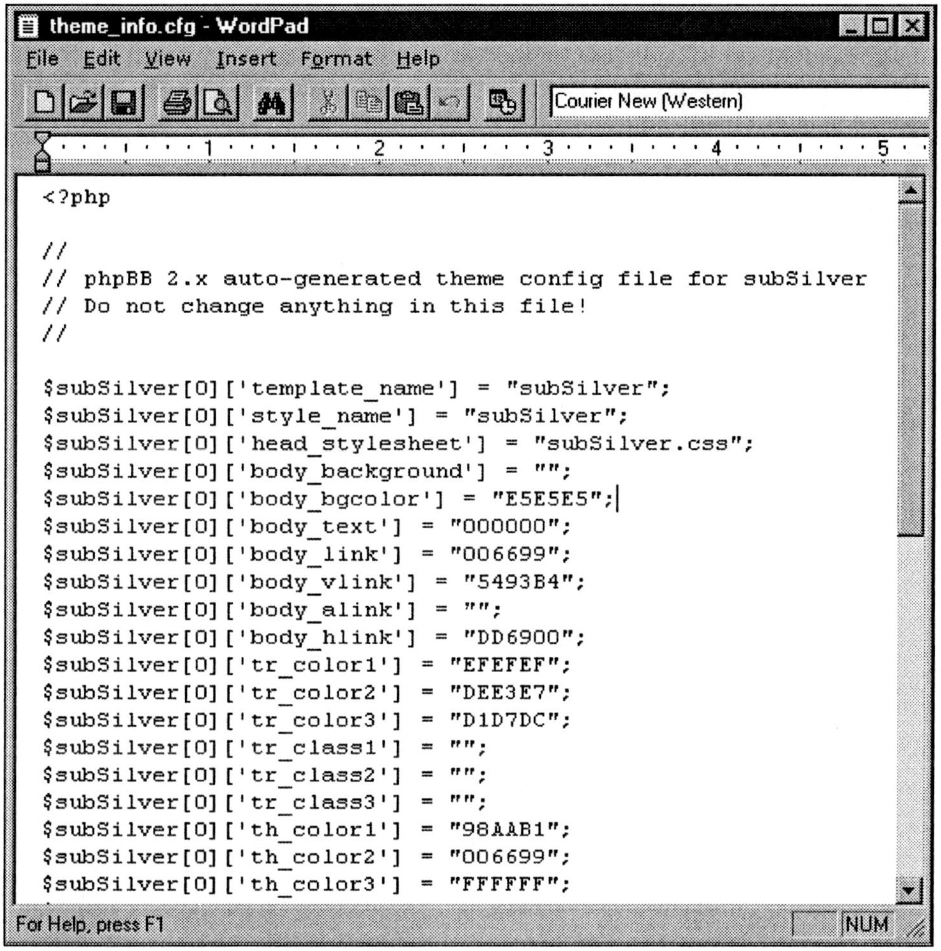

This screenshot shows a portion of an unaltered subSilver `theme_info.cfg`. Only our first option, `subSilver`, would be correct in this instance. Check each line of `theme_info.cfg` and make any corrections needed to the file or, if necessary, rename the style's `templates` directory. In certain cases, the latter will be an easier method of correcting the problem. Other styles will have different names for their directory and in `theme_info.cfg`, but the name must be the same in both places.

Configuration File Cannot Be Opened

Sometimes phpBB may have trouble finding the configuration file for a template element. When this happens, either during installation or normal forum operations, the forum will present the user with a Critical Error message, as shown in the following figure, mentioning the name of the template. That name is a very important part of this error message, because it is telling you what name phpBB has used to look for the configuration file. When the name of the template is shown as subSilver, phpBB could not find a file called `subSilver.cfg` in the `templates/subSilver` directory. Similarly, the name subBook means phpBB looked for `subBook.cfg` in the `templates/subBook` directory. The pattern here should be clear:

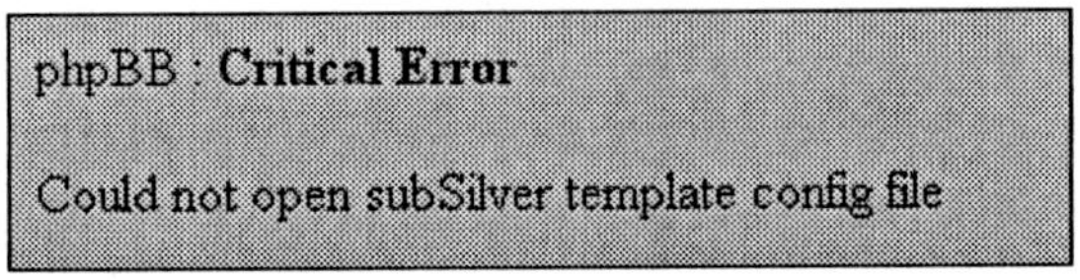

To repair this error, you need to ensure that phpBB can find the file in question. As with the error when the style does not appear in Styles Administration, the names of the actual file and directory must be exactly the same as that in the error message. `subbook` is not the same as `subBook`. First, look in the `templates` directory and ensure that there is a subdirectory with the template name. Next, look inside that subdirectory for the template configuration file. If either the directory or file is named incorrectly, renaming them to the correct spelling should fix the error.

If there is no `templates` subdirectory that comes even close to having the correct name, there are two ways to fix the error temporarily. The first method is to rename another subdirectory (and the template configuration file inside it) to the name phpBB is trying to find. When doing this, be sure to write down the original name for a quick change-back later. The second and better method is to copy another template and rename it. The steps for this are the same as those in the *Creating a Copy Style* section earlier in this chapter, except you will not need to edit `theme_info.cfg`. With the problem repaired for the moment, you can try to uninstall the problem style or work out a more lasting solution like replacing the `templates` files of the style.

Removing an Installed Style

At some point, you may decide that you want to remove a style you have added to your phpBB forum. This is a much simpler process than installing styles. There are two steps to removing a style: deleting the style and theme information from the database and deleting the `templates` directory of the style.

In the Administration Control Panel, scroll the navigation menu down to the Styles Admin section. Clicking the Management link will load a Styles Administration page, listing the styles currently installed on your forum. It looks very similar to the installation page you have already seen. By clicking the Delete link next to a style, you will remove all information related to that style in your forum's SQL database. You will be asked to confirm the deletion before it actually happens. Any users that have selected a style in their profiles will automatically have their selection changed when that style is deleted. Their profile setting will be altered to the style selected as the Board Default on the General Configuration page of the Administration Control Panel.

> If you only have one style installed on your forum, you cannot delete it. You also cannot delete the Board Default style.

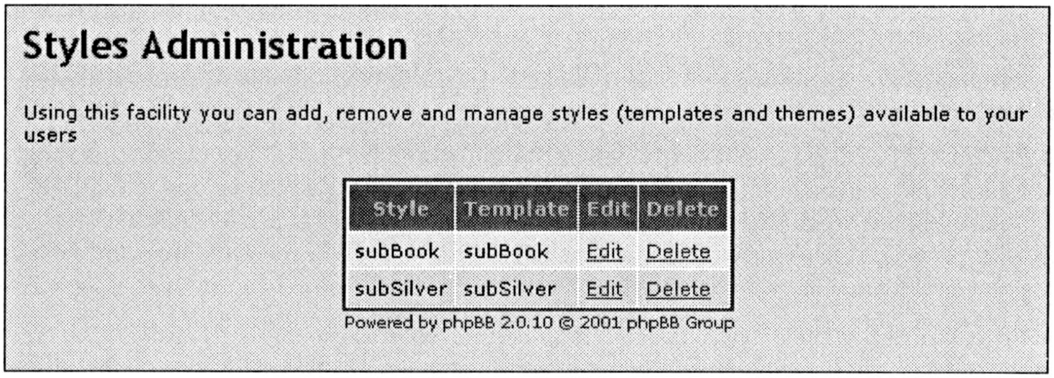

The second aspect of removing a style calls for deleting that style's related subdirectory of the `templates` directory. This will typically be done through the same means by which you copied the style into `templates` when installing it. Since it is possible to have multiple styles that use a single template or image set element with different themes, you should make certain that removing these files will not damage any styles you have not deleted in the Administration Control Panel.

Create or Customize

So far, we have only looked at installing new styles that already exist. This is only one of the ways in which we can alter the appearance of a phpBB, however. Two of our other options are creating a completely new style or customizing one already installed, like subSilver. Both of these options have some benefits and some drawbacks.

Creating a new style can really bring life to a forum. If your forum has a look that is unlike any other, your visitors are more likely to remember it. You probably remember some of the unique-looking websites you have visited in the past yourself. Also, you do not have to spend time looking through hundreds of existing styles for something you like or one that will fit nicely with the subject matter of your forum. Sometimes you may not even be able to find a style appropriate to your subject! The temptation to create your own style is great.

On the other hand, creating a new style is a lot of work! There are many graphics required for normal phpBB operations, and you will probably want to replace most of them with your own. You may even want to create new graphics and alter the template files to create new visual effects. Essentially, you would be designing an entire website. If you are not an experienced web designer or graphic artist, you may find the task to be a bit beyond your current skill level.

When you customize an existing style, you will save a lot of time over creating a new one. The existing structure will already be complete, other than any changes you want to make. You can quickly replace any images or colors to alter the mood of the forum, as you will see later in this chapter. The work of the original style creator will serve as a guideline to help you develop your knowledge. Then again, if you customize a style, that same existing structure will limit you unless changed greatly. Chances are that the customized style will bear some resemblance to the original, and many people will know that at first glance.

So which method is better? It really depends on how much you want to change the look of a forum. There is a good chance you can find an existing style to customize that will not limit you too much. If you look at enough styles, however, you will find that many of them are based, at least in part, on the original subSilver style. For something unique, you will have to create a new style.

In the rest of this chapter, we will learn to customize an existing style. However, the examples will use the subBook style created earlier in the chapter. This approach will allow us to preserve the original subSilver style of your forum, while making any changes we choose to the subBook copy.

In Chapter 6, we will deal with designing a completely new style in detail.

> If you did not create and install subBook earlier or replace all the uses of the subSilver name in subBook's template files, you may wish to do so now. You can work with subSilver if you like, but this may cause your forum to appear much different from the examples and screenshots in later chapters.

Customizing Through the Stylesheet

The quickest way to overhaul the look of a forum is to change its colors, fonts, and other visual (but non-graphical) decorations. When we looked at the basic elements of a style earlier, we learned that a theme defines and controls these concepts through the formatting rules of a **Cascading Style Sheet (CSS)**. CSS formatting rules add stylistic data, such as specifications for fonts, colors, sizes, borders, and spacing to a document structured with a markup language like HTML. Since phpBB creates documents of this kind to display a forum, the preferred method for changing these parts of the outward appearance of the forum is CSS.

CSS rules can be stored in three different places: in an external CSS file such as `subBook.css`, in `overall_header.tpl`, or in a combination of the `overall_header.tpl` method with some database storage. subSilver uses the combination method, and therefore subBook will also do the same.

Editing the Stylesheet in the Admin Panel

We can look at the database storage portion of the combination method first. It allows us to edit certain aspects of the stylesheet through the Administration Control Panel. The values entered into the administration feature are placed into the SQL database and later retrieved for use on every page phpBB displays.

To access the stylesheet-editing tool, visit the Styles Admin section of the Administration Control Panel, and click the Management link. This loads the same Styles Administration page you saw when exploring the means of removing installed styles. However, we are now interested in the Edit link instead of the Delete link. Clicking Edit will load the Edit Theme page, which provides a simple form for changing colors, fonts, text sizes, and a few other theme aspects.

Time For Action—Editing the Stylesheet

1. Locate the line labeled Background Color on the page.
2. There is a form field on this line containing the text E5E5E5. Delete that text.
3. Type CC0000 in the form field. Use the number zero, not the capital letter O.
4. Scroll down to the bottom of the page and press the Save Settings button.
5. On the next page, click the word Here in the text Click Here to return to Style Administration. This returns you to the Styles Administration page, where your change will be reflected.

What Just Happened?

As the name suggests, the Edit Theme page allows you to alter some aspects of the forum's theme. Each aspect that can be altered has a matching form field, such as Background Color for the background color of forum pages. By replacing E5E5E5 with CC0000, you altered the page background color from a light gray to red. If you replace CC0000 with E5E5E5 and Save Settings again, the change will be reversed.

Editing Other Theme Components

You can change more than just the background color of pages. The first two options on the Edit Theme page actually allow you to modify two aspects of the style, even though Theme may be used in their labels. Alterations to the Theme Name will be reflected in board style selection lists and Styles Administration. Selecting a new Template can change the entire layout of a forum while keeping the current color scheme. All templates in your forum's `templates` directory will be listed in this selection box, even if they are not currently used in an installed style.

The remaining thirty-eight options are presented in a three-column format. The first column, Theme Element, describes the individual settings while the second column holds the current values. When you install a new style, some values may or may not be provided automatically; it varies from style to style. These two columns are the most relevant to your needs.

The third column, Simple Name, can hold some extra descriptive information about the use of these settings. If you look at the Edit Theme page for subSilver, you can see this in action. Unfortunately, phpBB does not have a method of importing Simple Name data when installing new styles, so this column is often ignored. You can enter short descriptions of your own, but otherwise only subSilver will use this column:

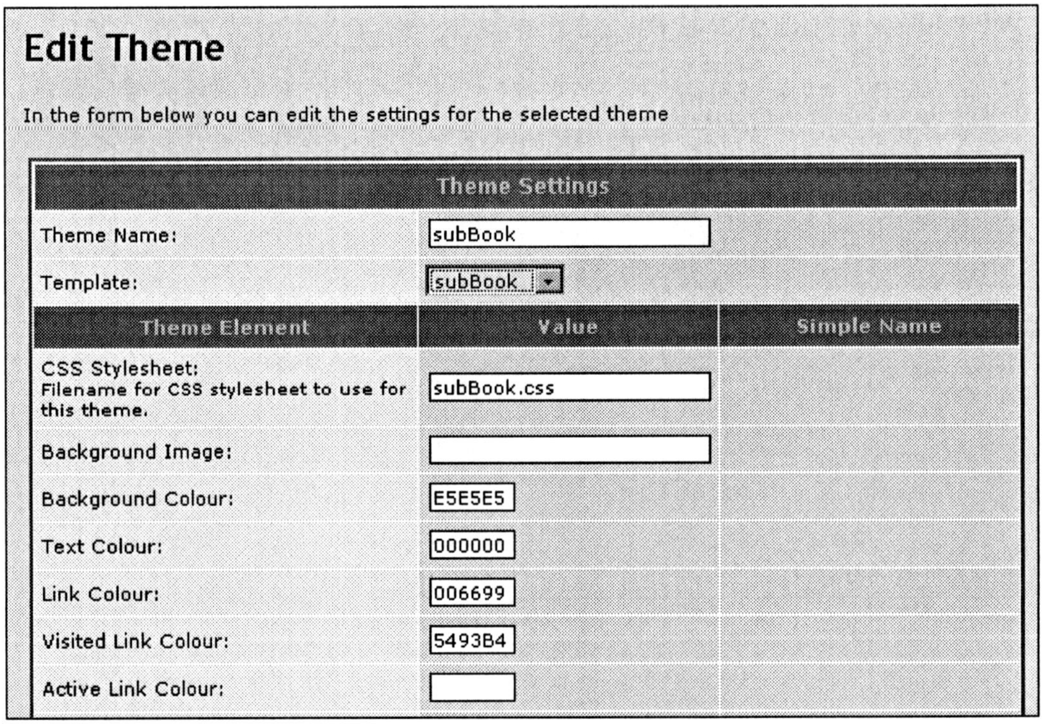

Since there are so many options on this page, let us concentrate on the types of values that can be entered, the settings used most often, and the ones you would most likely want to change. Many settings are alternative versions of others, so looking at every single one in detail is not necessary. All of the options are listed in a table at the end of this section.

> Not all templates will use every setting in the same way. Some templates also do not use all of the settings provided. You should consider the descriptions provided here as a general guide to the ways the settings *can* be used, but not how they *must* be used. There is a fair amount of flexibility here, and some templates make use of that.

Allowed Values

There are several types of values that can be entered and most settings accept only one type. Those restricted to one kind of value can be grouped under filename, color, font size, and font face settings. All other settings accept filename, color, and CSS class name values, but only one kind of value can be used in each group of these settings.

The filename settings—CSS Stylesheet and Background Image—should only be used with the names of existing files in the `templates` directory of a style. It is possible to use a file that is not in a `templates` subdirectory, but this often requires some editing of multiple template files. Some styles, including subSilver, will not use one or both of this pair when first installed. Make sure a value is filled in for CSS Stylesheet regardless, as you may find yourself needing it later. Background Image is optional.

Color settings require a hexadecimal color code. Hexadecimal color codes, sometimes called HTML color codes, are combinations of six letters and numbers that represent a color, usually prefaced with a pound symbol (#). Many websites provide charts and lists that show examples of these codes. When entering a hexadecimal color code into the color settings of this page, you must not include the pound symbol. The color settings will accept only six character values, so including the pound will cause the last character of the code to be cut off! That can lead to some weird color effects. You may be tempted to enter a color name, such as red or green, for the color settings. If you do so, however, you will get some strange results. Lists of the different hexadecimal codes are available on many websites. Two good lists can be found at `http://www.htmlgoodies.com/tutors/colors.html` and `http://webmonkey.wired.com/webmonkey/reference/color_codes/`.

Font size settings are limited to simple integer numbers like 9, 10, or 15. These will usually be related to a font size in pixel or point measurements, but the type of measurement can vary with each style. Since some styles may also use percentage measurements, you may want to leave these settings alone until you have determined the type of units used in the stylesheet.

The last of the restricted value settings—font faces—accepts comma-separated lists of typeface names. An example of a good value is Verdana, Arial, Helvetica, sans-serif. If you want to include a name that consists of more than one word in the list, place it inside single or double quotes: for example, 'Verdana', 'Trebuchet MS'. You can also use a single name, but it is a better idea to use a list. When a list is provided, the first font that is installed on the viewer's computer will be used.

The more flexible settings allow you to use filenames, colors, or CSS class names for values, as already stated. Filename values operate under the same restrictions as those for filename-specific settings. Color values can be hexadecimal color codes, including the pound symbol this time, or simple names like blue. **CSS class names** are names of Cascading Style Sheet formatting rules. They will usually be short names made of all lowercase letters and numbers. The formatting rules named will be used to control the display of everything that the theme element controls.

Commonly Used and Altered Elements

You have already learned about a few settings, such as font sizes and faces, in the previous section. Now let us examine some more useful options in the Edit Theme page.

Table Cell Colors

The Table Cell Color 1, Table Cell Color 2, Table Cell Class 1, and Table Cell Class 2 elements are interesting because they are perhaps the most commonly used. Any aspect of phpBB that displays data in table rows, such as the member list, forums, and topics, can use these elements to achieve an alternating row color effect. For compatibility with phpBB's internal coding, Table Cell Class 1 often has a value of row1 and Table Cell Class 2 a value of row2. This is a sort of unspoken standard, but one that is not always used.

Font Colors

Two options that many forum administrators like to change, but often cannot locate without help, are Font Color 2 and Font Color 3. All font color settings are used to color a variety of text, but these two are used for the special colors given to administrator and moderator usernames on the forum in several locations like online user lists. Font Color 3 assigns the administrator names' color, and Font Color 2 details moderator name color.

Again, these colors are used in other places as well, so be sure to look around the forum if you change them. It is very easy to change the name colors to something nice only to find your table headers or code BBCodes have become unreadable.

Once you have edited the elements to your preferences, you should click the Save Settings button at the bottom of the Edit Theme page to store the new values in the database. You will be shown a confirmation message that the settings have been updated, and the new settings should be reflected on any page loaded after that message.

The following table lists the names of theme elements and defines them:

Theme Element Name	Description
CSS Stylesheet	Filename for a Cascading Style Sheet file.
Background Image	Image used as a background for the forum. Not used in subSilver.
Background Color	Color of page backgrounds.
Text Color	Default text color of all pages.
Link Color	Default color of all unvisited links.
Visited Link Color	Color for all links that have been visited.

Theme Element Name	Description
Active Link Color	When clicking a link, it switches color. Not used in subSilver.
Hover Link Color	When moving the mouse pointer over a link it changes to this color.
Table Row Color 1	Background color for table rows, often very light.
Table Row Color 2	Another, usually medium, table row background color.
Table Row Color 3	Third row background color, rarely used and is often the darkest.
Table Row Class 1	CSS class name for table rows. Not used in subSilver.
Table Row Class 2	Class name for a second set of rows. Not used in subSilver.
Table Row Class 3	Class name for a third row set. Not used in subSilver.
Table Header Color 1	Color for table headings. Also used for page borders in subSilver.
Table Header Color 2	Second heading color. Also used for table borders in subSilver.
Table Header Color 3	Third heading color. Also used for inner table borders in subSilver.
Table Header Class 1	CSS class name for table heading cells.
Table Header Class 2	Class name for a second set of table heading cells.
Table Header Class 3	Class name for a third heading set.
Table Cell Color 1	Background color of various common table cells.
Table Cell Color 2	Alternative table cell background color.
Table Cell Color 3	Another table cell background color. Not used in subSilver.
Table Cell Class 1	CSS Class name for table cells. Often used to alternate row colors.

Theme Element Name	Description
Table Cell Class 2	Second Class name for cells. Often used to alternate row colors.
Table Cell Class 3	Third possible class name. Not used in subSilver.
Font Face 1	Default type face for most text.
Font Face 2	Second type face, sometimes for topic titles.
Font Face 3	Third type face. Often used for code BBCode tags.
Font Size 1	Smallest font size.
Font Size 2	Medium font size.
Font Size 3	Largest font size, used for most text, including posts.
Font Color 1	Quote BBCode text color.
Font Color 2	Code BBCode text color. Also moderator username color.
Font Color 3	Table header cell text color. Also administrator user name color.
Span Class 1	A CSS class name for use in HTML span tags. Not used in subSilver.
Span Class 2	Another class name for span tags. Not used in subSilver.
Span Class 3	Third class name for span tags. Not used in subSilver.

Changing CSS Styles to Change the Look of Your Site

The second portion of the combined stylesheet storage method deals with CSS-formatting rules placed in the `overall_header.tpl` file of a template. These formatting rules, or **CSS classes**, control many aspects of the forum's display. By editing the CSS classes directly, you can create a broader range of design changes than are possible through the Edit Theme utility.

The first step is to locate the CSS classes in `templates/subBook/overall_header.tpl`. Open that file in WordPad and scroll down to a line that contains `<style type="text/css">`. All of the CSS classes are between this line and another containing

`</style>`. Each of the classes has two major parts: a class name, also known as a selector, and a declaration block.

The **class name** is a short and descriptive name that will be used to associate the individual classes with elements of forum pages. Names may be the same as those of HTML tags, such as `body`, `td`, `hr`, or `font`, or author-created names preceded by a period, such as `.postbody` or `.quote`. A combination of the two, such as `td.row1` is also acceptable. You will also see classes containing names separated by commas; this is a shortcut for applying one class to all of the named elements.

Declaration blocks consist of one or more declaration lines enclosed in curly brackets. Each **declaration line** holds a property name and value separated by a colon and ends with a semicolon. Several declaration lines can actually be placed on one line of text, as long as a semicolon ends each declaration, and you will see several such cases in the files. Property names and values specify the actual formatting features like colors, borders, and so on. Here is a sample line for underlining text:

```
text-decoration: underline;
```

Most styles' stylesheets will also include comment lines starting with `/*` and ending with `*/` that explain what display elements of the forum each class will affect. Comment lines do not affect any layout features themselves. An entire class might resemble this sample.

```
td.row2
{
    color: black;
    /* White Background */
    background-color: #FFFFFF;
}
```

Until you reach a point where you are adding new features to your forum, you should not need to alter class names very much, if at all. On the other hand, editing the declaration blocks will let you do just about anything. By examining the existing entries in the file, you will get a good idea of what you can do by adding or removing declaration lines in each class.

> Hundreds of possible combinations of property names and values exist. There are also some types of class names not covered here or used in subSilver and subBook. For more information about Cascading Style Sheets beyond the scope of this book, check out these resources:
>
> 184 Manually selected Style Sheet Resources:
> `http://www.cbel.com/style_sheets/`
>
> W3Schools CSS Tutorials: `http://www.w3schools.com/css/`
>
> css-discuss Wiki `http://css-discuss.incutio.com/`

In `overall_header.tpl`, you will see many declaration lines containing special **template variables** like `{T_BODY_BGCOLOR}`. Template variables are a special feature of phpBB used to substitute data into the layout generated from the template files. Some recognizable characteristics of template variables are names beginning and ending with curly brackets and containing only letters, numbers, underscores, and periods. You will not see template variables whose names contain semicolons, colons, or most other special characters. Any template variables in the stylesheet will be replaced with the "theme element" values of the Edit Theme utility; they are where the combination of the database and `overall_header.tpl` come into play. For a listing of the template variables and their matching theme element names, consult the table at the end of this section.

Template variables can be applied to classes for other types of theme elements, as well. For an example, look at the first class in subBook's `overall_header.tpl`. This body class, which affects the HTML <body> tag and thus an entire webpage, uses several table color elements in scrollbar-related declaration lines. These lines will change the colors in certain parts of your web browser's scrollbar, if the browser supports them. The scrollbar properties are not part of the standard CSS features and only function in certain browsers, such as Microsoft's Internet Explorer. Netscape and Mozilla browsers ignore the scrollbar properties.

For an interesting example of how you can change the look of your forum, locate the `.bodyline` class. This would be on a single line about eight lines below the body class. Near the end of the line, you can see the `border` property, which manages the border around the forum pages. It should currently have values that create a solid, one pixel wide, light blue border, with the color changeable in Edit Theme. Now, replace the word `solid` with `dashed`. Save this change and look at your forum's index page—it now has a dashed line for a border. You can also try `dotted`, `ridge`, and `groove` for some other effects. By altering the number portion of the `1px` code in the same area, you can increase and decrease the width of the border. Try `10px` and `dotted` together for an unusual view.

> The stylesheet code found in `subBook/overall_header.tpl` is duplicated in `subBook/simple_header.tpl` and, with some changes, in `subBook/admin/page_header.tpl`. Any changes applied to one file should also be made in the others, if you want to keep the same look across all parts of the forum.

Using External Stylesheets

By placing a stylesheet in `overall_header.tpl`, phpBB gives you a lot of control through the Edit Theme page, but it comes at a cost. The stylesheet has to be freshly loaded on every page, and this can slow down a very busy forum. An alternative is to use an external stylesheet file, such as `subSilver.css` and `subBook.css`. Web browsers do not refresh external stylesheets as often, resulting in smaller page sizes and faster loading times. This type of stylesheet does not support the Edit Theme utility, however, so the utility is rendered almost useless. Edit Theme will still control administrator and moderator username colors and, depending on the style, row classes and colors.

To enable the external stylesheet for subBook, find the following line in `templates/subBook/overall_header.tpl`:

```
<!-- link rel="stylesheet"
href="templates/subBook/{T_HEAD_STYLESHEET}" type="text/css" -->
```

This line is an HTML comment line due to the `!--` and `--` character sequences near the beginning and end. Like the Cascading Style Sheet comment lines, it has no effect on the page layout. By removing the comment characters, you can have the line become a reference to the external stylesheet file. The line should then look like this:

```
<link rel="stylesheet" href="templates/subBook/{T_HEAD_STYLESHEET}"
type="text/css">
```

You should also delete all the CSS classes in `overall_header.tpl`, or they will override the same classes in the external stylesheet. If you have made any changes to those CSS classes, make identical changes in `subBook.css` before deleting the code from `overall_header.tpl`. You will find the same classes in `subBook.css`, but you cannot use template variables in external stylesheet files. If you make these same changes in `simple_header.tpl` and `admin/page_header.tpl`, you can control the appearance of the entire forum from a single stylesheet file. Note that the final line in `admin/page_header.tpl` will be slightly different. You need to add `../` before `templates` in this line for the stylesheet to be displayed properly on pages using this file. Those pages are generally Administration Control Panel pages, which only you may see (unless you give other users administrator access). The final line for `admin/page_header.tpl` is:

```
<link rel="stylesheet"
href="../templates/subBook/{T_HEAD_STYLESHEET}" type="text/css">
```

The following table lists the template variables and related theme elements:

Template Variable	Theme Element Name
{T_HEAD_STYLESHEET}	CSS Stylesheet
{T_BODY_BACKGROUND}	Background Image
{T_BODY_BGCOLOR}	Background Color
{T_BODY_TEXT}	Text Color
{T_BODY_LINK}	Link Color
{T_BODY_VLINK}	Visited Link Color

Template Variable	Theme Element Name
{T_BODY_ALINK}	Active Link Color
{T_BODY_HLINK}	Hover Link Color
{T_TR_COLOR1}	Table Row Color 1
{T_TR_COLOR2}	Table Row Color 2
{T_TR_COLOR3}	Table Row Color 3
{T_TR_CLASS1}	Table Row Class 1
{T_TR_CLASS2}	Table Row Class 2
{T_TR_CLASS3}	Table Row Class 3
{T_TH_COLOR1}	Table Header Color 1
{T_TH_COLOR2}	Table Header Color 2
{T_TH_COLOR3}	Table Header Color 3
{T_TH_CLASS1}	Table Header Class 1
{T_TH_CLASS2}	Table Header Class 2
{T_TH_CLASS3}	Table Header Class 3
{T_TD_COLOR1}	Table Cell Color 1
{T_TD_COLOR2}	Table Cell Color 2
{T_TD_COLOR3}	Table Cell Color 3
{T_TD_CLASS1}	Table Cell Class 1
{T_TD_CLASS2}	Table Cell Class 2
{T_TD_CLASS3}	Table Cell Class 3
{T_FONTFACE1}	Font Face 1
{T_FONTFACE2}	Font Face 2

Template Variable	Theme Element Name
{T_FONTFACE3}	Font Face 3
{T_FONTSIZE1}	Font Size 1
{T_FONTSIZE2}	Font Size 2
{T_FONTSIZE3}	Font Size 3
{T_FONTCOLOR1}	Font Color 1
{T_FONTCOLOR2}	Font Color 2
{T_FONTCOLOR3}	Font Color 3
{T_SPAN_CLASS1}	Span Class 1
{T_SPAN_CLASS2}	Span Class 2
{T_SPAN_CLASS3}	Span Class 3

Customizing through Images

Another major part of a forum's appearance is created using images. **Forum images** can be divided into two main categories: those that are just for looks, and those that serve some function. The former might include a forum's logo or menu link images, while examples of the latter would be new post indicators and posting buttons. By replacing any of these images, you can create a new user interface and adapt your forum's design at the same time. If you are a graphic artist or experienced in creating your own images, you can create some awesome images to liven up your forum.

You can also download new graphics from phpBB communities, of course. Both `phpBB.com` and `phpBBHacks.com`, which offer style downloads as mentioned previously, also offer some graphic sets. Some of their image downloads are rank and emoticon images, but you can find packs of normal forum buttons too. A few style authors have also made special PSD image packs available, which can be used to create new images for their styles using Adobe Photoshop and other image editors. PSD packs for styles you install, if available, may be useful when adding new features to your forum later.

Installing New Images to Change the Look of Your Site

There are two ways to install new images to a phpBB forum. The first is to replace an existing image. Replacing an image entails finding or creating an image, renaming it with the same filename as an image already used on your forum, deleting the existing image, and putting the new image in the same location. This is a quick way of getting new graphics on your forum, but it will limit you to the same type of image previously in place. If you have a JPEG image, like a digital photo, that you want to use for a New Topic button in subSilver or subBook, you would have to convert it to a GIF image, losing some picture quality in the process. For cases like this, it's better to use the second method of installing new images: adding an image with a new filename.

In order to get phpBB to detect the new filename, however, you may have to edit the template configuration file of the style in which you are installing the new image. If you will recall from earlier in the chapter, these files have a name matching that of a `templates` subdirectory, such as `subSilver.cfg` or `subBook.cfg`, and list many of the graphics found on a forum. The entries in this list usually resemble these examples:

```
$images['name'] = "$current_template_images/image.gif";
$images['name'] = "$current_template_images/{LANG}/image.gif";
```

If you open `subBook.cfg` in WordPad, you should see several lines in this format. Generally speaking, you should only edit the parts of a line after the last backslash and before the last quotation mark, which would be `image.gif` in the example. If your new image is not inside the `images` subdirectory of the style's directory, like `templates/subBook/images`, then you would need to replace `$current_template_images` with the correct path to the image. It is usually easier to simply put the new file in the style's `images` directory. The special `{LANG}` placeholder allows phpBB to use different versions of an image in support of multiple languages.

The one image you might expect to find in the configuration file—the forum's phpBB logo—is actually not there. To change the filename for the logo, you will have to edit `overall_header.tpl`. The HTML image tag for the logo resembles:

```
<img src="templates/subBook/images/logo_phpBB.gif" border="0"
alt="{L_INDEX}" vspace="1" />
```

Notice the phpBB logo is the `logo_phpBB.gif` file. Most people want to change the logo quickly, so this is a good file to experiment with replacing or renaming.

Hacking phpBB

Altering the look of your forum is only one aspect of customizations that you can perform with phpBB. For some interesting changes, you'll most likely want to add some completely new features to your forum. You may also want to remove some features that you do not plan to use. To add new features, remove existing features, or otherwise alter the abilities of a phpBB forum, you will have to edit the code of the PHP script files that are the heart of phpBB. You may also need to edit or add new template files to the styles installed on a forum, as well. The process of making these kinds of changes is called **modifying** or **hacking** phpBB.

MODs and Hacks

There are many sets of instructions for altering phpBB's features available at online phpBB communities. Such downloads may include step-by-step instructions for altering core phpBB files or the SQL database, adding new forum files, or any combination of those three categories. These downloads are commonly called MODs or Hacks. **Hack** was the original term used during the era of phpBB 1 and is still used extensively in some phpBB communities. With the advent of phpBB 2.0, the term **MODs,** from a shortened form of the word modifications, also became popular. To avoid confusion, the term **modification** will be used in this chapter.

phpBB Modification

What exactly does a modification include? That will depend on the scope of the modification. Very simple modifications typically include one text file containing instructions for altering an existing phpBB file. More complex modifications may also include new files to be added to phpBB and a special installer file. Some extremely complex modifications typically include all of these, plus already edited copies of the original phpBB files. All these files will be placed together in a compressed file, typically in the ZIP format.

While a group of developers created phpBB, modifications are typically the work of individual phpBB users that needed the effect created by the modification. phpBB is open source and released under the GNU General Public License so, it and any derivative works (like modifications) can be freely distributed to others at no charge. Modification authors make their works available to others in the hope that other forum administrators will benefit from them and eventually contribute back to the larger phpBB community. Therefore, there is a large and diverse group of modifications created in different coding methods and writing styles. Some modifications are also released in developmental stages, and you should be careful about using those. They often contain bugs, security holes, or incomplete features that may annoy your forum's visitors.

The best places to find large selections of phpBB modification downloads are:

- phpBBHacks.com: `http://www.phpbbhacks.com/`
- phpBB Official Site: `http://www.phpbb.com/`

Many modification authors will also release their works on their own websites or other phpBB communities. If possible, make sure you only download modifications described as compatible for the version of phpBB you are using. There are many releases of phpBB 1 and phpBB 2, but not all modifications will work with every phpBB release. phpBB 1 modifications, mainly found only at `phpBBHacks.com` now, will not work on any phpBB 2 release. Some phpBB 2 modifications will work only with early or later versions of phpBB 2.0.

Installing a Modification

When you find and download a modification you wish to install, you need to follow a series of steps to place the new code in your forum and activate it fully. Like many other things, the exact steps needed vary with each modification. There is a standard way of proceeding that is common to all modifications, however. To begin with, let's install this simple modification. It adds a button to each user's posts that allows others to quickly search for all posts by that user.

```
#
#-----[ OPEN ]------------------------------------------
#
templates/subSilver/viewtopic_body.tpl

#
#-----[ FIND ]------------------------------------------
#
          //--></script><noscript>{postrow.ICQ_IMG}</noscript></td>

#
#-----[ IN-LINE FIND ]------------------------------------------
#
</noscript>

#
#-----[ IN-LINE AFTER, ADD ]------------------------------------------
-
#
{postrow.SEARCH_IMG}

#
#-----[ SAVE/CLOSE ALL FILES ]------------------------------------------
---
#
# End
```

Time For Action—Installing a Small Modification

1. Locate the `templates/subSilver/viewtopic_body.tpl` file of your forum. Open this file in your text-editing program.
2. Use the text-editing program's search feature to locate this line of text in the file. In many programs, this feature can be accessed from the menus or by pressing *Ctrl+F* on Windows systems.

```
//--></script><noscript>{postrow.ICQ_IMG}</noscript></td>
```

3. Now, locate the text `</noscript>` within that line.
4. Directly after `</noscript>`, type a space and the text {postrow.SEARCH_IMG}. The final version of the line should look like this example:

```
//--></script><noscript>{postrow.ICQ_IMG}</noscript>
{postrow.SEARCH_IMG}</td>
```

5. Save and close the file. If necessary, upload it to your website, replacing the existing file there. You may repeat all of these steps with the `templates/subBook/viewtopic_body.tpl` file, if you wish.
6. Go to your forum and look at any post. You should see a new Search image below the post.

What Just Happened?

Congratulations, you have just installed your first phpBB modification! The majority of modifications contain a series of instructions similar to those on the previous page. Authors intend you to use these instructions as a basic guide to adding the modification to your phpBB files. By placing a little bit of new code inside your `viewtopic_body.tpl` file, you have enabled the search button that can be shown with forum posts.

Installing a Downloaded Modification

After you have downloaded a modification that you wish to install, you must first decompress the downloaded file if it is a ZIP file or another archive file format. When you do so, one or more new files, and possibly directories containing more files, will be created. When there is only one file, it will typically be a simple text file that you can open in WordPad. The name of the file is usually `readme.txt`, `install.txt`, `install.mod`, or something like that. For the sake of example, let's use `install.txt`.

> If a modification contains an `install.mod` file, you may not be able to open this file by double clicking on it like other files. The file extension `.mod` has been used by a popular music file format for years, so music players like WinAMP usually try to open double clicked `.mod` files. In these cases, you will have to open the file through WordPad's File | Open menu.

The `install.txt` will contain all the instructions for installing the modification's changes, as well as the author's credits and notes about the changes. Larger modifications may include both a `readme.txt` and an `install.txt` file. In those cases, it's usually a good idea to examine `readme.txt` before doing anything else, as it may contain special instructions beyond those found in `install.txt`.

A few modifications are simply written out in paragraph form, but the majority use a common template of a header and simple commands called actions. The modification header will contain basic information such as the modification's name, version number, author, description, and an estimation of installation difficulty and time. Important notes about the modification and its history might also be found here, so be certain to read the header fully. **Actions** describe steps of the modification installation using a header containing a brief, descriptive name followed by one or more lines of code.

Here is an example of an action header, as it may appear in a file of instructions.

```
#
#-----[ ACTION NAME ]------------------------------------------
#
```

The actual name of each action will replace the text ACTION NAME. There are many kinds of actions, each of which has a different meaning. When used in a set of instructions, action names are usually typed entirely in capital letters.

> Remember to back up any file you are instructed to alter before doing anything to that file. Refer to the *Editing phpBB Files* section earlier in this chapter if you need to refresh your memory.

The Copy Action

This action, labeled **Copy**, is an instruction to place files into certain new locations. Typically, the files to be copied are part of the modification and must be uploaded to your forum. Sometimes they already exist in the forum and just need to be moved, but special cases like that should be noted in the modification's instructions.

```
#
#-----[ COPY ]------------------------------------------
#
db_update.php to db_update.php
functions_new.php to includes/functions_new.php
templates/*.* to templates/subSilver/*.*
```

Above is an example of a typical Copy action. Each line lists a file to copy on the left and the destination of the copy on the right. Unless otherwise noted, the destination path will be relative to your forum's main directory. With the example, you would place `db_update.php` in the main directory, alongside `viewtopic.php` and `profile.php`, `functions_new.php` inside the `includes/` directory, and all the files in the modification's `templates/` directory inside the forum's `templates/subSilver/` directory. The special notation `*.*` is a quick way of saying *all files within this directory.*

The SQL Action and Editing the Database

When a hack adds new features, they are often tracked in some manner by the SQL database of the forum. In order to get this working, you will need to make changes to the database. Modification authors will include these changes using one or more of three methods. The first method, and most popular in more recently created modifications, is to include an installer script file. Installer files are special files with a `.php` filename extension that can make database changes for you. They are typically named `install.php` or `db_update.php`, but the name can have some variety. To use these files, you normally only need to place them in your forum's directory structure (the Copy action handles that) and run the file.

This part might be confusing to you. People learning how to install modifications often ask, "What does it mean to *run* the file?" To run a `.php` file, you need to visit it in your web browser like a normal web page. A good comparison comes from thinking of your forum's `viewtopic.php`, which displays all topics. Every time you read a topic in the forum, you are running the `viewtopic.php` file. Just visiting your uploaded `db_update.php` file will begin the process of editing the database. Some complicated installers may walk you through several steps.

> Many installer scripts will not work unless you log in to the forum using an administrator account before running the file. Always be sure to log in first, and delete the installer file *immediately* after running. Leaving an installer script in place can be a major security risk!

A second method of including database changes is to place a list of SQL query commands in the installation instructions under an SQL action. The third method places the same kind of list in a separate text file, which might be named `sql.txt` or `schema.sql`. Other names are possible, but the important thing to note is that any file with an extension of `.sql` is a text file containing SQL queries. When either of these two methods is used, you will need to do one of two things: create your own installer script or run the changes manually.

It is not very hard to create your own installer script. In fact, there are generators that can create a `db_update.php` file for you! One such generator can be found at `http://www.phpbbhacks.com/forums/db_generator.php`. Simply copy the SQL queries from the SQL action or file and paste them into this or another generator, submit the form, and you will be presented with the code of a `db_update.php` file. You can download the file directly from that page, place it in your forum, and run the file in the same way you would run an author-supplied installer.

> Some SQL queries may not be compatible with `db_update.php` generators. These will usually produce installer scripts that display parse errors when run. If this happens, visit a friendly phpBB support forum and ask for help with making the queries compatible.

In order to make database changes manually, you can use phpMyAdmin or another similar database management utility. However, you may need to edit the SQL queries before you can do this. When you installed phpBB, you had an option to enter a database table prefix. phpBB uses the value of this option for the beginning of all database table names. Each query in a modification should mention a database table name such as `phpbb_posts` or `phpbb_config`. If your chosen table prefix were `myforum_`, you would need to change the table names to `myforum_posts` and `myforum_config` before using the queries. Installer script files will typically make this change automatically, so you should consider generating one if you are uncomfortable with this process. These are some queries as they might appear before and after changing the table prefix:

```
CREATE TABLE phpbb_tracker (
   tracker_id mediumint(8) DEFAULT '0' NOT NULL,
   tracker1 tinyint(1) DEFAULT '0' NOT NULL,
   tracker2 varchar(40) NOT NULL,
   PRIMARY KEY (tracker_id),
);
CREATE TABLE myforum_tracker (
   tracker_id mediumint(8) DEFAULT '0' NOT NULL,
   tracker1 tinyint(1) DEFAULT '0' NOT NULL,
   tracker2 varchar(40) NOT NULL,
   PRIMARY KEY (tracker_id),
);
INSERT INTO phpbb_tracker (tracker_id, tracker1, tracker2)
   VALUES (1, 3,'Some text');
INSERT INTO myforum_tracker (tracker_id, tracker1, tracker2)
   VALUES (1, 3,'Some text');
```

With the queries in the proper format, open phpMyAdmin and, if necessary, select your database in the left column. Click on the SQL tab or Query Window link. Either of these will load a page containing a large text box. Copy the SQL queries from the modification instructions or text file and paste them into this box. A click of the Go button should run the queries on the database automatically.

The Open Action

This simple action tells you the name and location of a file you need to edit. You should open this file in WordPad, or your favorite text-editing program, and be prepared to make changes to it. If you have not already backed up the file, do so now. All the other actions that follow an Open action should be preformed on the file listed in this action until you reach the end of the instructions or another Open action.

```
#
#-----[ OPEN ]------------------------------------------
#
includes/functions.php
```

The Find Action

Each Find action is followed by one or more lines of code that should be contained within the file in the last Open action. Your goal is to locate this code, which is supposed to be an easy task. Most text-editing programs, including WordPad, have a Find or Search function that makes searching the entire file quick and easy. The Find function should be accessible through the menus of the program or, in Windows programs, by pressing *Ctrl+F*.

Unfortunately, there are some problems that can make finding lines a chore. First, several versions of phpBB have been released. Each version has certain code changes, so phpBB 2.0 will have some modifications for early releases where the Find code is very different than the code in the latest version. In these cases, it is often best if you do not install the modification unless the relevant changes between versions seem minor. Another problem is that some modifications try to find code that has been changed, or even removed, by other modifications already. Some authors have tried to bypass this problem by only listing the first few characters of each line to find. That practice has created yet another problem due to misinterpretation of the actions that follow Find instructions. Finally, some lines of code appear more than once in some files. You may need to edit only a specific appearance or all instances.

How can we solve these problems? Sometimes it is not very easy. If you cannot locate some Find code, the first solution to try is searching for smaller portions of the code. Suppose you have a hard time locating the line of this instruction:

```
#
#-----[ FIND ]------------------------------------------
#
'SOME_TPL_VARIABLE' => $some_php_variable,
```

Looking for a key part of the line, like `SOME_TPL_VARIABLE`, may allow you to find the line even if it has already been changed by another modification or version of phpBB. The ability to adapt lines of code is a key skill when installing modifications and you may need to develop this skill over time.

When dealing with lines or blocks of code that appear in a file several times, keep in mind that most modifications are written based on a top-to-bottom order. Say you have instructions containing two Find commands for one file, with the code of the second appearing twice in the file. The author usually means for you to locate the first appearance following the code of the first Find command.

The Addition Actions

Three actions can add a new code to a file: **Before, Add**; **After, Add**; and **Replace With**. Each of these addition actions will always follow a Find action, and operate in reference to the code in the Find action. In the case of Before, Add actions, the code following the action should be placed into the file on a line before the code of the Find action. For After, Add actions, the codes go onto a line after the Find action's code. A Replace With action will delete the Find action's code and substitute the new code for the old.

For the most part, these are simple steps. There is one point about both Before, Add and After, Add actions that cannot be stressed enough, and that is *always place the new code on a new line, separate from all other code*. Some modification authors, as has been mentioned, include only partial lines of code in their Find actions. The problem with this practice is that modification users tend to add new code right after that in a Find action, on the same line. This places new code right in the middle of the original code, creating a series of syntax errors that can make a forum inaccessible. If you always add code before or after Find code by inserting it on a completely new line, you should be able to avoid this problem.

To illustrate how the code of a file should look, here are some sample action sequences and the correct resulting code. For the sake of these examples, assume a file containing the following code has already been referenced in an Open action.

```
<?php

$number1 = $number2 = $number3 = 0;
$number1 = $x + $y;
$number2 = $y + $z;

$total = $number1 + $number2 + $number3;
echo 'The total is: ' . $total;

?>
```

First, a simple Find and After, Add combination:

```
#
#-----[ FIND ]------------------------------------------
#
$number1 = $x + $y;
$number2 = $y + $z;
#
#-----[ AFTER, ADD ]------------------------------------------
#
$number3 = $a + $b;
```

This sequence should create:

```
$number1 = $number2 = $number3 = 0;
$number1 = $x + $y;
$number2 = $y + $z;
$number3 = $a + $b;

$total = $number1 + $number2 + $number3;
```

A Find and Before, Add combination is next:

```
#
#-----[ FIND ]------------------------------------------
#
$number1 = $x + $y;
$number2 = $y + $z;
#
#-----[ BEFORE, ADD ]------------------------------------------
#
$my_array = array('a' => 1, 'b'=> 2, 'x' => 3, 'y' => 4, 'z' => 5);
while( list($key, $value) = each($my_array) )
{
    $$key = $value;
}
```

After applying this sequence, the file would contain:

```
$number1 = $number2 = $number3 = 0;
$my_array = array('a' => 1, 'b'=> 2, 'x' => 3, 'y' => 4, 'z' => 5);
while( list($key, $value) = each($my_array) )
{
    $$key = $value;
}
```

```
$number1 = $x + $y;
$number2 = $y + $z;
```

A Find action followed by a Replace With action could be:

```
#
#-----[ FIND ]------------------------------------------
#
$total = $number1 + $number2 + $number3;
#
#-----[ REPLACE WITH ]------------------------------------------
#
$average = ($number1 + $number2 + $number3) / 3;
```

That sequence would transform the end of the file into this snippet of code.

```
$average = ($number1 + $number2 + $number3) / 3;
echo 'The total is: ' . $total;

?>
```

Finally, here is another version of the earlier Find and After, Add sequence. This time, the Find action contains only portions of the lines. The result of applying the sequence should be the same as if the full lines were given.

```
#
#-----[ FIND ]------------------------------------------
#
$number1 =
$number2 =
#
#-----[ AFTER, ADD ]------------------------------------------
#
$number3 = $a + $b;
```

The In-Line Actions

Despite what you have just learned about the importance of adding code on new lines, sometimes you will need to change a piece of code within a line. The In-Line actions are used for this. There are four of these: **In-Line Find**; **In-Line Before**, **Add**; **In-Line After**, **Add**; and **In-Line Replace With**. Ideally, you will see a Find action with a long line of code, followed by an In-Line Find with a short snippet of that line, then one of the other three In-Line actions. Use them just as you would their normal counterparts, but this time do not add the new code on a separate line. You will actually insert the code inside the current line. In several modifications that use In-Line actions, you may have to change a line in several different places.

Using the same short file above, here is an example of an In-Line Replace With action sequence that edits two parts of one line.

```
#
#-----[ FIND ]------------------------------------------
#
echo 'The total is: ' . $total;
#
```

```
#-----[ IN-LINE FIND ]------------------------------------------
#
 total
#
#-----[ IN-LINE REPLACE WITH ]----------------------------------------
---
#
 average
#
#-----[ IN-LINE FIND ]------------------------------------------
#
$total
#
#-----[ IN-LINE REPLACE WITH ]----------------------------------------
---
#
$average
```

That sequence alters the end of the file to look like:

```
$average = ($number1 + $number2 + $number3) / 3;
echo 'The average is: ' . $average;

?>
```

The Last Action

Almost every modification's instructions end with a variation of this action:

```
#
#-----[ SAVE/CLOSE ALL FILES ]----------------------------------------
---
#
# End
```

This is the last step of the instructions. It serves as a reminder to save your changes, close any remaining open files, and transfer edited files to your forum if necessary. Once you have done those things, you should be finished with the modification installation. You should thoroughly test the installation with your administrator account, a normal user account, and, if necessary, a moderator account. Many modifications add features that work differently for accounts with different permissions. For testing purposes, it is best if you only install one modification at a time. If you were to install three or four modifications simultaneously and you encounter an error in your forum, you might have a hard time tracking down the cause.

The following table provides a quick reference of the modification Action:

Action Name	Definition
Copy	Copies one or more files from one location to another.
SQL	Runs one or more SQL queries on your forum's database. These should usually be completed before installing the remainder of the modification.

Action Name	Definition
Open	Opens the file in preparation for editing. Every action following this until the last action, or another Open action, should be performed on this file. It is followed by a single filename.
Find	This locates the code in the file and is followed by code.
After, Add	Places the following code *on a new line after* the code in the preceding Find action. It always follows a Find action.
Before, Add	Places the following code *on a new line before* the code in the preceding Find action. It always follows a Find action.
Replace With	Deletes the code found in the preceding Find action and puts the following code in its place. It always follows a Find action.
In-Line Find	Usually follows a Find action. Locates the following code inside a longer line of code.
In-Line After, Add	Places the following code *after* the code in the preceding In-Line Find, *on the same line of code.* It always follows an In-Line Find action.
In-Line Before, Add	Places the following code *before* the code in the preceding In-Line Find, *on the same line of code.* It always follows an In-Line Find action.
In-Line Replace With	Deletes the code in the preceding In-Line Find and put this code in its place on the same line of code. It always follows an In-Line Find action.
Save/Close All Files	Signals the end of file changes and reminds you to save your changes. It is always the last action of a modification.
Add SQL	This is an older form of the SQL action, with the same meaning as that action.

The Trouble with Templates

One very important aspect of modification installation remains, just when you thought you had finished it. When you install modifications, you will see that almost all of those modifying or adding template files will only mention the subSilver template in their instructions. By this time, you should have installed at least one other template on your forum. With so many templates existing, it is not practical for authors to mention all of them in their instructions. Since every phpBB forum has subSilver installed at some point, and many templates are built from subSilver, only that one template gets mentioned, with an unspoken understanding that it is really a reference to all templates.

The trouble with templates is that you have to install every modification's template file changes to all your installed templates, even though the instructions do not tell you to do this. Also, if you install modifications and later install new templates, you have to apply the modifications to those templates. Should you forget to modify a template, any forum members using that template will not be able to access the modification's features unless they switch to another that you did edit.

Another problem in this area is the code of the templates themselves. While many templates are created from subSilver, quite a few are not. The latter kinds tend to have some very different markup language coding in their files. It can seem nearly impossible to locate code in a Find action unless you break it down into individual template variables. You might actually have to rewrite the new template files or code to match the look of the alternative templates, too. It can be quite a headache.

Uninstalling Modifications

Occasionally, you may have a need to remove a modification after installing it. Maybe you've found that two modifications are conflicting with each other or a modification does not live up to your expectations. Whatever the reason, uninstalling tends to be easier than installing.

There are two methods of removing a modification's changes to your files. Since you created backups before editing any of your files, you can replace your current files with those backup copies. This reverts the forum's files to the same condition they were in before the modification was installed. If you have made changes to the files other than installing this modification, then you should not restore the backup files. Doing so in such a case will cause your other changes to be lost.

The second method is to go through the modification's instructions as if installing, but invert the action commands. For example, if the instructions have a Find action followed by an After, Add action, you would locate and delete the After, Add code. In the case of a Find and Replace With combination, you would search for the Replace With code, remove it, and place the Find code at that location. To further illustrate these concepts, the following example removes the Search button added to posts in the earlier modification installation exercise.

Time For Action—Uninstalling a Small Modification

1. Locate and open the `templates/subSilver/viewtopic_body.tpl` file of your forum in a text-editing program.
2. Use the text-editing program's search feature to locate this line of text in the file. Again, most programs allow accessing such a feature from their menus or by pressing *Ctrl+F* on Windows systems.

```
//--></script><noscript>{postrow.ICQ_IMG}</noscript>
{postrow.SEARCH_IMG}</td>
```

3. Now, locate the text {postrow.SEARCH_IMG} within that line.
4. Delete this text and the single space before it. The line should once again look as it originally did:

```
//--></script><noscript>{postrow.ICQ_IMG}</noscript></td>
```

5. Save and close the file. If necessary, upload it to your website, replacing the existing file there. You may repeat all of these steps with the templates/subBook/viewtopic_body.tpl file, if you wish.
6. Go to your forum and look at any post. You should see that the Search image is no longer shown.

What Just Happened?

By reversing the actions you took to install the Search button modification, you have removed it from your forum. Instead of finding the original code and adding to it, you searched for the modified code. Then you removed the extra code added by the original modification. This restored the altered file to its original state.

Removing Other Changes

The need to remove new files and database changes is common to both methods of removing file changes reviewed before the previous example. New files added by a modification are quick and easy to deal with: just delete them. Removing database changes is a more complex aspect of uninstallation; however, phpMyAdmin is a handy tool for making this simple. When a modification has added a new table or a new column in a table, you can locate this addition in phpMyAdmin and click a Delete link, which often takes the form of a trash can icon, next to it. phpMyAdmin will ask you to confirm the deletion (or dropping, as it is called when dealing with tables or columns); do so and the change will be gone.

Example Modifications

Thousands of modifications for phpBB have been released for public use in the years since phpBB first appeared. Think of almost any feature you might like to add to or remove from a phpBB forum, and there will probably be at least one modification for that already. New modifications are created and released each week so the possibilities for customizing a forum through this method are endless.

One of the most popular modifications is the massive **File Attachment Mod**, which contains over 140 files. It adds a new feature to phpBB's posting forums allowing users to upload files that will be attached to and displayed with their posts. Another commonly used example is Modify Profile, formerly known as Add New Field to Profile. This modification is an instruction guide for adding new information fields to user registration and profile-editing forms. Many different kinds of fields can be added, ranging from simple text entry boxes to drop-down selection lists. The data stored in the new field can also be displayed in public profiles, topics, posts, and other places throughout a forum.

Dozens of modifications alter or add new BBCodes. User and administration management tools, online games, stores, chat rooms, recent topics, download systems, phpBB bug fixes or upgrades, and website portals are examples of some other widely used modifications.

These lists are only scratching the surface when it comes to describing the types of modifications available for your use. It will definitely be worth your time to check out a few websites that list modifications; you will find something that you want to install at your forum if you look closely enough. Chances are you will find many things to use in customizing your forum.

Moving Elements

Some layout alterations can be made to your forum without taking the time to search for a detailed modification. While you can find modification downloads for some of these, modifications often don't deal with layout issues very well. The differences in templates, and sometimes those created by other modifications, often force forum administrators to rearrange their layout without any help. In order to move elements like this, you will need to have at least a basic knowledge of HTML coding.

You might have noticed that subSilver and subBook have some statistical data and a login box at the bottom of their forum index pages. One popular change that you can make is to move one or more of those elements to another part of the page. By finding the layout code that creates them in `index_body.tpl` and placing it closer to the top of the file, you can emphasize that your users should log in or the number of users and posts on your forum.

Adding New Elements to Your Forum

Creating new areas in your forum will usually require a full modification, complete with instructions. There are a couple of simple things that can be done without a modification, however. One of these is to add a new link to your forum's header menu.

Time For Action—Adding a Menu Link

1. Locate and open the `templates/subBook/overall_header.tpl` file for editing. You can use the `subSilver overall_header.tpl` file instead, if you like.
2. Find the line in this file containing the code `<!-- BEGIN switch_user_logged_out -->`. There will be several tab spaces at the beginning of the line.
3. Insert the following code on a new line before the code you just located:

```
 <a href="{U_VIEWONLINE}" class="mainmenu"><img
src="templates/subBook/images/icon_mini_members.gif" width="12"
height="13" border="0" alt="{L_WHO_IS_ONLINE}" hspace="3"
/>{L_WHO_IS_ONLINE}</a></span> 
```

4. Save your changes to the file and view your forum. You may need to reload or refresh the forum page, but you should see a new Who is Online link with the other links near the top of the forum.

What Just Happened?

The menu links of your forum, like Profile, FAQ, and Search, are created by HTML stored in the `overall_header.tpl` template file. By duplicating a line or series of lines that creates one of these links and altering the line a little, you can create a new menu link. In this case, the new link points to the `viewonline.php` file, which displays a list of users currently visiting the forum. If these steps were written up as a modification, they might look like this:

```
#
#-----[ OPEN ]------------------------------------------
#
templates/subBook/overall_header.tpl
#
#-----[ FIND ]------------------------------------------
#
<!-- BEGIN switch_user_logged_out -->
 <a href="{U_REGISTER}" class="mainmenu"><img
src="templates/subBook/images/icon_mini_register.gif" width="12"
height="13" border="0" alt="{L_REGISTER}" hspace="3"
/>{L_REGISTER}</a></span> 
<!-- END switch_user_logged_out -->
#
#-----[ BEFORE, ADD ]------------------------------------------
#
 <a href="{U_VIEWONLINE}" class="mainmenu"><img
src="templates/subBook/images/icon_mini_members.gif" width="12"
height="13" border="0" alt="{L_WHO_IS_ONLINE}" hspace="3"
/>{L_WHO_IS_ONLINE}</a>
</span> 
#
#-----[ SAVE/CLOSE ALL FILES ]------------------------------------------
---
#
# End
```

Adding New Languages

Another common change made by forum administrators is the installation of new language files. If you plan to have many visitors who are fluent in languages other than English or cannot read English, you might want to download and install a language pack from phpBB.com's Downloads section. Each language pack adds a new option to the Board Language drop-down list in user profiles and the Administration Control Panel. Selecting that option will cause the forum to be displayed in that language. Posts will not be translated, but many links and other default text will.

When adding language packs, you should keep in mind that you may have to edit the new language files. Some modifications will include new language files or instructions for editing language files. If you add a new language and do not copy these changes to that language, then some text will not appear on your forum. This situation is similar to that for modifications and templates; you must edit every language, even if the modification's instructions only mention one.

Summary

phpBB is excellent and powerful forum software in many areas. Customization possibilities are one of the strongest. With the skills and knowledge you've gained in this chapter, you can give your forum a complete face-lift or expand its features beyond anything you might have imagined. Specifically, you learned:

- A phpBB style creates the appearance of a forum
- Editing a style's components allows you to change any aspect of the appearance
- Modifications are instructions for changing phpBB's features, and usually have a special format
- How to install and remove styles and modifications downloaded from websites
- Methods of editing any of phpBB's files and solving errors

Later chapters will expand on these topics somewhat by discussing details of creating your own styles and modifications.

5

Forum Administration

In the previous chapters you've read about how your board works and how to customize the way it looks. Some advanced topics were skipped so that you could concentrate on the most important and widely used phpBB features. It's now time to master phpBB, and go through details that will make you a real power-phpBB-admin.

In this chapter you'll learn about:

- Making your board multi-lingual
- Configuring avatars
- Managing smilies
- Assigning ranks
- Forum permissions
- User permissions
- Usergroups and group permissions
- Database backups and restore—a second look
- The human side—moderators, flamewars, and banning

Making Your Board Multi-Lingual

phpBB is developed to support multiple languages in the same board. The whole interface (screens, messages, buttons, e-mails, and so on) is translated into more than 50 languages. The translators are not members of the phpBB team, but are native-speaking volunteers, and this guarantees that the translations are correct and ready to be installed on your board. Thus, you provide a better service for your community, giving them an interface they feel more comfortable with.

Time For Action—Adding Spanish Support to Your Forum

1. Go to the phpBB.com downloads page `http://www.phpbb.com/downloads.php`.

2. Scroll down to the Language & Image Packs section and locate the Español (Spanish) row:

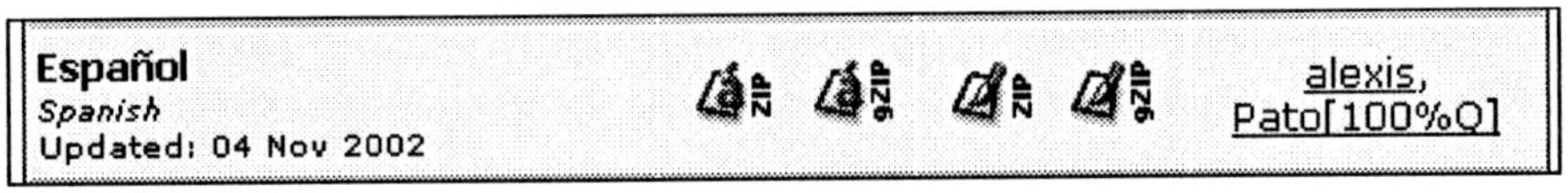

3. Choose your preferred compression type—ZIP or GZIP—and download the two archives in the selected format. Let's choose the ZIP format as an example. The first ZIP file contains the texts for the phpBB interfaces, and the second one contains the interface graphics, such as the buttons for a new post, quote, and so on. These graphics are provided for the default subSilver theme only.
4. Uncompress the first file, `lang_spanish.zip` (and FTP it if you're using a hosted service), into the `language` directory within your phpBB directory. This should create a `lang_spanish` subdirectory under `language`.
5. Uncompress the second file, `subSilver_spanish.zip`, to a selected directory. When you do this, you'll notice that it has a nested directory structure, and in your selected directory, you'll have a `subSilver/images/lang_spanish` path.
   If you follow this path, you'll find a number of GIF files.
6. Copy (and/or FTP) the last directory (`lang_spanish`, the one that contains all the GIF files) into your corresponding phpBB directory, `templates/subSilver/images`.

What Just Happened?

After you have successfully uncompressed the ZIP archives and copied their content, your forum structure will look like the following screenshot:

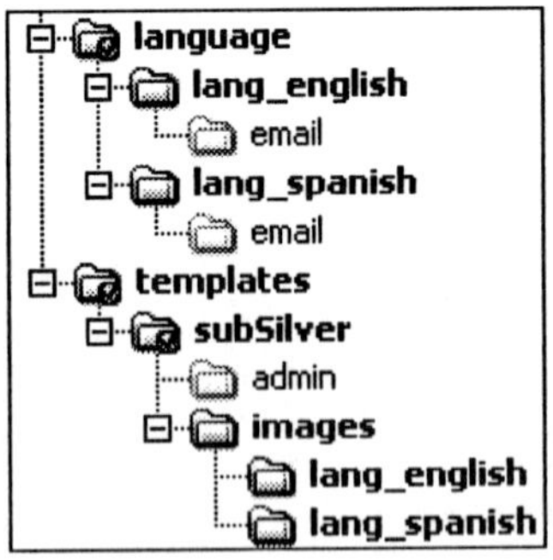

Now if you log in to your forum and access your profile, you'll see that the Board Language dropdown now has two values, as shown in the illustration:

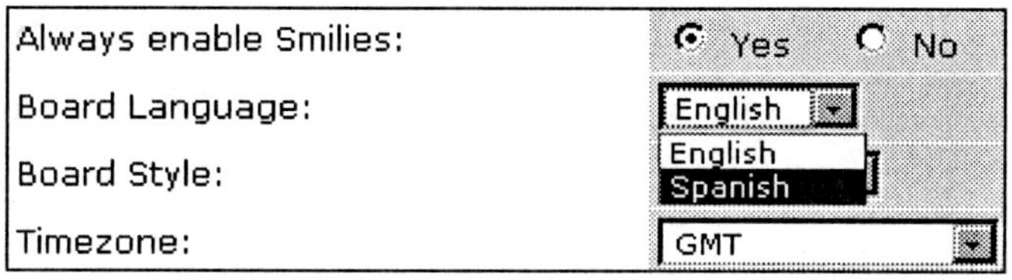

If you change your preference to Spanish, you'll see the whole board with a Spanish interface. ¡Hola!

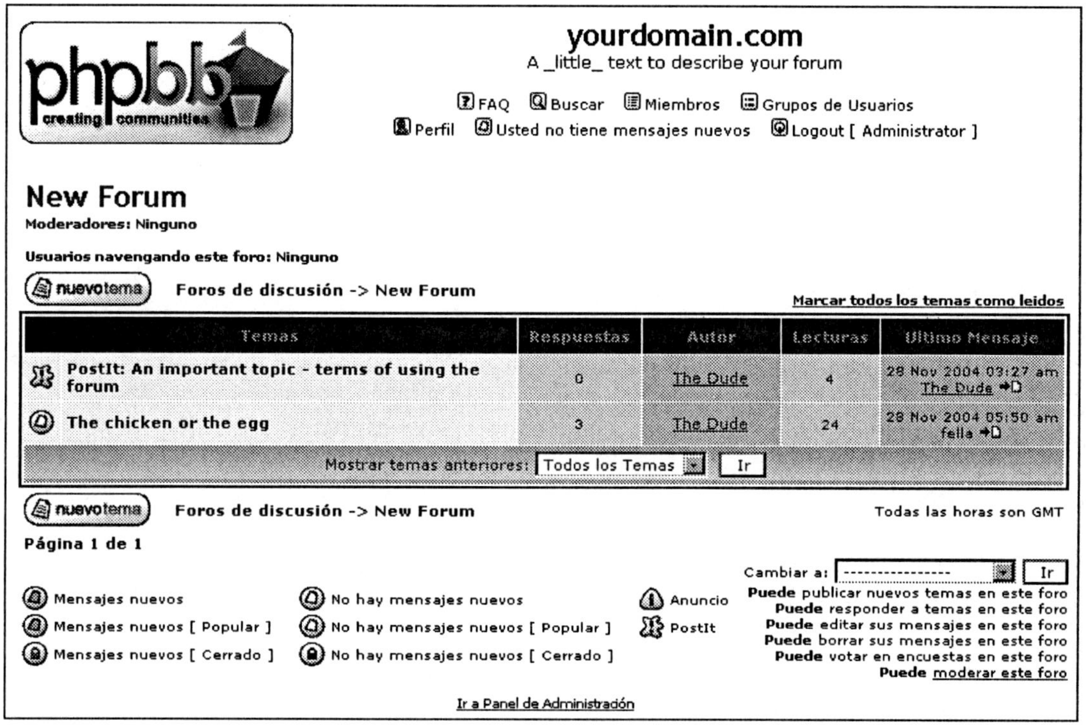

Now you have two languages installed, but English is still the default language for the board. If your community is mainly Spanish speaking, you can consider changing the default language. To do that you need to go to the Administration Panel and follow the Configuration link under General Admin.

Avatars: Enabling and Configuring

Avatars are those small images that reside under the username in all postings and are also displayed when viewing a user's profile. They are not enabled by default in phpBB, but can be enabled pretty easily using the Administrator Panel.

There are three options for the use of avatars, and they are not exclusive; you can select any number of them.

- Option one is to enable the so-called **gallery avatars**: The images that can be used as avatars are selected by you and hosted on the same server on which phpBB runs. Users can select their preferred avatar only from the offered images.
- Option two is to enable **remote avatars**: The avatar image can reside on any server on the Internet and the users are just linking to it, using image's URL address (starting with `http://`).
- Option three is to allow users to **upload avatars**: The users copy their images to your server, and phpBB reads them from there when displaying a post.

All these options have pros and cons to consider when making a decision.

- **Remote avatars** are your safest bet in terms of server security; it's all in the hands of the users, and your board is not responsible for hosting or managing the images. However, some users may want to use images that are on their hard drives and are nowhere to be found on the Internet. Also, because of the dynamic nature of the Internet, many pages and even whole sites appear and disappear in a single day. This means that an image your user selected today may not be available tomorrow, and some browsers (like Internet Explorer) will display a broken image icon instead, which is not pretty. Or even if an avatar is available but hosted on a slow site, it may slow the whole page down. There may be issues when the board members use avatars hosted on servers that don't allow hotlinking. Moreover, you don't have control over the sizes of the avatars. Somebody can put a real big picture as an avatar and ruin the whole look of a topic.
- With **gallery avatars**, you have control over the size of the images, because you're the one selecting them. The drawbacks are that these images will increase your bandwidth usage and will be too restrictive for the users, as they can only pick an image from pre-defined choices.
- **Uploaded avatars** can lead to increased bandwidth, which can be an issue for heavily used boards with a lot of users. Another issue might be that some hosts may not allow you to use file uploads, because of the general concern that anything that a user does to a server can be potentially dangerous. Apart from that, uploaded avatars have quite a few benefits, like defining the size in pixels and the disk size in bytes for the images. With the uploaded avatars, users are free to use any possible image they can lay their hands on, not only those images available on the Internet.

To configure the avatars, you need to log in as an administrator, go to the Administrator Panel, and bring up the general configuration form:

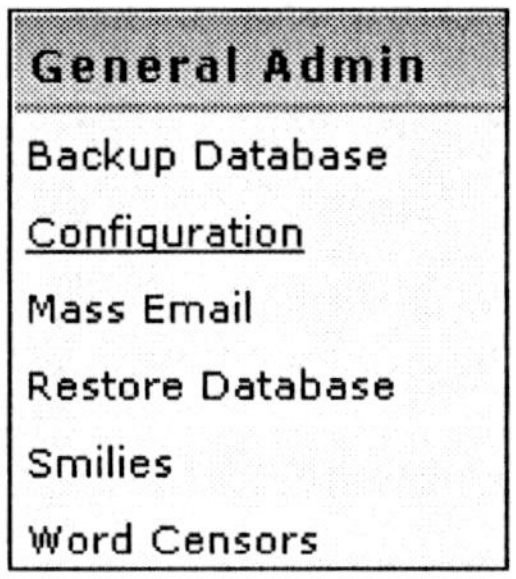

Here's what the avatars section in the configuration form looks like:

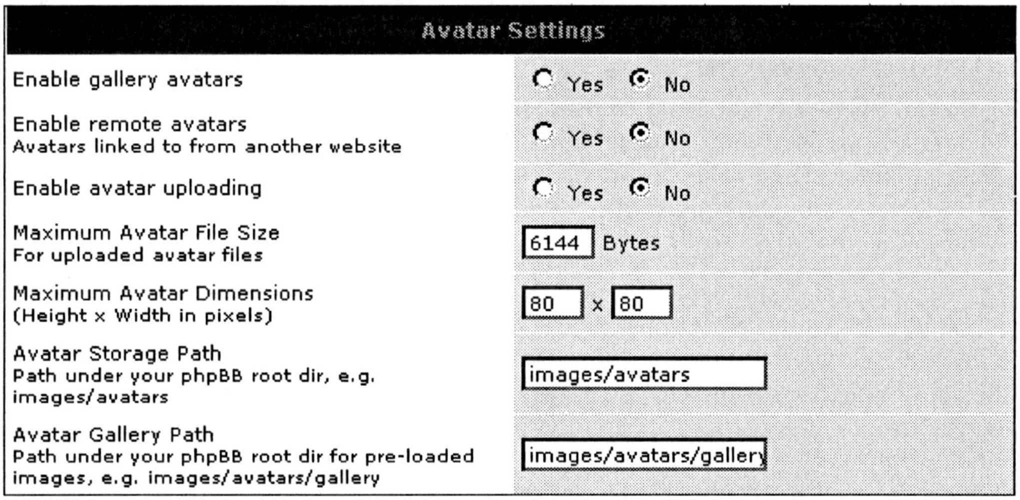

The first three fields represent the three avatar options discussed. The next three fields are applicable to uploaded avatars only, and the very last field is for gallery avatars only.

To feel more comfortable with the avatar options, the best thing to do is just to enable all three options and play around with the avatars. After that, you can make your choice.

Getting gallery avatars

You can get avatars for your gallery from `http://www.phpbb.com/styles/`. Click on Downloads, and then Avatars. Unzip the packages into a subfolder within the `avatars` directory you specified in the configuration (the default is `images/avatars/gallery`).

Don't forget permissions

If you enable avatar uploads, you have to make sure the directory specified to contain the images (the default is `images/avatars`) is writable, meaning `chmod 777` for Linux systems. Setting file permissions was explained in Chapter 2.

You can have categories of gallery avatars; actually you have to have at least one category. What does this mean? It means that you have to copy *all* your gallery avatars into sub-directories of the main avatar gallery directory. For example, you'd copy `dog.gif` and `cat.gif` to `images/avatars/gallery/pets`, even if you host a pet-lovers site and `pets` would be the only gallery you'll ever need. In any event, this feature helps you keep your galleries organized.

Managing Smilies

phpBB comes with a default set of smilies, but you can change the defaults or add new ones. In fact, your users may request that you add more smilies, because the defaults may not be enough for them to express their emotions. Or it's just that some of your members may be used to seeing different smilies in other boards that they visit, and miss those cute graphics in your board.

As you know already, **smilies** and **emoticons** are synonyms. "Smilies" is a more widespread term, while "emoticons" is probably more accurate, because not all of the small round faces are smiling. One other interesting thing is that the word "smilie" can be spelled as "smilie" *and* "smiley". phpBB prefers "smiley" but a Google search returned more results on "smilie", so it's apparently more often used. In this book, we've adopted "smilie".

phpBB gives you the ability to:

- Edit or delete an existing smilie
- Add new smilies one by one
- Add new smilies in batches using the special `.pak` files
- Create `.pak` files using your currently installed smilies; this is a good idea if you have created a number of smilies that you'd like to share with other phpBB administrators.

Smilies' Properties

Let's first see what a smilie consists of. Every smilie has:

- **An image**: Smilie images like  and  reside in the `images/smilies` directory of your board's directory structure.
- **A code**: The code is the sequence of characters a poster needs to type (or have them typed automatically by clicking the corresponding image) in order to display the selected smilie in a post. For the example icons in the previous bullet, the corresponding codes are :D and :?. Sometimes there can be several codes for one emoticon, and so there are several ways to include the same image in a post. You can use :D or :-D or :grin:, and the result will always be the  image.
- **An emotion**: This is a human-readable representation of the smilie. It may be displayed (depending on the browser) as a tool-tip when a reader holds the mouse over a poster's emoticon (in HTML terms, it is the `alt` attribute of the `img` tag).

Here's a pair of images showing an example. The left-hand illustration shows a posting at the moment of writing; the right-hand one shows how the posting is displayed (with the mouse over the smilie) in an Internet Explorer browser window:

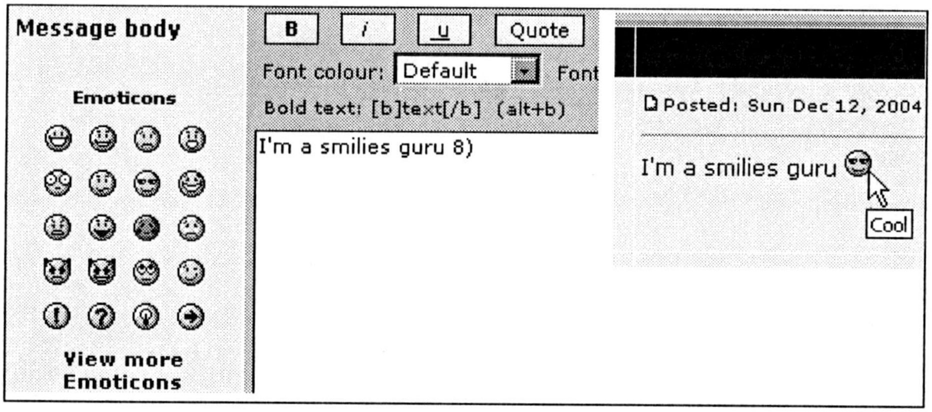

Smilies Administration Panel

All smilie operations are accessible through the Administration Panel using the Smilies link under the General Admin section:

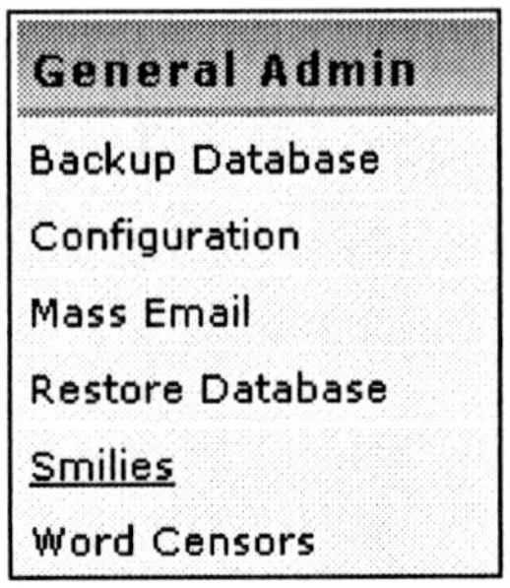

Clicking this link brings up a list of existing smilies:

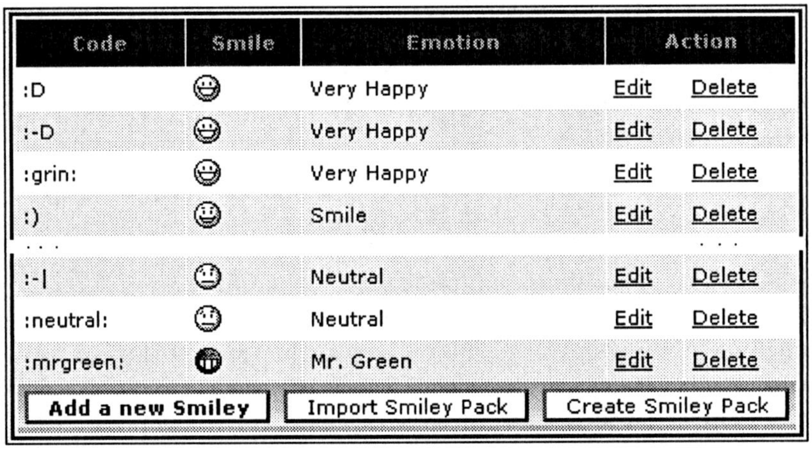

This illustration shows the listing cut down in the middle. The listing can grow pretty long as you add new smilies. You can see all the properties of the smilies—the code, the image, and the emotion they represent—as well as the possible actions that you can execute on them.

Before proceeding with the following exercises, it may be a good idea to make a backup of your `images/smilies` directory, just in case you want to revert to the default smilies.

Editing or Deleting a Smilie

To edit or delete a smilie, use the appropriate link next to the smilie in question.

Be careful when playing around, because when you click **Delete**, there will be no "Are you sure?" confirmation; the smilie will be removed permanently. Deleting a smilie means that it can no longer be used in postings; it also means that any older postings that use this emoticon will display the code, but not the image.

Deleting a smilie doesn't delete the actual image from the server, as chances are this image may be used for other smilies as well. For example, if you delete the smilie with the :-D code, the 😀 image won't be deleted, because it's also used in the :D smilie. Even if you delete all smilies that use a certain image, the image will stay on the server and can be used later on, by defining a new smilie.

To edit a smilie, use the Edit link next to it. This brings up a form with all the smilie properties, as shown on the illustration.

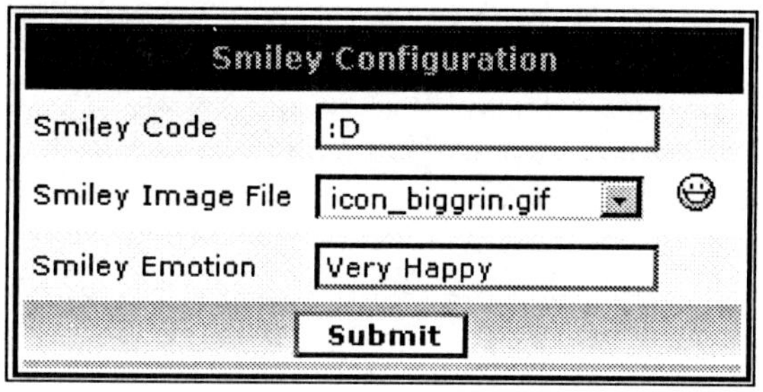

The Smilie Image File drop-down field lists all the files found in the `images/smilies` folder of your board installation. Selecting an image file from the dropdown displays this image next to the dropdown.

Adding New Smilies

The simplest way to add a new smilie is by using an existing image.

Time For Action—Adding a New Smilie Using an Existing Image

1. In the smilies admin panel, click the Add a new Smiley button. The same form as the one for editing is displayed.
2. In the first field, type :mg:.
3. In the second field (drop-down), select icon_mrgreen.gif.
4. In the last field, type Mr. Green.
5. Click Submit.

What Just Happened?

You created a new Mr. Green smilie using the same existing image. In other words, you defined a new way for the users to use this emoticon. Now the users can have Mr. Green displayed in their postings in two ways: by using either the default code, :mrgreen:, or the new one, :mg:.

Now let's add a completely new smilie. Let's say you took Mr. Green's icon and painted it all orange. Now let's call this guy Mr. Orange 😁 and name the file `mr_orange.gif`.

Time For Action—Adding a Custom Smilie

1. Copy/FTP the `mr_orange.gif` file to your `images/smilies` directory.
2. Go to the smilies admin panel and click the Add a new Smiley button.
3. In the first field, type :mrorange:.
4. In the second field select mr_orange.gif.
5. In the last field, type Mr. Orange.
6. Click Submit.

What Just Happened?

You've just added a brand new shiny smilie face to your board. You can see it now in the smilies listing.

Adding Smilies with a .pak File

You may be wondering how to create GIF files like the one used in the example above. Well, this is a topic that is outside the scope of the book, but you can find many tools and tutorials on the Internet. If you don't want to deal with the graphics, don't worry; there is good news for you. There are lots of smilie images out there on the Web, available for you do download and use in your board. To ease the installation, phpBB has a feature to add smilies in batches using the `.pak` files. This "pak" stands for "package".

If you visit `http://www.phpbb.com/styles`, click on Downloads, and then Smilies, you'll see a listing of smilie packages for you to choose from. Let's pick one of those packages to download, the one called More smilies.

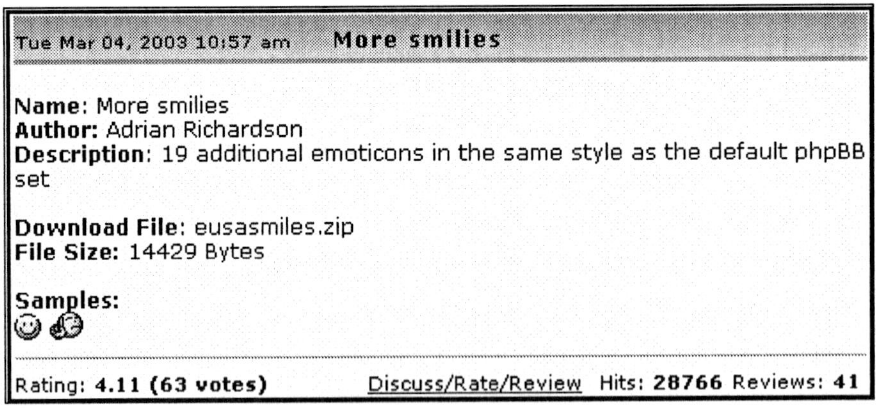

If you download `eusasmiles.zip` and uncompress it, you'll see that it contains a number of GIF files and one `eusa.pak` file. Don't be scared by the unknown extension of this file, it's just a plain text file. If you open it with any text-editing program (like Notepad or WordPad for Windows) and look at the file contents, you'll notice that it contains simply the smilie properties, divided by the sequence of characters `=+:`, used as a delimiter.

The last line of the file, for example, says:

```
eusa_silenced.gif=+:Silenced=+::-#
```

What this means is that :-# is the code for an emoticon that means Silenced and whose icon image is called `eusa_silenced.gif`.

Now let's use the provided `.pak` file to quickly add a bunch of new smilies to the board.

Time For Action—Adding Smilies Using a .pak File

1. Copy the uncompressed content (the GIF images and the `.pak` file) to the `images/smilies` directory of your bulletin board.
2. Go to the smilies admin area in the Administration Panel and click on the Import Smiley Pack button. You'll see the Smiley Pack Import form.

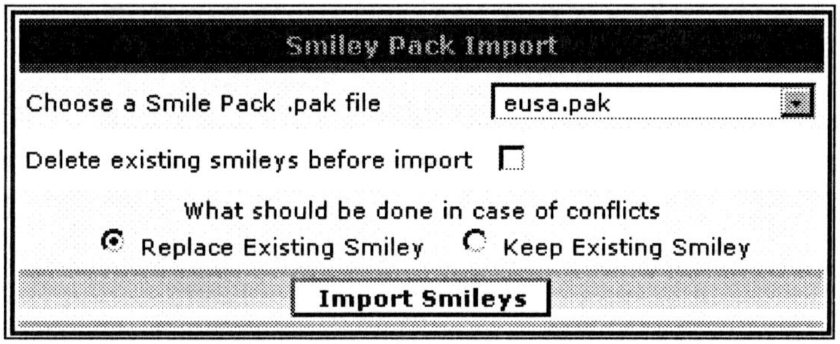

3. In the dropdown, choose eusa.pak.
4. Leave the other fields as they are. They represent your options of what to do with the existing smilies and how to handle conflicts, if any.
5. Click Import Smileys.

What Just Happened?

You've added a whole lot of new smilies in a single shot. You can see them now in the smilies listing, right after the Mr. Orange smiley you added in the previous exercise. Here's a part of what the new smilies listing will look like:

:mrorange:		Mr. Orange	Edit	Delete
=D>		Applause	Edit	Delete
#-o		d'oh!	Edit	Delete
=P~		Drool	Edit	Delete
:^o		Liar	Edit	Delete

Creating a .pak File

You can create a `.pak` file with your existing smilies configuration. You can use it for backup purposes or to share your icons. Let's say you've created not only Mr. Orange, but also Mr. White, Mr. Pink, Mr. Brown, and Mr. Blonde, and have added them by hand following the same procedure as for Mr. Orange.

:mrwhite:		Mr. White
:mrpink:		Mr. Pink
:mrbrown:		Mr. Brown
:mrblonde:		Mr. Blonde

Now let's create a `.pak` file that will contain the properties of all smilies you've added, so that you can share your smilies with other phpBB administrators.

> The images used in this chapter are available in the book's download area at `http://www.packtpub.com`.

Time For Action—Creating a .pak File

1. Go to the smilies admin and click the Create Smiley Pack button.
2. You get information about working with `.pak` files and an option to download the `.pak` file generated for you. Download it. The file is called `smilies.pak` by default, but you can always change its name to something else, like `reservoir_dogs.pak` for example.
3. The package file contains *all* the properties for all the smilies on your board, but you actually need only your *five* custom ones. So open the `.pak` file in a text editor and remove all unnecessary lines, leaving just your five lines. The `.pak` file contents now should look like:

```
mr_orange.gif=+:Mr. Orange=+::mrorange:
mr_white.gif=+:Mr. White=+::mrwhite:
mr_pink.gif=+:Mr. Pink=+::mrpink:
mr_brown.gif=+:Mr. Brown=+::mrbrown:
mr_blonde.gif=+:Mr. Blonde=+::mrblonde:
```

4. Zip this .pak file together with the five images.

What Just Happened?

You've created a .pak file containing all the smilies you've created. You can send it to other phpBB admins if they want to install your custom smilies.

Assigning Ranks

Ranks are another way of giving your community members a credit for their participation. Only one rank exists by default: the Site Admin rank. There are two types of ranks that you can create: **ranks by number of posts** and **special ranks**. The first type of ranks are automatic, and are assigned as a member keeps posting. The second type are not dependent on the number of posts, and you can assign them as you may find appropriate, using the user management facility in the Administration Panel.

Ranks are given names, typically something like New user, Enthusiast, Forum addict, and so on. Ranks can optionally have rank images. When viewing postings by a user, the name of the rank assigned to the user is displayed under the username, and the rank image is displayed under the rank name, above the avatar. Here's an example of how the author-info area of a posting looks when a rank is assigned:

In this illustration, The Dude is the username you already know from the previous chapters, Forum Wizard is the rank name, the five stars is the rank image, and the paintbrush daub is the user's avatar.

The following examples will help you get some hands-on experience on assigning ranks. For the sake of the first example, let's assume that you have created five rank images. The images are in GIF format and show one, two, three, four, and five blue stars respectively, like this:

- rank1.gif: ★
- rank2.gif: ★★
- rank3.gif: ★★★
- rank4.gif: ★★★★
- rank5.gif: ★★★★★

If creating GIF files is not your cup of tea, don't worry, you can download rank images from the Internet: one place to look is, of course, the phpBB.com site. Visit the styles section and click on Downloads followed by Rank Images. You can also find many rank images on the phpBBHacks site, at `http://www.phpbbhacks.com/rankimages.php`.

Time For Action—Creating Automatic Ranks

1. In the `images` directory of your board, create a subdirectory called `ranks`. This will keep rank-related images separate from the rest of the images.
2. Copy the files listed above (`rank1.gif` through to `rank5.gif`) to the newly created directory.
3. In the Administration Panel, click the Ranks link (the last link in the administration menu).
4. Click the Add new rank button.
5. You're presented with the Rank Administration form. Fill it out as shown on the illustration:

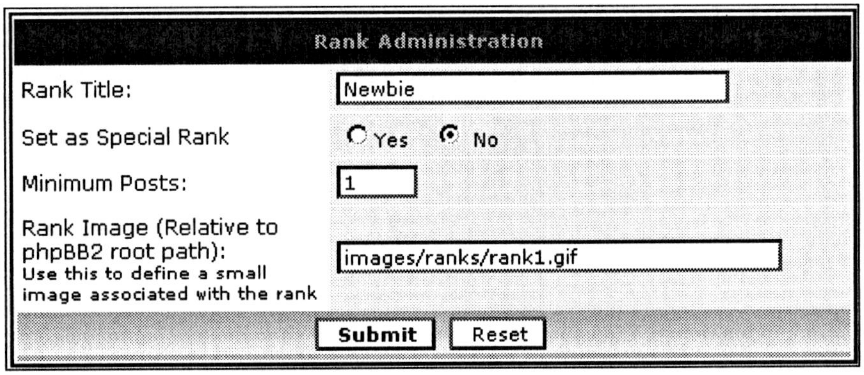

6. Click Submit.
7. Repeat steps 4 through 6 until you use all rank images. At the end you'll have your ranks setup as the following:

Rank Title	Minimum Posts	Set as Special Rank	Edit	Delete
Site Admin	-	Yes	Edit	Delete
Newbie	1	No	Edit	Delete
Oldie	5	No	Edit	Delete
Zealot	10	No	Edit	Delete
Guru	20	No	Edit	Delete
Forum Wizard	30	No	Edit	Delete
Add new rank				

What Just Happened?

You've successfully set up an automated ranking system that will display a rank name and a rank image after each member's username in the member's postings. The exact rank will be determined by phpBB based on the total number of posts by this member.

In practice of course you'd want to use a much bigger number of postings, but for testing the functionality this is enough.

Now let's take a look at the procedure for creating special ranks and how you can assign a special rank to the members you feel are special.

Time For Action—Creating and Assigning a Special Rank

1. In the ranks listing click Add new rank.
2. Fill out the form as shown:

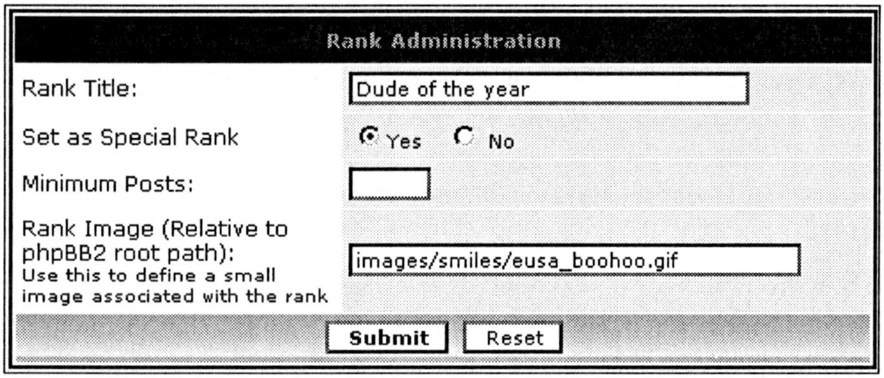

3. Click Submit
4. Now in the left menu, click the Management link in the User Admin section.
5. In the text field, type The Dude and click Look up user.
6. Scroll down to the bottom of the user admin form. In the Rank Title drop-down, select Dude of the year.
7. Click Submit.

What Just Happened?

Steps 1-3: You created a special rank, meaning that it's not related to the number of postings. The Minimum Posts field was left blank, as it's not applicable to special ranks. Actually, even if you do enter something in it, the value will be ignored by phpBB. In this example you didn't create a new rank image, but reused an existing smilie image instead.

Steps 4-7: You assigned the newly created special rank to a user. If you now visit the front-end of your board and find a posting by The Dude, you'll see the new rank.

Understanding Forum Permissions

Forum permissions were discussed in Chapter 3, but we'll now take a more insightful approach so that we'll be able to specify more precisely who can do what on your board.

Let's start with defining two important terms: **permission types** and **permission levels**.

Permission Types and Permission Levels

Permission types and **permission levels** are two important terms when dealing with phpBB permissions, and understanding these will help you when you think of how to assign and control privileges:

- **Permission types** are the actions that a user can do in the board, such as view, reply, vote, etc. When you think about permission types, think *what*, as in "What can be done?"
- **Permission levels** reflect restrictions about who can do a certain actions. Every user has at least one permission level. When you think about permission levels, think *who* as in "Who can do it?"

The following list discusses the permission types ("*What-s*") that exist, and the capabilities they provide to a user. (You already know what these actions mean, as they were described in detail in the previous chapters.)

- **View**: The user can see that a forum exists on the board front page.
- **Read**: The user can list forum topics, read the postings, view the members' profiles, and their contact info.
- **Reply**: The user can post in existing topics.
- **Post**: The user can start new topics.
- **Edit**: The user can edit their own postings.
- **Delete**: The user can delete his or her own postings, provided no one has replied to them yet.
- **Sticky**: The user can start sticky topics. This is dependent on the post privilege—if you cannot post, you certainly cannot post sticky topics.
- **Announce**: The user can start announcements. Just like the sticky type, the post privilege is a prerequisite.
- **Vote**: The user can vote in polls.
- **Poll create**: The user can create polls for others to vote in.

Permission levels, or "*Who-s*", can also be thought of as user types.

Here are the possible permission levels:

- **ALL**: Everybody who accesses the board; this includes members who are currently not logged in.
- **REG**: A member registered at the board and currently logged in.
- **PRIVATE**: A special permission level that is assigned individually. In order for a user on this level to communicate in privacy with others, this user has to be given private access to a private forum. This is the trickiest part of the permissions, so don't be scared if you don't understand it yet. There will be some examples to clarify this concept.
- **MOD**: A moderator who can do everything to a forum.
- **ADMIN**: A board administrator (someone like you, who can access the Administration Panel).

Simple and Advanced Mode of Setting Permissions

As you know already, there are two ways of setting permissions: simple mode and advanced mode. The simple mode has been discussed in Chapter 3, and as you know, gives you predefined permissions options.

If you access the advanced mode, you'll see all the possible permissions types and permission levels we discussed above. To do that, log in as an administrator, go to the Administrator Panel, under Forum Admin section click Permissions, look up any forum, and click Advanced Mode. Here's what you'll see:

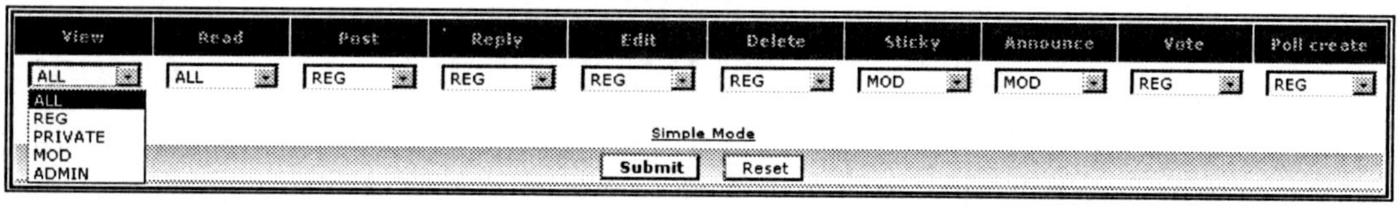

This screen shows all the permission types (displayed as table headers) and the permission levels (these are the values in the drop-down boxes). The advanced permissions shown in the above illustration would be displayed in simple mode as Registered, shown in the following illustration:

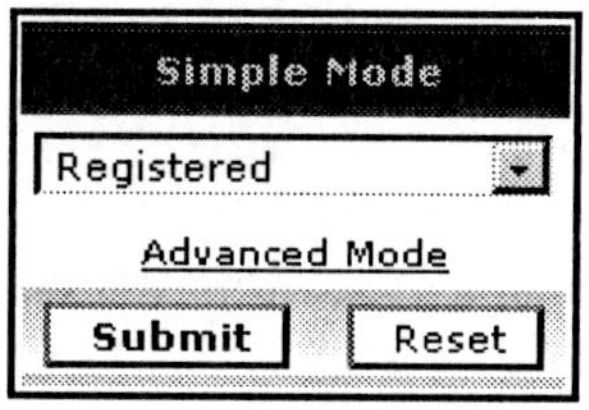

We have seen that the simple modes are a quicker and easier way of setting permissions. Let's now find out exactly *what* the simple modes— Public, Registered, Private, and Moderators—mean, and *which* advanced permissions settings they group together.

A rough idea about these modes is that they define who can post in the selected forum (for example, everybody can post in Public forums, but only logged-in members can post in Registered forums, and so on).

Except for the Public mode, all other simple modes have an option that includes [Hidden] in the name. This means that the users without sufficient privileges are unable to not just *post*, but even to *see* that such forums exist.

Here's a more detailed explanation of the simple mode permissions:

- Public: Everybody (permission level ALL) can see the public forum, read it, reply in topics, and start new topics. Registered and logged-in members (permission level REG) can even edit and delete their own postings, vote, and create polls.
- Registered: ALL can see and read the forum. REG can post, start topics, edit and delete their own postings, vote, and start polls.
- Registered [Hidden]: Same as above, except that ALL can no longer see nor read the forum—they have to register to be able to do so.
- Private: The forum is visible to ALL just to see it exists, but is PRIVATE, and only users who are explicitly allowed access to this forum can read postings, post, start topics, edit and delete their own postings, vote, and start polls. The next two sections of this chapter explain how to grant private access to users. Another specific thing about private forums is that the private members can also post sticky postings. Announcements, however, are still a "moderators-only" area.
- Private [Hidden]: Same as above, except that ALL can no longer see that this forum exists. It's a really protected and private forum.
- Moderators: same as Registered and Private, but only moderators can read, post, start topics, vote, and so on. A user has to be a moderator in this forum in order to use it. Being a moderator for any other forum doesn't mean the user can access this one.
- Moderators [Hidden]: Same as above except that ALL can't even see that such a forum exists.

The following table explains the same as the bullets point above, but in greater detail. You'll see that it is actually a pretty good way to understand permissions in general.

x	Public	Registered	Registered [Hidden]	Private	Private [Hidden]	Moderators	Moderators [Hidden]
View	ALL	ALL	REG	ALL	PRIVATE	ALL	MOD
Read	ALL	ALL	REG	PRIVATE	PRIVATE	MOD	MOD
Post	ALL	REG	REG	PRIVATE	PRIVATE	MOD	MOD
Reply	ALL	REG	REG	PRIVATE	PRIVATE	MOD	MOD
Edit	REG	REG	REG	PRIVATE	PRIVATE	MOD	MOD
Delete	REG	REG	REG	PRIVATE	PRIVATE	MOD	MOD
Sticky	MOD	MOD	MOD	PRIVATE	PRIVATE	MOD	MOD
Announcement	MOD	MOD	MOD	MOD	MOD	MOD	MOD
Vote	REG	REG	REG	PRIVATE	PRIVATE	MOD	MOD
Poll create	REG	REG	REG	PRIVATE	PRIVATE	MOD	MOD

When setting permissions it's always a good idea to choose one of the simple modes. They have been carefully selected by the phpBB team to match the most-used forum types. If you feel you need something different, you can always switch to advanced mode. In such a case, it's a good idea to first use a simple mode to set and save permissions, and then edit them again, and switch to advanced mode for fine-tuning.

Time For Action—Creating and Fine-Tuning a Private Forum

1. Log in as an administrator and go to the Administrator Panel.
2. Go to Management under Forum Admin.
3. Create a new category called Special forums, and then a new forum called The Dudes forum in this category.
4. Click on the Permissions link under Forum Admin.
5. Select The Dudes forum from the Select a Forum dropdown and click Look up Forum.
6. You are now in the Forum Permission Control area and Simple Mode.
7. Select Private [Hidden] and click Submit.
8. Repeat step 5.
9. Click Advanced Mode to switch to a more powerful editing form.

10. In the Sticky column, change the PRIVATE value to MOD.
11. Click Submit to save the settings.

What Just Happened

Steps 1-3: You've created a new category and a new forum.

Steps 4-7: You've set the forum permissions using the simple mode. You've set the permissions so that only special private members can see, read, post, etc., on the forum. The only thing private members cannot do is post announcements. (Of course if the users are not moderators, they can only edit or delete *their* postings, and not other private members' postings.)

Steps 8-11: You've set the permissions again, this time using advanced mode, and disallowed private members to post sticky posts.

Now if you visit the front page of your board, you'll see the new category and the new forum (because you're logged in as an administrator, and can see and do everything), but as soon as you log out, the forum and the whole category will no longer be visible.

In the next two sections we'll find out how to make a private forum visible for some members by making them private members.

Understanding User Permissions

You already know how to use the permissions area of the Administrator Panel to make a user a moderator; let's look at what *else* you can do. If you remember, user permissions are accessible through the Permissions link under the User Admin section:

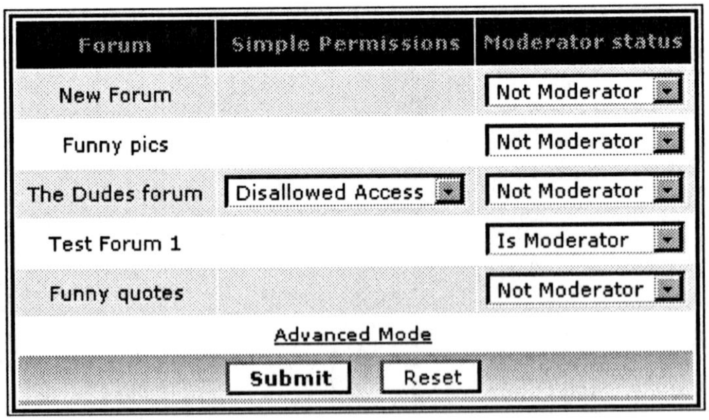

You see that along with setting the moderator status here, you can also specify user permissions for each forum (in other words, specify forum permissions that apply to a specific user only). Note that you can use this option only for *private forums*; for all other types of forums, the forum permissions are applied and the user permissions cannot override them.

> A *private forum* by definition has at least one permission type set to PRIVATE.

In the previous section, we created The Dudes forum as a private forum, so now in the user permission control area, we can allow or disallow a user from accessing the private forum. Allowing access means that this user becomes a private member and can do whatever private members are allowed to do—the user will have the permission types (for example read, post, etc.) that were set for the PRIVATE level in the forum's administration.

Time For Action—Making The Dude a Private User of The Dudes Forum

1. Log in as an administrator and go to the Administration Panel.
2. Select Permissions under User Admin.
3. Type The Dude and click Look up User. At this point, you see something similar to the previous illustration (at the beginning of this section).
4. On The Dudes forum row, change the first dropdown from Disallowed Access to Allowed Access.
5. Click Submit to save the permission settings.

What Just Happened?

You've allowed The Dude to access the private The Dudes forum. By doing this, you've made The Dude a private member of this forum and let him enjoy all the permission types that were set to PRIVATE on the forum's admin.

If you repeat steps 1-4 again and then click Advanced Mode, you'll see a screen like the following:

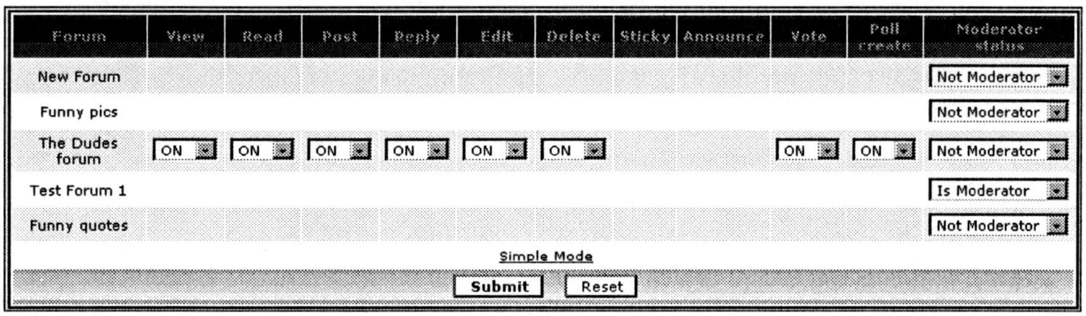

This Advanced Mode form allows you to be even more precise on per-user basis by turning off some permission types that are allowed by default for private members. You don't have options in the Sticky and Announce columns, because these permission types were set to MOD and not PRIVATE when setting up the forum permissions.

There is another way of restricting user privileges, and it has nothing to do with the permissions—the ability to allow or deny private messages and avatars on a per-user basis as well as to activate or deactivate a user. This can be done by editing a user's profile in the Administrator Panel (the Management link under User Admin section) and using the Special admin-only fields, shown in the following illustration:

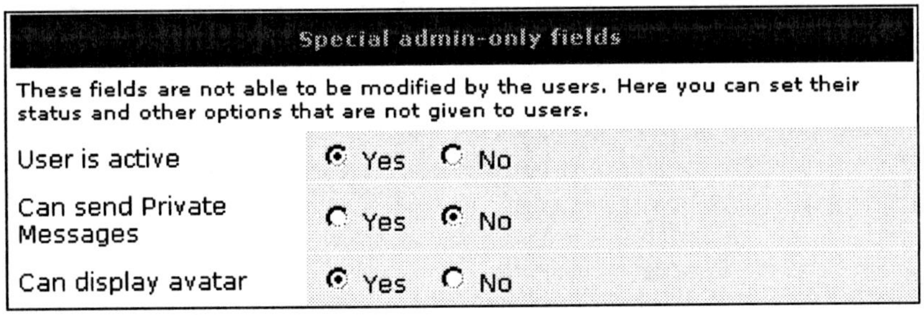

Usergroups and Group Permissions

Usergroups are a way for you to create groups of users, based on some criteria that you find appropriate. You don't have to use usergroups—in the default phpBB installation, no groups exist—but this can be a useful feature.

Users access the usergroups by using the Usergroups Usergroups top navigation menu icon. You as an administrator can also use this link; it gives you some administrative options as well. When accessed by a group moderator, this link also brings up the interface for moderating a group.

Every group has a moderator. This community member is responsible for managing the group, and is not to be confused with a forum moderator. Group moderators have no special privileges over the forum topics or postings; they have special privileges only for the group they are moderating. They can add and remove members from the group, can accept or deny membership applications and can change a group type.

What types of groups exist? A group can be open, closed, or hidden.

- An **open** group is visible for everybody and accepts new members. In order to become a member to the group, a user applies to join. The group moderator can accept or deny applications. He or she can also add members to the group without having those members to apply first.

- A **closed** group is a group that does not accept applications. The group moderator can still add new members.
- A **hidden** group is like the closed group, but is not displayed to the users. Only logged-in members of the group can see it. The group moderator adds new members.

Time For Action—Creating a New Group

1. Log in as an administrator and go to the Administration Panel.
2. Click on the Management link under the Group Admin menu section:

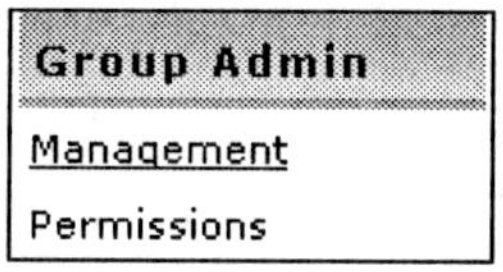

3. Click the Create New Group button.
4. Fill out the form as shown:

5. Click Submit.

What Just Happened?

You've successfully created a new usergroup called Test with the world-famous user The Dude as a moderator. This group is open and accepts membership applications.

If you now visit the front-end of the board, go to Usergroups, and view the information about the Test group, you'll see a screen like the following:

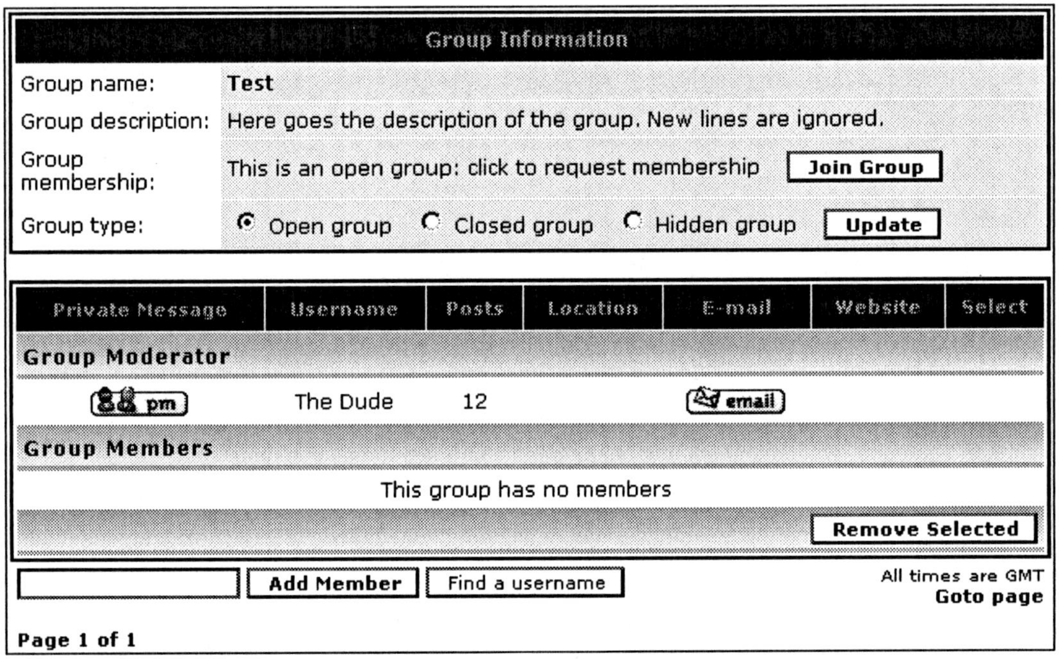

Because you're still logged in as an administrator, you see the group moderator options for changing the group type and adding/removing members. You don't see the membership applications interface, because no applications currently exist. Also, because you are not a member of this open group, you see the Join Group button.

Click the Join Group button to apply for a group membership. This sends the group moderator an e-mail advising that there is a new pending application. The moderator logs in, goes to the usergroup (the screen above), and accepts or denies this application. If the application is accepted, you become a member of the group and get an e-mail communicating that fact.

Time For Action—Editing a Group

1. You're still logged in as an administrator; go to the Administration Panel.
2. Under Group Admin, click Management.
3. The Test group is selected; click on Look up group.

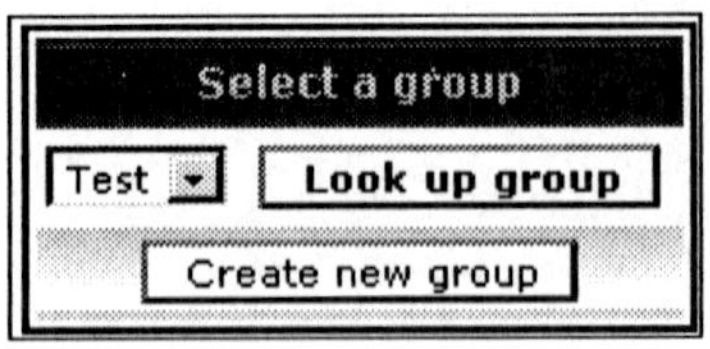

4. Change the name and the description of the group as shown. Also, change the Group status to Hidden group.

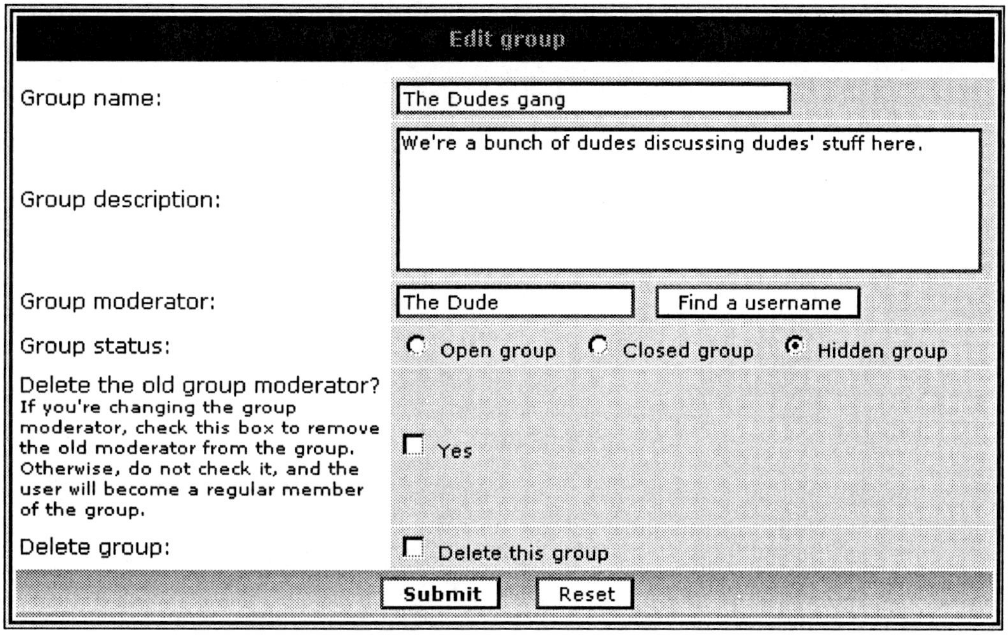

5. Click on Submit to save the changes.

What Just Happened?

You have successfully edited the group. It was a simple thing to do, just like creating the group. But this time you had two additional checkboxes on the Edit group form: you could delete the group, and when changing the group moderator, you could select whether the group's ex-mod stays in the group as a regular member or is removed from the group.

Group Permissions

The administrator has the option of setting group permissions. The group moderator doesn't have control over them. The group permissions work just like the user permissions. The only difference is that you can set a permission type once per group and it will apply to all members of the group. This can save you a lot of work. Although a member is part of a group and has group permissions, you can still override these permissions on a per-user basis. This means, for example, that you can specify that all members of a usergroup can post announcements, but then forbid this for a specific user of the group.

Group permissions are accessible through the Permissions link in the Group Admin section of the Administration Panel navigation menu:

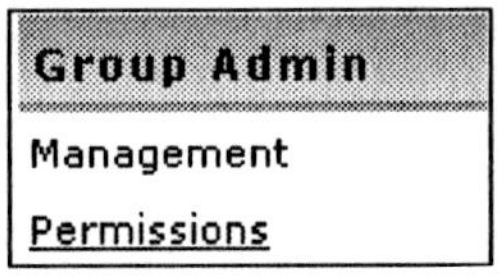

One common task you might want to do is to create a special hidden forum that can be used only by certain users (for example, a forum for moderators, where they can talk about board or user-related issues without those discussions being publicly available).

In order to do this, you:

- Create a Private [Hidden] forum.
- Create a private group.
- Give access to the group to use the private forum.

So far we have discussed the first two points. We've created a special private hidden forum called The Dudes forum and you've a hidden group called The Dudes gang. Now the last point: giving The Dudes gang access to The Dudes forum.

Time For Action—Setting Group Permissions

1. Log in as an administrator, and go to the Administration Panel.
2. Select Permissions under the Group Admin section of the navigation menu.
3. In the next screen, select The Dudes gang and click on Look up Group.
4. In the Group Permissions Control form, switch to Advanced Mode.

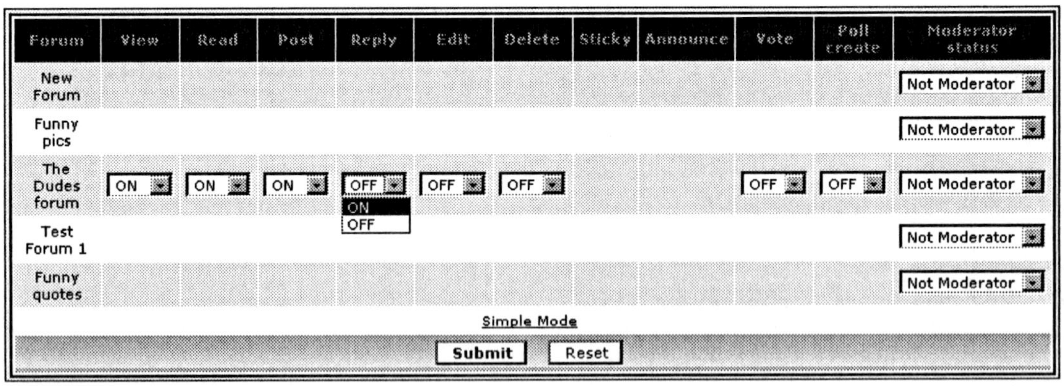

5. Change all dropdowns on The Dudes forum row from OFF to ON.
6. Click Submit to save the permission settings.

What Just Happened?

You've granted privileges for the whole The Dudes gang usergroup to be able to read, post, vote, etc., in The Dudes forum. Here are a few more points for you to think about and experiment.

- You can use the Advanced Mode for granting permissions by turning ON/OFF selectively; it's not necessary to turn all ON or all OFF.
- Simple Mode cannot be used for setting group permissions, not in the phpBB version this book is based on.
- Forum moderators and group moderators are completely independent of each other. The Dude is a group moderator of The Dudes gang, but is not a forum moderator in The Dudes forum.
- You can make everybody in a group a moderator by setting the group's Is Moderator status.
- Group permissions are a fast way to set permissions, but you can still use the user permissions to be more specific. User permissions override group permissions.
- You can have several usergroups with different access to a forum. For example, you can set up an open group called "Junior Dudes" that can only *read* The Dudes forum, while the good old The Dudes gang usergroup can still *post*.

Second Look into Database Backups and Restore

You already know how to use phpBB's backup and restore utilities. It was mentioned that they might not work as expected, if you have a very big database and your hosting provider has set some rules on server resources usage. So now let's take a look at using other means of achieving the same result. MySQL is the RDBMS used in this section; it's the most popular to run phpBB on.

Using phpMyAdmin

phpMyAdmin can be used for backing up and restoring you forum database. It has an export utility that can help you create an SQL dump of a table or a database or even *all* the databases on a server. An SQL dump is a text file that contains all the necessary SQL commands needed to create a copy of a table or a database. phpBB's database backup and restore utility uses the same SQL dumps.

If you're feeling nosy you can open an SQL dump with a text editor, and you'll see a whole bunch of SQL commands that start like this:

```
-- phpMyAdmin SQL Dump
-- version 2.6.0-rc2
```

```
-- http://www.phpmyadmin.net
--
-- Host: localhost
-- Generation Time: Dec 14, 2004 at 10:45 PM
-- Server version: 3.23.47
-- PHP Version: 4.3.0
--
-- Database: 'forums'
--

-- --------------------------------------------------------

--
-- Table structure for table 'phpbb_auth_access'
--

CREATE TABLE 'phpbb_auth_access' (
  'group_id' mediumint(8) NOT NULL default '0',
  'forum_id' smallint(5) unsigned NOT NULL default '0',
  'auth_view' tinyint(1) NOT NULL default '0',
  'auth_read' tinyint(1) NOT NULL default '0',
  'auth_post' tinyint(1) NOT NULL default '0',
  'auth_reply' tinyint(1) NOT NULL default '0',
  'auth_edit' tinyint(1) NOT NULL default '0',
  'auth_delete' tinyint(1) NOT NULL default '0',
  'auth_sticky' tinyint(1) NOT NULL default '0',
  'auth_announce' tinyint(1) NOT NULL default '0',
  'auth_vote' tinyint(1) NOT NULL default '0',
  'auth_pollcreate' tinyint(1) NOT NULL default '0',
  'auth_attachments' tinyint(1) NOT NULL default '0',
  'auth_mod' tinyint(1) NOT NULL default '0',
  KEY 'group_id' (`group_id`),
  KEY 'forum_id' (`forum_id`)
) TYPE=MyISAM;

--
-- Dumping data for table `phpbb_auth_access`
--
```

If this looks like an alien language to you, don't worry; you don't need to know any of that. It was just an example to give an idea of what SQL dumps look like. The important thing is to know how to create them and use them.

The good thing about phpMyAdmin is that it allows you to create SQL dumps of individual tables, not of the whole database in a single file. This is good—if you need to restore the database later on and your hosting provider has restrictions on the size of the files that you upload, then you may be able to work around the upload limit by splitting a possibly large database into several smaller SQL dumps.

Let's look at an example that will help you understand the procedure of database backups and restoring using phpMyAdmin. For the sake of this and the other examples further in this chapter, let's assume that the database that contains your board is named `forums`, your database username is `dbuser`, and your password to access the database is `dbpass`.

Time For Action—Creating an SQL Database Dump

You are currently on the front page for your "forums" database. It looks like the following illustration:

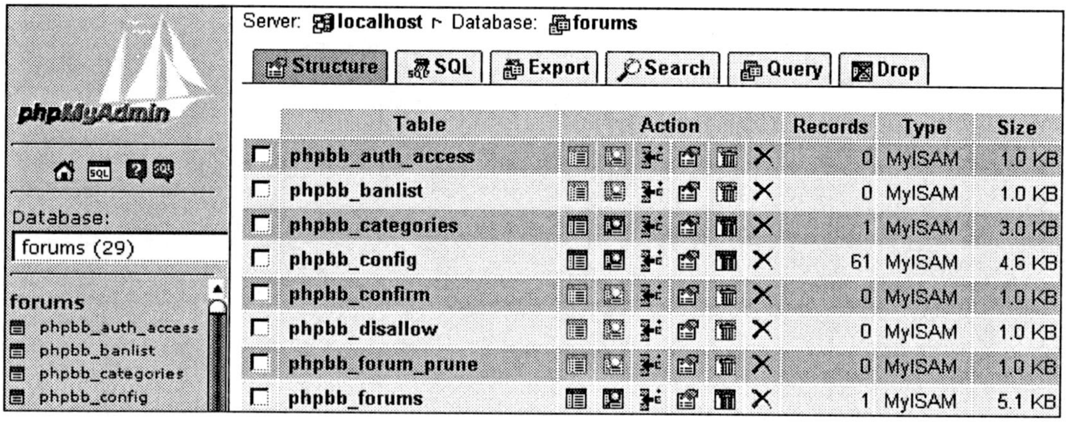

1. Click the  tab to be taken to a page that looks like the following:

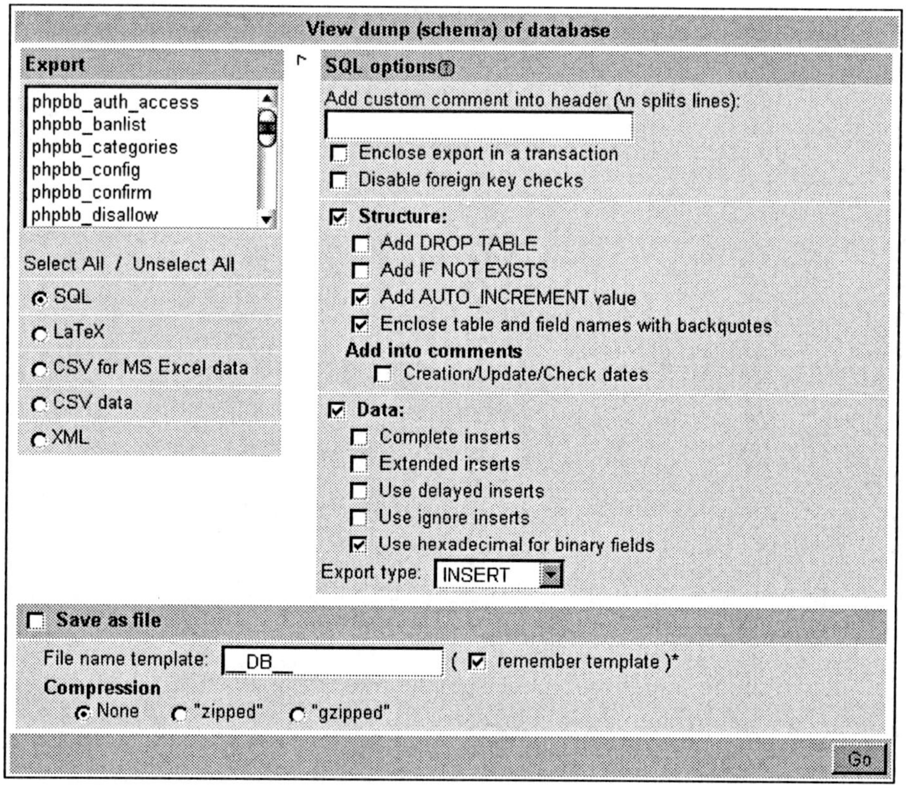

2. You can see all the tables in this database listed under Export in the top left corner. Here you can individually select which tables to dump. Click Select All to dump all tables.
3. Leave all other fields at their default values. Double-check to see that both Structure and Data checkboxes are selected.
4. Select the Save as file checkbox.
5. Click Go.
6. You'll be prompted with a file dialog window asking under what name and where to save the dump file. Use mydump.sql as the filename and save it where you think most appropriate (for example, a directory designed to contain all your backup dumps).

What Just Happened?

You've successfully created an SQL dump file of all the tables and data found in your board database. In step 2 you saw an example of how you can selectively pick which tables to include in the dump and this way create several smaller dumps that together hold all the database tables and data.

If you now click on the SQL tab, you'll be taken to a page that allows you to execute SQL queries.

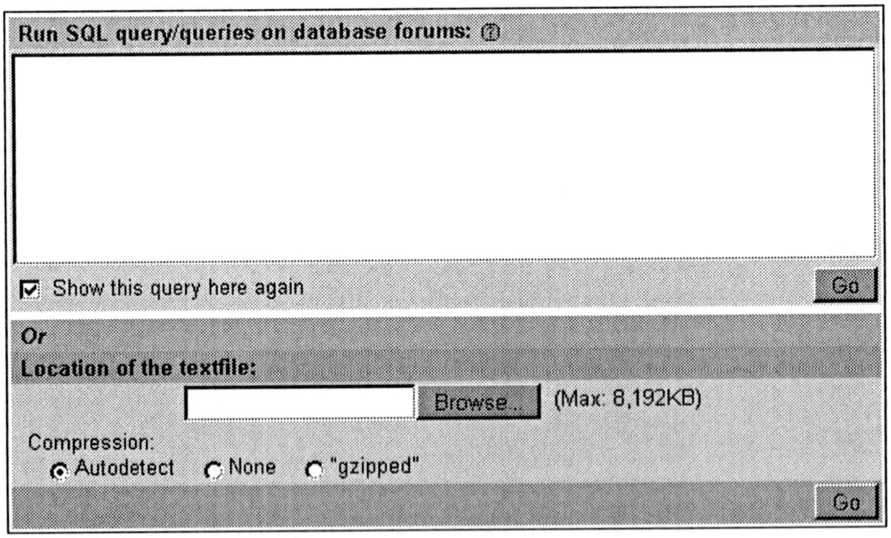

In the second half of the screenshot, under Location of the textfile title, you can upload a SQL dump to be executed into your database. This is the "restore" part of the operation.

It's usually done on a completely different server and a blank database (for example, when you switch hosting providers and move your board).

In the case shown in the illustration, you see that there is a limit of 8192KB (or 8MB); you cannot upload dumps bigger that this. If your SQL dump is larger, you have to split it into smaller chunks. Another good option would be to explain the situation to your provider (they might suggest that you FTP the file and they can take it from there and import it using tools like the command-line MySQL utilities.

Using MySQL Command-Line Tools

If you have access to MySQL from the command line, huge databases won't be a problem; you should be able to do your backups and to restore if needed. Chapter 2 already discussed connecting to MySQL from the command line, using the `mysql` utility. Here we discuss another utility: `mysqldump`.

Creating Backups with mysqldump

As the name suggests this is a utility for creating SQL dumps from a MySQL database. It has a lot of options which you can always investigate by calling the utility with the `--help` option, like this:

```
mysqldump --help
```

You can also read about this utility at `http://dev.mysql.com/mysqldump`, the MySQL online manual.

Here's an example of how to use the utility for creating a dump of your `forums` database:

```
mysqldump -u dbuser -pdbpass forums > mydump.sql
```

This line in plain English means "Create an SQL dump of the database called forums and write this dump to a file called mydump.sql, located in the current directory. To prove that I'm allowed to access this database, I give you my username which is dbuser, and my password, which is dbpass." Make note that the option `-p` and the password are glued together; there is no space like that between the `-u` option and the username.

If you have access on the server to create a scheduled task (a **cronjob**), you can have this command line executed daily for a fresh database copy. This command may vary depending on your server, mainly in the part after the right angle bracket, where the dump filename and its location are specified.

You can even go one step further and save hard-drive space by creating a compressed SQL dump and deleting the original dump, which can be large. On Linux systems you can use the `tar` archiver; the whole command that you can run as a cronjob would be something like:

```
mysqldump -u dbuser -pdbpass forums > mydump.sql ; tar cz mydump.sql -f
mydump.tgz ; rm -f mydump.sql
```

Now *that* is some real sysadmin-ing! Again if you want to translate this into plain English, it would mean "Create a SQL dump of my forums database and write it into mydump.sql. Compress mydump.sql and create mydump.tgz. Now delete the unneeded mydump.sql."

Using the mysql Utility to Restore a Database

To restore a database means to create a new database out of an existing SQL dump. Now that we have a `mydump.sql` that contains everything from the `forums` database, let's create a new database called `forums-copy` and have the contents copied there. You can do this in phpMyAdmin, but we'll see how to do it from the command line.

Time For Action—Creating a Database Copy from a SQL Dump

1. In the command line, type
   `mysql -u dbuser -pdbpass`
   and hit *Enter*.
2. Type `CREATE DATABASE 'forums-copy';`
   Hit *Enter*.
3. Type `\u forums-copy`.
   Hit *Enter*.
4. Type `\. mydump.sql`
   Hit *Enter*. If everything is fine, you'll see a lot of messages like this one:
   `Query OK, 1 row affected (0.00 sec)`

What Just Happened?

1. You connected to the database server.
2. You created a new database.
3. You selected the new database (`forums-copy`) to use it for the next operations.
4. You executed the `mydump.sql` file. Here you may need to adjust the path to the file, depending on where it's located.

Other Tools

Sometimes you may not use the command line MySQL tools or phpMyAdmin. Or the hosting provider's restrictions may make phpMyAdmin unusable for your huge dump. Don't despair, there's still hope! You can use some specially designed tools to deal with large databases. One such good tool is called BigDump, and can be downloaded free of charge from `http://www.ozerov.de/bigdump.php`.

It works around the server restrictions by taking small parts of your dump and executing them chunk by chunk until all the SQL commands are executed.

The Board's Human Side: Flamewars and Banning

Let's take a break from the sysadmin stuff and end this chapter with a look at the human side of running an online community. There are situations that you're most likely to encounter, which happen to almost every board admin, so it's good to be prepared or at least be aware that you're not alone.

Whatever your board is about, it's likely that it starts as a small board with a handful of nice fellows posting in it. Maybe the board will be an addition to your existing site; its forums might discuss the content of your site, where you'll answer questions and get suggestions.

If you happen to have a site with interesting content, your community is likely to grow gradually. As more and more people join in, more and more different opinions will be shared. An occasional flamewar can burst out, where some community members start exchanging hostilities. Do not panic! It's not you or your board or your site that is to blame for the flamewars. They just happen. They have been happening since the dawn of online communication, in Usenet groups, mailing lists, and so on. Flamewars are a part of the online communities; it's a human thing.

There can also be some community members that seem to like starting off new flamewars and look like they come to the board with the sole purpose of making the life of your community miserable. It happens. The anonymity provided by the Internet can make some folks behave quite differently from what they really are. You'll have to learn to live with this fact. But that doesn't mean that you'll have to tolerate such behavior. Some respected and valued community members may start limiting their participation and even leave the community for good, because of the bad behavior of those folks. This is something you don't want to happen.

It's tough in such situations and there's no recipe. You have to use your best judgment and you have to act like a leader and an example for your community. At some point you'll probably end up writing sticky postings like "Read me before you post", sort of terms of use. This is a good and a necessary step because it sets the ground rules. Without rules there's no right nor wrong, everybody can have a different understanding of what is acceptable behavior and what is not. You also need to be careful when writing these rules not to make them too restrictive. These rules need to be respected, that's why they are rules. So don't set impossible goals and wishlist items as rules; be a realist.

At some point the board may grow so much that you won't be able to follow what is happening all the time. You need someone to keep an eye on it. That's where moderators come into the picture. They are your best helpers with the board. They will volunteer their time to make the forums a better place for peaceful discussions. So choose them carefully. First, you have to trust your moderators. But chances are you've never even met those people, how can you trust them? Again, follow your gut feeling and use your best judgment.

Banning users is never an easy task. Try to avoid this as much as possible, because a banned user can find a way to register again and again using fake IP addresses and will keep abusing your community. And a banned user will be feeling and acting like a victim. So again, try to avoid banning as much as you can. Try to resolve any issues in a peaceful manner, try to listen to that user's problems and use banning as a last resort. But when you make the decision to ban someone, do it and be firm.

Here are some more tips that can help you with the board administration.

- Create a Private [Hidden] forum for your moderators. Let them talk about forum issues in privacy and make collective decisions.
- Create a Private [Hidden] forum that will serve as a recycle bin. Instead of deleting a thread, move it there. When only a few postings are to be deleted, but otherwise the topic is OK, split the postings in question into a new topic of their own and move this topic to the bin. The bin helps you have a history of what happened in case you need it. Grant your moderators access to the bin so that they can manage the topics moved there.
- When some board admins ban users, they do this temporarily and unban the troublemakers after let's say a week. Sometimes this helps.
- Users will complain about different things—you, the board, other users, and whatnot. Listen to what they have to say. But remember: there are a lot more people that are happy with the board, life, and everything. It's a normal behavior—when you're OK, you don't write a posting to say you're OK, but when you're angry about something, you write about it at once.
- Read the Netiquette book by Virginia Shea. It's available online at `http://www.albion.com/netiquette/book/`. It was written quite some time ago and it speaks about flamewars in Usenet groups and not in bulletin boards. So it's even more reassuring to see that you're not alone and your board is not the first one to experience such extremities. You'll recognize quite a few of your community members and situations described there and this is guaranteed to give you a good laugh. Such topics as the types of flames ("The Spelling Flame", "The Get-a-Life Flame") are really amusing.
- Again, there are no recipes, all the boards are different and unique, so use your best judgment and … be a leader. Good luck!

6
Creating Your Own Template

Making your own template can be not just very interesting, but also time consuming. There are many small details just waiting to be overlooked, and that is why I advise you not to rush through it too fast. Take your time, and the reward will come at the end.

As with many other design-related projects, one of the most challenging things about creating an appealing phpBB template is to get the idea for the layout. You might already have a homepage and would like to apply that layout, but many times I have seen people building the rest of their site around the layout of their phpBB template.

That is why, in this chapter, we will start from scratch by telling you how to go about getting the basic layout idea into building the entire template.

Let me start by saying that inspiration, and the whole creative process itself, is not some precious gift that very few people are endowed with. It is something everybody can learn in time, with practice and some patience. Find some layout ideas and tweak them until you are satisfied with the result; the more time you spend doing this, the more you will learn about yourself: what you like and what you don't. Soon you will have developed your own style that you can turn almost anything into.

There is a limitless amount of places to begin looking for your future phpBB template layouts; magazines, newspapers, advertisings, homepages, constructions, art, or even basic wallpapers are just *some* of the inspiration sources I have found useful. Spending half an hour in a coffee shop with a pen drawing lines on a napkin can reveal the most appealing layout of all. It all depends on how "far" you're willing to go with this, even though I doubt anyone can build a good template layout based on things like… a teapot!

For the kind of layout needed in a phpBB template, you should try to look for patterns you can use. For example, we need something that can show topics and posts, maybe with room for an image and a menu.

The template I'm going to build in this chapter is based on an idea I got from a newspaper. It wasn't that complicated really: just a photo, a headline, and some text, which I drew a sketch of on a piece of paper so I wouldn't forget. I liked the simplicity, the lines, and the rather big image. And even though it might not look like a phpBB template at first glance, I will try anyway, while showing you how to work around any obstacles that are bound to bump up on the way:

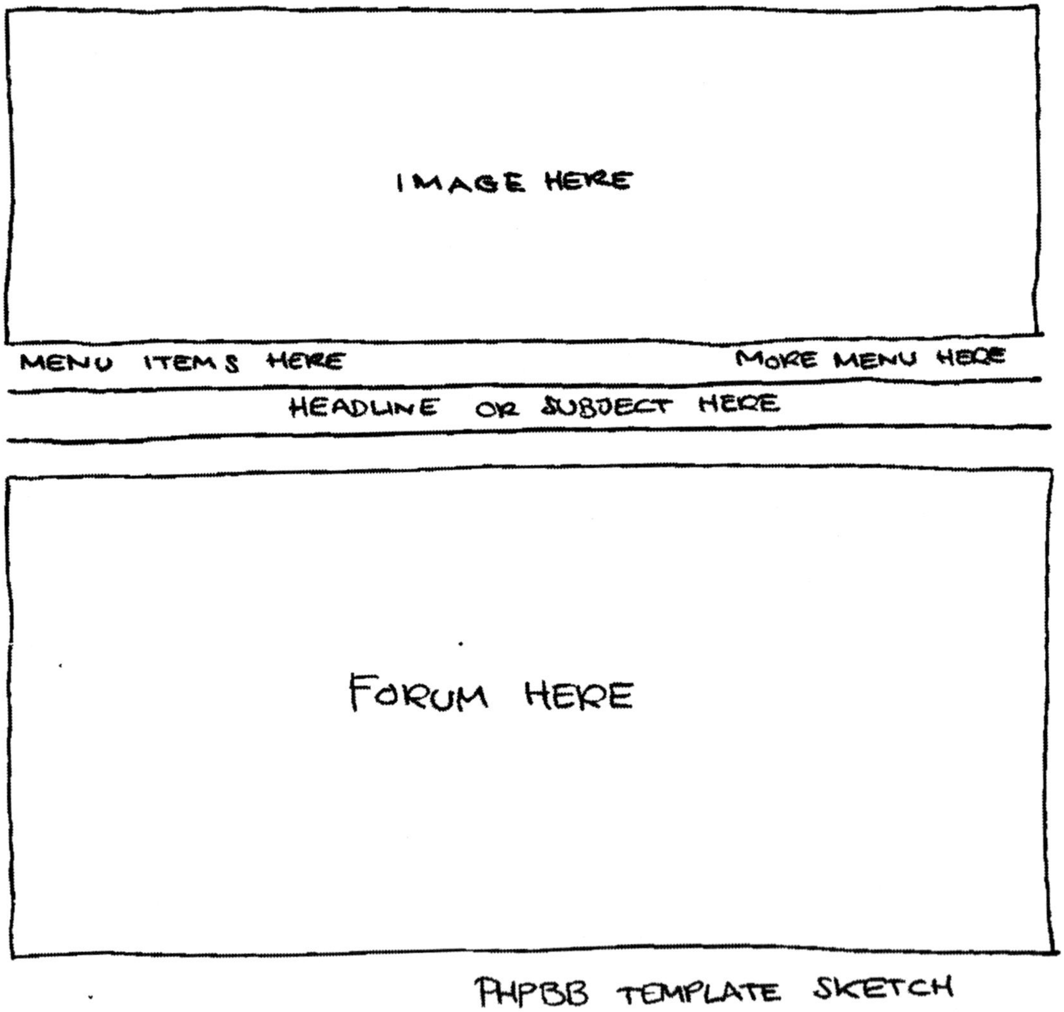

Sketching the Layout

The first thing I am going to do is to put together a rough, basic layout of the template in Photoshop. It doesn't have to be precise or exact, but enough to get an estimated look of the template. There are some important things that need to be decided upon first, starting with the width of the layout. Making it 100% wide is a very popular choice for HTML sites and templates, but it may not be such a good idea for this layout because of the image at the top. I need a fixed size. Also, in order to keep everything from getting too large, I have decided to shrink the entire layout down to a width of just 780 pixels. That will leave some "air" on the sides of the forum and also look more like a paper-based layout. With this width there are 20 pixels allocated to the scrollbar, for those who have screen resolution 800x600 pixels.

For the big image at the top, I had an old PSD image that I made for a Photoshop contest long time ago. I have always wanted to use this image for one of my projects and this seemed to be a good opportunity. The format of the image is 717x231 pixels, which fits nicely, neither too big nor too small.

Under the image will come the menu. The forum tables under the black lines won't look good with the same color as the background, so instead I give them a light gray shade.

It is hard to get a good color feeling going, since the colors of my PSD image don't match the rest of the template layout. After some trials with new background and forum colors that could match the image, I end up changing the image into an empty gray box, so as to match the light gray color of the forum. However, I still feel this is not the best solution; it looks much too empty.

Playing around with some Photoshop brushes eventually leads me to a brush with some paint spills, and with red color I manage to get something that looks like nosebleed. A bit morbid maybe, but it looks quite good, simple, and neat. I add the title 'NoseBleed' with a font I find well-fitted for the image, making it more dynamic.

There is no need to get into too many details at this early stage; it is quite easy to change images and colors later on if you get better ideas. After all, this is just a sketch!

I am still not sure if I want a colored background or maybe even a background image for the white "air" on each side of the forum, so I leave the option open. For now though, we keep it as simple as possible; all white.

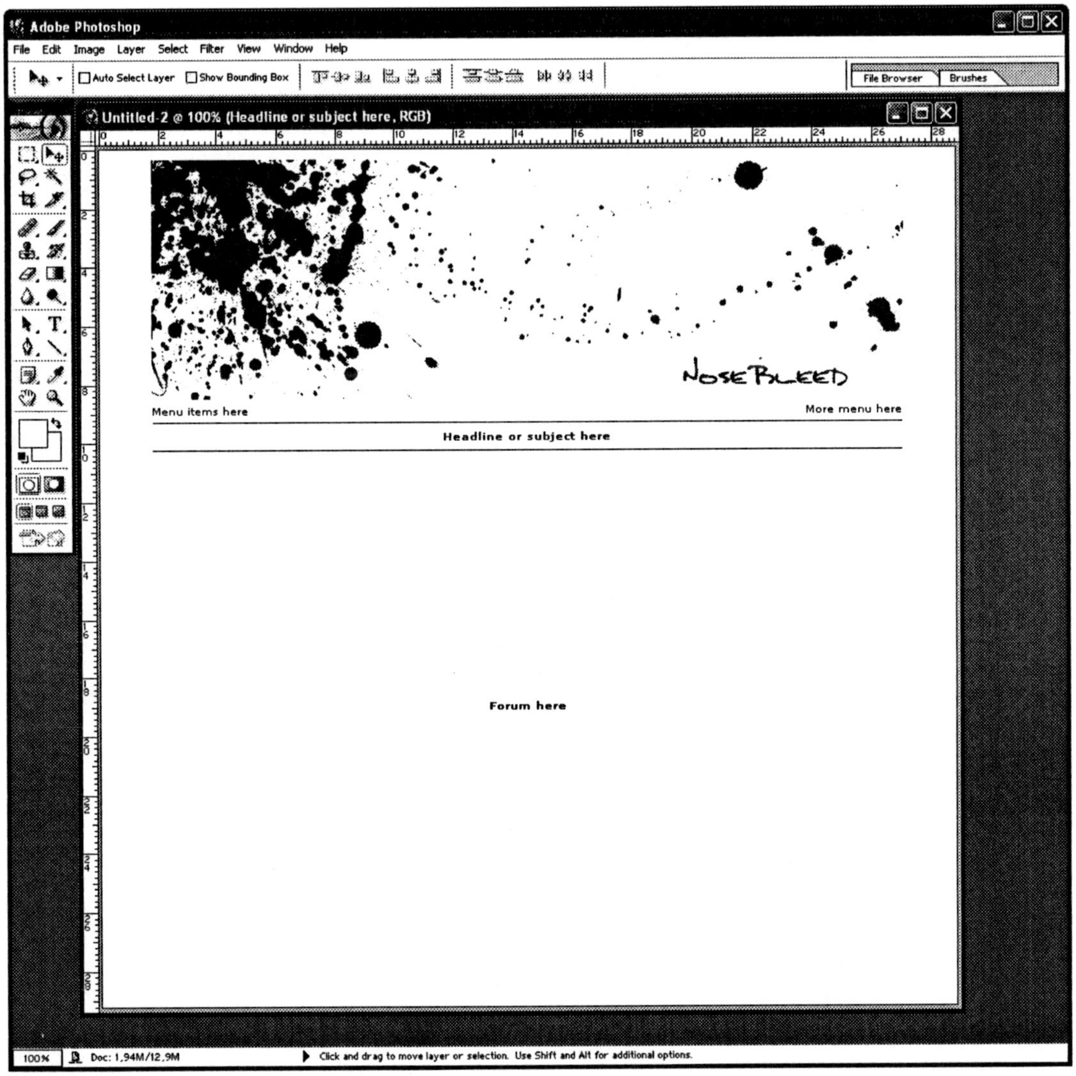

With the sketch finished, I cut out the image and save it as `top_image.jpg`, so that we can begin creating the template.

TPL Stands for Template

Each page in the browser is made up of three `.tpl` files, consisting of HTML code, cascading style sheet code (CSS), and phpBB variables. The first file is always the `overall_header.tpl`, and the last one is always the `overall_footer.tpl`. The middle of these three `.tpl` files displays the actual content of what we can see on that specific page. If, for example, we are viewing the index page of the forum, what we see is the code of `overall_header.tpl`, `index_body.tpl`, and `overall_footer.tpl` put together. Or if we go to the login page, the `.tpl` files shown are `overall_header.tpl`, `login_body.tpl`, and `overall_footer.tpl`, and so on. This is quite handy since we only need to edit one `.tpl` file, the `overall_header.tpl`, in order to make changes in the top part of all the pages shown by the browser.

Think of it as if you were to write a letter on a piece of business paper. The paper would already have the company name, logo, and address at the top (`overall_header.tpl`), and maybe also an address line at the bottom (`overall_footer.tpl`). You would write your individual message in the middle (the middle `.tpl` file). No matter how many letters you wrote, and no matter how different the content of the letters was, you would always have the same header and footer. It's the `.tpl` in the middle that brings the phpBB forum to life.

However, before we start editing any files, we make a copy of the `subSilver` folder in the phpBB templates directory, and name it `NoseBleed`. With a copy we can always go back and get hold of the original `.tpl` file, should something go wrong.

Making Your Template Folder

In order to make phpBB recognize the new `NoseBleed` folder as a unique template, we need to edit some of the files. In the folder, there is a file named `subSilver.cfg`, which we rename to `NoseBleed.cfg`. We also rename `subSilver.css` to `NoseBleed.css`, even though there is no need for this file right now. Lastly we need to replace every instance of `subSilver` in the `theme_info.cfg` file with `NoseBleed`. If you are using WordPad for this, you can press *CTRL+H* to bring up the Replace All window, making this a fast edit.

We can now upload and install the new template from the Administration Panel.

Editors for .tpl Documents

The code being used in the `.tpl` files is basically, as mentioned earlier, HTML code. If you already have some knowledge of basic HTML and CSS, you have nothing to fear, and if you don't, don't worry. We will go through the process with detailed explanations on the way.

For this chapter we are using Notepad to edit `.tpl` files. We could also use a WYSIWYG editor for editing, like Dreamweaver. It can have some advantages like being able to see an approximated view of the layout while coding. However, I don't recommend using the code that these editors can insert automatically, since there is a chance that phpBB can conflict with this kind of code. We could also use Word, WordPad, or any other text editor, as long as we remember to save the document as plain ASCII code, since phpBB can not read rich-text formatted `.tpl` files.

Start by opening the overall_header.tpl from the NoseBleed folder; this is the file that will contain the top layout appearing on every page. Remember not to be nervous if this is your first time with HTML; it's really not as difficult as it might seem at a first glance. At the top of the code you'll find the part telling your browser that this is an HTML document. We then have the title of the page, the CSS code, and then at the bottom, we have the HTML code that will display our layout. When phpBB loads a .tpl file, it fills in the phpBB variables from the database. These variables all have capital letters and always look like this: {PHPBB_VARIABLE}.

Between the <style type="text/css"> and </style> code tags, you will find all the CSS code, e.g.:

```
/* Name of poster in viewmsg.php and viewtopic.php and other places
*/
.name { font-size : {T_FONTSIZE2}px; color : {T_BODY_TEXT};}
```

If you put code between the /* and */ tags in CSS, it will be ignored by the browser. You can use this if you want to leave comments for yourself or others. The particular CSS style above is called .name. The dot before name is not a type error, but something you should be aware of when you're going to add your own style. A CSS style named .table would only affect those areas of your HTML document where it is applied, e.g.:

```
<span class="table">Some text here</span>
```

However, a CSS style named table with no dot would have an effect on every table of your HTML document.

But let us get started building our template!

Ready, Set, Go!

With the sketch at hand, the best way to create a template is to simply follow the sketch, starting from the top and working our way down to the bottom. As mentioned earlier, the overall_header.tpl always contains the top part of each page you'll see in the browser, so this is the one we will work on first. In subSilver, this file already shows an image and the menu, a good approach that we will keep the same for our own template.

Open the overall_header.tpl file and scroll down to where the <body> begins (the section up to this tag is the CSS, which we will get to later).

The first thing we need to do is to make sure that the template stretches out entirely in the browser. By default, the browser adds a margin to the top and to the left of the page, but we can get rid of this by setting the topmargin and leftmargin to zero. We can do this by modifying the <body> tag as follows:

```
<body bgcolor="{T_BODY_BGCOLOR}" text="{T_BODY_TEXT}"
      link="{T_BODY_LINK}" vlink="{T_BODY_VLINK}"
      leftmargin="0" topmargin="0">
```

The next thing worth noticing in the template is the <a name="top"></a> link tag. If we add the following link:

```
<a href="top">Go to top!</a>
```

... anywhere else in the template, the browser will take you (on clicking the link) to <a name="top"></a>, in this case to the top of our page, where it is located.

Then we have the table structure of the template. The first table starts with:

```
<table width="100%" cellspacing="0" cellpadding="10" border="0"
align="center">
<tr>
<td class="bodyline">
```

... but it apparently has no end. This is not an error; it is because this table surrounds the entire forum, including the content that will be loaded after the overall_header.tpl.

You can find the end of this table:

```
</td>
</tr>
</table>
```

... in the overall_footer.tpl file.

Next we change the width of the table surrounding the entire forum. This width is set to 100% in the subSilver template, but we only want it to be 780 pixels for our template. We also add a height of 100% to stretch the template from top to bottom in our browser:

```
<table width="780" height="100%" cellspacing="0"
      cellpadding="10" border="0" align="center">
<tr>
<td class="bodyline" valign="top">
```

The table will now cause all content inside it to appear ten pixels from the table borders, because of the size of the cellpadding. We changed the width to 780 pixels instead of 100%, and add the height 100%, in case we later decide on adding a background image or color on each side of the forum. Since the content, by default, is horizontally aligned in the middle of the table—which is now 100% in height—we need to align it so that it appears at the top. We can do this by adding a valign tag in the first <td> of the table.

After doing these modifications, the code of our table should look like this:

```
<table width="780" height="100%" cellspacing="0"
      cellpadding="10" border="0" align="center">
<tr>
<td class="bodyline" valign="top">
```

Adding the Banner Image

We now want to add top_image.jpg—the banner image that we made earlier—which we first upload to the NoseBleed/images/ template folder. Without beginning to change and edit the rest of the already existing table structure—which could easily turn out to be an editing task from hell—we simply add a new independent table instead, directly underneath the line above, a table that will contain nothing but our banner image:

```
<table width="717" height="231" border="0" align="center"
       cellpadding="0" cellspacing="0">
<tr>
<td>
  <div align="center">
  <a href="{U_INDEX}">
  <img src="templates/NoseBleed/images/top_image.jpg" border="0"
        alt="{L_INDEX}" vspace="1" />
  </a>
  </div>
</td>
</tr>
</table>
```

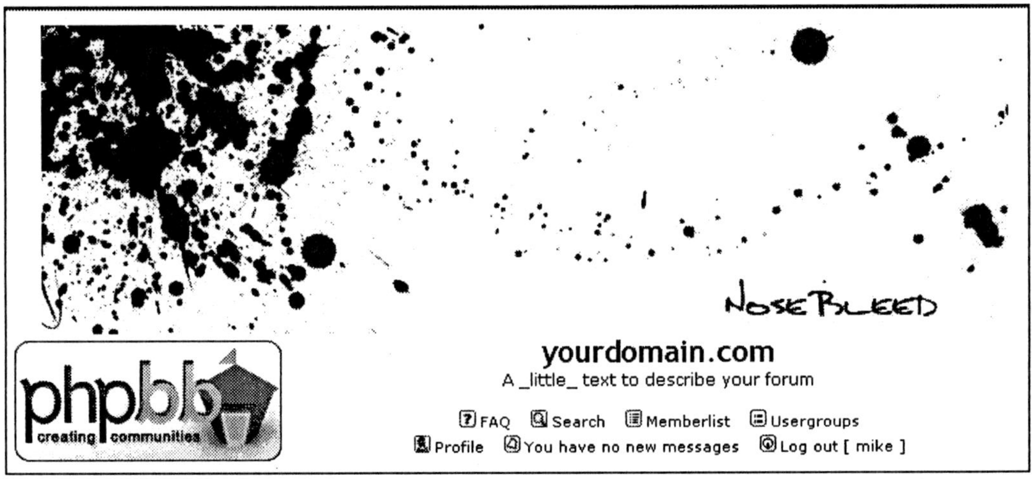

As you can see, I have added the <a href="{U_INDEX}"></a> link tag around the image, so that it works as a link back to the index page of the forum. This is similar to how subSilver also handles its own banner image. Basically, I just copied that part, using the same phpBB variable as was already given.

There are many variables like this one that we can use throughout the template, a list of all of which can be found at http://www.phpbb.com/styles/listvars.php.

Note that not all variables work in all the .tpl files. Most do, but some are meant for specific parts of the forum, like the registration page, the search page, etc.

Adding a Menu

The next thing we do is add the menu right under the top_image. Again we add a new table, below our banner image, this time with some temporary text that we will correct later. The text is added now to make it clearer when we start to add the real menu items.

```
<table width="715" height="20" border="0" align="center"
cellpadding="0" cellspacing="0">
<tr>
<td align="left">
   FAQ
   Search
   Memberlist
   Usergroups
   Profile
   You have no new messages
 </td>
 <td align="right">
   Log in
   Register
 </td>
 </tr>
</table>
```

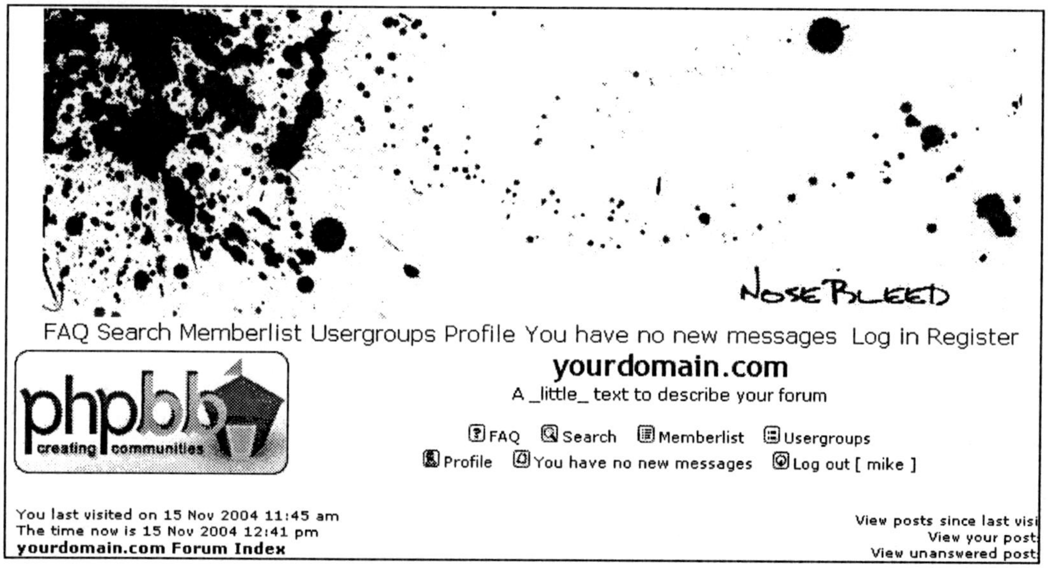

The sharp eye might have noticed that I made this table only 715 pixels wide instead of the 717 pixels that we'd decided on. The reason is just that it looks better this way, nothing more. I tried first with 717 pixels, but it then looked like the text was wider than the image. 715 pixels made it look more consistent.

In order to make the menu work, we need to turn each part of the menu into a link. For example, to make `FAQ` a link, `<a href="url">` and `</a>` tags are added around it, where `url` should be replaced with the address of the file that we are linking `FAQ` to. The same thing has to be done for the rest of the menu:

```
<table width="715" height="20" border="0" align="center"
       cellpadding="0" cellspacing="0">
<tr>
```

```
<td align="left">
  <a href="url">FAQ</a>
  <a href="url">Search</a>
  <a href="url">Memberlist</a>
  <a href="url">Usergroups</a>
  <a href="url">Profile</a>
  <a href="url">You have no new messages</a>
</td>
<td align="right">
  <a href="url">Log in</a>
  <a href="url">Register</a>
</td>
</tr>
</table>
```

To replace the `url` with the actual address of where we want the link to take us, we can simply look at the way the `subSilver` template already used it. By looking at the code, each `url` can be replaced with the correct phpBB variable. We can also replace the text of the menu with variables; this way a user using the forum in another language won't be forced to have English menu items. After replacing the text, our table is now:

```
<table width="715" height="20" border="0" align="center"
cellpadding="0" cellspacing="0">
<tr>
<td align="left">
  <a href="{U_FAQ}">{L_FAQ}</a>
  <a href="{U_SEARCH}">{L_SEARCH}</a>
  <a href="{U_MEMBERLIST}">{L_MEMBERLIST}</a>
  <a href="{U_GROUP_CP}">{L_USERGROUPS}</a>
  <a href="{U_PROFILE}">{L_PROFILE}</a>
  <a href="{U_PRIVATEMSGS}">{PRIVATE_MESSAGE_INFO}</a>
</td>
<td align="right">
  <a href="{U_LOGIN_LOGOUT}">{L_LOGIN_LOGOUT}</a>
  <a href="{U_REGISTER}">{L_REGISTER}</a></td>
</tr>
</table>
```

One thing to notice here is that users already logged in shouldn't be able to click **Register**. To prevent this, we can use the `<!-- BEGIN switch_user_logged_out -->` and `<!-- END switch_user_logged_out -->` tags. Everything between these tags will be shown only if the user is logged out, which is what we want for the **Register** menu. If we want something to be shown only when the user is logged in, we can use the tags `<!-- BEGIN switch_user_logged_in -->` and `<!-- END switch_user_logged_in -->` instead.

Personally, I see no reason why users not logged in should see the **Profile** and **Private Messages** menu, so I'm going to use these tags also to prevent guests from trying to access the profile and private messages menu.

> An important note about these tags is that they only work if they are on their own lines in the code; phpBB simply won't recognize them if they aren't.

The table should now look like this:

```
<table width="715" height="20" border="0" align="center"
cellpadding="0" cellspacing="0">
<tr>
<td align="left">
  <a href="{U_FAQ}">{L_FAQ}</a>
  <a href="{U_SEARCH}">{L_SEARCH}</a>
  <a href="{U_MEMBERLIST}">{L_MEMBERLIST}</a>
  <a href="{U_GROUP_CP}">{L_USERGROUPS}</a>
<!-- BEGIN switch_user_logged_in -->
  <a href="{U_PROFILE}">{L_PROFILE}</a>
  <a href="{U_PRIVATEMSGS}">{PRIVATE_MESSAGE_INFO}</a>
<!-- END switch_user_logged_in -->
</td>
<td align="right">
  <a href="{U_LOGIN_LOGOUT}">{L_LOGIN_LOGOUT}</a>
<!-- BEGIN switch_user_logged_out -->
  <a href="{U_REGISTER}">{L_REGISTER}</a>
<!-- END switch_user_logged_out -->
</td>
</tr>
</table>
```

After saving the files, and uploading them (unless you are testing them locally), you'll see that it looks pretty good, except maybe for the font of the temporary text:

In order to change the font and colors of the template, I would like to introduce you to the Cascading Style Sheet (CSS).

CSS

If you look in the original subSilver menu you will notice that all of the links are surrounded by `<span class="mainmenu">` and `</span>` tags. This is a reference to the CSS code, and if you look higher up in the code of the `overall_header.tpl`, where the CSS is located, you can find this (reformatted here for the book):

```
/* The register, login, search etc links at the top of the page */
.mainmenu { font-size : {T_FONTSIZE2}px;
            color : {T_BODY_TEXT}
}
a.mainmenu { text-decoration: none;
             color : {T_BODY_LINK};
}
a.mainmenu:hover { text-decoration: underline;
                   color : {T_BODY_HLINK};
}
```

Here we can change everything we want about the way the menu is displayed. The first line, surrounded by the `/*` and `*/` tags, is just a comment to help us out and is not used by the browser. The second line determines how the text, in this example, should be displayed, and the last two lines describe how the text should be displayed if it is a link. The variables are set from within the Admin Panel of the forum. Personally I like to add the CSS code for when a link has been visited, so I can be certain I don't suddenly get different colors or font sizes. The code is called `a.mainmenu:visited` and could be inserted either on its own line or as a part of the code already written, separated by a comma, as follows:

```
/* The register, login, search etc links at the top of the page */
.mainmenu { font-size : {T_FONTSIZE2}px;
            color : {T_BODY_TEXT}
}
a.mainmenu,a.mainmenu:visited { text-decoration: none;
                                color : {T_BODY_LINK};
}
a.mainmenu:hover { text-decoration: underline;
                   color : {T_BODY_HLINK};
}
```

We could also add a definition for `a.mainmenu:active` if we want to define how the link should look when someone clicks on it.

With these definitions for our menu style, our table looks like this:

```
<table width="715" height="20" border="0" align="center"
cellpadding="0" cellspacing="0">
<tr>
<td align="left">
  <a href="{U_FAQ}" class="mainmenu">{L_FAQ}</a>
  <a href="{U_SEARCH}" class="mainmenu">{L_SEARCH}</a>
  <a href="{U_MEMBERLIST}" class="mainmenu">{L_MEMBERLIST}</a>
  <a href="{U_GROUP_CP}" class="mainmenu">{L_USERGROUPS}</a>
<!-- BEGIN switch_user_logged_in -->
  <a href="{U_PROFILE}" class="mainmenu">{L_PROFILE}</a>
```

```
  <a href="{U_PRIVATEMSGS}"
class="mainmenu">{PRIVATE_MESSAGE_INFO}</a>
<!-- END switch_user_logged_in -->
</td>
<td align="right">
  <a href="{U_LOGIN_LOGOUT}" class="mainmenu">{L_LOGIN_LOGOUT}</a>
<!-- BEGIN switch_user_logged_out -->
  <a href="{U_REGISTER}" class="mainmenu">{L_REGISTER}</a>
<!-- END switch_user_logged_out -->
</td>
</tr>
</table>
```

We are almost finished with the menu now. The only thing that doesn't look good is the menu items being too close to each other. In HTML, multiple spaces will only display as one space, but a way around this is to add the ` ` code instead, which in fact is just a spacing. It has the advantage that as many continuous spaces can be added as wanted.

We add two spacings between each menu item, and the span class `mainmenu`, in order to make the spacings the same font size as the font used in the menu.

The finished table looks like this:

```
<table width="715" height="20" border="0" align="center"
cellpadding="0" cellspacing="0">
<tr>
<td align="left" class="mainmenu">
  <a href="{U_FAQ}" class="mainmenu">{L_FAQ}</a>
    
  <a href="{U_SEARCH}" class="mainmenu">{L_SEARCH}</a>
    
  <a href="{U_MEMBERLIST}" class="mainmenu">{L_MEMBERLIST}</a>
    
  <a href="{U_GROUP_CP}" class="mainmenu">{L_USERGROUPS}</a>
<!-- BEGIN switch_user_logged_in -->
   
  <a href="{U_PROFILE}" class="mainmenu">{L_PROFILE}</a>
    
  <a href="{U_PRIVATEMSGS}"
class="mainmenu">{PRIVATE_MESSAGE_INFO}</a>
<!-- END switch_user_logged_in -->
</td>
<td align="right" class="mainmenu">
  <a href="{U_LOGIN_LOGOUT}" class="mainmenu">{L_LOGIN_LOGOUT}</a>
<!-- BEGIN switch_user_logged_out -->
   
  <a href="{U_REGISTER}" class="mainmenu">{L_REGISTER}</a>
<!-- END switch_user_logged_out -->
</td>
</tr>
</table>
```

We are now done with the tables in `overall_header.tpl` and can delete the left-over original subSilver table code.

It is time to enter the Admin Panel; we need to fix the text colors on the menu and this is where things might start to get a bit more confusing.

Let me start by saying that we do not need to use the Admin Panel settings of the forum in order to change the layout; we could just as easily edit the CSS code directly, without using variables. For example, say we wanted the text in the menu to be a little smaller, black, and when hovering the mouse over it, still black but underlined. The easiest way to achieve this would be to change the CSS to:

```
/* The register, login, search etc links at the top of the page */
.mainmenu { font-size : 11px;
            color : black
}
a.mainmenu { font-size : 11px;
             text-decoration: none;
             color : black;
}
a.mainmenu:visited { font-size : 11px;
                     text-decoration: none;
                     color : black;
}
a.mainmenu:hover { font-size : 11px;
                   text-decoration: underline;
                   color : black;
}
```

However, this way we would have to edit the `overall_header.tpl` every time we wanted to change something. This might be an OK solution for you personally, but if you are planning on releasing the template publicly, it might not be such a good idea. Not everyone feels comfortable editing CSS code, and besides, if we have the option of changing these things from the Admin Panel, we might as well do it.

In the Administration Panel, by selecting the template under Styles Admin and Management and editing it, you will find the variables used in the CSS. For example, the `{T_FONTSIZE2}` refers to `Font Size 2:`, which is set to `11`. If you wanted your `.mainmenu` to have a smaller font, change it to `10` here. However, this would mean that everywhere else in the CSS that the `{T_FONTSIZE2}` appears, it would be font size `10`—not exactly what we wanted.

Instead, it is easier to use `{T_FONTSIZE1}` in the CSS, which refers to `Font Size 1:` in the Admin Panel, which is already font size `10`.

The `Text Color:` in the Admin Panel is set to `000000`, which might be a bit too dark on a white background like this. So we are changing it to a value of `111111` to soften it a little.

The `Link Color:` is set to `006699`, which we are changing to a red color with a value of `9F0002`, the same value as for the brush in the `top_image.jpg`. We will also use this value for the 'visited', 'active', and 'hover' link settings.

That is all we need for now, and we can save these settings and return to the forum.

The menu now has red text because it is using the link variables of the Admin Panel. If we want them black at all time, we need to change the following in the CSS code:

```
/* The register, login, search etc links at the top of the page */
.mainmenu {
  font-size : {T_FONTSIZE2}px;
  color : {T_BODY_TEXT}
}
a.mainmenu {
  text-decoration: none;
  color : {T_BODY_LINK};
}
a.mainmenu:hover {
  text-decoration: underline;
  color : {T_BODY_HLINK};
}
```

... to:

```
/* The register, login, search etc links at the top of the page */
.mainmenu {
  font-size : {T_FONTSIZE1}px;
  color : {T_BODY_TEXT}
}
a.mainmenu {
  font-size : {T_FONTSIZE1}px;
  text-decoration: none;
  color : {T_BODY_TEXT};
}
a.mainmenu:visited {
  font-size : {T_FONTSIZE1}px;
  text-decoration: none;
  color : {T_BODY_TEXT};
}
a.mainmenu:hover {
  font-size : {T_FONTSIZE1}px;
  text-decoration: underline;
  color : {T_BODY_TEXT};
}
```

The menu is now with black text as wanted. Notice that we add the `font-size : {T_FONTSIZE1}px;` code to all the link definitions. This is something we don't normally have to do since it is already defined in `.mainmenu`, but I have experienced that sometimes, if a user installs a new template with a CSS that only defines the font size in the `.mainmenu`, the template would use the font size from the previously installed template. It sounds strange, but this is something I have seen and it was not very pretty. There might be other ways to solve the problem, but this one has worked for me.

The gray background color and the borders around the forum don't seem to match the rest. Changing the `Background Color:` in the Admin Panel from `E5E5E5` to `FFFFFF` solves the first problem, but there are still some borders we need to get rid off. If you run into problems like this one, the best thing to do is to go back into the code for the `.tpl` file and find out what caused it. In this case, the borders are coming from a CSS in the first table called `bodyline`:

```
<table width="780" height="100%" cellspacing="0" cellpadding="10"
border="0" align="center">
```

```
<tr>
<td class="bodyline" valign="top">
```

In the CSS code we have:

```
/* This is the border line & background color round the entire page
*/
.bodyline {
  background-color: {T_TD_COLOR2};
  border: 1px {T_TH_COLOR1} solid;
}
```

Easy fix though, since only changing the border to `0px` takes care of the problem.

We are now ready to edit the `index_body.tpl`, which displays the forum's index page.

Modifying the Forum Index in index_body.tpl

The first table in the `index_body.tpl` file looks like this:

```
<table width="100%" cellspacing="0" cellpadding="2" border="0"
align="center">
<tr>
<td align="left" valign="bottom"><span class="gensmall">
<!-- BEGIN switch_user_logged_in -->
  {LAST_VISIT_DATE}<br />
<!-- END switch_user_logged_in -->
  {CURRENT_TIME}<br /></span><span class="nav">
  <a href="{U_INDEX}" class="nav">{L_INDEX}</a></span>
</td>
<td align="right" valign="bottom" class="gensmall">
<!-- BEGIN switch_user_logged_in -->
  <a href="{U_SEARCH_NEW}" class="gensmall">{L_SEARCH_NEW}</a>
  <br />
  <a href="{U_SEARCH_SELF}" class="gensmall">{L_SEARCH_SELF}</a>
  <br />
<!-- END switch_user_logged_in -->
  <a href="{U_SEARCH_UNANSWERED}"
class="gensmall">{L_SEARCH_UNANSWERED}</a>
</td>
</tr>
</table>
```

It displays a range of variables: when the logged-in user last visited, the current time, a link to posts that the user hasn't read yet, and unanswered posts. We don't want to display these variables on top of the index page, so we simply copy the entire table, delete it, and paste it at the bottom of the `.tpl` instead. That way we can deal with it later.

For the top of the page, according to the layout idea, there should be two black lines under the menu with some text inside. This is a detail that should continue throughout the template, and something we have to build into all of the `.tpl` files.

The next table in `index_body.tpl` looks like this:

```
<table width="100%" cellpadding="2" cellspacing="1" border="0"
class="forumline">
<tr>
<th colspan="2" class="thCornerL" height="25" nowrap="nowrap">
   {L_FORUM} 
</th>
<th width="50" class="thTop" nowrap="nowrap">
   {L_TOPICS} 
</th>
<th width="50" class="thTop" nowrap="nowrap">
   {L_POSTS} 
</th>
<th class="thCornerR" nowrap="nowrap">
   {L_LASTPOST} 
</th>
</tr>
<!-- BEGIN catrow -->
<tr>
<td class="catLeft" colspan="2" height="28">
  <span class="cattitle">
  <a href="{catrow.U_VIEWCAT}" class="cattitle">{catrow.CAT_DESC}</a>
  </span>
</td>
<td class="rowpic" colspan="3" align="right">
   
</td>
</tr>
<!-- BEGIN forumrow -->
<tr>
<td class="row1" align="center" valign="middle" height="50">
  <img src="{catrow.forumrow.FORUM_FOLDER_IMG}" width="46"
height="25" alt="{catrow.forumrow.L_FORUM_FOLDER_ALT}"
title="{catrow.forumrow.L_FORUM_FOLDER_ALT}" />
</td>
<td class="row1" width="100%" height="50">
  <span class="forumlink">
  <a href="{catrow.forumrow.U_VIEWFORUM}"
class="forumlink">{catrow.forumrow.FORUM_NAME}</a>
  <br />
  </span>
  <span class="genmed">
  {catrow.forumrow.FORUM_DESC}
  <br />
  </span>
  <span class="gensmall">
  {catrow.forumrow.L_MODERATOR} {catrow.forumrow.MODERATORS}
  </span>
</td>
<td class="row2" align="center" valign="middle" height="50">
  <span class="gensmall">
  {catrow.forumrow.TOPICS}
  </span>
```

```
</td>
<td class="row2" align="center" valign="middle" height="50">
  <span class="gensmall">
  {catrow.forumrow.POSTS}
  </span>
</td>
<td class="row2" align="center" valign="middle" height="50"
nowrap="nowrap">
  <span class="gensmall">
  {catrow.forumrow.LAST_POST}
  </span>
</td>
</tr>
<!-- END forumrow -->
<!-- END catrow -->
</table>
```

This is the forum itself, with all the topics and categories, and this is what we want appearing at the top. On the first line, we can see that the table has a `class="forumline"` attribute. This is what creates the border around the table, and is what we want to modify. Jumping back to the CSS code of the `overall_header.tpl`, we can find:

```
/* This is the outline round the main forum tables */
.forumline {
  background-color: {T_TD_COLOR2};
  border: 2px {T_TH_COLOR2} solid;
}
```

The `{T_TD_COLOR2}` variable refers to **Table Cell Color 2**: in the Admin Panel, currently set to `FFFFFF`, a bright white. `{T_TH_COLOR2}` is the **Table Header Color 2**: that's set to 006699, a blue color. We can change this code any way we like to suit the frame around the table, but for this template, in order to keep it as simple as possible, and make it match the layout idea, we don't want any borders right now. The easiest thing to do would be to just remove the `class="forumline` attribute from the table, but if later we decide we want borders anyways, it would mean we have to go into all the `.tpl` files and add the attribute again manually—too much work! Instead, we change the CSS to:

```
/* This is the outline round the main forum tables */
.forumline {
  /*
  background-color: {T_TD_COLOR2};
  border: 2px {T_TH_COLOR2} solid;
  */
}
```

The table width is set to 100% now, which we change to 717 to match the image. We also add an `align="center"` attribute to make it centered on the page.

The first part of the table now looks like:

```
<table width="717" align="center" cellpadding="2" cellspacing="1"
border="0" class="forumline">
<tr>
<th colspan="2" class="thCornerL" height="25" nowrap="nowrap">
   {L_FORUM} 
</th>
```

```
<th width="50" class="thTop" nowrap="nowrap">
   {L_TOPICS} 
</th>
<th width="50" class="thTop" nowrap="nowrap">
   {L_POSTS} 
</th>
<th class="thCornerR" nowrap="nowrap">
   {L_LASTPOST} 
</th>
</tr>
```

In the code, we can find the classes called thCornerL, thTop, and thCornerR. These are the ones displaying the blue background with orange text in the first row of our table. In our CSS code, we find them here:

```
/* Header cells - the blue and silver gradient backgrounds */
th {
  color: {T_FONTCOLOR3};
  font-size: {T_FONTSIZE2}px;
  font-weight : bold;
  background-color: {T_BODY_LINK};
  height: 25px;
  background-image: url(templates/subSilver/images/{T_TH_CLASS2});
}
```

... here:

```
th.thHead,th.thSides,th.thTop,th.thLeft,th.thRight,th.thBottom,th.thC
ornerL,th.thCornerR {
  font-weight: bold;
  border: {T_TD_COLOR2};
  border-style: solid;
  height: 28px;
}
```

... and here:

```
th.thHead,td.catHead {
  font-size: {T_FONTSIZE3}px;
  border-width: 1px 1px 0px 1px;
}
th.thSides,td.catSides,td.spaceRow {
  border-width: 0px 1px 0px 1px;
}
th.thRight,td.catRight,td.row3Right {
  border-width: 0px 1px 0px 0px;
}
th.thLeft,td.catLeft { border-width: 0px 0px 0px 1px; }
th.thBottom,td.catBottom { border-width: 0px 1px 1px 1px; }
th.thTop { border-width: 1px 0px 0px 0px; }
th.thCornerL { border-width: 1px 0px 0px 1px; }
th.thCornerR { border-width: 1px 1px 0px 0px; }
```

That's quite a mouthful! But don't despair; it is easier than it looks. If we start with the top left part of our table, the thCornerL class, we can follow it down the CSS code: First of all, it is a part of the th class, simply because we can find <th colspan="2" class="thCornerL" height="25" nowrap="nowrap"> in the table. In the CSS code for th, we can find the font color, the font size, the font weight, the background color, the height of the th, and the background image.

Further down, we find more definitions for th.thCornerL, with a border color, a border style, and a height of 28 pixels. We also get the exact definition of how the borders are displayed with th.thCornerL{border-width: 1px 0px 0px 1px; }, which is the size of the border on each side, clockwise starting from the top.

To change it, it is easiest to start from the bottom. We know that we want black lines above and below this section, so we can start by changing the CSS to:

```
th.thCornerL { border-width: 1px 0px 1px 0px; }
```

Going up in the CSS, we find border: {T_TD_COLOR2};, which in the Admin Panel refers to Table Cell Color 2, currently set to FFFFFF. Changing this color to black will change every instance in the CSS where {T_TD_COLOR2} is being used. And since we want that white table cell color, we need to do something different. Changing the border: {T_TD_COLOR2}; to border: {T_BODY_TEXT}; would give us the color of the text which we earlier set to black. That's one solution. The bad thing about this is that if we later want to change the font color, but not the black lines, we have to come back and edit the CSS again. Instead, we can add 111111 to the Table Cell Color 3 field (it's not being used yet) in the Admin Panel, and change the CSS to border: {T_TD_COLOR3};.

Following the CSS higher up, we find that in the th part there is a background image. If we want a background image behind this part of the table, we should keep this code. However, for this template we decided to go for a white background with black text, so again we add the /* and */ markers around the background image and the background color. After changing the font color and the font size, the CSS now looks like:

```
/* Header cells - the blue and silver gradient backgrounds */
th {
  color: {T_BODY_TEXT};
  font-size: {T_FONTSIZE1}px;
  font-weight : bold;
  /*
  background-color: {T_BODY_LINK};
  */
  height: 25px;
  /*
  background-image: url(templates/subSilver/images/{T_TH_CLASS2});
  */
}
```

... and:

```
th.thHead,th.thSides,th.thTop,th.thLeft,th.thRight,th.thBottom,th.thC
ornerL,th.thCornerR {
  font-weight: bold;
  border: {T_TD_COLOR3};
  border-style: solid;
  height: 28px;
}
```

... and:

```
th.thHead,td.catHead {
  font-size: {T_FONTSIZE3}px;
  border-width: 1px 1px 0px 1px;
}
th.thSides,td.catSides,td.spaceRow { border-width: 0px 1px 0px 1px; }
th.thRight,td.catRight,td.row3Right { border-width: 0px 1px 0px 0px;
}
th.thLeft,td.catLeft { border-width: 0px 0px 0px 1px; }
th.thBottom,td.catBottom { border-width: 0px 1px 1px 1px; }
th.thTop { border-width: 1px 0px 0px 0px; }
th.thCornerL { border-width: 1px 0px 1px 0px; }
th.thCornerR { border-width: 1px 1px 0px 0px; }
```

Changing the `thTop` and `thCornerR` to have black lines similar to `thCornerL` is the last step needed to be done for now, and this can be done here:

```
th.thTop { border-width: 1px 0px 1px 0px; }
th.thCornerL { border-width: 1px 0px 1px 0px; }
th.thCornerR { border-width: 1px 0px 1px 0px; }
```

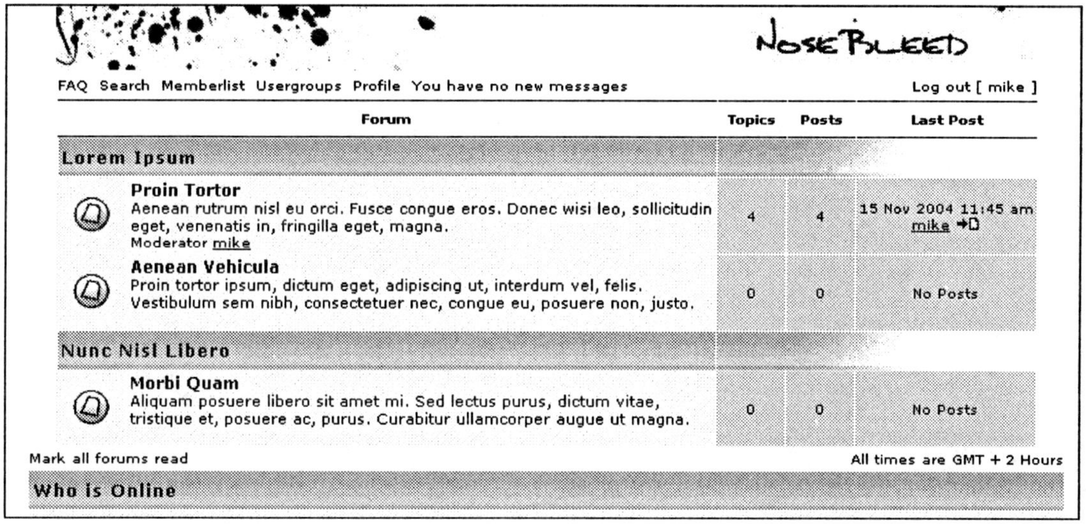

The rest of the table looks like this:

```
<!-- BEGIN catrow -->
<tr>
<td class="catLeft" colspan="2" height="28">
  <span class="cattitle">
  <a href="{catrow.U_VIEWCAT}" class="cattitle">{catrow.CAT_DESC}</a>
  </span>
</td>
<td class="rowpic" colspan="3" align="right">
   
</td>
</tr>
```

```
<!-- BEGIN forumrow -->
<tr>
<td class="row1" align="center" valign="middle" height="50">
  <img src="{catrow.forumrow.FORUM_FOLDER_IMG}" width="46"
height="25" alt="{catrow.forumrow.L_FORUM_FOLDER_ALT}"
title="{catrow.forumrow.L_FORUM_FOLDER_ALT}" />
</td>
<td class="row1" width="100%" height="50">
  <span class="forumlink">
  <a href="{catrow.forumrow.U_VIEWFORUM}"
class="forumlink">{catrow.forumrow.FORUM_NAME}</a>
  <br />
  </span>
  <span class="genmed">
  {catrow.forumrow.FORUM_DESC}
  <br />
  </span>
  <span class="gensmall">
  {catrow.forumrow.L_MODERATOR} {catrow.forumrow.MODERATORS}
  </span>
</td>
<td class="row2" align="center" valign="middle" height="50">
  <span class="gensmall">
  {catrow.forumrow.TOPICS}
  </span>
</td>
<td class="row2" align="center" valign="middle" height="50">
  <span class="gensmall">
  {catrow.forumrow.POSTS}
  </span>
</td>
<td class="row2" align="center" valign="middle" height="50"
nowrap="nowrap">
  <span class="gensmall">
  {catrow.forumrow.LAST_POST}
  </span>
</td>
</tr>
<!-- END forumrow -->
<!-- END catrow -->
</table>
```

The `catrow` and the `forumrow` determine the categories and forum topics found in the database; they use the above HTML code to display the categories and topics, until there are no more to be found, like a loop. If we start with the first table row, we find where the name of the category is displayed:

```
<tr>
<td class="catLeft" colspan="2" height="28">
  <span class="cattitle">
  <a href="{catrow.U_VIEWCAT}" class="cattitle">{catrow.CAT_DESC}</a>
  </span>
</td>
<td class="rowpic" colspan="3" align="right">
   
</td>
</tr>
```

Again, we hunt in our CSS code for the classes being used, starting with `catLeft`:

```
td.cat,td.catHead,td.catSides,td.catLeft,td.catRight,td.catBottom
{
  background-image: url(templates/subSilver/images/{T_TH_CLASS1});
  background-color:{T_TR_COLOR3};
  border: {T_TH_COLOR3};
  border-style: solid;
  height: 28px;
}
```

Notice that `catLeft` is not the only class in this line. If we wanted all the other classes to look like this, except the `catLeft` class, the easiest way would be to just remove this class from the list and turn it into its own class underneath. But since all these classes are more or less only about displaying a background color and image, we leave the class where it is and change them all at once.

For this template, we don't use much from what is determined in these classes, so we change it to:

```
td.cat,td.catHead,td.catSides,td.catLeft,td.catRight,td.catBottom
{
  /*
  background-image: url(templates/subSilver/images/{T_TH_CLASS1});
  background-color:{T_TR_COLOR3};
  border: {T_TH_COLOR3};
  border-style: solid;
  */
  height: 28px;
}
```

We are keeping the height for now.

The next class we hunt for is called `rowpic`. What it actually does for our forum is simply displays a background image other than the one in `catLeft`, so the approach is the same. You can use this if you want to have an image background behind your category text, different from the image you would get from `catLeft`. But since we don't need any image there, we can remove that class from the table.

After doing this, our table should look like:

```
<tr>
<td class="catLeft" colspan="5" height="28">
  <span class="cattitle">
  <a href="{catrow.U_VIEWCAT}" class="cattitle">{catrow.CAT_DESC}</a>
  </span>
</td>
</tr>
```

The category description is determined by the `cattitle` class, and we can find it in the CSS here:

```
/* Forum category titles */
.cattitle {
  font-weight: bold;
  font-size: {T_FONTSIZE3}px;
```

```
    letter-spacing: 1px;
    color : {T_BODY_LINK}
  }
  a.cattitle {
    text-decoration: none;
    color : {T_BODY_LINK};
  }
  a.cattitle:hover {
    text-decoration: underline;
  }
```

There is not much to change here except the font, which is a little too big; so the spacing of one pixel between each letter in the word has to go. We can also add an `a.cattitle:visited` class.

The class now looks like:

```
  /* Forum category titles */
  .cattitle {
    font-weight: bold;
    font-size: {T_FONTSIZE2}px;
    color : {T_BODY_LINK}
  }
  a.cattitle {
    text-decoration: none;
    color : {T_BODY_LINK};
  }
  a.cattitle:visited {
    text-decoration: none;
    color : {T_BODY_LINK};
  }
  a.cattitle:hover {
    text-decoration: underline;
  }
```

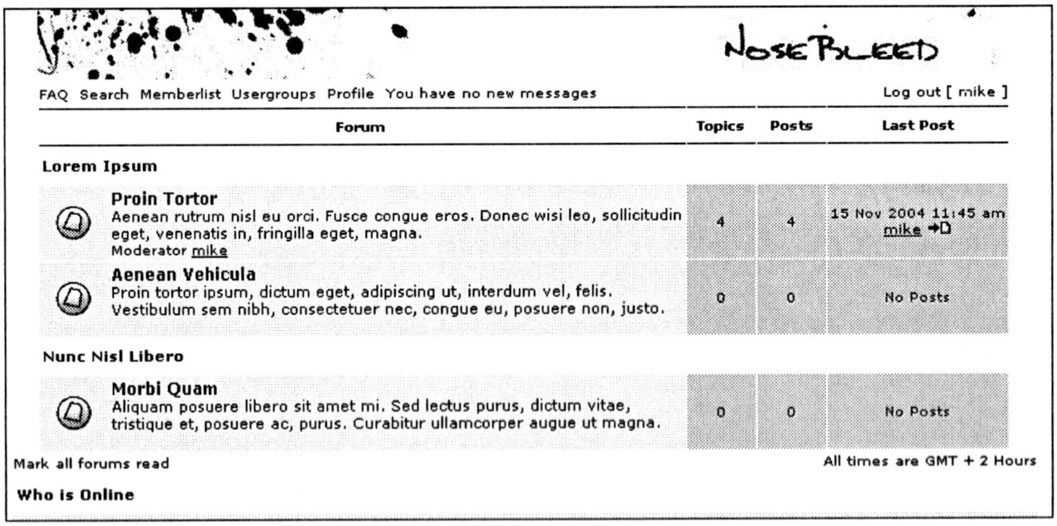

Moving down in our `.tpl`, we find the forum row.

```
<!-- BEGIN forumrow -->
<tr>
<td class="row1" align="center" valign="middle" height="50">
  <img src="{catrow.forumrow.FORUM_FOLDER_IMG}" width="46"
height="25" alt="{catrow.forumrow.L_FORUM_FOLDER_ALT}"
title="{catrow.forumrow.L_FORUM_FOLDER_ALT}" />
</td>
<td class="row1" width="100%" height="50">
  <span class="forumlink">
  <a href="{catrow.forumrow.U_VIEWFORUM}"
class="forumlink">{catrow.forumrow.FORUM_NAME}</a>
  <br />
  </span>
  <span class="genmed">
  {catrow.forumrow.FORUM_DESC}
  <br />
  </span>
  <span class="gensmall">
  {catrow.forumrow.L_MODERATOR} {catrow.forumrow.MODERATORS}
  </span>
</td>
<td class="row2" align="center" valign="middle" height="50">
  <span class="gensmall">
  {catrow.forumrow.TOPICS}
  </span>
</td>
<td class="row2" align="center" valign="middle" height="50">
  <span class="gensmall">
  {catrow.forumrow.POSTS}
  </span>
</td>
<td class="row2" align="center" valign="middle" height="50"
nowrap="nowrap">
  <span class="gensmall">
  {catrow.forumrow.LAST_POST}
  </span>
</td>
</tr>
<!-- END forumrow -->
```

The classes of `row1`, `row2`, and `row3` in the CSS determine the background colors for our template. They are defined by `{T_TR_COLOR1}`, `{T_TR_COLOR2}`, and `{T_TR_COLOR3}`, which again are defined in the Admin Panel by Table Row Color 1, Table Row Color 2, and Table Row Color 3. From the layout idea, we have already decided on light gray, to match the `top_image` of the template. We don't need to change anything in the CSS code, but from the Admin Panel, we add the new values of `F3F3F3`, `EBEBEB`, and `E3E3E3`, with the first color being the same as in the `top_image.jpg` and the others, slightly darker.

Next in our table are the folder images, defined by the `{catrow.forumrow.FORUM_FOLDER_IMG}` variable. We don't want to change anything here. Later in the chapter we will see how to make new icons and images. The `forumlink` class determines what the font of the text describing the forum should look like. In the CSS we find the following:

```
/* Forum title: Text and link to the forums used in: index.php */
.forumlink {
  font-weight: bold;
  font-size: {T_FONTSIZE3}px;
  color : {T_BODY_LINK};
}
a.forumlink {
  text-decoration: none;
  color : {T_BODY_LINK};
}
a.forumlink:hover {
  text-decoration: underline;
  color : {T_BODY_HLINK};
}
```

There isn't much to change here, except maybe the font size from `{T_FONTSIZE3}` to `{T_FONTSIZE2}`, and the hover color from `{T_BODY_HLINK}` to `{T_BODY_LINK}`. `{T_BODY_HLINK}` is the hover setting of links from the Admin Panel, but there is no need for a different color for this. The changed class now looks like:

```
/* Forum title: Text and link to the forums used in: index.php */
.forumlink {
  font-weight: bold;
  font-size: {T_FONTSIZE2}px;
  color : {T_BODY_LINK};
}
a.forumlink {
  text-decoration: none;
  color : {T_BODY_LINK};
}
a.forumlink:visited {
  text-decoration: none;
  color : {T_BODY_LINK};
}
a.forumlink:hover {
  text-decoration: underline;
  color : {T_BODY_LINK};
}
```

As you might have noticed by now, it is not all that difficult to change the CSS, and I will try to spare you from a detailed description for the rest of the chapter.

The next thing to change is the size of the `genmed` class to `{T_FONTSIZE1}` in the CSS, to make it a little smaller.

We are almost finished with this table now, but the text in the table row is really close to the edges. I am not too happy about that, and one way to solve this problem is to change the `cellpadding` value from 2 to 4 in the table. Another way would be to add a padding definition to a CSS class or even to make a new class and then add it to the table. We go for the first solution here.

Finally, to spice up the forum a bit, we add a rollover effect on the table row, meaning that it will change color when you move the mouse over it, and at the same time the whole table row will work as a link.

Our table should now look like:

```
<table width="717" align="center" cellpadding="4" cellspacing="1"
border="0" class="forumline">
<tr>
<th colspan="2" class="thCornerL" height="25" nowrap="nowrap">
   {L_FORUM} 
</th>
<th width="50" class="thTop" nowrap="nowrap">
   {L_TOPICS} 
</th>
<th width="50" class="thTop" nowrap="nowrap">
   {L_POSTS} 
</th>
<th class="thCornerR" nowrap="nowrap">
   {L_LASTPOST} 
</th>
</tr>
<!-- BEGIN catrow -->
<tr>
<td class="catLeft" colspan="5" height="28">
  <span class="cattitle">
  <a href="{catrow.U_VIEWCAT}" class="cattitle">{catrow.CAT_DESC}</a>
  </span>
</td>
</tr>
<!-- BEGIN forumrow -->
<tr>
<td class="row1" align="center" valign="middle" height="50">
  <img src="{catrow.forumrow.FORUM_FOLDER_IMG}" width="46"
height="25" alt="{catrow.forumrow.L_FORUM_FOLDER_ALT}"
title="{catrow.forumrow.L_FORUM_FOLDER_ALT}" />
</td>
<td class="row1" width="100%" height="50"
   onmouseover="this.style.backgroundcolor='{T_TR_COLOR2}';
   this.style.cursor='pointer';"
   onmouseout=this.style.backgroundcolor=""
   onclick="window.location.href='{catrow.forumrow.U_VIEWFORUM}'">
  <span class="forumlink">
  <a href="{catrow.forumrow.U_VIEWFORUM}"
class="forumlink">{catrow.forumrow.FORUM_NAME}</a>
  <br />
  </span>
  <span class="genmed">
  {catrow.forumrow.FORUM_DESC}
  <br />
  </span>
  <span class="gensmall">
  {catrow.forumrow.L_MODERATOR} {catrow.forumrow.MODERATORS}
  </span>
</td>
<td class="row2" align="center" valign="middle" height="50">
  <span class="gensmall">
  {catrow.forumrow.TOPICS}
  </span>
</td>
<td class="row2" align="center" valign="middle" height="50">
  <span class="gensmall">
```

```
    {catrow.forumrow.POSTS}
    </span>
  </td>
  <td class="row2" align="center" valign="middle" height="50"
  nowrap="nowrap">
    <span class="gensmall">
    {catrow.forumrow.LAST_POST}
    </span>
  </td>
  </tr>
  <!-- END forumrow -->
  <!-- END catrow -->
  </table>
```

The next table in our `index_body.tpl` file displays the link for "mark all forums" and the time and time-zone for the forum:

```
  <table width="100%" cellspacing="0" border="0" align="center"
  cellpadding="2">
  <tr>
  <td align="left">
    <span class="gensmall">
    <a href="{U_MARK_READ}" class="gensmall">{L_MARK_FORUMS_READ}</a>
    </span>
  </td>
  <td align="right">
    <span class="gensmall">
    {S_TIMEZONE}
    </span>
  </td>
  </tr>
  </table>
```

It looks quite good; the only thing to change is the width from 100% to 717 pixels; also, we want to change the `gensmall` class in the CSS to have black links instead of red, similar to what we did with the `mainmenu` class.

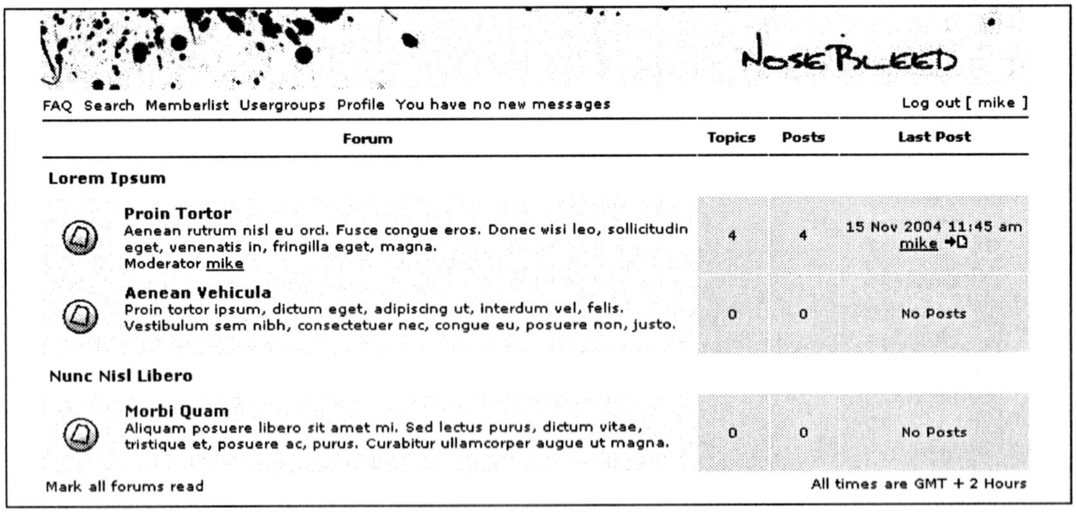

This takes care of the main part of the forum.

The next part of the `index_body.tpl` file is the table that displays who is online and other relevant information about the forum users. This table is found only in this `.tpl` file, and in my opinion it is not really a part of the forum itself, but more is of something extra being added. For this reason we insert this part at the bottom of the page, and also add here all the extra links we removed from the top of the file. We can add it all in a table, giving it the class of `thTop` so that it will have black lines above and below it, like we have with the menu.

To add a little space around the table, we insert an extra table row with a height of ten pixels at the beginning and end of the table.

The new table looks like:

```
<table align="center" width="717" border="0" cellspacing="0"
cellpadding="0">
<tr height="10"><td>&nsbp;</td></tr>
<tr>
<th colspan="2" class="thTop" height="25" nowrap="nowrap">
<table width="717" cellspacing="0" cellpadding="2"
       border="0" align="center">
<tr>
<td align="left" valign="bottom">
  <span class="gensmall">
<!-- BEGIN switch_user_logged_in -->
  {LAST_VISIT_DATE}
  <br />
<!-- END switch_user_logged_in -->
  {CURRENT_TIME}
  <br />
  </span>
  <span class="nav">
  <a href="{U_INDEX}" class="nav">{L_INDEX}</a>
  </span>
</td>
<td align="right" valign="bottom" class="gensmall">
<!-- BEGIN switch_user_logged_in -->
  <a href="{U_SEARCH_NEW}" class="gensmall">{L_SEARCH_NEW}</a>
  <br />
  <a href="{U_SEARCH_SELF}" class="gensmall">{L_SEARCH_SELF}</a>
  <br />
<!-- END switch_user_logged_in -->
  <a href="{U_SEARCH_UNANSWERED}"
class="gensmall">{L_SEARCH_UNANSWERED}</a>
</td>
</tr>
</table></th>
</tr>
<tr height="10"><td>&nsbp;</td></tr>
</table>
```

We can now delete the table (the one we moved from the top in the beginning) at the bottom of the `.tpl` file.

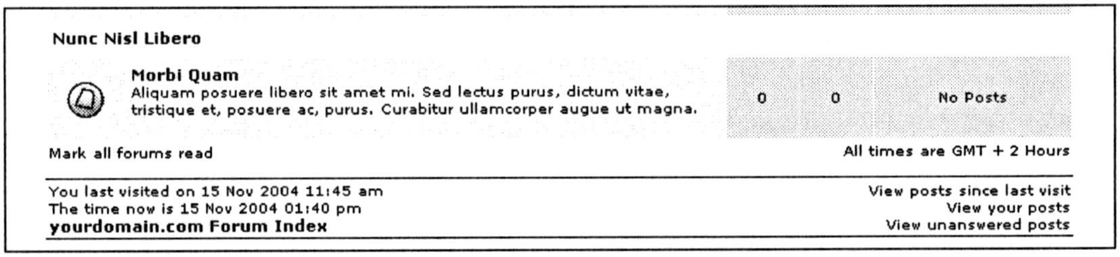

We can now deal with the next table, which displays the information about the users of the forum. There are only a few things changes here: the width should be 717 pixels instead of 100%, and we need to add an `align="center"` tag.

Under this table is another table, with a variable displaying the number of active users in the past five minutes. Changing the width and aligning it like the above table corrects this table as well.

Next we have the login table, surrounded by `<!-- BEGIN switch_user_logged_out -->` and `<!-- BEGIN switch_user_logged_out -->` tags to make sure only users that are *not* logged in can see the table. If you want the login information to appear at the top of your site, just copy and paste this where you want it. For this template it is fine where it is now though, and again the only changes necessary are the width and the alignment.

There is one thing to notice here: the `<form...>` element. In some browsers, by adding a form, the element will also add a margin above and under it, almost making it look like you added a line break in the HTML code above and under the form. To prevent this, add this class in the CSS:

```
/* Form */
form {
  margin: 0px;
  padding: 0px;
}
```

Now we can add line breaks manually, above and under the form, and be sure it displays evenly in different browsers.

The last part of the `index_body.tpl` file shows the icons of the forum. We will come back to this later in the chapter, and leave it unchanged for now. The following screenshot shows what our forum looks like with the changes made up until now:

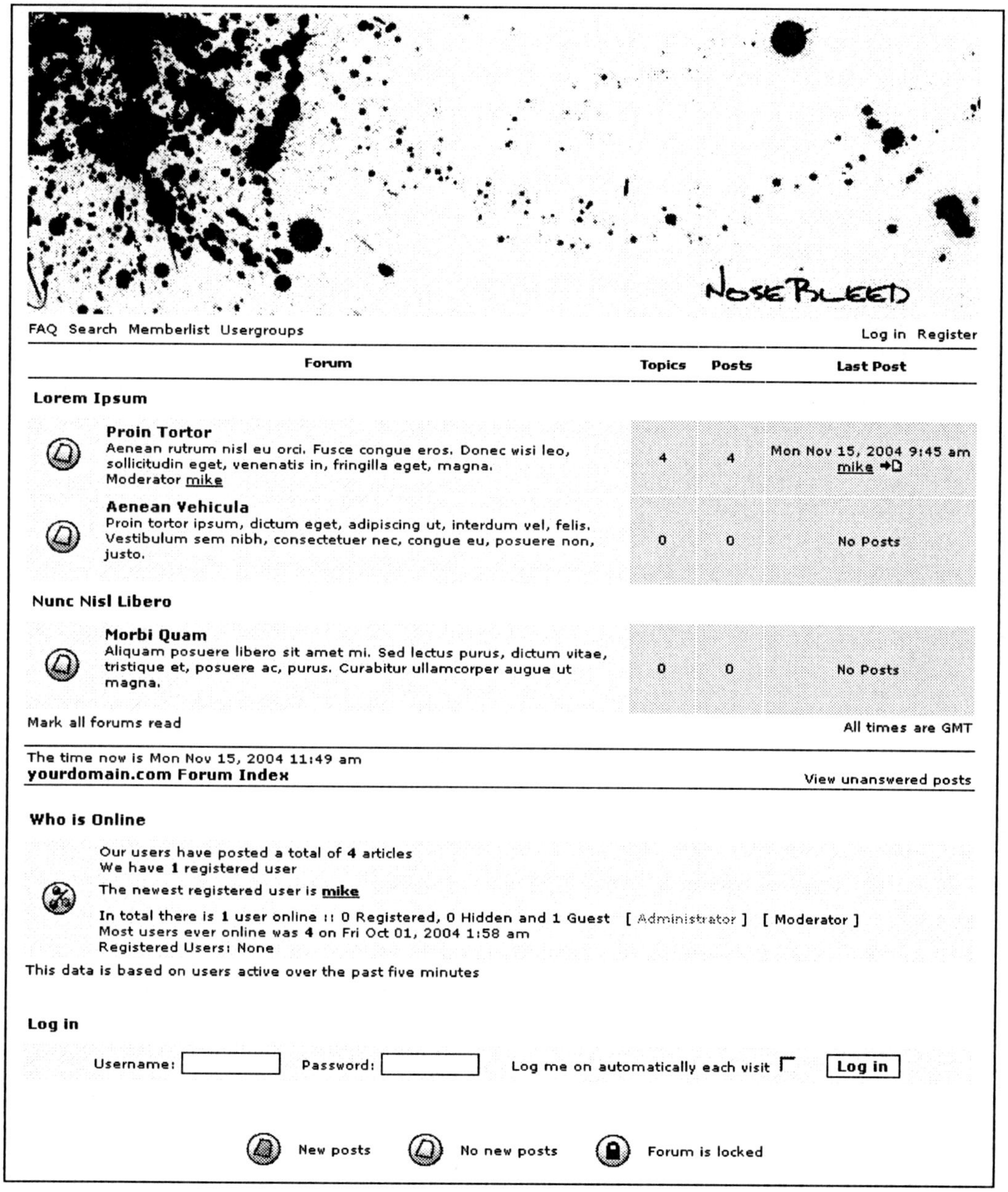
NoseBleed
FAQ Search Memberlist Usergroups
Log in Register
Forum
Topics
Posts
Last Post
Lorem Ipsum
Proin Tortor
Aenean rutrum nisl eu orci. Fusce congue eros. Donec wisi leo, sollicitudin eget, venenatis in, fringilla eget, magna.
Moderator mike
4
4
Mon Nov 15, 2004 9:45 am
mike
Aenean Vehicula
Proin tortor ipsum, dictum eget, adipiscing ut, interdum vel, felis. Vestibulum sem nibh, consectetuer nec, congue eu, posuere non, justo.
0
0
No Posts
Nunc Nisl Libero
Morbi Quam
Aliquam posuere libero sit amet mi. Sed lectus purus, dictum vitae, tristique et, posuere ac, purus. Curabitur ullamcorper augue ut magna.
0
0
No Posts
Mark all forums read
All times are GMT
The time now is Mon Nov 15, 2004 11:49 am
yourdomain.com Forum Index
View unanswered posts
Who is Online
Our users have posted a total of 4 articles
We have 1 registered user
The newest registered user is mike
In total there is 1 user online :: 0 Registered, 0 Hidden and 1 Guest [Administrator] [Moderator]
Most users ever online was 4 on Fri Oct 01, 2004 1:58 am
Registered Users: None
This data is based on users active over the past five minutes
Log in
Username:
Password:
Log me on automatically each visit
Log in
New posts
No new posts
Forum is locked

Modifying the Forum Body in viewforum_body.tpl

The next file we edit is the `viewforum_body.tpl` template. This is the file displaying the content of the forum after the index. Here is how our forum looks like before editing the `.tpl` file:

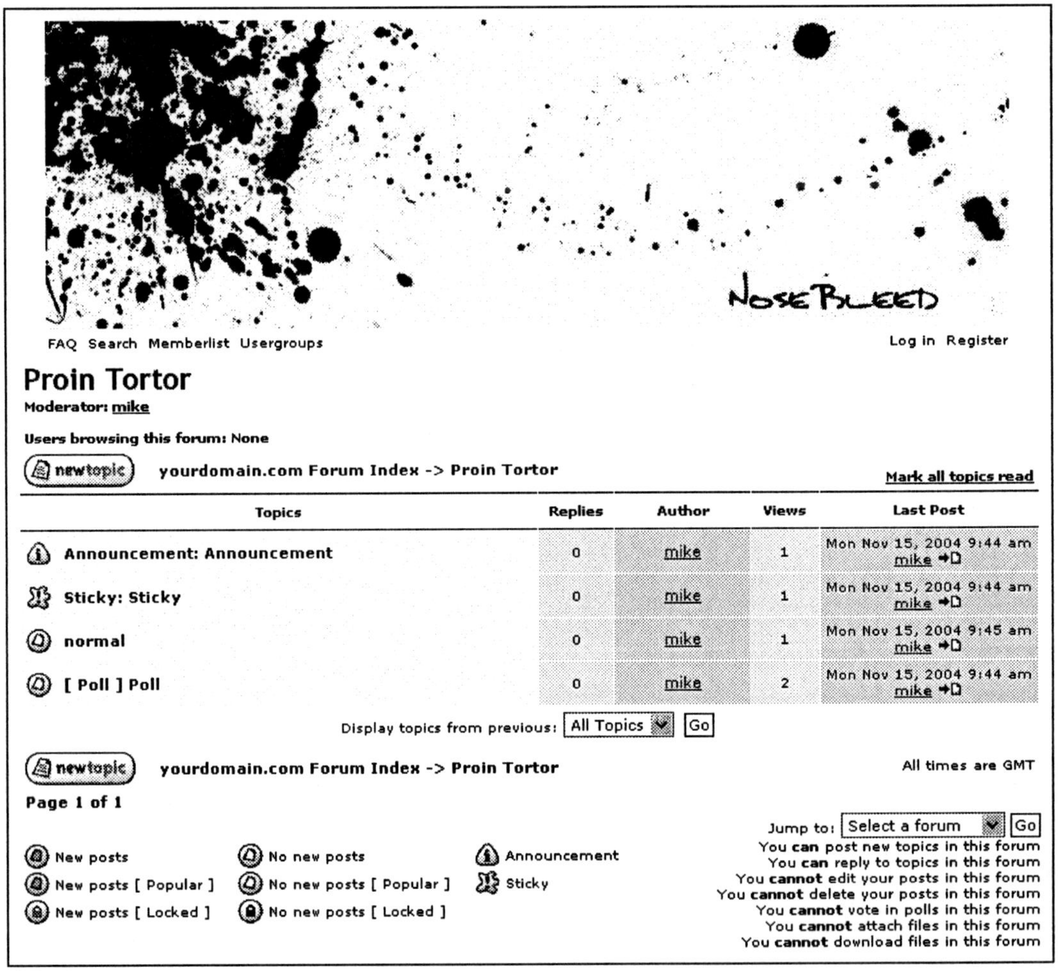

The first line of code in `viewforum.tpl` is a form object, which we leave unchanged. And, as with the `index_body.tpl`, we move the first table to the end of the file, so that we can get the black lines appearing at the top, right under the menu. In the start of the code, we now have the following table:

```
<table border="0" cellpadding="4" cellspacing="1" width="100%"
class="forumline">
<tr>
```

```
<th colspan="2" align="center" height="25" class="thCornerL"
nowrap="nowrap">
   {L_TOPICS} 
</th>
<th width="50" align="center" class="thTop" nowrap="nowrap">
   {L_REPLIES} 
</th>
<th width="100" align="center" class="thTop" nowrap="nowrap">
   {L_AUTHOR} 
</th>
<th width="50" align="center" class="thTop" nowrap="nowrap">
   {L_VIEWS} 
</th>
<th align="center" class="thCornerR" nowrap="nowrap">
   {L_LASTPOST} 
</th>
</tr>
<!-- BEGIN topicrow -->
<tr>
<td class="row1" align="center" valign="middle" width="20">
  <img src="{topicrow.TOPIC_FOLDER_IMG}" width="19" height="18"
alt="{topicrow.L_TOPIC_FOLDER_ALT}"
title="{topicrow.L_TOPIC_FOLDER_ALT}" />
</td>
<td class="row1" width="100%">
  <span class="topictitle">
  {topicrow.NEWEST_POST_IMG}{topicrow.TOPIC_TYPE}
  <a href="{topicrow.U_VIEW_TOPIC}"
class="topictitle">{topicrow.TOPIC_TITLE}</a>
  </span>
  <span class="gensmall">
  <br />
  {topicrow.GOTO_PAGE}
  </span>
</td>
<td class="row2" align="center" valign="middle">
  <span class="postdetails">
  {topicrow.REPLIES}
  </span>
</td>
<td class="row3" align="center" valign="middle">
  <span class="name">
  {topicrow.TOPIC_AUTHOR}
  </span>
</td>
<td class="row2" align="center" valign="middle">
  <span class="postdetails">
  {topicrow.VIEWS}
  </span>
</td>
<td class="row3Right" align="center" valign="middle" nowrap="nowrap">
  <span class="postdetails">
  {topicrow.LAST_POST_TIME}
  <br />
  {topicrow.LAST_POST_AUTHOR} {topicrow.LAST_POST_IMG}
  </span>
</td>
</tr>
<!-- END topicrow -->
```

```
<!-- BEGIN switch_no_topics -->
<tr>
<td class="row1" colspan="6" height="30" align="center"
valign="middle">
  <span class="gen">
  {L_NO_TOPICS}
  </span>
</td>
</tr>
<!-- END switch_no_topics -->
<tr>
<td class="catBottom" align="center" valign="middle" colspan="6"
height="28">
  <span class="genmed">
  {L_DISPLAY_TOPICS}: {S_SELECT_TOPIC_DAYS} <input
type="submit" class="liteoption" value="{L_GO}" name="submit" />
  </span>
</td>
</tr>
</table>
```

Again, we change the width from 100% to 717 pixels, and center-align it.

Under the black lines, the forum starts with the gray rows. But to make it fit better with the index page, we add an extra table row with two links: one to go back to the index page, and one to display the name of the selected forum. Instead of having the first link displaying the full name of the index page, we put instead a < sign to keep it short, which we add in the code with `<`. The top part of the table should now look like this:

```
<table border="0" cellpadding="4" cellspacing="1" width="717"
class="forumline" align="center">
<tr>
<th colspan="2" align="center" height="25" class="thCornerL"
nowrap="nowrap">
   {L_TOPICS} 
</th>
<th width="50" align="center" class="thTop" nowrap="nowrap">
   {L_REPLIES} 
</th>
<th width="100" align="center" class="thTop" nowrap="nowrap">
   {L_AUTHOR} 
</th>
<th width="50" align="center" class="thTop" nowrap="nowrap">
   {L_VIEWS} 
</th>
<th align="center" class="thCornerR" nowrap="nowrap">
   {L_LASTPOST} 
</th>
</tr>
<tr>
<th colspan="6" align="left" height="28" class="nav" nowrap="nowrap">
  <a href="{U_INDEX}" class="nav">&lt;</a>
    
  <a class="nav" href="{U_VIEW_FORUM}">{FORUM_NAME}</a>
</th>
</tr>
```

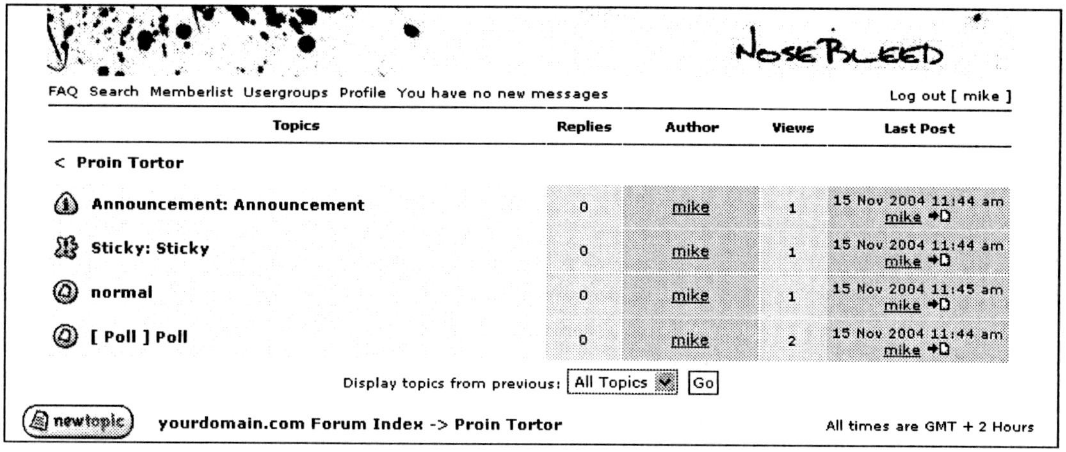

The next part of the table looks like:

```
<!-- BEGIN topicrow -->
<tr>
<td class="row1" align="center" valign="middle" width="20">
  <img src="{topicrow.TOPIC_FOLDER_IMG}" width="19" height="18"
alt="{topicrow.L_TOPIC_FOLDER_ALT}"
title="{topicrow.L_TOPIC_FOLDER_ALT}" />
</td>
<td class="row1" width="100%">
  <span class="topictitle">
  {topicrow.NEWEST_POST_IMG}{topicrow.TOPIC_TYPE}<a
href="{topicrow.U_VIEW_TOPIC}"
class="topictitle">{topicrow.TOPIC_TITLE}</a>
  </span>
  <span class="gensmall">
  <br />
  {topicrow.GOTO_PAGE}
  </span>
</td>
<td class="row2" align="center" valign="middle">
  <span class="postdetails">
  {topicrow.REPLIES}
  </span>
</td>
<td class="row3" align="center" valign="middle">
  <span class="name">
  {topicrow.TOPIC_AUTHOR}
  </span>
</td>
<td class="row2" align="center" valign="middle">
  <span class="postdetails">
  {topicrow.VIEWS}
  </span>
</td>
<td class="row3Right" align="center" valign="middle" nowrap="nowrap">
  <span class="postdetails">
  {topicrow.LAST_POST_TIME}
  <br />
```

```
    {topicrow.LAST_POST_AUTHOR} {topicrow.LAST_POST_IMG}
    </span>
  </td>
  </tr>
  <!-- END topicrow -->
```

This section will loop for every topic, between the `<!-- BEGIN topicrow -->` and the `<!-- END topicrow -->` tags. Notice that the rows have the background colors of the CSS classes `row1`, `row2`, `row3`, and `row3right`. There are a few things we could change, the first being the row color, and the second, the font size for the author of the topic. This row is darker than the two surrounding ones; it doesn't look very good, so we change it to the class of `row2`. As far as concerns the font, this row uses the `name` span class, which we change to `{T_FONTSIZE1}` in the CSS.

The red and bold font of the topic doesn't look very good either, so we modify it to the small and normal default black font that we also used in the index.

This class is called `topictitle`, and in the CSS it looks like:

```
/* titles for the topics: could specify viewed link colour too */
.topictitle,h1,h2 {
  font-weight: bold;
  font-size: {T_FONTSIZE2}px;
  color : {T_BODY_TEXT};
}
a.topictitle:link {
  text-decoration: none;
  color : {T_BODY_LINK};
}
a.topictitle:visited {
  text-decoration: none;
  color : {T_BODY_VLINK};
}
a.topictitle:hover {
  text-decoration: underline;
  color : {T_BODY_HLINK};
}
```

... which we change to:

```
/* titles for the topics: could specify viewed link colour too */
.topictitle,h1,h2 {
  font-size: {T_FONTSIZE1}px;
  color : {T_BODY_TEXT};
}
a.topictitle:link {
  text-decoration: none;
  color : {T_BODY_TEXT};
}
a.topictitle:visited {
  text-decoration: none;
  color : {T_BODY_TEXT};
}
a.topictitle:hover {
  text-decoration: underline;
  color : {T_BODY_TEXT};
}
```

We are almost done with this section. It is worth mentioning that when an Announcement, Sticky, or Poll post is posted, it will display the matching text in front of the name of the topic using a variable named {topicrow.TOPIC_TYPE}. To match the link color, we would like this text to be red instead of black, but at the same time would like it to use the class of topictitle, like the rest of the text. To solve this, we add <span style="color: {T_BODY_LINK}"> and </span> tags around it, which will change only the color of the text and not the size or other attributes.

Finally once we add the rollover effect as in the index page, the section should now look like this:

```
<!-- BEGIN topicrow -->
<tr>
<td class="row1" align="center" valign="middle" width="20">
  <img src="{topicrow.TOPIC_FOLDER_IMG}" width="19" height="18"
alt="{topicrow.L_TOPIC_FOLDER_ALT}"
title="{topicrow.L_TOPIC_FOLDER_ALT}" />
</td>
<td class="row1" width="100%"
    onmouseover="this.style.backgroundcolor='{T_TR_COLOR2}';
    this.style.cursor='pointer';"
    onmouseOut=this.style.backgroundcolor=""
    onclick="window.location.href='{topicrow.U_VIEW_TOPIC}'">
  <span class="topictitle">
  {topicrow.NEWEST_POST_IMG}
  <span style="color: {T_BODY_LINK}">
  {topicrow.TOPIC_TYPE}
  </span>
  <a href="{topicrow.U_VIEW_TOPIC}"
class="topictitle">{topicrow.TOPIC_TITLE}</a>
  </span>
  <span class="gensmall">
  <br />
  {topicrow.GOTO_PAGE}
  </span>
</td>
<td class="row2" align="center" valign="middle">
  <span class="postdetails">
  {topicrow.REPLIES}
  </span>
</td>
<td class="row2" align="center" valign="middle">
  <span class="name">
  {topicrow.TOPIC_AUTHOR}
  </span>
</td>
<td class="row2" align="center" valign="middle">
  <span class="postdetails">
  {topicrow.VIEWS}
  </span>
</td>
<td class="row3Right" align="center" valign="middle" nowrap="nowrap">
  <span class="postdetails">
  {topicrow.LAST_POST_TIME}
  <br />
  {topicrow.LAST_POST_AUTHOR} {topicrow.LAST_POST_IMG}
```

```
      </span>
   </td>
   </tr>
   <!-- END topicrow -->
```

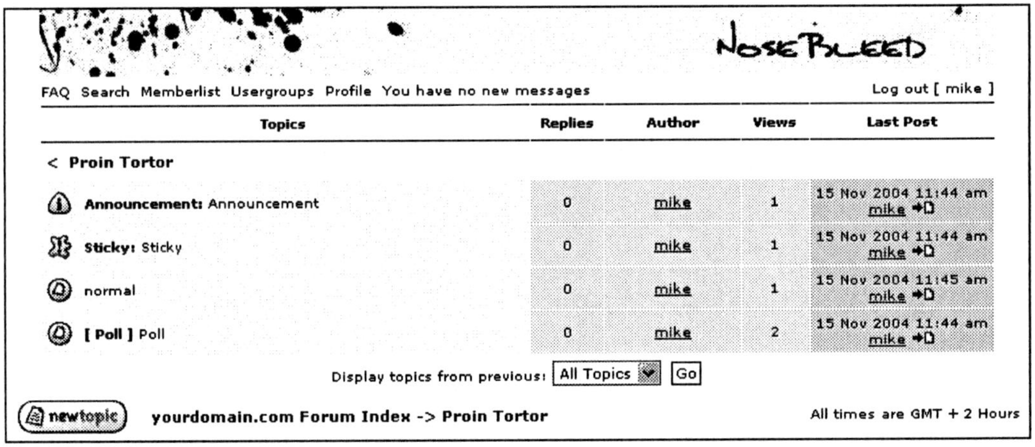

The next part of the table looks like this:

```
<!-- BEGIN switch_no_topics -->
<tr>
<td class="row1" colspan="6" height="30" align="center"
     valign="middle">
  <span class="gen">
  {L_NO_TOPICS}
  </span>
</td>
</tr>
<!-- END switch_no_topics -->
```

This is what will be displayed if there are no topics in the forum. Again, the font size is a little too big and there are two ways to change it; either change the `<span class="gen">` to `<span class="gensmall">`, or change the CSS of gen to use a different font size. Here, we do the latter since this template will probably always need the gen class to be a smaller size.

The table row looks empty and narrow as it is now, and so it needs to be a bit larger; we just add some line breaks here, and this part of the table is done:

```
<!-- BEGIN switch_no_topics -->
<tr>
<td class="row1" colspan="6" height="30" align="center"
valign="middle">
  <span class="gen">
  <br />
  {L_NO_TOPICS}
  <br />
  <br />
  </span>
</td>
```

```
</tr>
<!-- END switch_no_topics -->
```

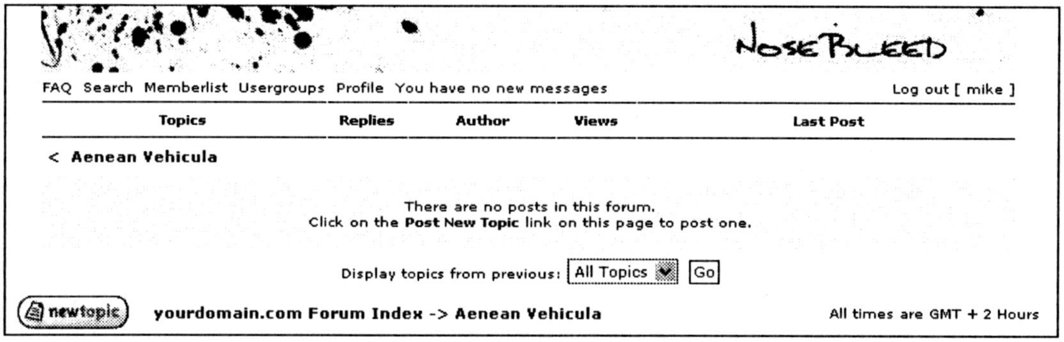

The last part of the table looks like this:

```
<tr>
<td class="catBottom" align="center" valign="middle" colspan="6"
height="28">
  <span class="genmed">
  {L_DISPLAY_TOPICS}: {S_SELECT_TOPIC_DAYS} <input
type="submit" class="liteoption" value="{L_GO}" name="submit" />
  </span>
</td>
</tr>
</table>
```

Instead of using the gray background colors of `row1`, `row2`, or `row3`, the table uses a class called `catBottom`. We find it in our CSS here:

```
td.cat,td.catHead,td.catSides,td.catLeft,td.catRight,td.catBottom {
  /*
  background-image: url(templates/subSilver/images/{T_TH_CLASS1});
  background-color:{T_TR_COLOR3};
  border: {T_TH_COLOR3};
  border-style: solid;
  */
  height: 28px;
}
```

We have already changed this code earlier when we removed the background color and image from our menu. We didn't need it then, and so we added the `/*` and `*/` comment markers around it. That was only for our `catLeft` and `catRight` classes, and now we need something different for our `catBottom`. To solve this, we must remove the `catBottom` class from this area and add it below with its own code:

```
td.cat,td.catHead,td.catSides,td.catLeft,td.catRight {
  /*
  background-image: url(templates/subSilver/images/{T_TH_CLASS1});
  background-color:{T_TR_COLOR3};
  border: {T_TH_COLOR3};
  border-style: solid;
  */
```

```
    height: 28px;
}
td.catBottom { background-color:{T_TR_COLOR3}; }
```

We give it the background color of {T_TR_COLOR3}, which is the same as row3, the darkest of the gray tones.

Fixing the Size of the Jump Menu

The last thing to fix in this table is the font size of the jump menu and the button next to it. The properties for both the jump menu and the button are under select and input in the CSS:

```
/* Form elements */
input,textarea, select {
  color : {T_BODY_TEXT};
  font: normal {T_FONTSIZE2}px {T_FONTFACE1};
  border-color : {T_BODY_TEXT};
}
```

All we need to do is change the font size to {T_FONTSIZE1}.

We align the td to the right instead of keeping it centered, to make the menu appear on the right side.

In the index_body.tpl file we had a table after the main table, and it looked like this:

```
<table width="717" cellspacing="0" border="0" align="center"
cellpadding="2">
<tr>
<td align="left">
  <span class="gensmall">
  <a href="{U_MARK_READ}" class="gensmall">{L_MARK_FORUMS_READ}</a>
  </span>
</td>
<td align="right">
  <span class="gensmall">
  {S_TIMEZONE}
  </span>
</td>
</tr>
</table>
```

We use this again, except that this time we change the {L_MARK_FORUMS_READ} variable to {L_MARK_TOPICS_READ}, and then paste it in here.

After this table in the index_body.tpl, came the table with the black lines above and below it, and it looked like this:

```
<table align="center" width="717" border="0" cellspacing="0"
cellpadding="0">
<tr height="10"><td></td></tr>
<tr>
<th colspan="2" class="thTop" height="25" nowrap="nowrap"><table
width="717" cellspacing="0" cellpadding="2" border="0"
align="center">
```

```
<tr>
<td align="left" valign="bottom">
  <span class="gensmall">
<!-- BEGIN switch_user_logged_in -->
  {LAST_VISIT_DATE}
  <br />
<!-- END switch_user_logged_in -->
  {CURRENT_TIME}
  <br />
  </span>
  <span class="nav">
  <a href="{U_INDEX}" class="nav">{L_INDEX}</a>
  </span>
</td>
<td align="right" valign="bottom" class="gensmall">
<!-- BEGIN switch_user_logged_in -->
  <a href="{U_SEARCH_NEW}" class="gensmall">{L_SEARCH_NEW}</a>
  <br />
  <a href="{U_SEARCH_SELF}" class="gensmall">{L_SEARCH_SELF}</a>
  <br />
<!-- END switch_user_logged_in -->
  <a href="{U_SEARCH_UNANSWERED}"
class="gensmall">{L_SEARCH_UNANSWERED}</a>
</td>
</tr>
</table></th>
</tr>
<tr height="10"><td></td></tr>
</table>
```

We copy this table from `index.tpl` and paste it in here. Instead of using the variables used there, we use the ones we have from the original first table (the table that was earlier moved to the end of the file). The table then looks like:

```
<table align="center" width="717" border="0" cellspacing="0"
cellpadding="2">
<tr height="10"><td></td></tr>
<tr>
<th colspan="2" class="thTop" height="25" nowrap="nowrap">
<table align="left" width="100%" border="0" cellspacing="0"
cellpadding="0">
<tr>
<td align="left" valign="top">
  <span class="gensmall">
  {L_MODERATOR}: {MODERATORS}
  <br />
  {LOGGED_IN_USER_LIST}
  </span>
</td>
<td align="right" valign="top">
  <span class="gensmall">
  {PAGE_NUMBER}
  <br />
  {PAGINATION}
  </span>
</td>
</tr>
```

```
<tr align="left" valign="top">
<td colspan="2">
  <span class="nav">
  <a href="{U_INDEX}" class="nav">{L_INDEX}</a>
    ~  
  <a class="nav" href="{U_VIEW_FORUM}">{FORUM_NAME}</a>
  </span>
</td>
</tr>
</table>
</th>
</tr>
<tr height="10"><td></td></tr>
</table>
```

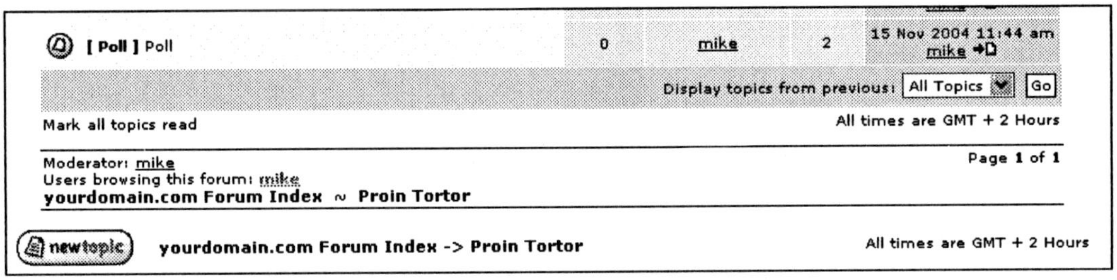

The next table looks like this:

```
<table width="100%" cellspacing="2" border="0" align="center"
        cellpadding="2">
<tr>
<td align="left" valign="middle" width="50">
  <a href="{U_POST_NEW_TOPIC}"><img src="{POST_IMG}" border="0"
alt="{L_POST_NEW_TOPIC}" /></a>
</td>
<td align="left" valign="middle" width="100%">
  <span class="nav">
     
  <a href="{U_INDEX}" class="nav">{L_INDEX}</a> -> <a class="nav"
href="{U_VIEW_FORUM}">{FORUM_NAME}</a>
  </span>
</td>
<td align="right" valign="middle" nowrap="nowrap">
  <span class="gensmall">
  {S_TIMEZONE}
  </span>
  <br />
  <span class="nav">
  {PAGINATION}
  </span>
</td>
</tr>
<tr>
<td align="left" colspan="3">
  <span class="nav">
  {PAGE_NUMBER}
  </span>
```

```
</td>
</tr>
</table>
</form>
```

This table contains the New Topic button and the end tag of the form, but we do not really need to use the other variables again, and can cut down the table to this:

```
<table width="715" align="center" border="0" cellspacing="0"
cellpadding="0">
<tr>
<td>
  <a href="{U_POST_NEW_TOPIC}"><img src="{POST_IMG}" border="0"
alt="{L_POST_NEW_TOPIC}" /></a>
</td>
</tr>
</table>
</form>
```

Then we have the table with the jump box. We only need to change the width and the alignment, but here again we add an extra table row with a height of ten pixels, just to get some space between the different areas.

The last table displays the icons and the list of what the user can do in this topic, and we only fix the width for now.

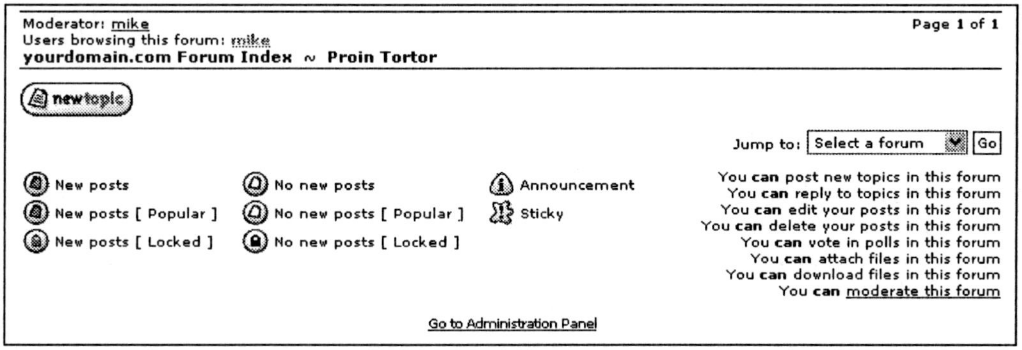

And this leads us to the end of `viewforum_body.tpl`.

And the Story Continues

The rest of the `.tpl` files need the same kind of editing: locate the class in the CSS, copy the tables from previously edited files whenever possible, and use the phpBB variables specific for the `.tpl` you are working with. You should have a pretty good idea of how to do this by now, and instead of explaining every `.tpl` in detail for the rest of the chapter, we will sum up their functions here.

Starting from the first file throughout the `NoseBleed` folder:

agreement.tpl

This is the first page forum visitors encounter when they want to register. It explains the registration agreement terms and checks for the visitor's age.

bbcode.tpl

This is the file that phpBB uses to display quotes and code, e-mail links, images in posts, URLs, and more. If, for example, you do not like the way quotes are displayed, this is the file you need to edit.

confirm_body.tpl

This file is displayed if the user has to confirm something with either 'yes' or 'no'.

error_body.tpl

This file displays error messages.

faq_body.tpl

This file displays the FAQ section.

forumIE.css

This is for additional CSS code, with IE-specific formatting definitions.

groupcp_info_body.tpl

This file displays usergroup information and members.

groupcp_pending_info.tpl

This file displays to the group moderators for them to allow or forbid pending users to join the usergroup.

groupcp_user_body.tpl

This file displays an overview of all the usergroups, as well as *which* usergroup the user belongs to.

index.htm

This file displays an image made by the designer of the template. It is included and displayed to prevent visitors of the site from viewing the files in the folder.

index_body.tpl

This is the main page for your forum.

jumpbox.tpl

This file displays the jump box.

login_body.tpl

This file displays the way the forum looks when someone wants to log in.

memberlist_body.tpl

This file displays the registered users of the forum.

message_body.tpl

This file displays a confirmation message from phpBB to the user; e.g., after changing your profile and clicking the submit button, you will be shown this file, to confirm that your profile has been updated.

modcp_body.tpl

This file is used when a moderator wants to moderate a post.

modcp_move.tpl

This file is used when a moderator wants to move a topic.

modcp_split.tpl

This file is used when a moderator wants to split a topic.

modcp_viewip.tpl

This file is used when a moderator wants to see the IP number of the user that posted the selected post.

subSilver.tpl

This is the configuration file of your template and should be renamed to the template's name, e.g. `NoseBleed.tpl`. It tells phpBB where it can find the different images and icons for the template.

subSilver.css

This is the CSS file of the template, and should be renamed to the template's name if you want to reuse it. By default, it is not being used; instead, the CSS code is located at the beginning of the `overall_header.tpl` file. Later, in *Final Touches* section of this chapter, you will see how to move the CSS to its own file, which is something you might want to do if you are trying to save bandwidth.

overall_footer.tpl

This file is displayed at the bottom of almost all pages. It contains the link to the Admin Panel and the phpBB copyright note.

overall_header.tpl

This file is displayed at the top of almost all pages. By default it has the CSS code at the beginning of the file.

posting_body.tpl

This file displays when the user is posting a new post. It also contains JavaScript code for a pop-up window, used when the user wants to see all the emoticons he or she can use in the post.

posting_poll_body.tpl

This file displays how to add a poll to the post, and is loaded from `posting_body.tpl` with the variable `{POLLBOX}`.

posting_preview.tpl

This file displays how a preview of the post looks, and is loaded from `posting_body.tpl` with the variable `{POST_PREVIEW_BOX}`.

posting_smilies.tpl

This file displays in the pop-up window all the emoticons that a user can use in his or her post. This file uses `simple_header.tpl` and `simple_footer.tpl` instead of `overall_header.tpl` and `overall_footer.tpl`.

posting_topic_review.tpl

This file appears in an iframe in `posting_body.tpl`, using the `{TOPIC_REVIEW_BOX}` variable. This file uses `simple_header.tpl` and `simple_footer.tpl` instead of `overall_header.tpl` and `overall_footer.tpl`.

privmsgs_body.tpl

This file displays all your private messages.

privmsgs_popup.tpl

Whenever a user receives a new private message, a small pop-up window telling him or her about it will appear when he or she visits the forum.

This file uses `simple_header.tpl` and `simple_footer.tpl` instead of `overall_header.tpl` and `overall_footer.tpl`.

privmsgs_preview.tpl

This file displays a preview of your private message, loaded from `posting_body.tpl` with the `{POST_PREVIEW_BOX}` variable.

privmsgs_read_body.tpl

This file displays when a user is reading a private message.

profile_add_body.tpl

This file displays when a visitor registers, and it is used to gather information like username, password, location, etc. This file is also displayed if the user wants to change his or her profile settings.

profile_avatar_gallery.tpl

This file displays a list of avatars that the user can choose from, to add to his or her profile setting.

profile_send_email.tpl

This file displays when a user is sending an e-mail to another user of the forum.

profile_send_pass.tpl

This file displays how to retrieve a forgotten password.

profile_view_body.tpl

This file displays the profile of a registered user.

search_body.tpl

This file displays when a user is searching a post or topic.

search_results_posts.tpl

This file displays only a list of posts containing the searched for word or expression.

search_results_topics.tpl

This file displays only a list of topics containing the searched for word or expression.

search_username.tpl

This file displays, in a pop-up window, when searching for a username. It is loaded from `posting_body.tpl` with the variable `{U_SEARCH_USER}`. This file uses `simple_header.tpl` and `simple_footer.tpl` instead of `overall_header.tpl` and `overall_footer.tpl`.

simple_footer.tpl

This file replaces the `overall_footer.tpl` in pop-up windows and iframes.

simple_header.tpl

This file replaces the `overall_header.tpl` in popup windows and iframes. Sometimes, copying the CSS from `overall_header.tpl` and pasting it into `simple_header.tpl` is enough to make the look of the pop-up windows and iframes match the rest of the template.

theme_info.cfg

This is the configuration file for the template. The first time it is installed, the template uses the default values of colors, fonts, etc., from this file. If you plan on releasing your templates for other people, be sure you have the correct values in this file. You do not need to type all these values in manually. If you go to the Admin Panel, under Styles Admin and select Export, phpBB will create a new `theme_info.cfg` file with all the font and color settings from the Admin Panel. You can download and use this file instead.

viewforum_body.tpl

This file displays the list of topics in the selected forum.

viewonline_body.tpl

This file displays the list of users and guests on the forum.

viewtopic_body.tpl

This file displays the topics on your forum.

viewtopic_poll_ballot.tpl

This file displays the poll ballot in the topic. It is loaded from `viewtopic_body.tpl` with the `{POLL_DISPLAY}` variable.

viewtopic_poll_result.tpl

This file displays the result of the poll in the topic. It is loaded from `viewtopic_body.tpl` with the `{POLL_DISPLAY}` variable.

The Admin Folder

The files in the `admin` folder of the template control how the Admin Panel is displayed. They use `page_header.tpl` and `page_footer.tpl` instead of `overall_header.tpl` and `overall_footer.tpl`. Sometimes, copying the CSS from `overall_header.tpl` and pasting it into `page_header.tpl` is enough to make the Admin Panel match the rest of the template.

Icons and Images

All the icons and images of the template are located in the `images` folder. This folder contains another folder, which contains the specific language images. There is one thing to notice here: the icon for Delete is universal and is displayed only by an X in the image. If we want our image to display actual text such as Delete instead, we should place the image in the specific language folder, in this case the `lang_english` folder. Since phpBB will not look for the Delete image in the language folder, we need to edit the `NoseBleed.cfg` file. Going down in the code we find this:

```
$images['icon_delpost'] = "$current_template_images/icon_delete.gif";
```

This is the path phpBB is using for this image. Adding the `{LANG}`language variable, we can specify the new path:

```
$images['icon_delpost'] =
"$current_template_images/{LANG}/icon_delete.gif";
```

Making all the new images and icons might scare off many people, but there is a bright side to this: we do not have to start from scratch.

At `http://www.phpbb.com/downloads.php#subSilver` the original SDK files can be downloaded, and then edited with Photoshop, GIMP, Paint Shop Pro, and other programs. An easy solution if we are only interested in changing the font color, font size or background.

For the `NoseBleed` template, this file is downloaded and the font and the background of the icons changed, but the little icons for the language buttons are kept the same.

To simplify the use of icons and images even more, all the icons that are used for no new topics are changed into blank GIF files; only new topics will have an icon. We've also removed the no new topic icons from the `index_body.tpl` and `viewforum_body.tpl` files explanation, since they were just blank icons now.

Final Touches

The template is pretty much finished now, and the only thing left to do is test it for errors and optimize it. Remember to check for links pointing to the `subSilver` directory, since these need to be changed to our new template folder.

We can also change the administrator and moderator colors on the index page with Font Color 2 and Font Color 3 in the Admin Panel.

One way to optimize the template is to place the CSS in its own file, saving us bandwidth and making the forum load faster. For this, open the forum in your browser, right-click somewhere on the site, and select View Source (in IE) or View | Source or Sourcecode (in other browsers). Copy all the CSS code between the `<style type="text/css">` and `</style>` tags and paste it into the CSS file of the template. Upload the new CSS file and delete the CSS code from the `overall_header.tpl`. At the top of the `overall_header.tpl`, you'll find:

```
<!-- link rel="stylesheet"
href="templates/subSilver/{T_HEAD_STYLESHEET}" type="text/css" -->
```

... which you need to change to:

```
<link rel="stylesheet" href="templates/NoseBleed/{T_HEAD_STYLESHEET}"
      type="text/css">
```

The `{T_HEAD_STYLESHEET}` variable uses the default name of the CSS file, in this case `NoseBleed.css`. If you want to name the CSS file something else, replace this variable with the name of the CSS file you want to use instead.

Summary

We have covered a lot of things, and yet we have only just begun. The HTML, JavaScript, and CSS code explained in this chapter is merely just a narrow introduction. With continued work, you will discover new tricks and gain more knowledge, resulting in even better coding. However, I hope that by now you have gained the basic skills and courage to make your own templates. It might seem like an overwhelming task, and there is no doubt that it will take some time to complete, but when you first get started you will see that it is not so difficult.

There are several active template development communities where you can always find help, comments, and people to test your templates; both the phpBB community at `http://www.phpbb.com/phpBB/` and the phpBBHacks.com support forums at `http://www.phpbbhacks.com/forums/` are places with very helpful people.

7

Creating a New MOD

As your community grows, you may find that you need to expand the capabilities of your forum. You might need to introduce new BBCode tags, file attachments, photo galleries, or some new administration tool. Almost anything that you would need can be added by installing a modification, as you learned in Chapter 4. The key word here is *almost*. Eventually you may need a feature and find yourself unable to locate an existing modification for it. When this happens, you have two options: ask someone for help in locating a modification or create a new one yourself. In this chapter, you will learn:

- What modifications are
- Skills and tools you need to create a modification
- How to create a simple modification
- Ways to make your modification available to other phpBB users

Introduction to MODs and Hacks

As you may recall from Chapter 4, modifications are most commonly known as **MODs** or **Hacks**, and are downloads containing files that add, remove, or alter features on a phpBB forum. You also learned that there are thousands of modifications available for download and how to install a modification on your forum. These things were presented to you from the viewpoint of a modification *user*, but now it is time to look at them from the flip side, as a MOD or Hack *author*.

The most basic form of a standard modification is a simple text file containing instructions for editing a forum's files. These instructions are typically formatted using a modification template, consisting of a header and list of actions. Slightly more complex modifications also have commands for editing the forum database in the same file or a SQL query installer such as a `db_update.php` file. Modifications that are even more complex include new forum files as well. All of the files are placed together in a compressed archive file (usually a ZIP file) and are made available for download on the World Wide Web.

Before You Begin

To create a modification, you need to have some skills and tools to make development and testing of modifications easier. Your exact needs will depend on the scope and purpose of the modifications you develop. Smaller modifications generally require a more basic setup, but large modifications are sometimes better left to professionals.

Building Your Skillset

As you already know, phpBB operates on a combination of four programming languages: PHP: Hypertext Preprocessor, Structured Query Language (SQL), Hypertext Markup Language (HTML), and JavaScript. If you have never heard of these before, don't worry! You do not have to be a highly experienced programmer to start creating modifications. Many people have actually learned the basics of programming by working with phpBB. As you develop modifications, you will become more familiar with phpBB and these languages. Essentially, you can (and will) learn as you go.

PHP: Hypertext Preprocessor, better known simply as PHP, is the main programming language used for almost every task in phpBB. As you may have noticed, *php*BB is even named after this language. Every file in your forum that has a name ending in `.php` contains PHP code, as do a few other files. Knowledge of PHP is one of the most essential skills in creating modifications, so you may want to take the time to locate and read some tutorials on basic PHP programming. You will also want to bookmark the online PHP manual, located at `http://www.php.net/manual/`. The manual is also available for download and is useful for offline work. Take the time to read the first three to four chapters of the manual. They focus on important details like code syntax that you will see time and time again.

Structured Query Language, or SQL, is coding used to access an SQL database. Your forum's PHP files use **SQL queries** (or commands written in SQL coding) to store information in, and later retrieve it from, several database tables. If you want to create a modification that tracks some data, like a page hit counter, you will need to know how to write some SQL queries. You should try to locate a manual for your site's database software to learn the correct structure of queries. Most software will support an official standard form of SQL, but may add unique extensions to the standard. The manual for MySQL, which is the most popular database choice for phpBB, is available at `http://www.mysql.com/`.

Hypertext Markup Language is not really a programming language. As the name suggests, HTML is used for marking up the display of documents. In this case, those documents are forum pages. You learned in Chapter 4 that HTML code, or that of another markup language, used to display your forum is stored in template files located within directories such as `templates/subSilver`. The closest thing you can find to a manual for HTML is the World Wide Web Consortium's HTML 4.01 specification at `http://www.w3.org/TR/html401`. There is an abundance of easier to understand HTML tutorials that can be located through any major search engine, however.

Lastly, **JavaScript** is a client-side scripting language that phpBB uses for certain types of user interaction. Client-side scripting languages are programming languages that run on the remote user's computer, even though the code is located on your website. JavaScript code will be run within the confines of the viewer's web browser and is therefore not something you can always rely on.

Most modern web browsers have features that allow disabling of JavaScript or certain JavaScript operations. Several older browsers do not support JavaScript at all. Most modifications do not use JavaScript code, but some are based entirely on JavaScript. As with HTML, there are many online tutorials and websites devoted entirely to teaching aspects of this language.

Beyond the programming languages, you will also need a passing familiarity with the purpose of each phpBB file. This is one skill that will definitely be formed as you work with phpBB, but there are some online resources in phpBB communities that will be helpful. In those communities, you will also find members that are experienced MOD and Hack authors. Some of them can often give useful advice on a wide range of issues related to these subjects, so do not hesitate to ask for help if you need it.

The Right Tools for the Job

Anyone can create a new modification, but it will be much easier if you have the right materials and working environment. Most authors use specialized tools that provide many helpful features. There are several types of resources you should get if you plan to create many modifications.

The first and most important resource is phpBB itself. Many authors will create a second phpBB installation, sometimes on their own computers, for testing and developing code. One benefit of this approach is that any problems arising during the development will not affect a live website that people are currently visiting. Greater control of the testing environment is usually another factor that authors favor.

The downside of creating a phpBB installation on your own computer is that you might have to install several other pieces of software first. Those include a web server program, such as Apache, the PHP language, an SQL database package, and possibly other software as well. Some authors will use a package that contains more than one of these. For example, EasyPHP from `http://www.easyphp.org` installs and manages Apache, PHP, and MySQL. With all three of those installed, you should be able to install phpBB.

It is always a good idea to keep a completely unaltered copy of phpBB on hand for backups and reference. You should make certain you are working with the latest version of phpBB 2.0 to ensure that you have the most secure and up-to-date code. On the other hand, keep in mind that not all communities are based on the latest phpBB version. Over eleven updates to phpBB 2.0 have been released and some people do not have the time to upgrade with each release.

If you release the modification to the public, some of those forum administrators may try to use it and ask you for help if they encounter a problem in that phpBB version. For these reasons, you may also want to have copies of older phpBB versions around, even if you do not test your modification on those versions. Every release of phpBB can be downloaded from the following web pages:

- The phpBB Project Filelist on SourceForge: `http://sourceforge.net/project/showfiles.php?group_id=7885`
- phpBBHacks' phpBB downloads: `http://www.phpbbhacks.com/phpbbinfo.php`

When developing your modification, ensure that you do so using an unmodified installation of phpBB. If you create the modification on a forum where other modifications have already been installed, those modifications may adversely affect the development process. They may add code that causes your modification to behave differently than if those modifications were absent. Since you cannot anticipate what modifications have already been installed on another person's forum, distributing a modification developed on a hacked phpBB installation is an invitation to problems. You might also accidentally include code from another modification in your own modification's installation file. That can cause any number of unexpected reactions.

> It is possible that you might develop a modification that *does require* the presence of another, such as a portal add-on block. In such cases, only the absolutely required modifications should be installed on your testing forum.

Another very important tool to use is a good program for editing phpBB files. For the simple work of installing a modification like that in Chapter 4, Microsoft WordPad was all you needed. You can continue to use WordPad for this chapter, but if you intend to develop several modifications, you will probably want something with a wider range of useful features.

There are many text-editing programs that have syntax-highlighting features that make coding much easier. With syntax highlighting, different aspects of code are displayed in different colors. This feature can allow you to spot incorrect code just by looking at the colors used in a file. Other features like multiple line searching, find and replace, or code auto-completion can also save time. You can find listings and reviews for many text-editing programs with these features at the PHP-Editors site, `http://www.php-editors.com/`.

> Microsoft WordPad will be sufficient for completing the examples presented in this chapter.

Creating a Simple MOD: A New BBCode Tag

One of the best ways to learn is through hands-on experience, so now it is time for you to create your very first phpBB modification. As you follow along in this section, you will progress through the entire process of creating modifications. Since this is your first modification, the focus will be on adding a simple but useful new feature: a new BBCode tag. Modifications of this type have been in development since the very early releases of phpBB. You will follow the same process that has traditionally been used to create many BBCode tags over the years. If you downloaded this modification from a website, it would be just a single file of instructions, without any extra files or database alterations.

Step 1—Determine Your Goal

The first step of any project is to figure out exactly what it is you intend to achieve. Maybe you want to rearrange the display of topics. Or perhaps add a new entry in the registration form. Whatever you choose, you need to know what you are trying to do before you can actually do it.

As you now know, the goal of this modification will be to add a new BBCode tag to your forum. By installing BBCode modifications, you give forum members new ways of formatting their posts. phpBB includes BBCodes for bold, italic, and underlined text, text colors and sizes, images, bulleted and numbered lists, and several other formatting options when first installed. You can download modifications for dozens of different new tags. Some examples include glowing, shadowed, highlighted, moving, and blinking text. The [s] BBCode tag that we will add to the forum creates struck-through text, which is a series of normal words with a line through the middle of each character. The effect of the Strike BBCode can be seen in the following screenshot:

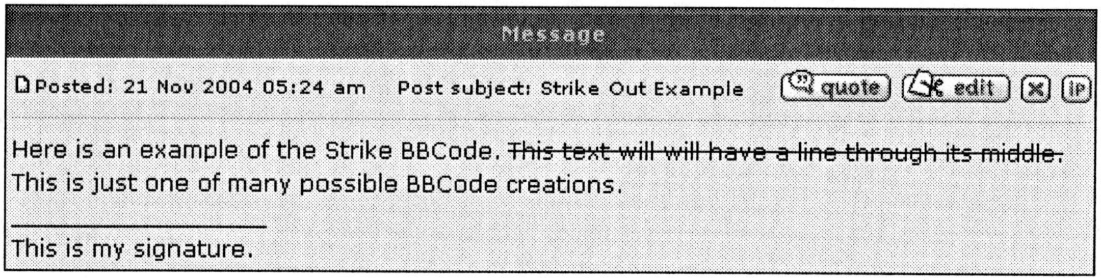

Step 2—Plan Your Database Changes

When creating a modification that tracks some new kind of information, you'll usually have to edit or create a database table through SQL queries. The Strike BBCode does not require any database changes, but this is such an important part of modification creation that it still needs to be addressed. The types of database changes that an author decides to make often determine the remaining structure of the modification.

There are generally three types of database changes used in most modifications: adding a new database table column, adding an entire database table, and adding new data into a table. Which of these changes you make will depend very much on what the modification does. If you are simply adding a new field to user registration and profiles, you would add a new column to the users database table, typically called `phpbb_users`. To record information about the websites people visited before reaching your forum, you would need a new database table. When your modification has configuration features that should be changed in the Administration Control Panel, adding new data to the `phpbb_config` table would be expected.

All of your database changes can be made using phpMyAdmin or similar database-management software. You can either write your own SQL queries and execute them through phpMyAdmin's SQL tab, or accomplish the same ends through a series of point and click operations that phpMyAdmin provides.

Step 3—Choose Your Files

Your modification will need to edit phpBB files, and possibly add new ones, to accomplish your goal. At this point, you need to decide which files are the best ones to edit, and make backups of those files. If your modification needs to add new files, you need to decide what each file will be named and where it will be placed within phpBB's directory structure. Certain types of new files will need to be located in certain places. If you need to add a new section to the Administration Control Panel, for instance, you will have to add at least one file in phpBB's `admin` directory. The Appendices of this book include descriptions of the phpBB files and directories that should be helpful in this step.

To add a BBCode tag, including our Strike BBCode, only two files need to be edited: `includes/bbcode.php` and `templates/subSilver/bbcode.tpl`. These files manage all BBCode operations in phpBB. `bbcode.tpl` contains HTML code for each BBCode tag in a special format, and `bbcode.php` replaces BBCode tags with that HTML code in posts. The latter file also does any special processing needed to format text correctly.

However, we will also edit some other files. If you have made a post on any phpBB forum, you have undoubtedly noted the posting form contained special buttons that, when clicked, inserted BBCode tags into the posting form. Forum members love these buttons, so we will add one for the Strike BBCode too. Three other files will need to be edited for this: `posting.php`, `language/lang_english/lang_main.php`, and `templates/subSilver/posting_body.tpl`. The following screenshot shows a final version of the posting form after adding a Strike button:

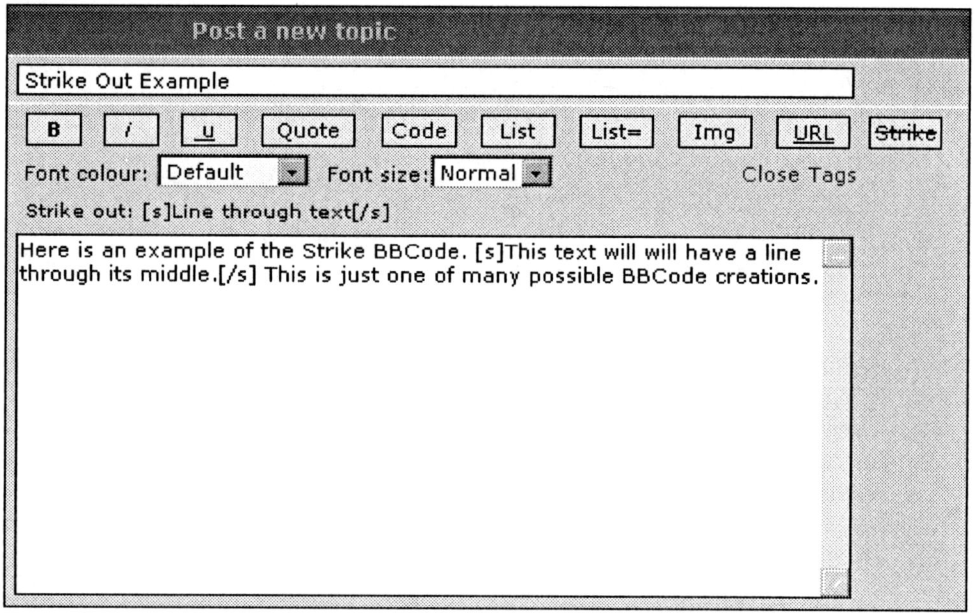

Step 4—File Editing and Creation

At last, the good part. During this step, you should be editing the existing phpBB files chosen in the previous step and creating any new files needed. The new files would be filled with code to create whatever type of effects might be needed by the modification. Since the Strike BBCode does not need any new files, we can focus on altering those listed in Step 3. As you'll see, this step can be quite long for even a simple modification. To create the Strike BBCode, you will need to do the following:

- Develop code to process the BBCode tags in posts
- Modify existing HTML code that will replace the tags in the posts
- Build a button for the posting form, complete with a mouse-hover tool tip
- Learn how and why each step is included
- Examine some alternative methods of creating the Strike BBCode

> When creating or editing PHP files, it is a good idea to follow phpBB's coding standards. Doing so makes your code easier for others to read and use. A copy of these guidelines is included in phpBB downloads and can also be found online at `http://area51.phpbb.com/docs/guide-coding.html`.

The first file to edit, `includes/bbcode.php`, processes BBCode tags once before a post is inserted into the database, and then again each time the post is displayed. Several **PHP functions** are used to accomplish this. Functions are snippets of code used to perform a task, usually one that needs to be repeated often or used in several different places. A basic function might look like the following example:

```
function do_some_thing($string)
{
    // Lines of code inside the function perform some task
    $string = 'Some random text';
    return $string;
}
```

This is a very simple function named `do_some_thing()`. It merely stores the words `Some random text` in a variable called `$string`, and then returns the value of `$string` to the code that uses the function. You can recognize functions by their first line of code, which always starts with the word `function`. This is followed by the name of the function, in turn followed by a set of parentheses that may contain arguments (if any). A **variable** is a name for a piece of data or other value of some sort. Variables always begin with a **dollar sign**, $. Some functions in `bbcode.php` include `load_bbcode_template()`, `prepare_bbcode_template()`, `bbencode_second_pass()`, `bbencode_first_pass()`, and `make_clickable()`. Many of the functions are preceded by **comment lines**, which describe the purpose of the code without actually affecting anything.

The `bbencode_second_pass()` and `bbencode_first_pass()` functions contain code that must be expanded to add any BBCode tag. `bbencode_first_pass()` must add a special, unique identification string to each BBCode tag in every post before that message is placed into the forum's database for later retrieval. `bbencode_second_pass()` will replace the altered BBCode tag with matching HTML stored in `bbcode.tpl`. You need to add some code so that each function recognizes the Strike BBCode. Since `bbencode_second_pass()` is actually listed before `bbencode_first_pass()` in the file, you should edit `bbencode_second_pass()` first. This is not really a requirement, but editing files in a "top to bottom" manner is usually a good practice.

Time For Action—The First Edit

1. Locate the following lines within the `bbencode_second_pass()` function of `includes/bbcode.php`. It is the only place these lines appear in the file together:

```
// [u] and [/u] for underlining text.
$text = str_replace("[u:$uid]", $bbcode_tpl['u_open'], $text);
$text = str_replace("[/u:$uid]", $bbcode_tpl['u_close'], $text);
```

2. Highlight (or select) these lines. Copy them and paste a duplicate set of lines into the file beneath the existing lines. The code should now look like this (after our duplication):

```
$text = str_replace("[/b:$uid]", $bbcode_tpl['b_close'], $text);

// [u] and [/u] for underlining text.
$text = str_replace("[u:$uid]", $bbcode_tpl['u_open'], $text);
```

```
$text = str_replace("[/u:$uid]", $bbcode_tpl['u_close'], $text);
```

```
// [u] and [/u] for underlining text.
$text = str_replace("[u:$uid]", $bbcode_tpl['u_open'], $text);
$text = str_replace("[/u:$uid]", $bbcode_tpl['u_close'], $text);
```

```
// [i] and [/i] for italicizing text.
```

3. In the first duplicated line, replace the tags `[u]` and `[/u] for underlining` with the `[s]` and `[/s] for strike` out.
4. Within the second duplicated line, change `[u:$uid]` to `[s:$uid]` and `u_open` to `s_open`.
5. Alter the third duplicate line's `[/u:$uid]` to read `[/s:$uid]` and `u_close` to `s_close`. Your duplicate lines should look like these examples when fully edited:

```
// [s] and [/s] for strike out text.
$text = str_replace("[s:$uid]", $bbcode_tpl['s_open'], $text);
$text = str_replace("[/s:$uid]", $bbcode_tpl['s_close'], $text);
```

What Just Happened?

You have now finished making the alterations needed for the `bbencode_second_pass()` function to work with your Strike BBCode tag. With this done, let us take a moment to look at the lines you have changed and some important points about them.

The lines that you duplicated are part of the Underline BBCode tag. Duplicating the lines allows you to maintain a working Underline BBCode while altering the second set of lines to create Strike. The Strike BBCode is actually very similar to Underline, so you will use lines of code related to that as a basis for many of the coming file alterations as well. Each line will become a unique part of the Strike BBCode as it is transformed by the changes you make.

The first line you made a copy of and then edited was:

```
// [u] and [/u] for underlining text.
```

A pair of forward slashes, `//`, at the beginning of this line mark it as a comment line. This particular comment line says that the next two lines are dealing with the opening and closing underline BBCode tags, or `[u]` and `[/u]`. You replaced the tags `[u] and [/u] for underlining` in the comment with the tags `[s] and [/s] for strike` out. Now the comment line has been updated to reflect the changes that will follow for the other copied lines.

The other two lines are PHP code that is used to process posts before they are displayed on your forum, and as such can be rather delicate things. Make certain that your final lines match the examples given exactly. If you edit these in the wrong way, you may see an error message on your forum later. Be especially careful with the double and single quotation marks and the `$uid` variables. These should not be changed at all when editing these lines.

The [s:$uid] and [/s:$uid] edits are related to the BBCode format that will allow users to access the Strike BBCode, [s] and [/s]. That may not have been clear when editing the lines, but you should see the correlation now. The s_open and s_close edits are also significant, but their exact purpose is best examined later when you have edited bbcode.tpl.

Time For Action—The Second Edit

1. Locate the following lines within the bbencode_first_pass() function of includes/bbcode.php. Again, this is the only place the lines appear in the file in this direct order.

```
// [u] and [/u] for underlining text.
$text = preg_replace("#\[u\](.*?)\[/u\]#si",
"[u:$uid]\\1[/u:$uid]",
                              $text);
```

2. Duplicate the lines in the same manner as the previous *Time For Action.*
3. Locate the comment line identical to that of the earlier code. Edit it in the same way as described in the previous *Time For Action* example. After doing this, your file should resemble the following.

```
$text = preg_replace("#\[b\](.*?)\[/b\]#si",
"[b:$uid]\\1[/b:$uid]",
                              $text);

// [u] and [/u] for underlining text.
$text = preg_replace("#\[u\](.*?)\[/u\]#si",
"[u:$uid]\\1[/u:$uid]",
                              $text);

// [s] and [/s] for strike out text.
$text = preg_replace("#\[u\](.*?)\[/u\]#si",
"[u:$uid]\\1[/u:$uid]", $text);

// [i] and [/i] for italicizing text.
```

4. On the second line duplicated here, change [u\] to [s\], [/u\] to [/s\], and [u:$uid]\\1[/u:$uid] to [s:$uid]\\1[/s:$uid]. Now fully altered, these lines will be:

```
// [s] and [/s] for strike out text.
$text = preg_replace("#\[s\](.*?)\[/s\]#si",
"[s:$uid]\\1[/s:$uid]", $text);
```

What Just Happened?

After completing the changes to bbencode_second_pass(), you have now moved on to the bbencode_first_pass() function. Here we again used existing code of the Underline BBCode as the basis of your Strike BBCode. You saw another comment line identical to that in the first set of changes in this file and also altered it in the same manner as the other.

Only one other line was edited here, and this important line will process posts containing the Strike BBCode tags before the posts are stored in the forum's SQL database. The main purpose of the line is to add the `$uid` variables to the tags for later reference. You need not worry about this too much, but be aware that it is one of phpBB's many built-in security measures. When displaying posts, phpBB will treat those without a `$uid` added here as plain text.

That was the last change required in `includes/bbcode.php`. Now you are ready to move on to the second file to be edited, `templates/subSilver/bbcode.tpl`. This file contains several snippets of HTML code that create the visual effects of each BBCode. The functions stored in `includes/bbcode.php` read this file and replace the BBCode tags like `[s]` and `[/s]` with snippets.

Time For Action—Editing BBCode HTML

1. Locate the following lines in `templates/subSilver/bbcode.tpl`:

```
<!-- BEGIN u_open --><span style="text-decoration: underline"><!--
END u_open -->
<!-- BEGIN u_close --></span><!-- END u_close -->
```

2. Copy these lines and paste a duplicate set into the file, just as you did with the `includes/bbcode.php`.
3. Replace both instances of `u_open` in the first duplicate line with `s_open`.
4. On the same line, replace `underline` with `line-through`.
5. On the second line, change both occurrences of `u_close` to `s_close`.
6. The final, complete code should be:

```
<!-- BEGIN s_open --><span style="text-decoration: line-through"><!--
END s_open -->
<!-- BEGIN s_close --></span><!-- END s_close -->
```

What Just Happened?

To create the HTML that will be displayed in place of the Strike BBCode's `[s]` and `[/s]` tags, we once again used the existing code for the Underline BBCode. If you take a moment to look at the other code snippets in this file, you may notice that most of them begin with some text like `<!-- BEGIN u_open -->` and end with text similar to `<!-- END u_close -->`. These are HTML comments, as marked by the `<!--` and `-->` character sequences. phpBB uses these comments to mark the beginning and ending of each snippet of code for a single BBCode tag. For the Underline BBCode, `[u]` is replaced with the `u_open` code and `[/u]` is replaced with the `u_close` code. You may also remember editing `u_open` and `u_close` in the `includes/bbcode.php` file, where you changed them to `s_open` and `s_close` respectively. As a result, `s_open` and `s_close` must also be used in the HTML comments here.

One more change was needed here, and it creates the actual striking effect. The Underline BBCode uses a Cascading Style Sheet property called `text-decoration` to draw a line below text. The code for this is `text-decoration: underline`. The text-decoration property also supports a value of *line-through*, which renders text with a line marked horizontally through the middle. So, by changing `underline` in your `s_open` line to *line-through*, you created the Strike BBCode.

This completes the changes required to use the Strike BBCode; you can now make posts on your forum using the `[s]` and `[/s]` tags. However, you would have to type the tags in manually. Many, if not most, forum users prefer the point-and-click convenience of buttons in the posting form over manual entry of BBCode tags, so now you should create a new button for the Strike BBCode.

To start, we can look at the components of a BBCode button. Each button does two things: insert the BBCode tags into the message body when clicked, and display a line of help text, between the BBCode controls and the message area, when hovered over with the mouse pointer. The majority of the code for these tasks is in `templates/subSilver/posting_body.tpl`, but the help text is partially set up in `language/lang_english/lang_main.php` and `posting.php`. The latter two files have very small changes, so it is easiest to edit them first.

Time For Action—Adding a Language String

1. Find the following line in your forum's `language/lang_english/lang_main.php` file. Duplicate it as you have with other lines in previous examples:

```
$lang['bbcode_f_help'] = 'Font size: [size=x-small]small
text[/size]';
```

2. Change the `bbcode_f_help` portion of the line to `bbcode_st_help`.
3. Replace the text between the last two single quotes with: `Strike out: [s]Line through text[/s] (alt+t)`.
4. The altered line now appears as:

```
$lang['bbcode_st_help'] = 'Strike out: [s]Line through text[/s]
(alt+t)';
```

What Just Happened?

Most of the built-in text that's displayed on the public portions of a phpBB forum is stored in `language/lang_english/lang_main.php`. This file is part of phpBB's multi-lingual support, one of the factors that has made phpBB very popular worldwide. Help text for all of the BBCode buttons is one of the many things you can find in the `lang_main.php`. The line you just located and copied contains the help text for the Font Size BBCode. The other lines of help text are above this one, and you have placed the new help text of the Strike BBCode below this line.

> There is a `lang_main.php` file for each language installed on a forum. If you want to locate this line in a file for a language other than English, search for the `$lang['bbcode_f_help']` portion of the line.

If you compare this line to the other help text lines, you will notice some clear differences. The `f` in `bbcode_f_help` is replaced with a different letter on the other lines. This part of the line is a name that is used to reference the help text later, so it needs to be unique from all other names here. A line with the name `bbcode_s_help` already exists, so you cannot use that letter here. Instead, we can use the letters `st`. There is no need to limit ourselves to only one letter. The text between the second pair of single quotes on each line is the actual text that will be displayed on the posting form. None of the present lines are really fitting for the Strike BBCode, so you can rewrite this text in the new line. The only restrictions on the content of the help text are that they cannot contain single or double quotation marks.

The next file we will look at, `posting.php`, handles many aspects of making posts on a forum. For the moment, we only care about one of these: the creation of the posting form. The form is created using a combination of phpBB's language and template systems. We have already added the help text to the language system, so now we need to incorporate it into the template system.

Time For Action—Adding a Template Variable

1. Find the following line in `posting.php` and duplicate it for editing:
   ```
   'L_BBCODE_F_HELP' => $lang['bbcode_f_help'],
   ```
2. Replace `bbcode_f_help` with `bbcode_st_help` to match the changes you made in the language file.
3. Alter the `F` in `L_BBCODE_F_HELP` to a matching `ST`.
4. The final line incorporating these alterations is:
   ```
   'L_BBCODE_ST_HELP' => $lang['bbcode_st_help'],
   ```

What Just Happened?

In this last example, you added a new template variable. It will represent the help text for the Strike BBCode and make that text available to the template system. phpBB sends information to the template system using lines like the following:

```
$template->assign_vars(array(
    'L_INFO' => $l_info,
    'MESSAGE' => $message,
    'MORE' => $more)
);
```

The first and last line of this code, along with the closing parenthesis on the `'MORE'` line, are required for the file to function, so you should leave them alone. If you needed to add a section of code to send data to the template system in a file that did not already do so, you would need to include these lines when editing the file. Fortunately, `posting.php` already has them, so we move on to the other lines, which specify the actual information to be sent. The `'L_INFO'` line, is a good example. It sends the value of a variable, `$l_info` in this case, to the template system with the name `L_INFO`. This tells the template system that all instances of `{L_INFO}` in a template file should be replaced with the value of the variable. `{L_INFO}` is called a **template variable** because it is replaced with some value by the template system. `L_INFO` is the **name** of the template variable.

> It is an accepted convention that most template variables and their names are written in all uppercase letters, numbers, or underscores, and do not contain other characters. This is mostly not required, but you should not use a period in the name of a template variable. The period is considered a special, reserved character in template variable names.

The third file we need to alter to add a BBCode button, `templates/subSilver/posting_body.tpl`, is also the most complicated. Only one line needs to be added in the files you edited previously, but this time there are several changes (some of them rather awkward). This is one of several sections of phpBB that was not designed with ease of expansion in mind. Many schools of thought on the proper way to add a new BBCode button in this file exist, but most require replacing large parts of this file or installing another modification first.

Time For Action—Adding a Posting Form Button

1. Open the `templates/subSilver/posting_body.tpl` file and locate the following line. Duplicate it as usual. This time, however, place the duplicated line *before* the existing code. The order of the lines does not really matter, but it will create a useful example later on in the chapter.

```
f_help = "{L_BBCODE_F_HELP}";
```

2. In the copy of the line, you should replace the template variable with that for the Strike help line. Also remove the lowercase `f` at the beginning of the line and add `st` in its place. This is the easiest change in this file. The resulting lines would be:

```
st_help = "{L_BBCODE_ST_HELP}";
f_help = "{L_BBCODE_F_HELP}";
```

3. Now find the following (rather long) line of code. Depending on the settings of your text editor, it may be wrapped onto two or more lines when displayed on your screen. Do your best to find the entire line.

```
bbtags = new
Array('[b]','[/b]','[i]','[/i]','[u]','[/u]','[quote]','[/quote]',
'[code]','[/code]','[list]','[/list]','[list=]','[/list]','[img]',
'[/img]','[url]','[/url]');
```

4. Add the following lines after the `bbtags` line that you just found.

```
// Begin further bbtags indexing at 22 to avoid font size/color
conflicts.
bbtags[22] = '[s]';
bbtags[23] = '[/s]';
```

5. The altered code now looks like:

```
bbcode = new Array();
```

```
bbtags = new
Array('[b]','[/b]','[i]','[/i]','[u]','[/u]','[quote]','[/quote]','[c
ode]','[/code]','[list]','[/list]','[list=]','[/list]','[img]','[/img
]','[url]','[/url]');

// Begin further bbtags indexing at 22 to avoid font size/color
conflicts.
bbtags[22] = '[s]';
bbtags[23] = '[/s]';

imageTag = false;
```

6. Locate and duplicate the following HTML code in the file:

```
<td><span class="genmed">
   <input type="button" class="button" accesskey="w"
name="addbbcode16" value="URL" style="text-decoration: underline;
width: 40px" onClick="bbstyle(16)" onMouseOver="helpline('w')" />
</span></td>
```

7. Alter the duplicated line to look like the following.

```
<td><span class="genmed">
   <input type="button" class="button" accesskey="t"
name="addbbcode22" value="Strike" style="text-decoration: line-
through; width: 44px" onClick="bbstyle(22)"
onMouseOver="helpline('st')" />
</span></td>
```

What Just Happened?

Now you have added the actual button in the posting form and completed the file changes for the Strike BBCode modification. Since this last *Time For Action* example was much longer, a detailed look at the changes is in order now, beginning with the additions after the long `bbtags` line.

That particular line is where several authors would begin to alter the file in different manners. Some of these alternatives will be examined later, but for now a simple addition after this line keeps the Strike BBCode as simple as possible. Using this method has a few benefits and disadvantages that will also be addressed later in the chapter.

With that code added, you moved on to the final alteration of this file: adding the actual button! Every change related to the button that you have made up to this point was geared toward making the button work, but not making the button itself. You duplicated and edited the code for the URL button, which is the last in the row of buttons on the posting form. These lines are HTML code, with the middle line being HTML for a clickable form button.

There was no need to alter the first or last line here. However, the middle line needed several changes to make it unique from the other buttons. The HTML for the button contains several attributes, in the form of *name="value"* pairs. All of these attributes except the first two, `button` and `class`, were changed when you finished. Let's go through a complete break down of these changes now.

The first attribute you may have noticed is `accesskey`. Access keys are a method of allowing a user to "click" a button without actually touching it. By pressing a special key (*Alt* on Windows or the Apple key on Macintosh systems) in combination with the key for the letter defined as an access key, the user triggers the effect of the button. When a user on your forum presses *Alt+B* at the posting form, the Bold BBCode tag is inserted into the post as if they had clicked the form button for that BBCode. During the process of adding new buttons, you should change the value of this attribute to a letter or digit that is not already used on your posting form. The letter "t" is a good not-in-use choice on unmodified forums, so `accesskey="w"` was changed to `accesskey="t"`.

Next up is the `name` attribute. It provides a unique name for the button that can be referenced inside JavaScript code. There is a large amount of JavaScript at the top of this file, and it works with the buttons and message body to add BBCodes, keep track of open BBCode tags in the message, and change the text displayed on the buttons. The value of `name` is used to access the buttons, especially for changing the text. When a user clicks on a BBCode button to insert an opening tag, like [b], an asterisk is added to the button to remind you that the tag is open. The value of this attribute will be similar for all your BBCode buttons—`addbbcodexx`, where `xx` is some even number. If you recall, we used "22" when adding code related to the `bbtags` line earlier. This is the first place it comes into play (the number is important for reasons we'll discuss later). The name of this button must be `addbbcode22`, so `name="addbbcode16"` was altered to `name="addbbcode22"`. Skipping ahead slightly to the `onClick` attribute, `16` was again replaced with `22`.

The third attribute, `value`, is simply the text displayed on the BBCode button. Since you are creating a Strike BBCode, `"Strike"` seems like a logical choice to display. `value="URL"` is thus replaced with `value="Strike"`.

The `style` attribute allows you to apply specific Cascading Style Sheet properties to HTML elements having that attribute. With BBCode buttons, `style` is usually used to demonstrate the effect of the BBCode and control the width of the button. You altered the `text-decoration` property from `underline` to `line-through`, as you did in `bbcode.tpl`. Increasing the `width` property from `40px` (forty pixels) to `44px` is also recommended to ensure that the asterisk of the Strike button can be seen when added.

The final attribute, `onMouseOver`, triggers the display of the help line text. The complete attribute is `onMouseOver="helpline('w')"`, but you need to be careful when editing this one. Only the `w` *inside* the single quotes should be changed. If you think back to the other help-line related changes, you may recall that you were often replacing the letter `f` with `st`. This is the same situation, but you are replacing a `w` now.

At last, you have finished all the file editing needed to use your new Strike BBCode! Congratulations on making it this far.

Pros and Cons of the Strike BBCode Methods

As mentioned earlier, there are a few advantages and disadvantages to some of the methods we just used when editing `posting_body.tpl`. Some of the changes could have been made in several different ways. To better understand how the BBCode buttons work and why there are different methods of creating BBCodes, let's look at some alternatives.

When creating a BBCode modification such as Strike, many authors would require that another modification, the Multi BBCode MOD, be installed on the forum first. This modification replaces and extends much of the BBCode system in `posting_body.tpl` and other files with the goal of making additional BBCodes easier to install. In fact, if an author wishes to distribute a BBCode modification at phpBB's official website, that modification is *required* to rely on the Multi BBCode MOD. One disadvantage of the process you just completed is that it was designed independently of Multi BBCode. The resulting modification is thus likely to be incompatible with the other modification.

Another possible alternative to the method you have learned centers on the `bbtags` code near the top of the file. You added two new lines after this code, but for a long time there has been a very different method considered as a standard way of editing this area. This method called for the `bbtags` code to be edited within that line. With that type of alteration, the `bbtags` line would be changed to the following by the Strike BBCode:

```
bbtags = new
Array('[b]','[/b]','[i]','[/i]','[u]','[/u]','[quote]','[/quote]','[c
ode]','[/code]','[list]','[/list]','[list=]','[/list]','[img]','[/img
]','[url]','[/url]','[s]','[/s]');
```

The `bbtags` line of code creates an **array**, or a stack of data, containing all the possible BBCode tags—except the size and color tags—and their closing tag counterparts, numbered in the order listed on the line. The numbering starts at 0; `[b]` would be number 0, `[/b]` would be number 1, and so on. The Strike BBCode's `[s]` becomes number 18 in this scheme.

However, this creates a problem. Remember that you used `addbbcode22` as the value of the `name` attribute in the HTML for the Strike button? Using the method just described, you would need to use `addbbcode18`. If you search through `posting_body.tpl`, you will find that `addbbcode18` is already used for the name of the Font Color drop-down list and `addbbcode20` is likewise used for Font Size. Since the value of `name` must be unique, editing the `bbtags` line directly forces you to also change the `name` attributes of the Font Color and Size lists. You would have to do that for every BBCode installed, which is quite a lot of repetitive work if you add several BBCodes.

When you added new lines for `[s]` and `[/s]` after the `bbtags` line, the new lines assigned the Strike tags to numbers 22 and 23 respectively. Essentially, you skipped the numbers 18 through 21, which were used by the Size and Color BBCodes.

This removed the need to edit the HTML for Size and Color. If you wanted to add new BBCodes using the method presented in this chapter, your code might look like this example. Notice how the number is incremented once on each line.

```
bbtags[22] = '[s]';
bbtags[23] = '[/s]';
bbtags[24] = '[flash]';
bbtags[25] = '[/flash]';
bbtags[26] = '[hide]';
bbtags[27] = '[/hide]';
```

Step 5—Break It and Fix It

With the changes for your first modification completed, the next step is to test your changes. While testing, do everything you can think of that might cause a problem in the modification. Any problems that do appear need to be fixed before someone else can find them. Lack of proper testing can be very dangerous, and in some cases might create new security holes in your forum.

Try to test out every aspect of the Strike BBCode. Try making a new topic, previewing a post, and even replying to and editing posts containing the BBCode. Check out every aspect of the posting form, from the buttons to the help line. If you have multiple styles installed on your forum, make sure you have edited the template files for every style, and test the BBCode and button on all of them. When there are multiple languages, test those as well!

You should not find any problems with the Strike BBCode, since it is a very simple modification. However, even simple modifications need thorough testing. There are many places where the lack of a single comma can make parts of a forum inaccessible.

Make Your MOD Accessible to the World

Once you have created a modification, you may wish to distribute it to other phpBB forum operators. Many modifications are made freely available by their authors as a way of giving something back to the global phpBB community. Not all modifications are free, of course, but those that are can often be found on several websites and may eventually even be translated to other languages.

There are several ways you can distribute a modification. You might write an essay or tutorial describing the changes made to install it, which could be similar to the previous pages of this chapter. The most widely used method is to create an installation file that uses simple instructions, like those explained in the section discussing modification installation in Chapter 4, to guide users through the changes.

You can also choose to make the modification available at one or more websites. Authors of multiple modifications usually have their own website dedicated to their works, often with phpBB-powered forums providing support and demonstrations. Several more general websites covering phpBB also carry modifications. The sites with the largest modification communities are `http://www.phpbb.com/`, the official phpBB website, and `http://www.phpbbhacks.com/`, the largest modification website. There are other websites offering modifications that you can use to distribute your work, including many based primarily on non-English languages.

Each of these large websites has its own rules regarding how modifications can be distributed on that site. phpBB.com has very strict rules, while phpBBHacks.com is much more relaxed. Both sites have forums with development areas that are available for help in creating and testing modifications, but are not used specifically for distributing any works. The two sites have a database of modifications for that purpose.

The modification database of phpBB.com can be found in its **Mods** section. To be included in this database, a modification must be submitted through a special form and has to pass a series of special validation procedures. The validation process tests several aspects of the download. If the modification fails in any those tests, which are conducted by the phpBB.com "MOD Team", it is rejected from inclusion on the website. Authors are typically informed of reason(s) for this rejection and are allowed to resubmit the work after making any required changes. In contrast, phpBBHacks.com allows authors to have more freedom in these areas with rules that are much less strict. Authors are expected to extensively test modifications before submitting them through a simple form.

> You can find links to all of phpBB.com's modification-submission requirements through the post at `http://www.phpbb.com/phpBB/viewtopic.php?t=160827`. The validation procedures are also described in posts at this forum.

Once you have decided where you wish to distribute your modification, look around that website for its specific rules and submission procedure. The process of distributing a modification at any given site generally encompasses the following steps:

1. Create the code, including any PHP, HTML, and so forth.
2. Assemble that code into a packaged collection (detailed in the next section).
3. If the site has a modification development forum, create a topic about the modification there. Other users may try it out and give you feedback, bug reports, or other advice.
4. Make any revisions to the code you desire based on the feedback, bug reports, etc., and then repeat steps 1-4 until you are satisfied that the modification is completely finished.
5. Submit the modification through the procedures available at the site.

Packaging Your MOD

Before making your modification available anywhere, it must first be collected into a set of files. This process of preparing your modification for distribution is called **packaging**. This typically involves creating the instruction file and placing it, along with any new forum files created for the modification, into a single ZIP file. Extremely large modifications often include other files, such as upgrading instructions, lists of tips or hints, and modified copies of original phpBB files that are also placed into this ZIP file.

In order to distribute a modification at phpBB.com, the instruction file must be created using a special "MOD Template" provided at that site. This template consists of three sections: a header, a list of several blank commands, and a footer containing an ending command. Each section is required; leaving out even one of them will cause the modification submission to be rejected. phpBBHacks.com accepts modifications created using this template or any other, including no template at all, as long as the instructions are understandable. Specific sections are also not required if a template is used. There is an official phpBBHacks.com template, but its use is optional. phpBB.com, however, only accepts modifications created with its own template.

The Strike BBCode modification you made earlier in this chapter could not be submitted at phpBB.com because it does not rely on the Multi BBCode modification, as required for all BBCode modifications listed there. Likewise, phpBBHacks.com would not accept it because Strike is not your original creation. However, creating an instruction file for this modification is still a good method of learning how to use the MOD Template in order to make installation files that can be submitted to phpBB.com and other sites.

Using the MOD Template Header

To begin, create a new text file. In most text editors for Windows, this involves opening the File menu and selecting New | New Text File or something similar. Save your new file with the name `strike.mod`. Most text files that you may be familiar with use a file extension of `txt`, resulting in a file name like `strike.txt`. phpBB.com requires modification instruction files to use the `.mod` file extension, also widely known as an extension for music files, instead.

Next, type the following lines in your file, or copy and paste them from the phpBB.com MOD Template. These lines compose the entire MOD Template header. If you type them in, be sure to match the exact grammar, spelling, and spacing of the MOD Template (in the printed book, the text appears wrapped). Changing any one of those aspects, even if you think them to be incorrect, will cause the modification to be rejected.

```
##############################################################
## MOD Title: mod_title_goes_here
## MOD Author: your_phpBB_username < your_email > (your_real_name)
your_url
## MOD Description: some_description_goes_here
## MOD Version: x.x.x
##
## Installation Level: (Easy/Intermediate/Advanced)
## Installation Time: x Minutes
## Files To Edit: file_1, file_2, file_3, etc
## Included Files: (n/a, or list of included/required files)
##############################################################
```

```
## For Security Purposes, Please Check: http://www.phpbb.com/mods/
for the
## latest version of this MOD. Downloading this MOD from other sites
could cause malicious code
## to enter into your phpBB Forum. As such, phpBB will not offer
support for MOD's not offered
## in our MOD-Database, located at: http://www.phpbb.com/mods/
##############################################################
## Author Notes:
##
##############################################################
## MOD History:
##
##   YYYY-MM-DD - Version x.x.x
##      - version notes go here
##
##############################################################
## Before Adding This MOD To Your Forum, You Should Back Up All Files
Related To This MOD
##############################################################
```

Several of these lines need to be edited for each modification. Let's take them one at a time, beginning at the top and working our way down. The header itself is organized into smaller sections by a few lines made completely of # characters. These separators should be left as presented.

MOD Title

The first line to change is the `MOD Title` line. As you have probably guessed, this is where you will place the name of the modification for all to see.

```
## MOD Title: mod_title_goes_here
```

The text `mod_title_goes_here` should be replaced with the correct name. In this case, you would type `Strike BBCode`.

MOD Author

Next is the `MOD Author` line, which lists the creators of the modification. Contact information can also be included here.

```
## MOD Author: your_phpBB_username < your_email > (your_real_name)
your_url
```

The line itself has four subparts that need to be altered. The first of these, `your_phpBB_username`, is to be replaced with the username of an account registered on the phpBB.com community forums. That same account would later be used to submit the modification. Second is the `< your_email >` section, which is a placeholder for your e-mail address. The arrow brackets here should not be removed, so the final version of this will resemble `< jon@doe.com >`. Next comes a location for your given name, in `(your_real_name)`. Again, the brackets (parentheses this time) should be left in place. Last but not least is `your_url`, a place for a website address that might contain a demonstration of the modification. Only the forum username entry is required. If you do not wish to enter your e-mail address, real name, or a website address, you can place `N/A` in those sections instead. Be sure to include the brackets, however. A final version of this line might be:

```
## MOD Author: MyAccount < jon@doe.com > (N/A) N/A
```

MOD Description

The third line you should edit is for the `MOD Description`. It is a fairly simple line.

```
## MOD Description: some_description_goes_here
```

The `some_description_goes_here` text should be replaced with one or two very short sentences describing the purpose of the modification. An example you can use here would be `Adds a strike out BBCode to posting`.

MOD Version

With the `x.x.x` of the `MOD Version` line, you can provide a three-part number describing this particular release of the modification. If for some reason you need to release more than one version, this number would be different for each of those releases.

```
## MOD Version: x.x.x
```

The first digit represents a stable release number, the second a minor addition number, and the third a simple alteration number. A modification that has a version number of 1.2.0 has seen one stable release followed by two releases with new features added. When a version number such as 2.3.4 is seen, that indicates two stable releases, three more releases with new features, and finally four other releases with minor changes (like small bug fixes). The version number of the first release of a modification submitted to phpBB.com is generally 1.0.0. Anything with a leading number less than one is considered to be a beta or alpha release. **Beta** and **alpha** releases are preview releases that may contain bugs, errors, or other problems. It might often be a bad idea to use beta or alpha releases on live forums.

Installation Level

`Installation Level` describes, in a single word, how difficult it will be to install the modification. `(Easy/Intermediate/Advanced)` would be replaced with just one of those words: `Easy`, `Intermediate`, or `Advanced`.

```
## Installation Level: (Easy/Intermediate/Advanced)
```

The Strike BBCode would be fairly `Easy` to install. Generally, the longer an installation file is, the higher the installation level of the modification.

Installation Time

Like the previous line, `Installation Time` deals with the difficulty of installing a modification. This time you should replace the `x` with a number representing the approximate number of minutes it might take to install a modification.

```
## Installation Time: x Minutes
```

For the Strike BBCode, `5` would be a fair, although slightly high, number. When in doubt, try to overestimate this number. Ideally, you should time yourself when installing the modification on a forum to get an idea of the time needed.

Files to Edit

The `Files to Edit` line lists every phpBB file edited by the modification. You may recall editing five files for the Strike BBCode: `posting.php`, `language/lang_english/lang_main.php`, `includes/bbcode.php`, `templates/subSilver/bbcode.tpl`, and `templates/subSilver/posting_body.tpl`. All these files would be listed here, with a comma separating one from the other. Since that is a rather long list, it would often be broken onto multiple lines in the file. Each line must start with ## like all of the other header lines.

```
## Files To Edit: file_1, file_2, file_3, etc
```

Included Files

This last line in the upper part of the header provides a list of all new forum files included in the modification. When there are no new files, as with the Strike BBCode, replace the parenthesized text with a simple `n/a`, which stands for not applicable.

```
## Included Files: (n/a, or list of included/required files)
```

phpBB.com's Security Notice

The next section of the header includes a security notice created by phpBB.com. This notice is required to appear in all modifications submitted to phpBB.com and should not be altered in any way. Even a small change, such as altering capitalization or line length, will result in the refusal of a submission.

```
## For Security Purposes, Please Check: http://www.phpbb.com/mods/
for the
## latest version of this MOD. Downloading this MOD from other sites
could cause malicious code
## to enter into your phpBB Forum. As such, phpBB will not offer
support for MOD's not offered
## in our MOD-Database, located at: http://www.phpbb.com/mods/
```

> Regardless of what the security notice may or may not imply, using a modification from other websites is not necessarily going to place intentionally harmful code into your forum. It can happen, but it is rare. Because there is a risk when installing any software you did not create, you should never install *any code* on your site unless you know what it does and what problems it may present. Security holes have been discovered even in earlier with phpBB, but such problems are rarely intentional.

Author Notes

Following the separator under the security notice is an `Author Notes` section. In this area you can add extra instructions or cautions related to using or installing the modification.

For example, you might explain what the modification does in more detail than in the MOD Description line. This is also a good place to mention post-installation tasks like changing settings found or added in the Administration Control Panel.

There are some things you should not include in the Author Notes section. Among these are addresses of other websites at which the modification can be found, contact information, licensing information, and installation instructions that can be covered by action commands (which you will see in a moment). Placing any one of these seemingly harmless things in the Author Notes can cause a modification to fail the validation process. The administration of phpBB.com has problems with links to other websites placed on their own; this is also reflected in their forum rules, which disallow most links of that type, and the security notice. The only contact information allowed by this template must be placed on the MOD Author line. All modifications released on phpBB.com are required to be released under the GNU General Public License that phpBB itself falls under. A copy of this license is included with phpBB, but do not mention it in this section.

After the Author Notes, an area is provided to describe each release of the modification. The MOD History is a list of every release, with dates in a year-month-day format as well as version numbers. The entries for the versions should provide brief descriptions of changes made from one version to another. For the first version of a modification, it is common to see a line saying "Initial version," "First release," or a similar short statement.

The MOD Template header ends with another section that should not be edited; this section is a quick reminder to the users of the modification, pointing out that they should make backups of files. A complete header for the Strike BBCode, with all of the changes you have made so far, should resemble the example after this paragraph. This would also be a good time to save your file. Save your work periodically to ensure that you do not lose everything you have accomplished due to an accident or, worse yet, a power failure:

```
##############################################################
## MOD Title: Strike BBCode
## MOD Author: MyAccount < jon@doe.com > (N/A) N/A
## MOD Description: Adds a strike out BBCode to posting.
## MOD Version: 1.0.0
##
## Installation Level: Easy
## Installation Time: 5 Minutes
## Files To Edit: posting.php, includes/bbcode.php,
##                language/lang_english/lang_main.php,
##                templates/subSilver/bbcode.tpl,
##                templates/subSilver/posting_body.tpl
## Included Files: n/a
##############################################################
## For Security Purposes, Please Check: http://www.phpbb.com/mods/
for the
## latest version of this MOD. Downloading this MOD from other sites
could cause malicious code
## to enter into your phpBB Forum. As such, phpBB will not offer
support for MOD's not offered
## in our MOD-Database, located at: http://www.phpbb.com/mods/
```

```
#################################################################
## Author Notes:
##
## Once this modification is installed on your forum, users can
include
## a strike out BBCode in their posts. The format of the BBCode is:
##     [s]This text will have a line through it.[/s]
## A button is also added to the posting form.
##
#################################################################
## MOD History:
##
##   2004-12-06 - Version 1.0.0
##      - Initial version.
##
#################################################################
## Before Adding This MOD To Your Forum, You Should Back Up All Files
Related To This MOD
#################################################################
```

Creating the List of Actions

The second major portion of your modification's instruction file, as defined by the MOD Template, is a list of actions. **Actions** are commands for making changes needed to install a modification. Each action is presented with a header followed by a file name, one or more lines of code, or other information. Action headers look like the following example, with the text `ACTION NAME` being replaced by the actual name of the command.

```
#
#-----[ ACTION NAME ]------------------------------------------
#
```

Consult the table under the *The Last Action* section in Chapter 4 for a list of the most commonly used actions and brief descriptions. phpBB.com allows the use of only twelve specific commands, all of which are listed in that table. The Add SQL action at the end of the table is not allowed for submissions to phpBB.com; you need to use the SQL action instead. Actions should generally be used in the order listed in the table. The Copy and SQL actions appear first, if needed, followed by an Open action, which in turn will proceed to combinations of the Find, Addition, and In-Line actions.

To create an action list for your instruction file for the Strike BBCode, review the steps you took in creating your modification. Since no new files were added, you will not need a Copy action. In the same vein, you did not make any database changes. That will render the SQL action unnecessary for these instructions. You edited five files, so you will need a matching Open action for each file.

The Open Action

The header of each Open action should be followed by a single line naming the file to be prepared for editing. Always include the full path to this file, relative to the main phpBB directory with this name. File paths in Open actions, and also Copy actions, should not start with something like `root/`, `phpBB2/`, or even a simple slash, `/`.

This is the correct Open action for the first file that was edited:

```
#
#-----[ OPEN ]------------------------------------------
#
includes/bbcode.php
```

> You do not have to list the files for editing in any specific order, but remember that Open actions are always followed by a Find action and *then* other actions.

The Find Action

The second thing you did, after opening that file, was to locate some code within it. You should instruct your modification's users to do the same by including that code in a Find action. This is the first Find action for the Strike BBCode:

```
#
#-----[ FIND ]------------------------------------------
#
	// [u] and [/u] for underlining text.
	$text = str_replace("[u:$uid]", $bbcode_tpl['u_open'], $text);
	$text = str_replace("[/u:$uid]", $bbcode_tpl['u_close'], $text);
```

The Addition Actions

After locating that code, it was duplicated and then altered to our needs. Several steps were involved in that process, but you do not need to describe every aspect of it in these instructions. Instead, you only want to give the user the final code and tell them where to place it, relative to the code in the Find action. The new code was placed after the code you located, so an After, Add action is needed here. If you had inserted the new code before the existing lines, then a Before, Add action would be appropriate. When removing old code and putting new code in the same location, use a Replace With action.

```
#
#-----[ AFTER, ADD ]------------------------------------------
#

// ---------------------------------------------
// Strike BBCode - Begin Code Addition

	// [s] and [/s] for strike out text.
	$text = str_replace("[s:$uid]", $bbcode_tpl['s_open'], $text);
	$text = str_replace("[/s:$uid]", $bbcode_tpl['s_close'], $text);

// Strike BBCode - End Code Addition
// ---------------------------------------------
```

You might notice that the After, Add action example includes some comment lines that you did not place into `includes/bbcode.php`. These lines mark the beginning and end of the code added by the modification. Although such lines are not required in your modification, try to add them whenever possible as a courtesy to the end users. If it becomes necessary to remove or upgrade your modification later, the users will be able to use lines such as these to quickly locate the code of the modification. You can format these lines any way you like; the format used here is just an example based on the author's personal style.

Create a set of a Find and After, Add action for the other changes you made to this file. The process is the same as that you just completed, and will complete the actions for `bbcode.php`. The resulting pair should resemble the following code:

```
#
#-----[ FIND ]------------------------------------------
#

   // [u] and [/u] for underlining text.
   $text = preg_replace("#\[u\](.*?)\[/u\]#si",
"[u:$uid]\\1[/u:$uid]", $text);

#
#-----[ AFTER, ADD ]------------------------------------------
#

// -------------------------------------------------
// Strike BBCode - Begin Code Addition

   // [s] and [/s] for strike out text.
   $text = preg_replace("#\[s\](.*?)\[/s\]#si",
"[s:$uid]\\1[/s:$uid]", $text);

// Strike BBCode - End Code Addition
// -------------------------------------------------
```

Additional Open, Find, and Addition Action Examples

We edited the `bbcode.tpl` file of your template; the next step is to create an Open action for it. A problem arises here: you need to include the path to the file, which will mention a template directory like `subSilver`. Suppose someone does not have `subSilver` present on their forum, but only other templates with different names. Will this prevent them from using your modification? Should you list instructions for every template?

The answer to both questions is a resounding "No". Anyone can use the modification on any template, although they may have to improvise a little if the content of the template files is extremely different from that of subSilver. There is no way you can predict what templates are installed on any forum, and there are hundreds of templates available (not counting private templates made for a single website!). Adding instructions for more than one template is impractical and more trouble than it is worth. The solution to this problem is to always base your modifications and their instructions on the subSilver template files, which are installed by default on every original phpBB 2.0 forum. Doing this is also required if you want your modification to appear on phpBB.com.

So, with all of that in mind, the Open action for `bbcode.tpl` would be:

```
#
#-----[ OPEN ]------------------------------------------
#
templates/subSilver/bbcode.tpl
```

You can again create a Find and After, Add instruction combination for the changes to this file. One important thing to remember is that you cannot include comment lines marking the new code in this file. Doing so would result in a forum displaying a **parse error**, which means there is incorrect syntax in a file or portion of code. A final set of commands for this file could be the following.

```
#
#-----[ FIND ]------------------------------------------
#

<!-- BEGIN u_open --><span style="text-decoration: underline"><!--
END u_open -->
<!-- BEGIN u_close --></span><!-- END u_close -->

#
#-----[ AFTER, ADD ]------------------------------------
#

<!-- BEGIN s_open --><span style="text-decoration: line-through"><!--
END s_open -->
<!-- BEGIN s_close --></span><!-- END s_close -->
```

Next in the list of files altered is the `language/lang_english/lang_main.php` file. A problem similar to that of the template file path also exists with language files. Files for non-English languages will have different file paths, such as `language/lang_dutch` or `language/lang_french`. For this situation, the resolution is also the same: use the files and file path of the default installed on forums, which is the English language. Including other languages in your instructions is usually allowed, but again, using the default is required if you want your work listed in phpBB.com's database.

The other actions for this file are the standard pair of a single Find and one After, Add action. Combined with the Open action, the full instructions for the file are:

```
#
#-----[ OPEN ]------------------------------------------
#
language/lang_english/lang_main.php

#
#-----[ FIND ]------------------------------------------
#

$lang['bbcode_f_help'] = 'Font size: [size=x-small]small
text[/size]';

#
#-----[ AFTER, ADD ]------------------------------------
#

// ---------------------------------------------------
// Strike BBCode - Begin Code Addition

$lang['bbcode_st_help'] = 'Strike out: [s]Line through text[/s]
(alt+t)';
```

```
// Strike BBCode - End Code Addition
// ------------------------------------------------
```

Moving along, the next file edited for the Strike BBCode was `posting.php`—just another Open, Find, and After, Add sequence:

```
#
#-----[ OPEN ]------------------------------------------
#
posting.php

#
#-----[ FIND ]------------------------------------------
#
    'L_BBCODE_F_HELP' => $lang['bbcode_f_help'],

#
#-----[ AFTER, ADD ]------------------------------------------
#

// ------------------------------------------------
// Strike BBCode - Begin Code Addition

    'L_BBCODE_ST_HELP' => $lang['bbcode_st_help'],

// Strike BBCode - End Code Addition
// ------------------------------------------------
```

Last but not least, the edits of `posting_body.tpl` were rather extensive compared to others in this modification. Since this is a template file, remember to use the path to subSilver template files in the Open action.

```
#
#-----[ OPEN ]------------------------------------------
#
templates/subSilver/posting_body.tpl
```

Do you remember the one time you duplicated code, but added it before an existing line instead of after that line? The reason for adding this before the line you copied was to create an example of using the Before, Add action instead of After, Add in this step of creating the instruction file. The only real difference, as far as appearance in the instructions, is that `AFTER` is replaced with `BEFORE`.

```
#
#-----[ FIND ]------------------------------------------
#
f_help = "{L_BBCODE_F_HELP}";


#
#-----[ BEFORE, ADD ]------------------------------------------
#

// ------------------------------------------------
// Strike BBCode - Begin Code Addition

st_help = '{L_BBCODE_ST_HELP}';
```

```
// Strike BBCode - End Code Addition
// ------------------------------------------------
```

Now you have another basic Find and After, Add action combination for the next alteration you made in this file.

```
#
#-----[ FIND ]------------------------------------------
#

bbtags = new
Array('[b]','[/b]','[i]','[/i]','[u]','[/u]','[quote]','[/quote]','[c
ode]','[/code]','[list]','[/list]','[list=]','[/list]','[img]','[/img
]','[url]','[/url]');


#
#-----[ AFTER, ADD ]------------------------------------------
#

// ------------------------------------------------
// Strike BBCode - Begin Code Addition

bbtags[22] = '[s]';
bbtags[23] = '[/s]';

// Strike BBCode - End Code Addition
// ------------------------------------------------
```

The actions for the last steps are, once again, Find and After, Add. This combination, as you may have noticed, is the one used most often in modification instructions. For this round, the procedure is the same, but notice that the comment lines in the After, Add instruction are very different.

```
#
#-----[ FIND ]------------------------------------------
#

          <td><span class="genmed">
            <input type="button" class="button" accesskey="w"
name="addbbcode16" value="URL" style="text-decoration: underline;
width: 40px" onClick="bbstyle(16)" onMouseOver="helpline('w')" />
            </span></td>

#
#-----[ AFTER, ADD ]------------------------------------------
#

<!-- Strike BBCode - Begin Code Addition -->
          <td><span class="genmed">
            <input type="button" class="button" accesskey="t"
name="addbbcode22" value="Strike" style="text-decoration: line-
through; width: 44px" onClick="bbstyle(22)"
onMouseOver="helpline('st')" />
            </span></td>
<!-- Strike BBCode - End Code Addition -->
```

Previously, the code snippets that were added with comment lines were lines of PHP or, earlier in this file, JavaScript code. This time you are adding HTML code instead. PHP and JavaScript have similar syntax for comment lines: anything after a pair of slashes, `//`, is a comment. HTML comments, however, begin with `<!--` and end with `-->`. If you used a PHP-style comment, like `// Strike BBCode - Begin Code Addition`, here, it would be displayed in plain text on the posting page.

> You might be tempted to use HTML-style comments in `bbcode.tpl`. Sadly, this is not allowed in that file because HTML comments are used by phpBB to parse the file itself. Also, avoid using in other template files any HTML comments that start with `<!-- BEGIN` or `<!-- END`. phpBB will think those are special template switches and usually report a parse error.

That ends the list of actions for this particular modification. Do not forget to save what you have completed so far!

Using Other Actions

Although the Strike BBCode only uses a few of the actions—Open; Find; After, Add; and Before, Add—you may need to use several of the other actions when creating your own original modifications. With that in mind, here are some examples of the other actions.

Copying Files—The Copy Action

When your modification includes new files, the first action that should appear in your list of commands is the Copy action. The Copy action indicates that users should upload the new files to their forum, and states the locations of these files. After the action header, you should include a line mentioning each file, including any folders that it might be in when the modification is uncompressed from a single file, and the path it should be placed in, relative to the forum's main directory. You will learn how to place files within folders inside a compressed file later in this chapter. There are some special shortcuts you can use in a Copy action, so now is a good time to look at an example action.

```
#
#-----[ COPY ]------------------------------------------
#
my_new_file.php to my_new_file.php
my_functions.php to includes/my_functions.php
new_tpls/new_file.tpl to templates/subSilver/new_file.tpl
language/lang_english/*.* to language/lang_english/*.*
```

Files included in the modification are listed on the left, then the word `to` is used as a separator followed by the file's correct position within the forum's structure. The first line of files is fairly simple in meaning: copy the `my_new_file.php` file to the main directory of a forum (the directory that contains files such as `viewtopic.php` and `posting.php`). On the second line, you are telling the user to place the remote copy of `my_functions.php` inside their forum's `includes/` directory. With the third line, you can see that the files being copied are in a folder named `new_tpls` here. After the directory names on the final line, the `*.*` shortcut means that the user would be copying *all files* within that directory. You can also use shortcuts like `*.php` or `*.tpl` to represent all files with a particular extension.

Altering the Database—The SQL Action

For making changes or additions to the SQL database of a forum, use the SQL action. Always include the SQL action near the top of your actions list; it should be the first or second action users complete. This action's header is followed by one or more SQL queries. Make sure that the queries you use are correctly structured and valid; they need to work exactly as presented. Note that most SQL actions will use queries created for MySQL databases, but this is not required. A sample of a SQL action that creates a simple database table could be:

```
#
#-----[ SQL ]------------------------------------------
#
CREATE TABLE phpbb_newtable (
   newtable_id int(8) NOT NULL default '0',
   newtable_item varchar(255) NOT NULL default '',
   PRIMARY KEY  (newtable_id)
);
```

Replacing Code—The Replace With Action

Sometimes you will need to alter an existing line of code instead of adding something before or after it. The Replace With action can be useful for this. Like the Before, Add and After, Add actions, Replace With will always follow a Find action. If you can use comment lines, it is also a good idea to include a commented out copy of the replaced lines in the Replace With action. That practice will make it easier for users to locate the code again later if another modification uses it in a Find action.

Suppose you wanted to replace the Underline BBCode with the Strike BBCode, instead of just adding the latter. In such a case, you might have a series of actions like these:

```
#
#-----[ FIND ]------------------------------------------
#

   // [u] and [/u] for underlining text.
   $text = preg_replace("#\[u\](.*?)\[/u\]#si",
"[u:$uid]\\1[/u:$uid]", $text);

#
#-----[ REPLACE WITH ]------------------------------------------
#
/* Original phpBB Code removed by Strike BBCode.
   // [u] and [/u] for underlining text.
   $text = preg_replace("#\[u\](.*?)\[/u\]#si",
"[u:$uid]\\1[/u:$uid]", $text);
*/
// ----------------------------------------------
// Strike BBCode - Begin Code Addition
```

```
    // [s] and [/s] for strike out text.
    $text = preg_replace("#\[s\](.*?)\[/s\]#si",
"[s:$uid]\\1[/s:$uid]", $text);

// Strike BBCode - End Code Addition
// ---------------------------------------------------
```

Modifying Portions of a Line—In-Line Actions

Do you remember the alternative methods of editing `posting_body.tpl` that were discussed after you created the Strike BBCode? Some of those make good examples of using the In-Line actions: In-Line Find; In-Line After, Add; In-Line Before, Add; and In-Line Replace With. In-Line actions are identical in use to their shorter named counterparts, with the exception that they always operate inside a single line of code. Typically when using these actions, you should start with a normal Find action, followed by an In-Line Find, and then one or more of the remaining three In-Line actions. Usually you will have a sequence such as Find, In-Line Find, and finally In-Line After, Add. This sequence would be used to add the `[s]` and `[/s]` Strike tags within the `bbtags` code line.

```
#
#-----[ FIND ]------------------------------------------
#
bbtags = new
Array('[b]','[/b]','[i]','[/i]','[u]','[/u]','[quote]','[/quote]','[c
ode]','[/code]','[list]','[/list]','[list=]','[/list]','[img]','[/img
]','[url]','[/url]');
#
#-----[ IN-LINE FIND ]----------------------------------------
#
'[/url]'
#
#-----[ IN-LINE AFTER, ADD ]------------------------------------
-
#
,'[s]','[/s]'
```

Adding the MOD Template Footer

To finish off the modification's instruction file, you need to add the footer of the MOD Template. The term "footer" is a bit misleading; you are actually placing one last action at the bottom of the file. All modifications submitted to phpBB.com must end with this action, and a variation of this is usually seen at the end of most other modifications as well. This action is explained in Chapter 4.

```
#
#-----[ SAVE/CLOSE ALL FILES ]--------------------------------------
---
#
# EoM
```

> `EoM` is an acronym for the phrase *End of MOD* or *End of Modification*. Some authors use `End` or another label instead of `EoM` when submitting hacks to sites other than phpBB.com.

The Completed Instruction File

With the full header, list of actions, and the footer compiled, you have finished the instruction file for the Strike BBCode. Here's a sample instruction file (text-wrapped here in the book) if you would like to compare your own to a working example (this file has also been included in the code download as `1132_07_strike.txt`).

```
##############################################################
## MOD Title: Strike BBCode
## MOD Author: Thoul < thoul@users.sourceforge.net > (Jeremy Rogers)
http://darkmods.sourceforge.net
## MOD Description: Adds a strike out BBCode to posting.
## MOD Version: 1.0.0
##
## Installation Level: Easy
## Installation Time: 5 Minutes
## Files To Edit: posting.php, includes/bbcode.php,
##                language/lang_english/lang_main.php,
##                templates/subSilver/bbcode.tpl,
##                templates/subSilver/posting_body.tpl
## Included Files: n/a
##############################################################
## For Security Purposes, Please Check: http://www.phpbb.com/mods/
for the
## latest version of this MOD. Downloading this MOD from other sites
could cause malicious code
## to enter into your phpBB Forum. As such, phpBB will not offer
support for MOD's not offered
## in our MOD-Database, located at: http://www.phpbb.com/mods/
##############################################################
## Author Notes:
##
## Once this modification is installed on your forum, users can
include
## a strike out BBCode in their posts. The format of the BBCode is:
##    [s]This text will have a line through it.[/s]
## A button is also added to the posting form.
##
##############################################################
## MOD History:
##
##   2004-12-06 - Version 1.0.0
##      - Initial version.
##
##############################################################
## Before Adding This MOD To Your Forum, You Should Back Up All Files
Related To This MOD
##############################################################

#
#-----[ OPEN ]------------------------------------------
#
includes/bbcode.php

#
#-----[ FIND ]------------------------------------------
#
```

```
    // [u] and [/u] for underlining text.
    $text = str_replace("[u:$uid]", $bbcode_tpl['u_open'], $text);
    $text = str_replace("[/u:$uid]", $bbcode_tpl['u_close'], $text);

#
#-----[ AFTER, ADD ]------------------------------------------
#

// ------------------------------------------------
// Strike BBCode - Begin Code Addition

    // [s] and [/s] for strike out text.
    $text = str_replace("[s:$uid]", $bbcode_tpl['s_open'], $text);
    $text = str_replace("[/s:$uid]", $bbcode_tpl['s_close'], $text);

// Strike BBCode - End Code Addition
// ------------------------------------------------

#
#-----[ FIND ]------------------------------------------
#

    // [u] and [/u] for underlining text.
    $text = preg_replace("#\[u\](.*?)\[/u\]#si",
"[u:$uid]\\1[/u:$uid]", $text);

#
#-----[ AFTER, ADD ]------------------------------------------
#

// ------------------------------------------------
// Strike BBCode - Begin Code Addition

    // [s] and [/s] for strike out text.
    $text = preg_replace("#\[s\](.*?)\[/s\]#si",
"[s:$uid]\\1[/s:$uid]", $text);

// Strike BBCode - End Code Addition
// ------------------------------------------------


#
#-----[ OPEN ]------------------------------------------
#
templates/subSilver/bbcode.tpl

#
#-----[ FIND ]------------------------------------------
#

<!-- BEGIN u_open --><span style="text-decoration: underline"><!--
END u_open -->
<!-- BEGIN u_close --></span><!-- END u_close -->

#
#-----[ AFTER, ADD ]------------------------------------------
#
```

```
<!-- BEGIN s_open --><span style="text-decoration: line-through"><!--
END s_open -->
<!-- BEGIN s_close --></span><!-- END s_close -->


#
#-----[ OPEN ]------------------------------------------
#
language/lang_english/lang_main.php

#
#-----[ FIND ]------------------------------------------
#

$lang['bbcode_f_help'] = 'Font size: [size=x-small]small
text[/size]';

#
#-----[ AFTER, ADD ]------------------------------------------
#

// -------------------------------------------------
// Strike BBCode - Begin Code Addition

$lang['bbcode_st_help'] = 'Strike out: [s]Line through text[/s]
(alt+t)';

// Strike BBCode - End Code Addition
// -------------------------------------------------


#
#-----[ OPEN ]------------------------------------------
#
posting.php

#
#-----[ FIND ]------------------------------------------
#
    'L_BBCODE_F_HELP' => $lang['bbcode_f_help'],

#
#-----[ AFTER, ADD ]------------------------------------------
#

// -------------------------------------------------
// Strike BBCode - Begin Code Addition

    'L_BBCODE_ST_HELP' => $lang['bbcode_st_help'],

// Strike BBCode - End Code Addition
// -------------------------------------------------


#
#-----[ OPEN ]------------------------------------------
#
templates/subSilver/posting_body.tpl
```

```
#
#-----[ FIND ]------------------------------------------
#
f_help = "{L_BBCODE_F_HELP}";


#
#-----[ BEFORE, ADD ]------------------------------------------
#

// -------------------------------------------------
// Strike BBCode - Begin Code Addition

st_help = '{L_BBCODE_ST_HELP}';

// Strike BBCode - End Code Addition
// -------------------------------------------------

#
#-----[ FIND ]------------------------------------------
#

bbtags = new
Array('[b]','[/b]','[i]','[/i]','[u]','[/u]','[quote]','[/quote]','[c
ode]','[/code]','[list]','[/list]','[list=]','[/list]','[img]','[/img
]','[url]','[/url]');


#
#-----[ AFTER, ADD ]------------------------------------------
#

// -------------------------------------------------
// Strike BBCode - Begin Code Addition

bbtags[22] = '[s]';
bbtags[23] = '[/s]';

// Strike BBCode - End Code Addition
// -------------------------------------------------

#
#-----[ FIND ]------------------------------------------
#

          <td><span class="genmed">
            <input type="button" class="button" accesskey="w"
name="addbbcode16" value="URL" style="text-decoration: underline;
width: 40px" onClick="bbstyle(16)" onMouseOver="helpline('w')" />
            </span></td>

#
#-----[ AFTER, ADD ]------------------------------------------
#

<!-- Strike BBCode - Begin Code Addition -->
          <td><span class="genmed">
            <input type="button" class="button" accesskey="t"
```

```
name="addbbcode22" value="Strike" style="text-decoration: line-through; width: 44px" onClick="bbstyle(22)"
onMouseOver="helpline('st')" />
              </span></td>
<!-- Strike BBCode - End Code Addition -->


#
#-----[ SAVE/CLOSE ALL FILES ]-----------------------------------------
---
#
# EoM
```

Creating a ZIP File

Now that you have an instruction file, you can place it into a ZIP file for distributing on websites. For a simple single file modification like this Strike BBCode, you could simply make it available as that one file. Larger modifications with multiple files, however, need to be packaged into a single compressed file. This makes them easier to distribute. As an example, consider the popular File Attachment modification, which contains over 140 individual files. Downloading these files one at a time would be a nightmare, so they are combined compressed into one ZIP file. Not only does this allow you to download the entire modification in one file, but the size of this file is significantly smaller and makes for an even faster download.

The actual process of creating a ZIP file will vary depending on the software used. There are many programs that can be used. Several were listed in Chapter 4's *Installing a New Style* section. The Windows XP and Mac OS X operating systems also have built-in abilities to create ZIP files. When you've chosen the software you will use, consult its Help files or website to determine how to create ZIP files with that software.

First, place all the files that need to be distributed as part of your modification in one folder and name this folder after the modification. For the Strike BBCode, you could create a `Strike` folder and place your `strike.mod` file in it. If the modification adds new forum files, you may wish to create folders within that first folder reflecting the correct locations of the new files, such as `templates/subSilver/`, for new template files, and place the additional files within those folders.

Once the files and folders are all arranged to your satisfaction, navigate to the folder containing the modification's folder (`Strike`, for the example). Right-click on the modification's folder to open the Windows context menu. There should be an entry in this menu for WinZip; hover over it with the mouse pointer to expand a submenu with several options for creating ZIP files. Click the Add to Strike.zip line to create a new file called `Strike.zip` containing all the files and folders within the `Strike` folder. The name used in Add to Strike.zip and `Strike.zip` will be different if you chose a different name for the modification folder. The image that follows illustrates using the context menu for this process. Test your new ZIP file by double-clicking the filename or icon. WinZip, or your chosen archive software, should open the file and allow you to extract the files.

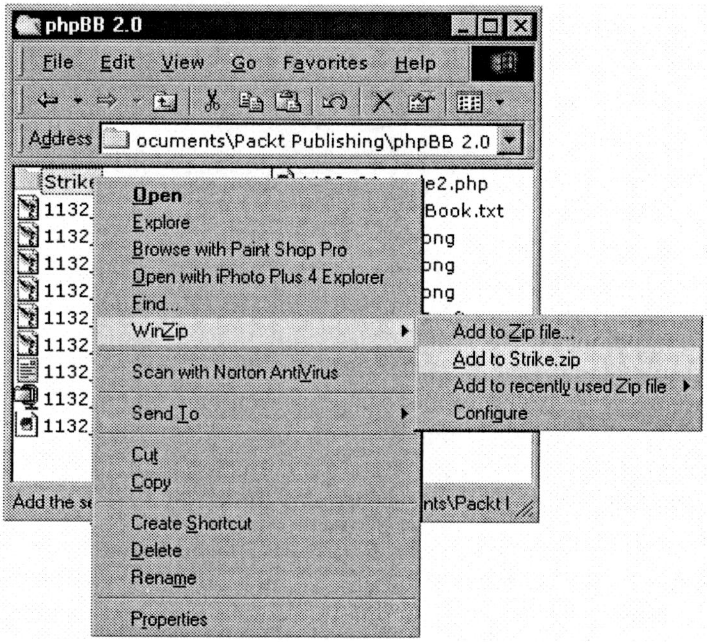

Submitting Your Modification

With all the files of your modification gathered into a package of one compressed file, you are finally ready to make it available to others. To submit the file to phpBB.com's modification database, you will need to log in to an account on that community's forums. If you do not already have an account there, you will need to register before you can submit any files.

Once logged in, click on the Mods image in the menu running across the top (of every page). This takes you to the website's modifications area, where you can find the modification database and documentation related to submitting and creating modifications. Click on the MODS-Database link on this page to view the categories of the database. All downloads in this database are gathered into sections based on the type of modification as you will see. Choose the most appropriate category for your modification—BBCode in the case of BBCode modifications—and click that category to view the downloads currently listed there. A list of links will be present on the left of the listing page. Click on the Add Link; this leads to the submission form.

The submission form has several fields for entering the same information that you placed into the header of your instructions file, such as MOD Author, MOD Description, Installation Time, and so on. You can also enter a private message for the modification validation team and other information related to the submission process. Clicking the Browse button on the last form entry will open a dialog window in which you can select the ZIP file on your computer. Submitting the form will upload the file from your computer. Make sure you do not close your web browser until the upload is complete, or your submission will not be received.

> You *cannot* submit the Strike BBCode to websites for reasons stated earlier in this chapter. However, you can distribute any original modifications you create.

When you submit a modification to phpBB.com's database, it is placed into a queue where it remains until reviewed by the site's MOD Team. Once it has been reviewed, the modification will either be listed in the database, or will be rejected, in which case you should receive a private message on the forum explaining why and what must be changed before you can resubmit. The validation may take some time, especially when there is a large backlog of unreviewed submissions, so you should be patient during this stage. This process has been known to take as long as six months in the past. If the modification is accepted and listed in the modification database, a topic announcing the release will be created in the community forums. You can use this topic for supporting the modification if any problems are found later.

The submission process for other sites is different. phpBBHacks.com has a much simpler procedure, for example. On that site, you only have to click a Submit link on the site's menu and then choose another link based on the type of download you are submitting. There are separate submissions forms for modifications and other downloads. The submission form at this site allows you to enter the same sort of information as phpBB.com's form: a title, description, version number, staff message, and so on. There are some other fields as well, such as phpBB version compatibility. One important difference is that you will not upload the modification using this form. Instead, you must first upload it to a website of your own and provide the URL of the uploaded file. As phpBBHacks.com allows authors to be responsible for testing their own work, this site does not have a detailed validation procedure. The submitted hacks are processed regularly, so your submission should appear within a few days. Again, however, try to be patient: there are times when the processing might take a little longer.

Since you have to upload the ZIP file containing the modification in order to submit it to phpBBHacks.com, you can also release it on your own website. Many modification authors do this, and may even set up a special phpBB forum on their sites. Such forums often help provide support for modifications, and demonstrations for curious users.

Summary

Creating modifications can be a very rewarding experience for you as a forum administrator. By making more modifications and making them progressively more complex, you can learn many things about the inner workings of phpBB and PHP programming. You will not only be able to improve the forums of an online community, but will also gain experience that can help you enhance other aspects. Some authors have even gone on to do work-for-hire, like writing chapters in phpBB books!

By progressing through the examples of this chapter, you learned:

- That modifications can be written using any combination of four major programming languages
- That developing should be done in a sound testing environment with the latest phpBB release
- How to create a brand-new BBCode for your community
- Skills and techniques that will allow you to create other modifications
- The methods of submitting your modification to two of the largest modification databases

8
Programming phpBB

We've learned a lot about installing phpBB, configuring it, and customizing it to suit our community's needs. It's now time for the last, most advanced chapter of the book, describing what you need to know in order to program new custom phpBB features.

PHP programming knowledge and some SQL knowledge are pre-requisites for a good understanding of the chapter, but even if you're not familiar with PHP, you can still skim through the examples, if only to whet your programming appetite. Who knows, maybe you'll like what you see and decide to learn some more PHP.

This chapter is not a comprehensive guide to the phpBB programming experience, but instead will concentrate on the most used phpBB libraries and functions. The chapter starts with a simple "Hello phpBB World" script and slowly moves on to include more complicated examples. At the end of the chapter, you'll develop an all-new phpBB script called "What's Up?", which displays the recent topics from all the forums in your board on a single screen, while respecting the user-specific privileges.

In this chapter you will learn about:

- Creating the "Hello phpBB World!" script
- Working with the database
- Using phpBB messages
- phpBB's multi-language system
- Using phpBB templates
- User authentication
- Other handy phpBB functions and coding standards
- Putting it all together to create a new phpBB add-on script

Hello phpBB World!

It's a tradition when you start learning a new programming language or technology; the first thing you learn to do is how to write a simple application that just displays "Hello World!". Let's see how to do this in phpBB.

First off, just to give you an idea of what the goal is, here's the result of executing the Hello World script, displayed in a browser.

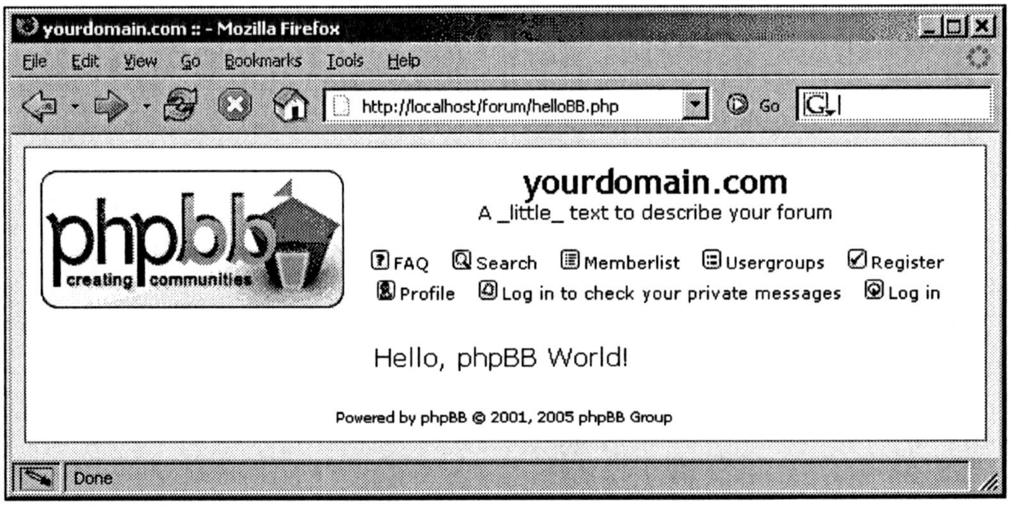

Here's the code to produce the result in the screenshot above.

```
<?php
// set IN_PHPBB constant and include the initialization script
define('IN_PHPBB', true);
$phpbb_root_path = './';
include($phpbb_root_path . 'extension.inc');
include($phpbb_root_path . 'common.'.$phpEx);

// Start session management
$userdata = session_pagestart($user_ip, PAGE_INDEX);
init_userprefs($userdata);

// include page header
include($phpbb_root_path . 'includes/page_header.'.$phpEx);

// say hello!
echo '<div align="center">Hello, phpBB World!</div>';

// include page footer
include($phpbb_root_path . 'includes/page_tail.'.$phpEx);
?>
```

In order to reproduce this on your board, you just need to create a new blank text file named, for example, `helloBB.php`, type the earlier code into the file, save it, and copy it to your board's root folder. You can then access the newly created script with your preferred browser (if your board is located at `http://www.yourdomain.com/forum`, you can go to `http://www.yourdomain.com/forum/helloBB.php` to access this script.

> The source code for this file (and for all the examples in the chapter) can be downloaded from `http://www.packtpub.com`.

Before reading the explanations, take a look at the code; take the time to read it and see if you can figure out what's happening in the script.

The script is divided into *five code blocks* delimited by empty lines. The actual work of the script is done in the *fourth* block—that's where the "Hello" is:

```
// say hello!
echo '<div align="center">Hello, phpBB World!</div>';
```

The rest of the script is setting up the phpBB environment for the actual work to be performed. Every script that you write should have the same flow, so you can use this script as a prototype for all your future scripts and just replace the "working" part with the functionality you require. This being said, you don't really need to know what's happening outside the fourth block but if you're curious, here's some more information.

Here's what's happening in the *first* block:

1. On the first line, a constant called `IN_PHPBB` is defined. This is a security measure that will be discussed in a bit more detail later in the chapter.
2. Then the phpBB root directory is defined, which in this case is the current directory since the script is located in the phpBB root.
3. Then a simple file called `extension.inc` is included. It only defines the extension of the PHP files on the server. Most likely the extension will be `.php`.
4. In the last line of the first block, a really important file—`common.php`—is included. This script is responsible for the most of the phpBB environment setup and configuration. You can look into its source for more details, but just to have a general idea, this script is responsible for initializing the forum configuration, establishing a database connection, and including the other libraries and functions that phpBB cannot do without.

The *second* block of code is responsible for calling two functions that deal with the session data and user preferences. The *third* and the *fifth* blocks are including respectively the header and the footer of the phpBB graphical user interface. The header is everything you see on the screenshot that is *before* the `Hello, phpBB World!` line, and the footer is everything *after* that. If you program a special script, for example a pop-up window script, you may not necessarily need the header and the footer.

Now that we know the basic structure of a phpBB script, let's move ahead and retrieve some data from the database.

Working with the Database

The database connectivity in phpBB is an important topic, so it needs special attention. This section gives you some background information about the database abstraction used in phpBB, and some examples of its use to retrieve data from your database.

Database Abstraction

As you know already, phpBB can work with different databases. To achieve this result without re-coding the whole system, phpBB employs a programming technique called **database abstraction**. This simply means that there are several scripts (classes), specific for each supported database system that in a different way achieve the same result. In this case, the other phpBB scripts don't need to know anything about the specific database system, they just call the functions (class methods) of the database abstraction class and it does the work on the specific database.

For example, to execute an SQL query on a MySQL database, PHP scripts use the `mysql_query()` function. To do the same on an MS Access database, `odbc_exec()` is used. So, as part of the database abstraction mechanism, phpBB is defining individual classes that work on different database systems: one class for MySQL, one for MS Access, and so on for the other supported RDBMS. The classes have different implementations, but share the same "public interface", meaning all classes have the same set of functions (methods). So when you want to execute an SQL query, all you need to do is use the `sql_query()` method from the phpBB database abstraction layer without having to understand how this method is implemented and what underlying database system is used. Abstracting and concentrating on the more important stuff, while leaving other classes responsible for some details—that's the beauty of the object-oriented programming!

In the `common.php` script (which we mentioned earlier) a database connection is established for you and the `$db` variable is defined, containing an object of the appropriate database class. Again, you don't care what type of database system is used; you only need to know the programming interface of the phpBB abstraction layer. This may sound like we're going into more trouble learning additional functions and how they work, but this is in fact a good thing, because this way you code once and then reuse your code on any database supported by phpBB.

One last thing about the database abstraction—the use of standard SQL commands. If you use any SQL commands or functions specific to a particular RDBMS, then be aware that this functionality may not exist in other systems. This shouldn't be a problem in general, because you don't just switch between different databases every day, but it's still something you should know.

Database Abstraction Working

Let's take a look at an example of how the phpBB database abstraction layer works. You'll create a script that shows a counter of how many words were used on the board forums so far. phpBB has a full text search system that stores all the used words into a database table. So for the purposes of the example, all you need to do is count the number of rows in this table.

To help visualize what you're aiming at, here's the result of the script execution:

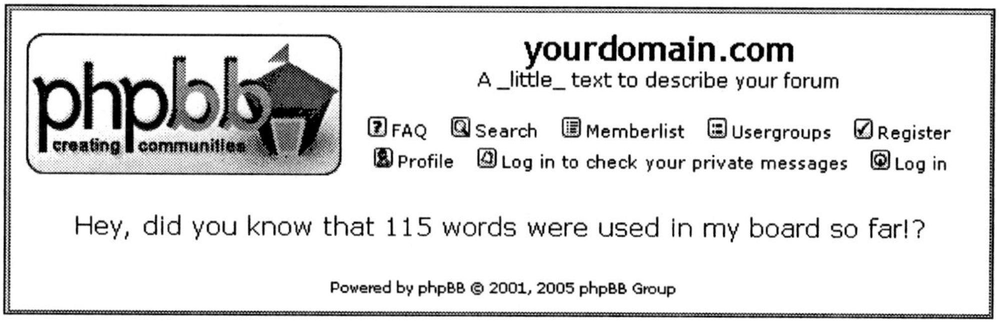

Here's the source code used to achieve it:

```
<?php
// set IN_PHPBB constant and include the initialization script
define('IN_PHPBB', true);
$phpbb_root_path = './';
include($phpbb_root_path . 'extension.inc');
include($phpbb_root_path . 'common.'.$phpEx);

// Start session management
$userdata = session_pagestart($user_ip, PAGE_INDEX);
init_userprefs($userdata);

// include page header
include($phpbb_root_path . 'includes/page_header.'.$phpEx);

// the main script work starts here
$sql = "SELECT COUNT(*) FROM " . SEARCH_WORD_TABLE;
$result = $db->sql_query($sql);
if ( !$result )
{
    message_die(GENERAL_ERROR, 'Cannot execute query', '', __LINE__,
__FILE__, $sql);
}
$row = $db->sql_fetchrow();
$word_count = $row[0];
echo '<div align="center">Hey, did you know that '. $word_count .'
words were used in my board so far!?</div>';
```

```
// end of the script work
// include page footer
include($phpbb_root_path . 'includes/page_tail.'.$phpEx);
?>
```

Save this code into a file called phpBBdb.php (or get it from the book's code download), copy the file to your phpBB root, and give it a try in your browser.

As you can see, this script follows the structure of the previous one, only the "working" part was changed. Let's discuss this part a bit.

First we start with a SQL query to be executed.

```
$sql = "SELECT COUNT(*) FROM " . SEARCH_WORD_TABLE;
```

In this query, SEARCH_WORD_TABLE is a constant that defines the name of the table that contains the full-text search data. If you remember, during the installation you could specify a table prefix for all the tables in the database. Using constants (such as SEARCH_WORD_TABLE, POSTS_TABLE, and so on) instead of hard-coded table names allows phpBB to offer this feature. You can see how all database-related constants (as well as other constants) are defined by looking at the includes/constants.php script. By default, the table prefix is phpbb_, so after the constant is replaced with its value, the query will look like SELECT COUNT(*) FROM phpbb_search_wordlist;.

Now let's take a look at the next the next line of code.

```
$result = $db->sql_query($sql);
```

This line executes the SQL query calling the sql_query() method of the instance of the appropriate DB abstraction class (which you didn't need to worry about).

This is followed by:

```
if ( !$result )
{
    message_die(GENERAL_ERROR, 'Cannot execute query', '',
                __LINE__, __FILE__, $sql);
}
```

These lines check whether the query was executed successfully. If not, an error message is displayed (you'll find out more about the messages in a bit). After the query is successfully executed, it's time to get the results of the execution. (The phpBB abstraction layer offers a variety of ways to do that, which will be discussed later.)

```
$row = $db->sql_fetchrow();
```

This line gets a row of results as an array and assigns it to a variable called $row. In this case, only one row (record), actually only one field, is returned. So $row[0] will contain the value that we want. The zero stands for offset zero in the row of returned results.

```
$word_count = $row[0];
```

The last thing left is to display the value using echo.

```
echo '<div align="center">Hey, did you know that '. $word_count .'
words were used in my board so far!?</div>';
```

Using the phpBB Database Abstraction Layer

We mentioned that there are several ways to retrieve data from the result of a query execution, after the query has been executed using `sql_query()`. Let's see the options.

Option 1

The example here used the `sql_fetchrow()` method. This method returns the results as both enumerated and associative array. The keys of the associative array are the field names in the result set—the same result as above could have been achieved by using:

```
$word_count = $row['COUNT(*)'];
```

Clearly, the above is not very typing-friendly. A better option would be to use:

```
$word_count = $row['words'];
```

This will work if the query is slightly modified to use `words` as an alias to `COUNT(*)`:

```
$sql = "SELECT COUNT(*) AS words FROM " . SEARCH_WORD_TABLE;
```

Option 2

Another way to get results from an executed query is by using the `sql_fetchrowset()` method. It works like `sql_fetchrow()`, except that it returns the data for all the records matched by a query. If you use `sql_fetchrow()`, you have to call this method in a loop until you reach the end of the result set, while `sql_fetchrowset()` returns all results and you loop through an array of results. The second option is somewhat friendlier, but consumes more memory because it requires copying the result set into the memory as an array. It's thus not recommended for use with queries that will return huge result sets, but is OK for smaller "everyday" queries.

To illustrate the difference, you can `print_r()` the results of both functions. From `sql_fetchrow()`, you'll get something like:

```
Array
(
    [0] => 71
    [COUNT(*)] => 71
)
```

.. and from `sql_fetchrowset()`, you'll get:

```
Array
(
    [0] => Array
        (
            [0] => 71
            [COUNT(*)] => 71
        )
)
```

Option 3

Another way to get the result from an executed query is by using `sql_fetchfield()`, which returns the result from one field only, and this field is referenced by name. To get the expected result from the previous example, you can use:

```
$word_count = $db->sql_fetchfield('COUNT(*)');
```

If you don't know the field name, but know its offset in the result-set row, you can use the `sql_fieldname()` method as follows:

```
$word_count = $db->sql_fetchfield($db->sql_fieldname(0));
```

Here again zero is the offset of the field you're interested in.

Using phpBB Messages

In the previous example, you already saw how phpBB messages are used. Now it's time to take a closer look at those messages and test them in action.

In order to see a phpBB message in action, you can simply use the previous example, but this time, introduce an invalid command in the SQL string; for example:

```
$sql = "HEY, GO AHEAD AND SELECT COUNT(*) FROM " . SEARCH_WORD_TABLE;
```

If you save the file that you've just modified as `phpBBmessage.php` and preview it in your browser, you'll see an error message caused by the invalid SQL string.

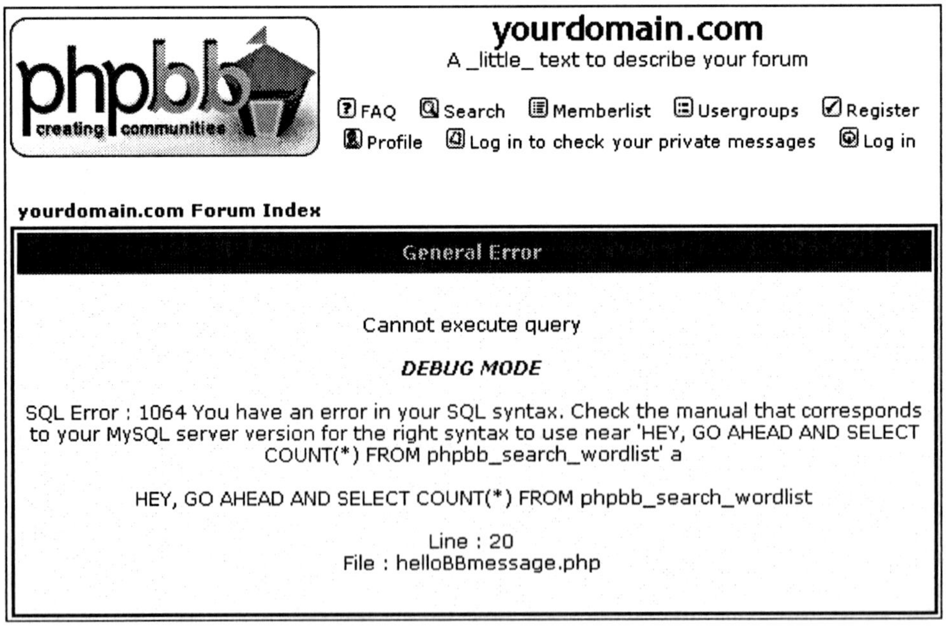

This message was caused by the following piece of code from the example:

```
if ( !$result )
{
    message_die(GENERAL_ERROR, 'Cannot execute query', '', __LINE__,
__FILE__, $sql);
}
```

Here the `message_die()` function available in phpBB was used. You see all the details of the error because the forum runs in debug mode. When in production (when your forum is live) it's a good idea to have the debug mode turned off. You can do this by changing a line in the `constants.php` script, located in the `includes` folder. The debug setup code is located at the very top of the `constants.php` script. Make sure the `DEBUG` constant is set to 0, as follows:

```
// Debug Level
//define('DEBUG', 1); // Debugging on
define('DEBUG', 0); // Debugging off
```

If the debug mode is disabled, the above message will be much less verbose:

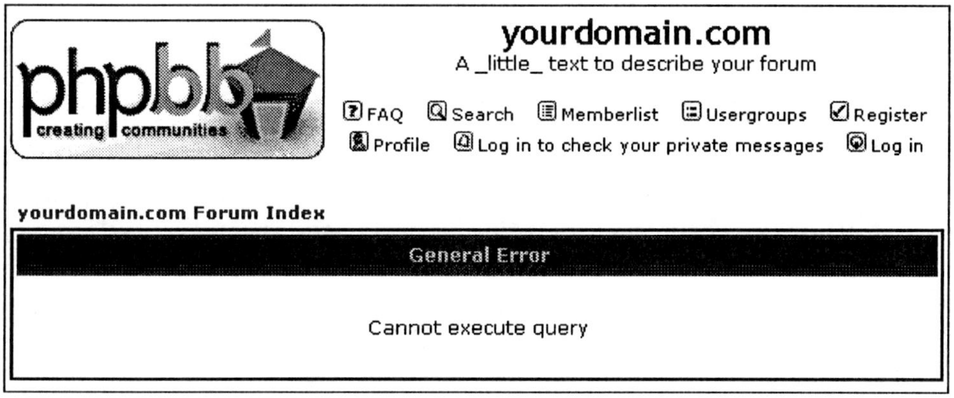

The `message_die()` phpBB function can be used for purposes other than for error messages. For instance, it can be used to display much nicer results from the database example discussed in the previous section of this chapter (`helloBBdb.php`). In this database example, change the line:

```
echo '<div align="center">Hey, did you know that '. $word_count .'
words were used in my board so far!?</div>';
```

to:

```
message_die(GENERAL_MESSAGE,
            'Hey, did you know that '. $word_count .' words were used
in my board so far!?',
            'Word count');
```

Save this as `helloBBmessage2.php` and view it in your browser. The result will be:

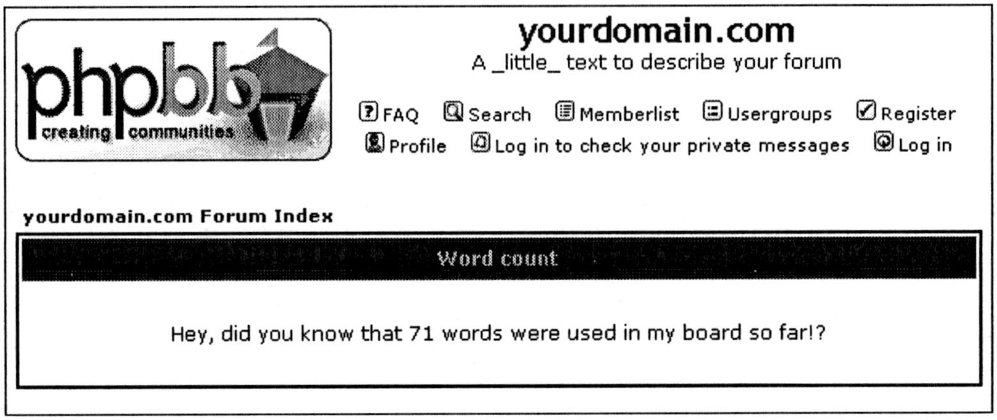

Here's some information about the six function parameters you can use when calling `message_die()`:

- **Message type**: Can be `GENERAL_MESSAGE`, `CRITICAL_MESSAGE`, `GENERAL_ERROR`, or `CRITICAL_ERROR`, depending on the severity of the message.
- **Message text**: Can be anything you want to communicate to the user.
- **Message title**: If you don't supply it, a default title will be used based on the message type. In the last example, the title was Word count.
- **Error line** (for debug mode only): This contains the line in the script where the error occurred. The way to pass this parameter is just to use the `__LINE__` PHP core constant.
- **Error file**: (for debug mode only): This is the filename of the script that caused the error. As with the previous parameter, just use `__FILE__` here.
- **SQL**: SQL string (if any) related to the error.

Of all the function parameters, only the first (message type) is a required parameter: the rest are optional.

Using phpBB's Multi-Language System

In the previous examples, a few texts were displayed to the user. The problem with these texts was that they were in English only, and might not be understood by visitors who browse your forums in a language other than English. To offer multi-lingual support your custom scripts, you can make use of phpBB's multi-language system.

The language folder of your phpBB installation contains sub-folders for each installed language, like `lang_english`, `lang_spanish`, etc. These folders have a number of files, but the one you'll be interested in the most, is called `lang_main.php`. This file contains static texts, defined as elements of an associative array called `$lang`. For example:

```
$lang['Guest'] = 'Guest';
$lang['Post_subject'] = 'Post subject';
$lang['View_next_topic'] = 'View next topic';
```

At the end of this file (before the "`That's all, Folks!`" comment) you can add your texts as new array elements. In the previous example (`helloBBmessage2.php`) two texts were used: `Word count` and `Hey, did you know that` *(number of words here)* `words were used in my board so far!?`. You can define them in `lang_main.php` as follows:

```
$lang['Word_count_title'] = 'Word count';
$lang['Word_count_message'] = 'Hey, did you know that
<strong>%d</strong> words were used in my board so far!?';
```

`%d` is used as a placeholder for the actual number of words, and it's to be replaced in your script. You can use anything as a replaceable placeholder, but phpBB team has adopted the usage of the PHP `printf()` function. For details on how `printf()` and `sprintf()` work, you can consult the PHP manual entries at `http://php.net/printf` and `http://php.net/sprintf`.

You've probably spotted a slight change in the text of the message. Well, just to make the message a bit different and at the same time to test how HTML is supported, the word count value `%d` was enclosed with the `<strong>` HTML tags to emphasize the number of words.

Now that your texts are in the `lang_main.php` file, they will be initialized automatically every time your script is accessed. So you can use them in your script by changing the call to `message_die()` to the following:

```
message_die(GENERAL_MESSAGE,
            sprintf($lang['Word_count_message'], $word_count),
            $lang['Word_count_title']);
```

Here's a complete listing of the modified script. You can save it as `helloBBlangs.php` and test it on your board. Don't forget the changes to `lang_main.php` and, if your board uses multiple languages, don't forget that you need to translate the texts and add them to the `lang_main.php` script in the corresponding languages' directories.

```
<?php
// set IN_PHPBB constant and include the initialization script
define('IN_PHPBB', true);
$phpbb_root_path = './';
include($phpbb_root_path . 'extension.inc');
include($phpbb_root_path . 'common.'.$phpEx);

// Start session management
$userdata = session_pagestart($user_ip, PAGE_INDEX);
init_userprefs($userdata);

// include page header
include($phpbb_root_path . 'includes/page_header.'.$phpEx);
```

```
// the main script work starts here
$sql = "SELECT COUNT(*) FROM " . SEARCH_WORD_TABLE;
$result = $db->sql_query($sql);
if ( !$result )
{
    message_die(GENERAL_ERROR, 'Cannot execute query', '', __LINE__,
__FILE__, $sql);
}
$row = $db->sql_fetchrow();
$word_count = $row[0];

message_die(GENERAL_MESSAGE,
            sprintf($lang['word_count_message'], $word_count),
            $lang['word_count_title']);
// end of the script work

// include page footer
include($phpbb_root_path . 'includes/page_tail.'.$phpEx);
?>
```

Here's the result of executing `helloBBlangs.php`:

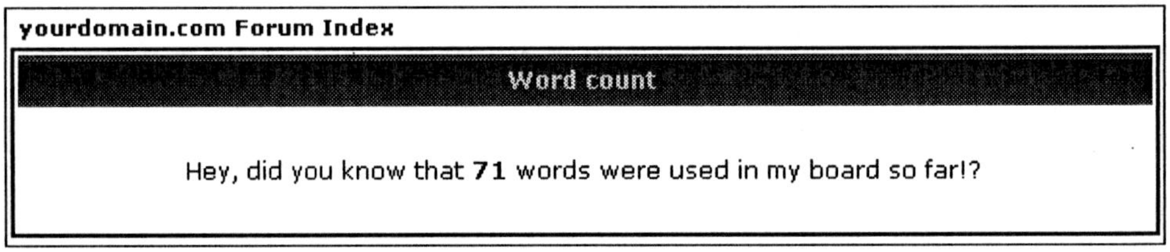

Using phpBB Templates

In the previous examples, there wasn't much graphical user interface work involved, but normally there will be, if you're developing new phpBB scripts or extending existing ones. Separating the programming code from the user interface is generally a good programming practice, often referred to as a "separation of logic from presentation". For web applications such as phpBB, this means having the PHP code and logic separated from the HTML code that is used to present the results to the user.

This is normally achieved by using the so called **templating systems** (templating engines), which consist of two parts:

- Static HTML template files that contain the rules of displaying the content; "rules" mean formatting, layout, and so on
- PHP logic to "fill-in the blanks" in the HTML templates

Using a templating engine allows for changing the face of a bulletin board completely, by changing the static HTML files only and not dealing with the programming logic, database access, and so on. Creating new templates was discussed in detail in Chapter 4.

phpBB has its own templating engine, which is discussed here in order to give you a basic understanding on how to use it in your scripts.

You can find the template library script (`template.php`) in the `includes` folder. This file contains the definition (the code) for a class called `Template` and you can see its implementation if you're interested. For the purposes of coding phpBB scripts, you only need to know how to use the library and not how it's actually coded (remember, that's the beauty of the object-oriented coding approach).

In order to use the template class, an instance (an object) of that class needs to be created. There is such an object created for you as part of the phpBB environment setup. As soon as you include the page header script, a variable called `$template` is initialized and it contains an object of the `Template` class.

A Simple Example

It is time to create a brand new, simple template. Create (or copy from the book code download) the following file (call it `wordcount.tpl` and place it in the `templates/subSilver` directory):

```
<span class="nav"><a href="{U_INDEX}"
class="nav">{L_INDEX}</a></span>
<div
    align="center"
    class="gen"
    style="border: solid 2px #006699; padding: 10px; margin-top:
5px;"
    >
    {WORD_COUNT_MESSAGE}
</div>
```

Before proceeding with the PHP code, take a look at the following screenshot; it shows the result of executing the example.

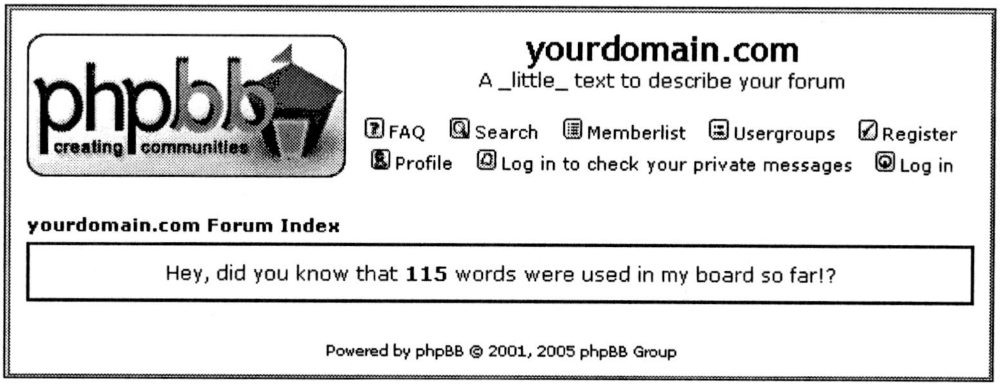

The template specified earlier is responsible only for the following part of the screenshot:

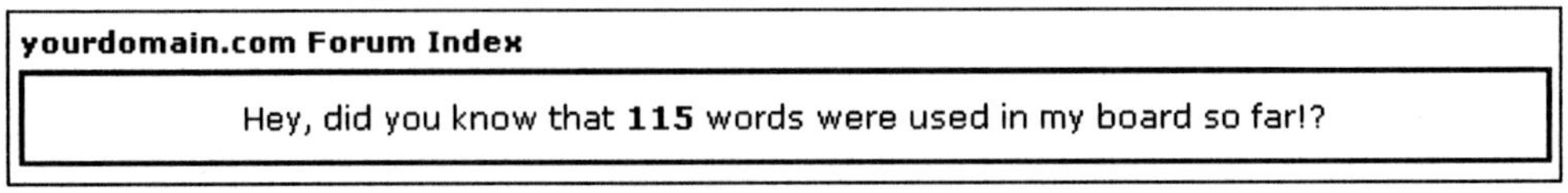

The rest is displayed by the default header and footer.

Let's see how to achieve this result. There are three parts to using the templating functionality in your scripts:

- First you specify the filename(s) that contain the static HTML, using `$template->set_filenames()`.
- Then you use PHP to replace the template variables with data by calling `$template->assign_vars()` or `$template->assign_block_vars()`. Having read Chapter 4, you're already familiar with the template variables and their syntax; they are enclosed by curly brackets and capitalized, like `{I_AM_A_VAR}`.
- Finally you call the `$template->pparse()` method to display the result.

Here's the PHP code that uses the `wordcount.tpl` template listed earlier:

```
// assemble the message text
$message_text = sprintf($lang['Word_count_message'], $word_count);

// set template file
$template->set_filenames(array('body' => 'wordcount.tpl'));

// assign template variables
$template->assign_vars(
    array(
        'WORD_COUNT_MESSAGE' => $message_text,
    )
);

// process, parse and display
$template->pparse('body');
```

There are two more template variables that were displayed in the result but were not assigned values using `$template->assign_vars()`—`U_INDEX` and `L_INDEX`. The reason you don't need to worry about them is that they were already assigned when the page header was processed. For more information and a full listing of the behind-the-scenes processed variables, open the `includes/page_header.php` script and scroll down to near the bottom of the file where the template variables are assigned.

To test the example, create a `helloBBtemplates.php` file with the following code and navigate to it in your browser (don't forget to also copy the `wordcount.tpl` template into the `templates/subSilver` directory):

```
<?php
// set IN_PHPBB constant and include the initialization script
define('IN_PHPBB', true);
$phpbb_root_path = './';
include($phpbb_root_path . 'extension.inc');
include($phpbb_root_path . 'common.'.$phpEx);

// Start session management
$userdata = session_pagestart($user_ip, PAGE_INDEX);
init_userprefs($userdata);

// include page header
include($phpbb_root_path . 'includes/page_header.'.$phpEx);

// the main script work starts here
$sql = "SELECT COUNT(*) FROM " . SEARCH_WORD_TABLE;
$result = $db->sql_query($sql);
if ( !$result )
{
    message_die(GENERAL_ERROR, 'Cannot execute query', '', __LINE__,
__FILE__, $sql);
}
$row = $db->sql_fetchrow();
$word_count = $row[0];

// assemble the message text
$message_text = sprintf($lang['Word_count_message'], $word_count);

// set template file
$template->set_filenames(array('body' => 'wordcount.tpl'));

// assign template variables
$template->assign_vars(
    array(
        'WORD_COUNT_MESSAGE' => $message_text,
    )
);

// process, parse and display
$template->pparse('body');
// end of the script work

// include page footer
include($phpbb_root_path . 'includes/page_tail.'.$phpEx);
?>
```

Using Loops in phpBB Templates

Often, assigning static template variables is not enough; you'll need the ability to perform dynamic assignments like using loops within a template (for example, listing all topics in a forum is performing a loop, listing all replies to a topic is also a loop, and so on). Let's consider an example to see how you can use loops.

The example displays the numbers from one to ten. To set up the loop in the template, use the **block variable** syntax.

```
<!-- BEGIN number_loop -->
    {number_loop.NUMBER}
<!-- END number_loop -->
```

Here number_loop is the name of the block and NUMBER is a variable. Note the dotted syntax to refer to a variable within a loop like {number_loop.NUMBER}. To make it a bit more interesting and to understand the difference between a variable within a block and outside a block, add another {NUMBER} variable, but this time not related to the loop. It will have a constant value during the loop iterations.

Here's the listing of the template (save it to a file called example2.tpl and place it in templates/subSilver):

```
<span class="nav"><a href="{U_INDEX}"
class="nav">{L_INDEX}</a></span>
<div
    align="center"
    class="gen"
    style="border: solid 2px #006699; padding: 10px; margin-top:
5px;"
    >
    <!-- BEGIN number_loop -->
        {NUMBER}{number_loop.NUMBER}
    <!-- END number_loop -->
</div>
```

Here's the PHP script (helloBBtemplates2.php) to parse the template:

```
<?php
// set IN_PHPBB constant and include the initialization script
define('IN_PHPBB', true);
$phpbb_root_path = './';
include($phpbb_root_path . 'extension.inc');
include($phpbb_root_path . 'common.'.$phpEx);

// Start session management
$userdata = session_pagestart($user_ip, PAGE_INDEX);
init_userprefs($userdata);

// include page header
include($phpbb_root_path . 'includes/page_header.'.$phpEx);

// the main script work starts here
// set template file
$template->set_filenames(array('body' => 'example2.tpl'));

// assign template variables in a loop
for ($i = 1; $i<=10; $i++)
{
    $template->assign_block_vars("number_loop",
        array(
            'NUMBER' => $i,
        )
    );
}
// assign a static variable
$template->assign_vars(
```

```
        array(
            'NUMBER' => '#',
        )
    );

    // process, parse and display
    $template->pparse('body');
    // end of the script work

    // include page footer
    include($phpbb_root_path . 'includes/page_tail.'.$phpEx);
    ?>
```

The result of executing `helloBBtemplates2.php` in a browser:

Using Conditions in phpBB Templates

Sometimes you'll want to display data to the user conditionally, depending on some "if" case (a "switch"). To do this using the phpBB templating engine, use the same **block variables** as when working with loops.

The next example is quite similar to the previous one; it lists the numbers from one to ten. But it uses an "if" case for even numbers in order to display them in bold font.

Here's the template. Save it as `example3.tpl` in `templates/subSilver`:

```
<span class="nav"><a href="{U_INDEX}" class="nav">{L_INDEX}</a>
</span>
<div
    align="center"
    class="gen"
    style="border: solid 2px #006699; padding: 10px; margin-top:
5px;"
    >
    <!-- BEGIN number_loop -->

        <!-- BEGIN odd_switch -->
         {NUMBER}{number_loop.odd_switch.NUMBER}
        <!-- END odd_switch -->
```

```
        <!-- BEGIN even_switch -->
         <strong>{NUMBER}{number_loop.even_switch.NUMBER}</strong>
        <!-- END even_switch -->

    <!-- END number_loop -->
</div>
```

Because you have nested blocks (a switch block within a loop block), when you reference a variable from the inner block, you need to specify both blocks' names, separated by a dot, like `{number_loop.odd_switch.NUMBER}`. Also note that there is no separate test for the even case—you simply use `else` to introduce an alternative block of code.

Here is the listing of the PHP script (save it as `helloBBtemplates3.php` in your root phpBB folder):

```
<?php
// set IN_PHPBB constant and include the initialization script
define('IN_PHPBB', true);
$phpbb_root_path = './';
include($phpbb_root_path . 'extension.inc');
include($phpbb_root_path . 'common.'.$phpEx);

// Start session management
$userdata = session_pagestart($user_ip, PAGE_INDEX);
init_userprefs($userdata);

// include page header
include($phpbb_root_path . 'includes/page_header.'.$phpEx);

// the main script work starts here
// set template file
$template->set_filenames(array('body' => 'example3.tpl'));

// assign template variables in a loop
for ($i = 0; $i <= 10; $i++)
{
    if ( $i % 2 )
    {
        $template->assign_block_vars("number_loop.odd_switch",
            array(
                'NUMBER' => $i,
            )
        );
    } else {
        $template->assign_block_vars("number_loop.even_switch",
            array(
                'NUMBER' => $i,
            )
        );
    }
}

// assign a static variable
$template->assign_vars(
    array(
        'NUMBER' => '#',
    )
);
```

```
// process, parse and display
$template->pparse('body');
// end of the script work

// include page footer
include($phpbb_root_path . 'includes/page_tail.'.$phpEx);
?>
```

Here's the script in action:

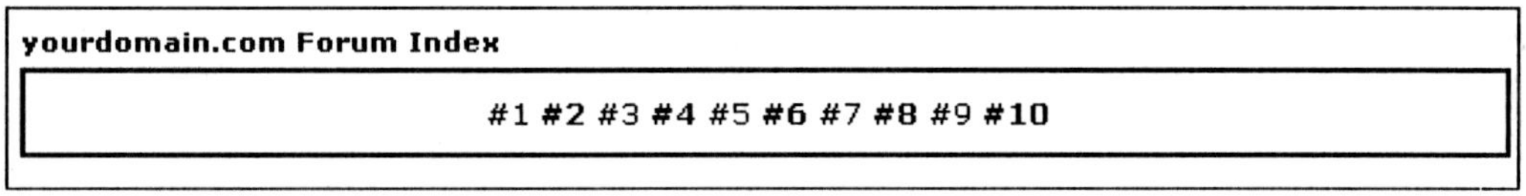

> To round off your knowledge on the phpBB templating engine, there is a comprehensive knowledge-base article at `http://www.phpbb.com/kb/article.php?article_id=200`.

User Authentication

When you develop new scripts or extend existing ones, it's likely that you'll need a way to verify a user's privileges (in other words, check if a user is allowed to do or view what your script provides); for example, if you develop a script to display postings from a hidden forum, you'll need to make sure that only users that are allowed access to this forum can see the postings.

There is one important user authentication function that is defined in `includes/auth.php`—the `auth()` function.

The `auth()` function returns an associative array that contains information about the privileges that are checked. You can check for individual privileges (permission types), like permission to view, read, post, vote, and so on; you can even check for all permission types at once. You can also check for privileges in a specific forum or in all forums.

There are three required parameters when you use the `auth()` function:

- **Permission type**: The possible values are the constants `AUTH_VIEW`, `AUTH_READ`, `AUTH_POST`, `AUTH_REPLY`, `AUTH_EDIT`, `AUTH_DELETE`, `AUTH_STICKY`, `AUTH_ANNOUNCE`, `AUTH_VOTE`, `AUTH_POLLCREATE`, or (to check for all permission types) `AUTH_ALL`.
- **Forum ID**: If you want to check for privileges in a specific forum, you specify its ID. To check for permissions in all forums, you use the `AUTH_LIST_ALL` constant.

- **User data**: An array of user information. You don't need to worry about this; there is a `$userdata` variable defined at the beginning of every script, in the session management part. So you just need to pass this variable as is.

The `auth()` function returns the results as associative arrays. Let's look at a few examples of how `auth()` can be used in order to get a better idea of the return values.

Using the Authentication Function

You can use the following code to play around and test how the authentication function works and what types of values it returns. Save this code as `helloBBauth.php` and load it in your browser:

```
<?php
// set IN_PHPBB constant and include the initialization script
define('IN_PHPBB', true);
$phpbb_root_path = './';
include($phpbb_root_path . 'extension.inc');
include($phpbb_root_path . 'common.'.$phpEx);

// Start session management
$userdata = session_pagestart($user_ip, PAGE_INDEX);
init_userprefs($userdata);

// include page header
include($phpbb_root_path . 'includes/page_header.'.$phpEx);

// check auth
$user_privileges  = auth(AUTH_ALL, AUTH_LIST_ALL, $userdata);
// display the return value
echo '<pre>';
print_r($user_privileges);
echo '</pre>';

// include page footer
include($phpbb_root_path . 'includes/page_tail.'.$phpEx);
?>
```

This script contains a call to the `auth()` function and then displays the results of the execution. You can start changing the parameters you pass to the `auth()` function and see how the return values are changed. You can also log in as a normal user, then log in as a moderator or an administrator, and then log out and see how the return values change.

Let's say your forum has a forum ID equal to 1, and this forum is set up as a **registered** forum, meaning that in the Administration Panel | Forum Admin | Permissions, its permissions were set to Registered using Simple Mode. This means that a user has to register and log in to be able to post. In this case to check the user privileges you can change the call to the `auth()` function in the previous example to:

```
$user_privileges  = auth(AUTH_ALL, 1, $userdata);
```

If you save the modified script as `helloBBauth2.php` and load it in your browser, you'll see the return value as:

```
Array
(
    [auth_view] => 1
    [auth_view_type] => anonymous users
    [auth_read] => 1
    [auth_read_type] => anonymous users
    [auth_post] => 0
    [auth_post_type] => registered users
    [auth_reply] => 0
    [auth_reply_type] => registered users
    [auth_edit] => 0
    [auth_edit_type] => registered users
    [auth_delete] => 0
    [auth_delete_type] => registered users
    [auth_sticky] => 0
    [auth_sticky_type] => moderators
    [auth_announce] => 0
    [auth_announce_type] => moderators
    [auth_vote] => 0
    [auth_vote_type] => registered users
    [auth_pollcreate] => 0
    [auth_pollcreate_type] => registered users
    [auth_mod] => 0
)
```

This result is displayed when you're not logged in. You see that only the `auth_view` and `auth_read` indices in the return value are set to `1`, the rest are `0`. This means that when you're not logged in, you only have the privilege to see that this forum exists and to read it.

Now if you log in as a regular user and visit `helloBBauth2.php` again, you'll see different return values:

```
Array
(
    [auth_view] => 1
    [auth_view_type] => anonymous users
    [auth_read] => 1
    [auth_read_type] => anonymous users
    [auth_post] => 1
    [auth_post_type] => registered users
    [auth_reply] => 1
    [auth_reply_type] => registered users
    [auth_edit] => 1
    [auth_edit_type] => registered users
    [auth_delete] => 1
    [auth_delete_type] => registered users
    [auth_sticky] => 0
    [auth_sticky_type] => moderators
    [auth_announce] => 0
    [auth_announce_type] => moderators
    [auth_vote] => 1
    [auth_vote_type] => registered users
    [auth_pollcreate] => 1
    [auth_pollcreate_type] => registered users
    [auth_mod] => 0
)
```

As you can see, now the only permission types set to 0 are `auth_mod`, `auth_sticky`, and `auth_announce`, because being logged as a regular user, you cannot moderate the forum or post stickies or announcements.

Checking for Poll-Creation Privileges

If all these associative array return values are giving you a headache, here's a friendlier way of displaying results from the calls to the `auth()` function. This example (`helloBBauth3.php`) tells you whether you can create polls in the forum with forum ID equal to 1. Test it when you're logged in and then when you're logged out.

```
<?php
// set IN_PHPBB constant and include the initialization script
define('IN_PHPBB', true);
$phpbb_root_path = './';
include($phpbb_root_path . 'extension.inc');
include($phpbb_root_path . 'common.'.$phpEx);

// Start session management
$userdata = session_pagestart($user_ip, PAGE_INDEX);
init_userprefs($userdata);

// include page header
include($phpbb_root_path . 'includes/page_header.'.$phpEx);

// check auth
$user_privileges  = auth(AUTH_POLLCREATE, 1, $userdata);

// display the result of the authentication
$message = '';
if ( $user_privileges['auth_pollcreate'] == 1 )
{
    $message = 'Great news! You can create polls in forum id #1!';
} else {
    $message = 'When you login, you\'ll be able to create polls in
forum id #1.';
}
message_die(GENERAL_MESSAGE, $message, 'Auth test');

// include page footer
include($phpbb_root_path . 'includes/page_tail.'.$phpEx);
?>
```

If you're logged in when you visit `helloBBauth3.php`, you'll see the following message:

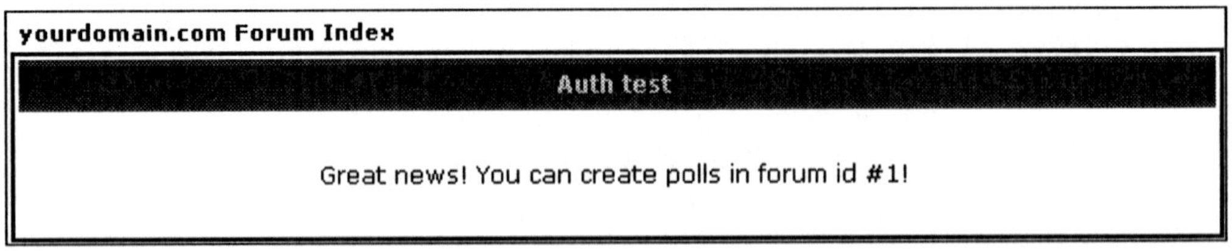

When you log out and come to the same page again, you'll see a changed message:

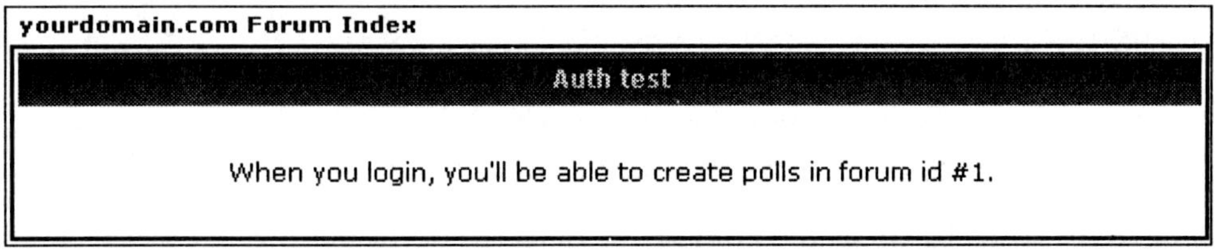

> Some code comments that serve as documentation on how the `auth()` function can be used; you can find these code comments before the function definition, at the top of the `includes/auth.php` file in your phpBB installation.

Tips and Tricks

This section describes some other phpBB functions that may come in handy. The functions listed are of two types: general functions (mostly contained in `includes/functions.php`), and posting-related functions that deal with processing BB code and smilies (these functions are defined in `includes/bbcode.php`). At the end of this section, there are some phpBB-specific coding guidelines and standards.

Miscellaneous Functions

These are some general-purpose functions that are shipped with phpBB.

Getting Board Statistics

Use this function to retrieve some board statistics data:

```
get_db_stat($mode)
```

The type of data this function returns depends of the parameter passed to it. This function can take only one of four pre-defined strings as a parameter. Here are the parameters, along with the returned values from the function (the last two options will give the stats for all forums, including hidden ones):

- `usercount`: When this parameter is passed, the function will return the total number of registered users.
- `newestuser`: When this is passed, the function will return an array with keys `username` and `user_id` containing the most recent registered user.
- `postcount`: This will give you the total number of posts.
- `topiccount`: This will give you the total number of topics created in your forums.

Here's an example usage of this function:

```
<?php
// set IN_PHPBB constant and include the initialization script
define('IN_PHPBB', true);
$phpbb_root_path = './';
include($phpbb_root_path . 'extension.inc');
include($phpbb_root_path . 'common.'.$phpEx);

// Start session management
$userdata = session_pagestart($user_ip, PAGE_INDEX);
init_userprefs($userdata);

// include page header
include($phpbb_root_path . 'includes/page_header.'.$phpEx);

// the main script work starts here
$newest_user = get_db_stat("newestuser");
message_die(
    GENERAL_MESSAGE,
    'My board has '
        . get_db_stat("usercount") . ' users, '
        . get_db_stat("postcount") . ' postings and '
        . get_db_stat("topiccount") . ' topics. '
        . 'Say \'Hi\' to the newest member - '
        . $newest_user['username'] .  '!',
    'Board stats - get_db_stats() demo'
);

// include page footer
include($phpbb_root_path . 'includes/page_tail.'.$phpEx);
?>
```

The output:

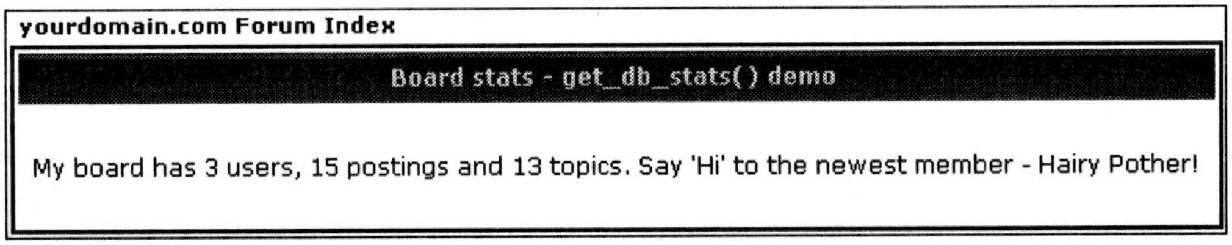

Retrieving User Information

Use this function for an array of information about a user:

```
get_userdata($user, $force_str = false)
```

It will return all the fields from the user's entry in the database table as an array with both associative and enumerated values.

Try the following piece of code into a script:

```
echo '<pre>';
print_r(get_userdata(2));
echo '</pre>';
```

This will display an array that starts like the following:

```
Array
(
    [0] => 2
    [user_id] => 2
    [1] => 1
    [user_active] => 1
    [2] => Administrator
    [username] => Administrator
    [3] => 2236c39cda27b2c5535ce82f3a1e28e0
    [user_password] => 2236c39cda27b2c5535ce82f3a1e28e0
    [4] => 1104479522
    [user_session_time] => 1104479522
. . .
)
```

Replace the 2 in the function call with any user ID or username you like. This function can take either a numeric ID or a username as a string.

If you pass the second parameter with value TRUE, the first parameter should be a *username*, and not an *ID*.

Encoding and Decoding IP Addresses

phpBB encodes all IP addresses it stores into the database. `encode_ip()` and `decode_ip()` are the two functions that serve this purpose. The first one takes a properly formatted IP address like `127.0.0.1` and returns an encoded representation of it. The second function takes an encoded string and returns the original IP address.

You can try these functions by using the following code:

```
// the main script work starts here
$ip = $_SERVER['REMOTE_ADDR'];
$encoded = encode_ip($ip);
$decoded = decode_ip($encoded);
message_die(
    GENERAL_MESSAGE,
    'I know you, your IP address is ' . $ip
        . '. This is encoded as ' . $encoded
        . ' and decoded back as ' . $decoded,
    'Encode/decode IP demo'
);
```

This will result in something like:

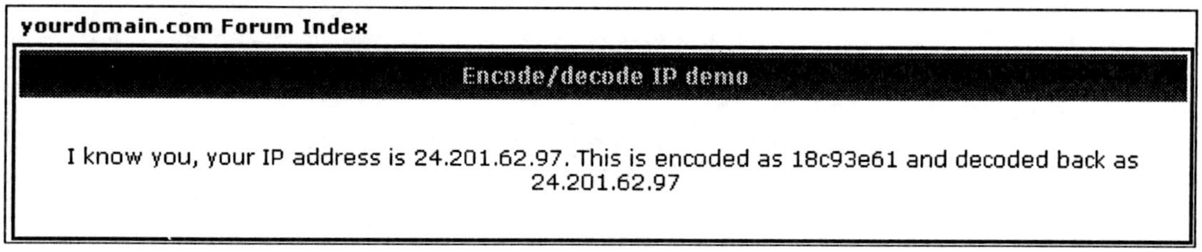

You can find the script to display this output in the book's code download, named `misc_encode_decode_ip.php`.

Displaying Dates

You can use the following phpBB function to display a formatted date:

```
create_date($format, $unix_timestamp, $timezone)
```

It's not only a wrapper around the `gmdate` PHP function (see `http://php.net/gmdate` for details), but also takes care of translating the date (months and weekdays) and takes account of the user's time zone and date format preferences set in the profile page.

A sample usage of the function would be to print the current date and time, using the user's preferred format and time zone. You can do that by using:

```
create_date($board_config['default_dateformat'], time(),
$board_config['board_timezone'])
```

This will return a string like: Mon Mar 14, 2005 8:56 am.

The book's code download has a script called `misc_create_date.php`, which shows how to use this function. You can also see the function used in the custom "What's Up" script at the end of the chapter.

Getting a List of Censored Words

The following function retrieves the list of censored words and their replacement words:

```
obtain_word_list(&$original_words, &$replacement_words)
```

The function accepts two parameters passed by reference. This basically means that you pass two empty arrays to this function and it populates these arrays with values.

We can use the word censoring as follows:

```
// the text to be filtered
$some_text = "I may contain naughty words.";
// empty arrays
$orig_word = $replacement_word = array();
// get the word lists
obtain_word_list($orig_word, $replacement_word);
// apply filters if there are ones
if ( !empty($orig_word) )
{
    $some_text = preg_replace($orig_word, $replacement_word,
$post_text);
    // now $some_text is filtered
}
```

Don't forget to use this functionality to filter not only post texts, but also topic titles, poll questions and answers, and anything else where you feel the need.

Preserving the Session in the Hyperlinks

The following function helps you preserve the user session by passing the session identifier in the URL for users that have their cookies disabled:

```
append_sid($url, $non_html_amp = false)
```

> You need to call this function every time you create a link to other pages in the forum, otherwise you'll lose the session ID of the user's visit and phpBB will create a new session for every page visited.

The second parameter of the function is optional; if it's `true`, the function will use "&" and not the correct HTML value "`&`" when constructing URL's parameters.

Example usage:

```
$url = 'viewtopic.php?t=12';
$url = append_sid($url);
```

Be careful if you use "#" (named anchors) in your URL; you need to add them *after* the call to `append_sid()` or otherwise the session ID will not be passed correctly.

Here's the incorrect way of doing it:

```
$url = 'viewtopic.php?p=21#21';
$url = append_sid($url);
```

And the correct way:

```
$url = 'viewtopic.php?p=21';
$url = append_sid($url) . '#21';
```

If you're interested in more details of the implementation of this function, look into the source file `includes/sessions.php`.

IN_PHPBB

`IN_PHPBB` is a constant, not a function. It was mentioned earlier and you have probably noticed that it's defined at the top of every script.

This is a security measure that doesn't allow include scripts to be accessed directly via a browser. In every include script, phpBB checks (and your script should too) if `IN_PHPBB` is defined. If it is not, this means somebody was trying to access the include scripts directly in the browser. They'll get an error message saying Hack attempt and won't be allowed to proceed further.

Postings-Related Functions

The following functions help you out when displaying a posting text.

Create Links Automatically

The following function will take any text and will make clickable all the strings that look like URLs or e-mails:

```
make_clickable($text)
```

An example:

```
$text = "Visit Packt at www.packtpub.com today";
$text = make_clickable($text);
echo $text;
```

This snippet will output the following HTML:

```
Visit Packt at <a href="http://www.packtpub.com"
target="_blank">www.packtpub.com</a> today.
```

Processing Smilies

The `smilies_pass($text)` function will replace all the smilie codes in a text with the HTML code for the corresponding image tags. See the following section for an example.

Displaying a Posting Body

In order to properly display a posting text you need to:

- Parse the BB code and convert it into HTML code
- Replace smilies
- Make links clickable
- Replace filtered words
- Convert new lines to HTML breaks

Look at the following example (it assumes that you have an array called `$row` that contains a database record from the posting texts table). Note that you need the **BB Code UID**, which is the key to transforming BB code into HTML.

```
// start
$post_text = $row['post_text'];
// BB code
$post_text = bbencode_second_pass($post_text, $row['bbcode_uid']);
// smilies
$post_text = smilies_pass($post_text);
// clickable links
$post_text = make_clickable($post_text);
// naughty words
$orig_word = $replacement_word = array();
obtain_word_list($orig_word, $replacement_word);
if ( !empty($orig_word) )
{
    $post_text = preg_replace($orig_word, $replacement_word,
$post_text);
}
$post_text = nl2br($post_text);
```

Note that in order for this piece of code to work, you need to include the `includes/bbcode.php` file in your script. This is normally done in the beginning of the script, as follows:

```
<?php
define('IN_PHPBB', true);
$phpbb_root_path = './';
include($phpbb_root_path . 'extension.inc');
include($phpbb_root_path . 'common.'.$phpEx);
include($phpbb_root_path . 'includes/bbcode.'.$phpEx);
```

Coding Guidelines

Coding standards and guidelines are always a good thing to have and follow. So it's a good idea to familiarize yourself with the phpBB coding standards and code your extensions following those standards. It's not mandatory (your code will still run even it does not adhere to the standards), but following pre-set standards can improve the maintainability of the code that you write. According to Sun Microsystems, "80% of the lifetime cost of a piece of software goes to maintenance" (source: *Code Conventions for the Java Programming Language* at `http://java.sun.com/docs/codeconv/`) and maintenance is much easier when coding conventions are employed. This is true even if you are the maintainer of your own code.

The idea behind using code conventions is to minimize the individual "handwriting" of a programmer, unifying how functions and variables are named, how code is indented, etc. When all programmers working on a project use the same style, one can easily read code written by another, because it looks consistent with the way you would have written it.

You can find the current phpBB coding standards and guidelines in the phpBB.com development area at `http://area51.phpbb.com/`.

Recent Postings MOD

This final section of the chapter is about creating a custom phpBB script called "Recent Postings" (or "What's Up") MOD. This script uses the techniques discussed earlier in this chapter and is designed to wrap up your knowledge on phpBB programming and the use of templates.

The Challenge

The script we're about to create will list the 15 most recent postings in all forums of the board. It can be very useful for you and the other forum junkies to have an overview page of what's happening in the board, without having to browse each forum individually. The same goes for moderators and administrators, the people that need to be up to speed with everything that's going on in the board.

The recent postings listing will respect user privileges, meaning that if a user doesn't have read access to a certain forum, the postings from this forum won't be present in the listing when viewed by this user.

To give you a more visual idea, here is a screenshot of the script in action:

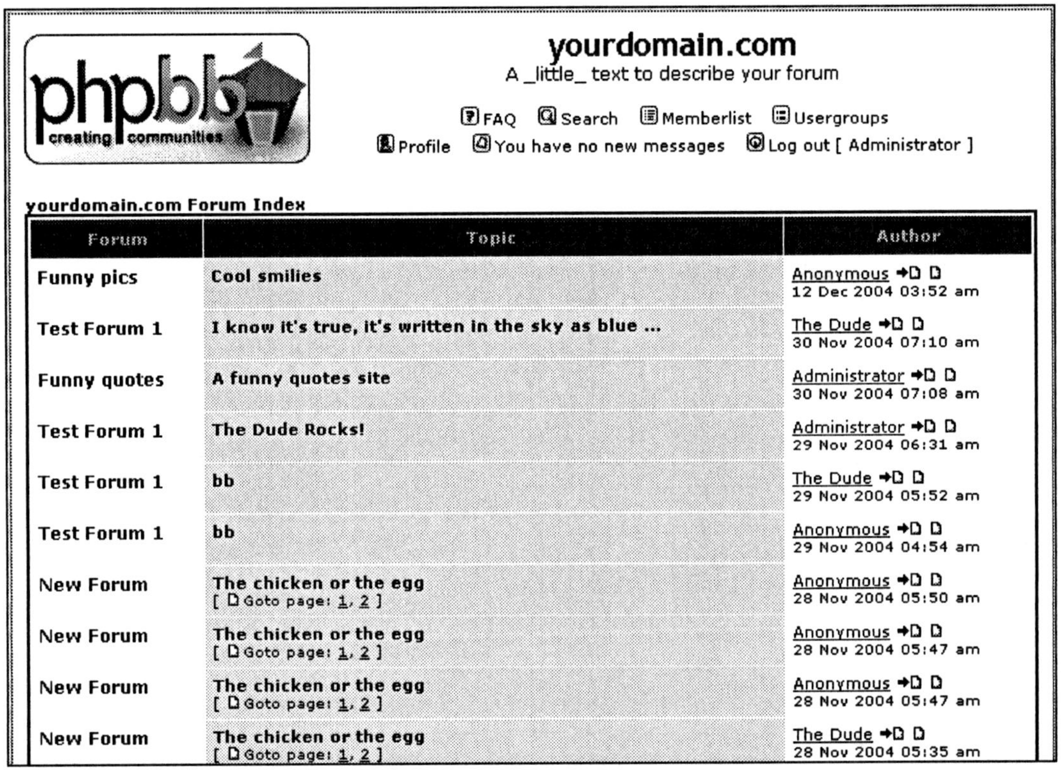

If users with moderator privileges in a certain forum are logged in and are viewing this page, they'll have a link to the moderator control panel for this forum, as shown:

There are two icons after the username in the right column. Clicking the first one takes the user to the posting, located in the View topic page (`viewtopic.php`). Clicking the second one doesn't load a new page, but expands the area below the posting title and shows the posting here in the same screen, with the BB code and the smilies processed properly. This is shown on the next illustration.

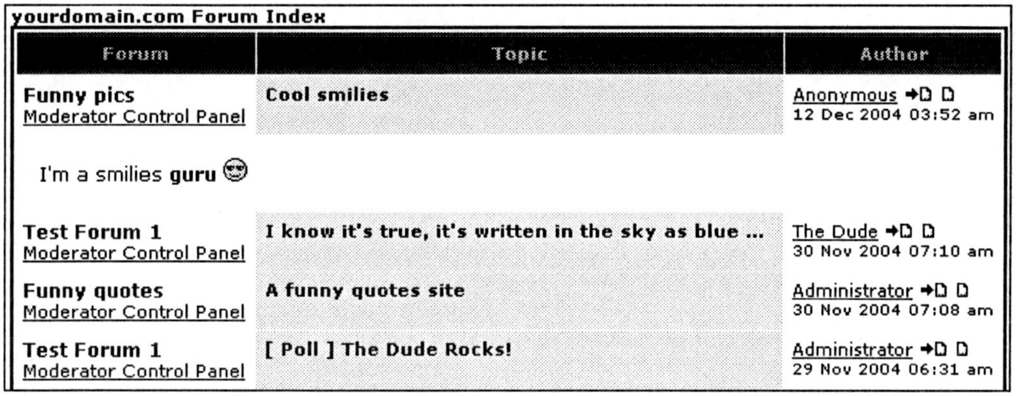

Clicking the same icon again (once a posting is expanded) collapses the additional area and hides the posting.

This is a convenient way to read the latest 15 posting in all forums, without leaving the page. To keep it simple, this script is not introducing new texts or graphics.

The Recent Postings MOD you're about to create consists of a PHP script and a template file. The PHP script is named `whatsup.php` and is hosted in the phpBB root, so if your board is installed in `http://www.yourdomain.com/forum/`, the scripts will be accessible at `http://www.yourdomain.com/forum/whatsup.php`.

The Template

The template for the script is named `whatsup.tpl` and is located in `templates/subSilver` directory. Here's its listing:

```
<span class="nav"><a href="{U_INDEX}"
class="nav">{L_INDEX}</a></span>

<table width="100%" cellpadding="5" cellspacing="1" border="0"
class="forumline">
  <tr>
    <th class="thCornerL" height="25"
nowrap="nowrap"> {FORUM} </th>
    <th width="50" class="thTop"
nowrap="nowrap"> {TOPIC} </th>
    <th class="thCornerR" nowrap="nowrap"> {POSTER} </th>
  </tr>
```

```
    <!-- BEGIN row -->
    <tr>
      <td valign="top" class="row1">
          <span class="forumlink">
              <a class="forumlink"
href="{row.U_FORUM}">{row.FORUM_NAME}</a>
          </span>
          <!-- BEGIN is_mod_switch -->
              <span class="name">
                  <br />
                  <a
href="{row.is_mod_switch.U_FORUM_MODCP}">{row.is_mod_switch.L_MOD}</a
>
              </span>
          <!-- END is_mod_switch -->
      </td>
      <td valign="top" class="row2">
          <span class="topictitle">
              {row.TOPIC_TYPE} <a class="topictitle"
href="{row.U_TOPIC}">{row.TOPIC_TITLE}</a>
          </span>
          <br />
          <span class="gensmall">{row.GOTO_PAGE}</span>
      </td>
      <td valign="top" class="row1">
          <span class="name"><a href="{row.U_POSTER}">{row.POSTER}</a>
{row.IMG_LATEST_POST}
          <a href="#" onclick="javascript:
document.getElementById('{row.POST_ID}').style.display =
(document.getElementById('{row.POST_ID}').style.display == 'none') ?
'' : 'none';">
          {row.IMG_VIEW_POST}</a>
          </span>
          <br />
          <span class="postdetails">{row.POST_DATE_TIME}</span>
      </td>
    </tr>
    <tr id="{row.POST_ID}" style="display:none">
      <td colspan="3" class="row1">
          <div class="postbody" style="padding: 10px;">
              {row.POST_TEXT}
          </div>
      </td>
    </tr>

    <!-- END row -->
</table>
```

There's nothing too specific for the template, it contains a table with three columns for Forum, Topic, and Author respectively. A loop block encloses two table rows (`<tr> ... </tr>`); the first one is the row that contains the forum name, the topic and the author information and links. The second one contains the posting. It's hidden by default (having `style="display:none"`) and gets shown/hidden on user request by a JavaScript linked to the second small icon (□).

There is also one nested block within the `row` block. It's called `is_mod_switch` and serves the purpose of handling an "if" case. The case is if the user has moderator privileges in the forum currently being listed. If yes, the link to the moderator control panel is displayed. This portion of the template is listed here:

```
<!-- BEGIN is_mod_switch -->
    <span class="name">
        <br />
        <a href="{row.is_mod_switch.U_FORUM_MODCP}">{row.is_mod_switch
.L_MOD}</a>
    </span>
<!-- END is_mod_switch -->
```

The Code

Now let's take a look at whatsup.php. The implementation starts like all other scripts discussed in the chapter, with a small difference: an additional file, bbcode.php, is included. It contains the necessary functions to work with the BBCode and the smilies:

```
<?php
define('IN_PHPBB', true);
$phpbb_root_path = './';
include($phpbb_root_path . 'extension.inc');
include($phpbb_root_path . 'common.'.$phpEx);
include($phpbb_root_path . 'includes/bbcode.'.$phpEx);
```

After including the required files comes the session management, which is similar to all the other scripts in this chapter:

```
// Start session management
$userdata = session_pagestart($user_ip, PAGE_INDEX);
init_userprefs($userdata);
```

Then comes the user authorization and privileges check:

```
// Start auth check
$user_can_read = array();
$user_can_read = auth(AUTH_READ, AUTH_LIST_ALL, $userdata);
```

This check verifies the user's read privileges for all the board's forums. Right after this there is a loop through the results of the authorization, so that an array of forum IDs is compiled. The array contains the IDs of the forums the user is allowed to read:

```
$allowed_forum_ids = array();
foreach ( $user_can_read AS $forum_id => $privileges )
{
    if ( !empty($privileges['auth_read']) )
    {
        $allowed_forum_ids[] = $forum_id;
    }
}
```

After the privileges are checked, we need some data from the database, for which we need to execute an SQL string. It is quite long as it joins five tables in order to retrieve the required information. The logic of the query is as follows:

- The most recent 15 entries from the **postings** table are selected. The way to get the most recent is to sort descending on the posting auto-increment ID.
- Based on the topic ID from the postings table, the **topics** table is joined to retrieve topic data such as title and topic type.
- Based on the forum ID from the postings table, the **forums** table is joined to retrieve forum data such as the name, and also to filter the allowed forums using the `$allowed_forum_ids` array that was already compiled.
- Based on the post ID from the postings table, the **posting texts** table is joined in order to retrieve the posting body.
- Finally based on the user ID from the postings table, the **users** table is joined as it contains the username of the poster, which is displayed in the listing.

```
// start SQL string
$sql = ' SELECT t.topic_title, t.topic_id, t.topic_replies,
t.topic_type, t.topic_vote, p.post_id, p.post_time, pt.post_text,
pt.bbcode_uid, f.forum_name, f.forum_id, u.username, u.user_id ';
$sql .= ' FROM ' . POSTS_TABLE . ' AS p ';
$sql .= ' LEFT JOIN ' . TOPICS_TABLE . ' AS t ON p.topic_id =
t.topic_id ';
$sql .= ' LEFT JOIN ' . FORUMS_TABLE . ' AS f ON t.forum_id =
f.forum_id ';
$sql .= ' LEFT JOIN ' . POSTS_TEXT_TABLE . ' AS pt ON p.post_id =
pt.post_id ';
$sql .= ' LEFT JOIN ' . USERS_TABLE . ' AS u ON p.poster_id =
u.user_id ';
$sql .= ' WHERE ';
$sql .= '   f.forum_id IN ('. implode(',', $allowed_forum_ids) .')';
$sql .= ' ORDER BY p.post_time DESC ';
$sql .= ' LIMIT 0, 15';
// end SQL string
```

After the SQL query is assembled, it's executed:

```
// execute query
$result = $db->sql_query($sql);
if ( !$result )
{
    // check for errors while executing the query
    message_die(GENERAL_ERROR, 'Cannot obtain latest post listing',
'',
                __LINE__, __FILE__, $sql);
}
```

After successful query execution, it's time to loop through the results and replace some template variables. Before the loop, we retrieve the list of censored words and their replacements. Remember that the filters were set up in the Admin panel.

```
// censored list
$orig_word = $replacement_word = array();
obtain_word_list($orig_word, $replacement_word);
```

The results loop starts:

```
// The loop through the results
while( $row = $db->sql_fetchrow($result) ) {
```

The first thing to do in the loop is to compile the "go to" links. These are the links like the ones shown in the following illustration.

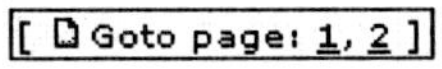

The code to retrieve these types of links is borrowed from a phpBB core script (`search.php`) without modifications—a good example of how you can learn from the phpBB application.

Next follows a check for some topic attributes—is this topic a sticky or an announcement and does it contain a poll? A `$topic_type` variable is assigned a value; this variable's value will be displayed before the topic name.

```
// check for topic type - announcement or sticky and/or poll
switch ( $row['topic_type'] )
{
    case POST_ANNOUNCE:
        $topic_type = $lang['Topic_Announcement'] . " ";
        break;
    case POST_STICKY:
        $topic_type = $lang['Topic_Sticky'] . " ";
    default:
        $topic_type = '';
}
if ( $row['topic_vote'] )
{
    $topic_type .= $lang['Topic_Poll'];
}
// end topic type check
```

Next the parsing of the posting body follows. It consists of processing the BB code, replacing the smilies codes with images, replacing any filtered words, and making clickable all strings that look like links or e-mail addresses:

```
// parse BBcode, smilies, filters, make links clickable
$post_text = $row['post_text'];
$post_text = bbencode_second_pass($post_text, $row['bbcode_uid']);
$post_text = smilies_pass($post_text);
$post_text = make_clickable($post_text);
if ( count($orig_word) )
{
    $post_text = preg_replace($orig_word, $replacement_word,
$post_text);
    $topic_title = preg_replace($orig_word, $replacement_word,
$row['topic_title']);
}
$post_text = nl2br($post_text);
```

At this point, all the data is retrieved and processed/compiled as necessary. It's now time to display it. So this is where the assignment of template variables within the `row` template block starts:

```
// assign row block variables
$template->assign_block_vars("row",
    array(
        'U_FORUM' => append_sid('viewforum.'.$phpEx . "?f=" .
                                $row['forum_id']),
        'FORUM_NAME' => $row['forum_name'],
        'U_TOPIC' => append_sid('viewtopic.'.$phpEx . "?t=" .
                                $row['topic_id']),
        'TOPIC_TYPE' => (empty($topic_type)) ? "" : "<strong>" .
                        $topic_type . "</strong>",
        'TOPIC_TITLE' => $topic_title,
        'GOTO_PAGE' => $goto_page,
        'POSTER' => $row['username'],
        'U_POSTER' => append_sid('profile.'.$phpEx .
"?mode=viewprofile&amp;u=" . $row['user_id']),
        'IMG_LATEST_POST' => '<a href="' .
append_sid("viewtopic.$phpEx?p=" . $row['post_id']) . "#" .
$row['post_id'] . '"><img src="' . $images['icon_latest_reply'] . '"
border="0" /></a> ',
        'IMG_VIEW_POST'    => '<img src="' . $images['icon_minipost']
. '" border="0" />',
        'POST_DATE_TIME' =>
create_date($board_config['default_dateformat'], $row['post_time'],
$board_config['board_timezone']),
        'POST_TEXT' => $post_text,
        'POST_ID' => $row['post_id'],
    )
);
```

What you may find interesting in this piece of code is the use of the phpBB functions `append_sid()` (for keeping the session ID in hyperlinks) and `create_date()` (for formatting the date). Their usage was already described earlier in the *Tips and Tricks* section of this chapter, but here you can see them in action.

Next is the `is_mod_switch`, providing moderators with a link to the forum's moderator control panel:

```
// process is_mod_switch block
if ( !empty($user_can_read[$row['forum_id']]['auth_mod']) )
{
     $template->assign_block_vars("row.is_mod_switch",
        array(
            'U_FORUM_MODCP' => 'modcp.'.$phpEx . "?f=" .
$row['forum_id'] . "&amp;sid=" . $userdata['session_id'],
            'L_MOD'          => $lang['Mod_CP'],
        )
     );
}
```

The loop through the results is now completed. All that remains to be done is:

- Include the page header
- Assign the template file
- Assign some global template variables ("global" meaning "outside the row loop")

- Parse and output the compiled template
- Include the page footer (tail)

Here is how it's done:

```
// header, body and footer
include($phpbb_root_path . 'includes/page_header.'.$phpEx);
$template->set_filenames(array(
    'body' => 'whatsup.tpl')
);
$template->assign_vars(
    array(
        'FORUM' => $lang['Forum'],
        'TOPIC' => $lang['Topic'],
        'POSTER' => $lang['Author'],
    )
);
$template->pparse('body');
include($phpbb_root_path . 'includes/page_tail.'.$phpEx);
```

And... that's it! This is how a completely new phpBB script is built from scratch. The following is the complete source code listing for the new phpBB feature, the `whatsup.php` script (included in the code download). Copy this to your board's root and you're done! And don't forget: `whatsup.tpl` should be copied to `templates/subSilver`.

```
<?php
define('IN_PHPBB', true);
$phpbb_root_path = './';
include($phpbb_root_path . 'extension.inc');
include($phpbb_root_path . 'common.'.$phpEx);
include($phpbb_root_path . 'includes/bbcode.'.$phpEx);

// Start session management
$userdata = session_pagestart($user_ip, PAGE_INDEX);
init_userprefs($userdata);

// Start auth check
$user_can_read = array();
$user_can_read = auth(AUTH_READ, AUTH_LIST_ALL, $userdata);

$allowed_forum_ids = array();
foreach ($user_can_read AS $forum_id => $privileges)
{
    if ( !empty($privileges['auth_read']) )
    {
        $allowed_forum_ids[] = $forum_id;
    }
}
// end auth check

// start SQL string
$sql = ' SELECT t.topic_title, t.topic_id, t.topic_replies,
t.topic_type, t.topic_vote, p.post_id, p.post_time, pt.post_text,
pt.bbcode_uid, f.forum_name, f.forum_id, u.username, u.user_id ';
$sql .= ' FROM ' . POSTS_TABLE . ' AS p ';
$sql .= ' LEFT JOIN ' . TOPICS_TABLE . ' AS t ON p.topic_id =
t.topic_id ';
```

```
$sql .= ' LEFT JOIN ' . FORUMS_TABLE . ' AS f ON t.forum_id =
f.forum_id ';
$sql .= ' LEFT JOIN ' . POSTS_TEXT_TABLE . ' AS pt ON p.post_id =
pt.post_id ';
$sql .= ' LEFT JOIN ' . USERS_TABLE . ' AS u ON p.poster_id =
u.user_id ';
$sql .= ' WHERE ';
$sql .= '    f.forum_id IN ('. implode(',', $allowed_forum_ids) .')';
$sql .= ' ORDER BY p.post_id DESC ';
$sql .= ' LIMIT 0, 15';
// end SQL string

// execute query
$result = $db->sql_query($sql);
if ( !$result )
{
    // check for errors while executing the query
    message_die(GENERAL_ERROR, 'Cannot obtain latest post listing',
'', __LINE__, __FILE__, $sql);
}
// censored list
$orig_word = $replacement_word = array();
obtain_word_list($orig_word, $replacement_word);

// The loop through the results
while( $row = $db->sql_fetchrow($result) )
{
    // goto page list
    $replies = $row['topic_replies'];
    $topic_id = $row['topic_id'];
    // reuse from the search page
    if ( ( $replies + 1 ) > $board_config['posts_per_page'] )
    {
        $total_pages = ceil( ( $replies + 1 ) /
$board_config['posts_per_page'] );
        $goto_page = ' [ <img src="' . $images['icon_gotopost'] . '"
alt="' . $lang['Goto_page'] . '" title="' . $lang['Goto_page'] . '"
/>' . $lang['Goto_page'] . ': ';

        $times = 1;
        for($j = 0; $j < $replies + 1; $j +=
$board_config['posts_per_page'])
        {
            $goto_page .= '<a href="' .
append_sid("viewtopic.$phpEx?" . POST_TOPIC_URL . "=" . $topic_id .
"&amp;start=$j") . '">' . $times . '</a>';
            if ( $times == 1 && $total_pages > 4 )
            {
                $goto_page .= ' ... ';
                $times = $total_pages - 3;
                $j += ( $total_pages - 4 ) *
$board_config['posts_per_page'];
            }
            else if ( $times < $total_pages )
            {
                $goto_page .= ', ';
            }
            $times++;
        }
```

```
        $goto_page .= ' ] ';
    }
    else
    {
        $goto_page = '';
    }
    // goto page list ends

    // check for topic type - announcement or sticky and/or poll
    switch ( $row['topic_type'] )
    {
        case POST_ANNOUNCE:
            $topic_type = $lang['Topic_Announcement'] . " ";
            break;
        case POST_STICKY:
            $topic_type = $lang['Topic_Sticky'] . " ";
        default:
            $topic_type = '';
    }
    if ( $row['topic_vote'] )
    {
        $topic_type .= $lang['Topic_Poll'];
    }
    // end topic type check

    // parse BBcode, smilies, filters, make links clickable
    $post_text = $row['post_text'];
    $post_text = bbencode_second_pass($post_text,
$row['bbcode_uid']);
    $post_text = smilies_pass($post_text);
    $post_text = make_clickable($post_text);
    if ( count($orig_word) )
    {
        $post_text = preg_replace($orig_word, $replacement_word,
$post_text);
        $topic_title = preg_replace($orig_word, $replacement_word,
$row['topic_title']);
    }
    $post_text = nl2br($post_text);

    // assign row block variables
    $template->assign_block_vars("row",
        array(
            'U_FORUM' => append_sid('viewforum.'.$phpEx . "?f=" .
$row['forum_id']),
            'FORUM_NAME' => $row['forum_name'],
            'U_TOPIC' => append_sid('viewtopic.'.$phpEx . "?t=" .
$row['topic_id']),
            'TOPIC_TYPE' => (empty($topic_type)) ? "" : "<strong>" .
$topic_type . "</strong>",
            'TOPIC_TITLE' => $topic_title,
            'GOTO_PAGE' => $goto_page,
            'POSTER' => $row['username'],
            'U_POSTER' => append_sid('profile.'.$phpEx .
"?mode=viewprofile&amp;u=" . $row['user_id']),
            'IMG_LATEST_POST' => '<a href="' .
append_sid("viewtopic.$phpEx?p=" . $row['post_id']) . "#" .
$row['post_id'] . '"><img src="' . $images['icon_latest_reply'] . '"
border="0" /></a> ',
```

```
                'IMG_VIEW_POST'     => '<img src="' .
$images['icon_minipost'] . '" border="0" />',
                'POST_DATE_TIME' =>
create_date($board_config['default_dateformat'], $row['post_time'],
$board_config['board_timezone']),
                'POST_TEXT' => $post_text,
                'POST_ID' => $row['post_id'],
            )
    );

    // process is_mod_switch block
    if ( !empty($user_can_read[$row['forum_id']]['auth_mod']) )
    {
            $template->assign_block_vars("row.is_mod_switch",
                array(
                    'U_FORUM_MODCP' => 'modcp.'.$phpEx . "?f=" .
$row['forum_id'] . "&amp;sid=" . $userdata['session_id'],
                    'L_MOD'          => $lang['Mod_CP'],
                )
            );
    }
}

// header, body and footer
include($phpbb_root_path . 'includes/page_header.'.$phpEx);
$template->set_filenames(array(
    'body' => 'whatsup.tpl')
);
$template->assign_vars(
    array(
        'FORUM' => $lang['Forum'],
        'TOPIC' => $lang['Topic'],
        'POSTER' => $lang['Author'],
    )
);
$template->pparse('body');
include($phpbb_root_path . 'includes/page_tail.'.$phpEx);
?>
```

Summary

This last chapter introduced you to the new and exciting world of phpBB programming. The chapter described in detail how to use different phpBB functions, how to use the phpBB database abstraction layer, the phpBB templating engine, and how to properly parse and display postings. Now you have the basic knowledge to start coding your own extensions to the phpBB core features. A number of examples were given, which are all available in the book's code download.

It's a good idea to start experimenting with the examples; tweak them a bit, and see how the results change. By doing so, you'll get a better understanding of how the different functions work, and probably some ideas will start taking shape as to how you can customize and extend the phpBB functionality. Happy phpBB-ing!

A

Directory Structure

A full download of phpBB 2.0 contains about three hundred files sorted into twenty-one directories. In order to do certain types of more advanced work with your phpBB forum, you will need to know which directories contain important files and what phpBB accomplishes with each file. Some directories and files are optional, while others are absolutely required for a forum to function correctly. This appendix provides a quick summary of each directory and the files it contains.

For the most part, you should never rename any directory or file. There are exceptions to this, of course, which may include installing modifications, customizing aspects of your forum, or some other instances noted elsewhere in this book. When you do change a name, be sure you understand what you are doing. Changing directory or file names without making other changes will usually cause errors to appear on your forum when it cannot find necessary files.

Required Directories

The majority of the directories created when you extract phpBB from a compressed file you have downloaded must be present on your website so that your forum works without errors. These basic required directories also contain most of the forum's necessary files, but you will find that some files within the required directories are actually optional.

The Root Directory

Your forum's main directory, which contains all the related files and other directories of the phpBB forum, is called the **root directory**. By default, this directory is named `phpBB2`. Renaming `phpBB2` is a common practice; some of the more popular names are `forums` and `boards`. No specific name is required; the internal code of phpBB will always refer to this name with a special shortcut notation.

The directories inside the root directory, and the files stored within those directories, will be examined individually. Contained in the root directory itself are many important files, most of which are constantly accessed directly by forum members. These files include other files, or add their contents to the current code, to perform certain necessary tasks.

Three exceptions are the `extension.inc`, `common.php`, and `config.php` files, which are included by the other files in the root directory. The following table lists the other files contained in the root directory and their uses, after which we examine the three more important files in detail.

File Name	Function of the File
`faq.php`	Lists frequently asked questions about forum operations.
`groupcp.php`	Lists and manages user groups.
`index.php`	Displays main page of forum, listing categories and forums.
`login.php`	Logs users in and out of the forum.
`memberlist.php`	Lists all forum members in a variety of ways.
`modcp.php`	Moderator Control Panel; used for managing topics and posts.
`posting.php`	Allows creation, editing, and deletion of posts.
`privmsg.php`	Sends, receives, and displays private messages.
`profile.php`	Interface for user account management. Calls other files for most work.
`search.php`	Search forums in a variety of manners.
`viewforum.php`	Lists of topics in a forum.
`viewonline.php`	View all users currently visiting the forums, along with pages viewed.
`viewtopic.php`	Lists posts within a topic.

extension.inc

As the first file called by all pages of your forum, `extension.inc` would seem to be one of the most important phpBB files of all. It is a very simple file, however, and rarely touched at all. The sole purpose of `extension.inc` is to define a variable, `$phpEx`, containing the file extension associated with PHP code files on a server. This extension is usually `.php`, which is also the default setting in `extension.inc`, so the file hardly ever needs to be altered. Some older servers that use PHP 3 might use the extension `.php3` instead of `.php`. If for some reason you must use one of these, you would need to change the file extension in this file and rename all files ending in `.php` so that their names end with `.php3`.

common.php

This file really "starts up" phpBB by initializing important variables, calling almost every file necessary for normal forum functions, and setting up forum configuration settings. Some special security measures for working with users' data are also performed here. In most cases, `common.php` will be the second file called by a phpBB page.

config.php

All the information your forum needs to access the SQL database is stored in the `config.php` file. That includes the address or name of the SQL server, your SQL username and password, and the name prefix of your database tables. All this data is entered when you install phpBB, and can later be altered by editing this file.

Administration Files

Usually, the first directory you will see within the root directory is called `admin`. The `admin` directory contains files that create phpBB's Administration Control Panel. Any file inside `admin` with a name that starts with `admin_`, such as `admin_styles.php`, will also be used to create the navigation menu shown in the Administration Control Panel. Many modifications add new administration sections by placing new `admin_` files here. All of the default `admin_` files (Administration Control Panel files) are described in the following table:

Administration File Name	Usage of File
`admin_board.php`	General configuration management.
`admin_db_utilities.php`	Basic phpBB database backup and restoration.
`admin_disallow.php`	Define usernames that are not allowed on a forum.
`admin_forum_prune.php`	Delete old posts from forums.
`admin_forumauth.php`	Manage general forum permission settings.
`admin_forums.php`	Create and manage forums and categories.
`admin_groups.php`	Create, edit, and delete user groups.
`admin_mass_email.php`	Send e-mail messages to all registered users.
`admin_ranks.php`	Management of user ranks.
`admin_smilies.php`	Add, remove, or alter emoticon images.

Administration File Name	Usage of File
`admin_styles.php`	Performs all style and theme administration.
`admin_ug_auth.php`	Define permission settings for specific users and user groups.
`admin_user_ban.php`	Ban users, e-mail addresses, or IP addresses.
`admin_users.php`	Administer user profiles.
`admin_words.php`	Specify words that will be automatically censored in messages.

Any original phpBB file in the `admin` directory that has a name without `admin_` prefixed is somehow involved in the displaying of the other pages. The `index.php` file has three functions: creating the frames of the control panel, building the navigation menu from `admin_` files, and displaying the entry page. One file used by every Administration Control Panel page is `pagestart.php`, which handles user-permission checking for the panel. It may also include `page_header_admin.php`, a file that creates the very top of administration pages. The matching `page_footer_admin.php` is used to terminate the processing of every administration page and make certain it is displayed.

Database Abstraction Layer Files

One of phpBB's features is the ability to work with several different types of SQL database software packages. That feature is provided by use of a **database abstraction layer**, which is a set of files used to create a common interface capable of accessing each supported software package. These files are located in the directory named db. One file is provided for each supported software package. Your forum only uses the file for your specific database, so you can delete the others to conserve a little server space. If any of these files are deleted, you will need to restore them should you decide to change database software packages later. The table that follows lists the files and their matching database software. The `index.htm` file in db is just a placeholder to prevent servers listing the contents of the directory. These placeholder files are present in several of phpBB's directories and are always named `index.htm`.

File Name	Database Software Supported
`db2.php`	This file is not used by phpBB 2.0.
`msaccess.php`	Microsoft Access via ODBC.

File Name	Database Software Supported
mssql.php	Microsoft SQL Server 7/2000.
mssql-odbc.php	Microsoft SQL Server via ODBC.
mysql.php	MySQL 3.2.
mysql4.php	MySQL 4.
oracle.php	Oracle 7 and 8 (removed in phpBB 2.0.14).
postgres7.php	PostgreSQL 7.

Included Files

As mentioned earlier, most pages that forum visitors access will include other PHP files and process the code of those files as part of the current page. A large number of these included files are stored in the forum's `includes` directory. Other than an `index.htm` placeholder, every file here is actually meant to be included by others. None of these files are ever likely to be accessed directly by your users. If someone does try to visit the files directly, they will only see a blank page or the Hacking Attempt message, depending on which file they choose. Almost all code contained in these files is in the form of functions or classes that will be referenced by the files including them. The following table shows the included files:

Included File Name	Usage or Contents of File
auth.php	Obtains user permission settings.
bbcode.php	Processes BBCode tags in messages.
constants.php	Defines many constants used in other files.
db.php	Includes a database abstraction layer file, based on forum configuration.
emailer.php	Contains a class for handing the sending of e-mails.
functions.php	Contains general functions used on many pages.
functions_admin.php	Functions used by the Administration and Moderator Control Panels.
functions_post.php	Processes messages for display and database storage.

Included File Name	Usage or Contents of File
functions_search.php	Performs many search-related tasks.
functions_selects.php	Creates HTML select code for drop-down lists.
functions_validate.php	Checks profile information for invalid or disallowed details.
page_header.php	Displays the forum header.
page_tail.php	Displays the forum footer and ends processing of scripts.
prune.php	Includes functions for deleting old forum topics.
sessions.php	Creates, updates, and deletes user sessions.
smtp.php	Sends e-mails via SMTP, which typically connects to another server.
sql_parse.php	Translates text files of SQL queries for use in database management.
template.php	Contains a class that parses template files into forum pages.
topic_review.php	Displays a Topic Review box on posting forms.
usercp_activate.php	Activates inactive user accounts.
usercp_avatar.php	Manages avatar galleries and uploads.
usercp_confirm.php	Creates visual confirmation images in the registration form.
usercp_email.php	Allows forum users to e-mail others through a forum interface.
usercp_register.php	Handles registration and profile editing, including form creation.
usercp_sendpasswd.php	Resets user account passwords.
usercp_viewprofile.php	Displays user profile information.

Installation Files

The install directory contains files used to install or upgrade phpBB. phpBB displays an error message if this directory is left in place after installation is completed, so you will have likely deleted the directory from your forum after completing the installation. When upgrading phpBB, you will need to recreate the install directory and place an upgrade installer file inside it. The name of the upgrade installer file will vary with each phpBB release, but is in the general format of update_to_2xxx.php, where 2xxx is replaced with the version number, or update_to_latest.php. An example would be update_to_2011.php. After upgrading, delete the install directory again.

A schemas directory may also be present inside install. The schemas files contain SQL queries that are used to create the forum's database tables and default data during installation. Early versions of phpBB 2.0 placed schemas inside the db directory.

Language Packs

Files that provide phpBB's multi-lingual support are located in the language directory. Each language is represented by a subdirectory named after the language and prefixed by lang_, such as lang_english, lang_dutch, lang_french, and so on. When first downloaded, phpBB only includes lang_english for English language files. Each language subdirectory contains several files that define the text used throughout the forum. Check the following table for a description of all default language files. New language files are often added by large modifications.

File Name	Contents of File
lang_admin.php	All text that appears only in the Administration Control Panel.
lang_bbcode.php	Creates the BBCode guide FAQ page.
lang_faq.php	Creates the main forum FAQ page.
lang_main.php	All the text that appears in the main areas of the forum.
search_stopwords.txt	Lists words omitted from forum searches and indexing.
search_synonyms.txt	Lists words used as synonyms for searched words.

Another subdirectory called email will also be present inside each language's directory, giving it a structure like language/lang_english/email. The files in email are templates for e-mail messages that the forum can send to users and administrators. The following table gives a description of each e-mail template:

File Name	Recipient	Used when...
admin_activate.tpl	Administrator	A user account must be activated.
admin_send_email.tpl	Users	An administrator mass e-mails forum members.
admin_welcome_activated.tpl	User	The user's account is activated by an administrator.
admin_welcome_inactive.tpl	User	The user registers and an administrator must activate the account.
coppa_welcome_inactive.tpl	User	The user registers and is under 13 years of age.
group_added.tpl	User	The user is added to a user group.
group_approved.tpl	User	The user requested to join a group and was added.
group_request.tpl	Group Moderator	A user requests to join the moderator's user group.
privmsg_notify.tpl	User	A new private message is received.
profile_send_email.tpl	User	A user e-mails another through the forum.
topic_notify.tpl	User	A topic the user is watching gets a new reply.
user_activate.tpl	User	The user must activate his/her account.
user_activate_passwd.tpl	User	The user requests a new password.
user_welcome.tpl	User	The user registers and account activation is turned off.
user_welcome_inactive.tpl	User	The user registers and must activate his/her account.

Template Storage

The last required directory is `templates`, which contains files associated with the styling system of phpBB. This is another directory that has the important files inside subdirectories. In this case, the subdirectories are named after the template file set they contain. phpBB ships with one set of template files, so the only directory in `templates` would be `subSilver`.

These template directories contain the images, stylesheets, configuration files, and template files used to display every page of a phpBB forum. Template files are text files, usually with the extension `.tpl`, containing markup code such as HTML. The major `.tpl` files are described in the table that follows. Usually, some other files such as Cascading Style Sheets (`.css` files) and template configurations (`.cfg` files) will also be present. These files typically have names based on the template, such as `subSilver.css` and `subSilver.cfg`.

File Name	Used to Display
`agreement.tpl`	Registration agreement page.
`bbcode.tpl`	None; used in special internal BBCode processing.
`confirm_body.tpl`	Confirmation (Do some thing?: Yes/No) pages.
`error_body.tpl`	Error messages displayed in forms.
`faq_body.tpl`	FAQ pages.
`groupcp_info_body.tpl`	Information about a user group.
`groupcp_pending_info.tpl`	Pending members of a user group.
`groupcp_user_body.tpl`	A user's user group memberships.
`index_body.tpl`	Main page of forum; index.php.
`jumpbox.tpl`	Forum navigation drop-down menu.
`login_body.tpl`	Login form.
`memberlist_body.tpl`	Member list pages.
`message_body.tpl`	Most error or success pages.
`modcp_body.tpl`	Lists of topics in the Moderator Control Panel.
`modcp_move.tpl`	Topic moving confirmation and forum list.
`modcp_split.tpl`	Topic splitting post list.

File Name	Used to Display
modcp_viewip.tpl	List of IP addresses associated with a post and user.
overall_footer.tpl	Normal page footers, such as copyright details.
overall_header.tpl	Normal page headers and site menus.
posting_body.tpl	Posting forms.
posting_poll_body.tpl	Poll areas of posting forms.
posting_preview.tpl	Post preview areas of posting forms.
posting_smilies.tpl	Pop-up smilies window, accessible from posting forms.
posting_topic_review.tpl	Topic review areas of posting forms.
privmsgs_body.tpl	Private Message folder listings.
privmsgs_popup.tpl	Private Message pop-up notification window.
privmsgs_preview.tpl	Preview area of private message posting form.
privmsgs_read_body.tpl	Text of a private message.
profile_add_body.tpl	Registration and profile editing forms.
profile_avatar_gallery.tpl	Avatar Gallery subcategories.
profile_send_email.tpl	E-mail sending form.
profile_send_pass.tpl	Lost password reset form.
profile_view_body.tpl	User profile pages.
search_body.tpl	Complete search form.
search_results_posts.tpl	Results of a search displayed as posts.
search_results_topics.tpl	Results of a search displayed as topics.
search_username.tpl	Pop-up user search window.

File Name	Used to Display
`simple_footer.tpl`	Smaller page footers, usually in pop-up windows.
`simple_header.tpl`	Smaller page headers, without site menus.
`viewforum_body.tpl`	Lists of topics in forums.
`viewonline_body.tpl`	Lists of users currently on the forums, and their visited pages.
`viewtopic_body.tpl`	Posts within a topic.
`viewtopic_poll_ballot.tpl`	Poll voting forms in topics.
`viewtopic_poll_result.tpl`	Poll result lists in topics.

Each template's directory can also contain as many subdirectories as the template author desires. The only required subdirectory is `admin`, such as `templates/subSilver/admin`. This directory will contain template files for displaying the Administration Control Panel, listed in the following table.

File Name	Used to Display
`admin_message_body.tpl`	Error and success messages.
`auth_forum_body.tpl`	Forum Permissions: permissions editor.
`auth_select_body.tpl`	Permissions: select a forum or group for editing.
`auth_ug_body.tpl`	Edit permissions of a user or user group.
`board_config_body.tpl`	General category: Configuration page.
`category_edit_body.tpl`	Editing a forum category's name and other details.
`db_utils_backup_body.tpl`	Database Utilities backup form.
`db_utils_restore_body.tpl`	Database Utilities restoration form.
`disallow_body.tpl`	Disallowed usernames page.
`forum_admin_body.tpl`	Basic forum details editing page.

File Name	Used to Display
forum_delete_body.tpl	Deleting a forum or category.
forum_edit_body.tpl	Editing a forum's name and other details.
forum_prune_body.tpl	Forum pruning area.
forum_prune_result_body.tpl	Details about a completed forum pruning.
forum_prune_select_body.tpl	Select a forum for pruning.
group_edit_body.tpl	Edit or create a user group.
group_select_body.tpl	Select a user group for editing.
index_body.tpl	Administration Panel entry page.
index_frameset.tpl	Administration Panel frames layout.
index_navigate.tpl	Administration Panel navigation menu.
page_footer.tpl	Page footers.
page_header.tpl	Page headers and stylesheet.
ranks_edit_body.tpl	Edit settings for a user rank or create a rank.
ranks_list_body.tpl	List all current ranks.
smile_edit_body.tpl	Add or alter an emoticon's settings.
smile_import_body.tpl	Install smilies from a pak file.
smile_list_body.tpl	List all smilies installed.
styles_addnew_body.tpl	Install a new style; list all uninstalled styles.
styles_edit_body.tpl	Create or edit a theme/style.
styles_exporter.tpl	Export theme settings for a template.
styles_list_body.tpl	List all installed styles.
user_avatar_gallery.tpl	Avatar Gallery; for editing a user's profile.

File Name	Used to Display
`user_ban_body.tpl`	Ban users utility.
`user_edit_body.tpl`	Edit a user's profile information.
`user_email_body.tpl`	Send a mass e-mail to users.
`user_select_body.tpl`	Select a user for editing.
`words_edit_body.tpl`	Add or edit a censored word.
`words_list_body.tpl`	List censored words.

Another common subdirectory is `images`, which may also contain more subdirectories, commonly named after language packs, such as `lang_english`. The language directories inside a template's directory typically hold images featuring typed text, such as reply or post buttons.

Optional Directories

In addition to the required directories you have just learned about, phpBB forums also include some directories that are optional. Some of these can be beneficial to have or useless in regards to the forum itself. Generally speaking, it is a good idea to delete these directories and their contents if you do not intend to use them on your website.

Cached Pages

One popular method of speeding up a forum is to add a caching system. **Caching systems** store code generated by the phpBB template system when a page is viewed, and then use that stored code when the page is viewed again. The speed boost comes from referencing the stored code; this is quicker than regenerating the code every time the page is viewed. The stored code is often saved in files in a `cache` directory. phpBB does not use a caching system by default, but does include a couple of optional systems, as you'll see a little later. A `cache` directory is provided for use with one of these options.

phpBB Documentation

phpBB's `docs` directory contains documentation files. By looking at these files, you can find such things as install and upgrade instructions, a copy of the license under which phpBB is released, and an FAQ about using phpBB. These files are not used by the forum in any way, so it is safe to delete this directory. Keep a copy of the files on your own computer in case you need to reference them later.

Images

The `images` directory is commonly used as a place to store image files for emoticons, ranks, and avatars. You can place those files in other locations within the forum's directory structure, but doing so usually requires changing some configuration settings in the Administration Control Panel. phpBB ships with `smilies` (containing the default emoticons) and `avatars` subdirectories inside `images`.

Other Directories of Note

Beyond both the optional and required directories in phpBB's structure, there are a few others. These are a bit unique. phpBB does not absolutely need to have them, but sometimes you do not really have a choice about including them or not. They are definitely worth a closer look.

Contributed Extras

A special `contrib` directory is included with phpBB. It contains some extra add-ons you have the option of installing on your forum. To learn about these add-ons, read the `README.html` file in your browser. The add-ons included vary with each phpBB release, but you can expect to see things like the template caching systems mentioned previously. phpBB will not use any add-ons or other files in this directory unless you actively install them to the forum.

As with the `install` directory, phpBB will display an error message if you leave the `contrib` directory in place on your website. In order for people to use your forum, you must delete `contrib` and all files within it.

Modification Files

At this point, you have already learned about all of the directories and files that come with phpBB. While reading, you may have noted that some sections said modifications may add files in certain areas. The truth is, modifications can do anything to the directory structure of your forum, including add new directories or files, move existing ones, or even remove some altogether.

Many modification authors have adopted a mutual standard of placing new files within a `mods` directory, which is added inside the root directory. phpBB does not include a `mods` directory when downloaded; this is a community-created concept. The `mods` directory typically has a subdirectory for each modification that adds files there, such as `prillian` for the Prillian messenger modification and `phpbb_fetch_all` for the phpBB Fetch All syndication modification. Using `mods` for new files keeps them grouped closely together and easy to find.

The use of `mods` is not practiced by all modification creators. Some will place new directories elsewhere in the forum structure. If you create modifications, you should place new files and directories wherever you feel comfortable. Unless you install modifications that use the `mods` directory, you do not need to create it. You will need to create the directories used by any modifications you install if those directories do not already exist.

> New language files are almost always placed within the `language` directories, even among authors that use the `mods` directory. Likewise, template files usually go within the `templates` directory. It is easier to keep track of—and use—these files when they are stored in these areas.

B
phpBB Resources

Here we've listed web links to further reading matter and interesting phpBB-related resources.

phpBB.com—Documentation and Support

phpBB.com is the number one site for phpBB-related information and updates. There you'll find everything you need to customize your board—templates, smilies, avatars, modifications, and so on. Here are some highlights from the site:

- `http://www.phpbb.com/support/guide/`
  The official phpBB userguide and the first stop to look for answers when in need.
- `http://www.phpbb.com/support/documents.php?mode=faq`
  Answers by board administrators to frequently asked phpBB questions. It is an addition to the FAQ you have on your user-oriented board.
- `http://www.phpbb.com/kb/categories.php`
  The knowledge base containing over 100 articles on phpBB, covering all sorts of questions—installation, administration, templates, and MODs.
- `http://www.phpbb.com/support/tutorials/`
  Presents phpBB tutorials as beautiful Flash animations. You can get the popcorn, sit, relax, and watch the movies.
- `http://www.phpbb.com/support/`
  The support homepage that lists all support options at a glance. It also contains the option of subscribing to the phpBB mailing list. It's highly recommended that you join the mailing list to stay updated with any security reports or updates.

- `http://www.phpbb.com/phpBB/`
  The phpBB community. Here you can meet fellow board admins, look for support and MODs, as well as ask (and answer) questions. It's a huge information base with more than a million postings.
- `http://www.phpbb.com/phpBB/viewtopic.php?t=128123`
  Provides the support request template. It contains the information to be provided when asking for support in the phpBB community support forums.

MODs and Styles

Here is a short list of resources that will help you with the customization of your board:

- `http://www.phpbb.com/phpBB/catdb.php?db=2`
  This is the place to download new templates and other graphics, like rank images, smilies, and other icons. As for the templates (also called 'styles'), you can see them in action so that you can decide which one to download. The demos for the templates are located at the following address: `http://www.phpbb.com/styles/demo.php`.
- `http://www.phpbb.com/mods/`
  This provides a list of available MODs for you to download. It also contains links to MODs-related documentation. The MODs listed at this address are created by enthusiasts outside the phpBB team, but are verified for security-related issues by the phpBB MOD team.
- `http://www.phpbbhacks.com`
  Probably the most popular place to look for MODs and styles, it has an active and friendly support community, as well as tutorials, tools, and more.

Programming

If you are coding your own MODs and templates or have decided to start doing it, then you'll find the following sites to be useful:

- `http://area51.phpbb.com/`
  This is the development area of the phpBB site. Here you can see screenshots of the future releases and read the guidelines to phpBB coding styles.
- `http://sourceforge.net/projects/phpbb/`
  This is the SourceForge homepage of the phpBB project. Like many other open-source projects, phpBB uses SourceForge's services for software project management, involving source files hosting, version control, and bug tracking.

- `http://cvs.sourceforge.net/viewcvs.py/phpbb/phpBB2/`
  This is a web interface to the phpBB CVS repository. **CVS (Concurrent Versioning System)** is the source control system adopted by the phpBB team. It allows you to download past versions of the software, see how the files changed over time, and download the bleeding-edge versions, which are under development. More information about what CVS is and how it works can be found at: `https://www.cvshome.org/`.
- `http://www.php.net`
  This is the homepage of the PHP programming language. You can download the PHP interpreter and read the installation documentation. If you're developing MODs, the PHP manual (`http://www.php.net/manual/`) should be of good help, especially with the user-contributed notes allowing other programmers to post their solutions to common programming problems.
- `http://www.mysql.com`
  This is the homepage of the MySQL database. The MySQL Reference Manual is located at: `http://dev.mysql.com/doc/mysql/`.
- `http://www.postgresql.org/`
  This is the home of the PostgreSQL database system, probably the second most popular database system used for phpBB.
- `http://www.phpbb.com/styles/listvars.php`
  This provides a comprehensive list of all template variables. The most interesting part of the list is the first part, general variables, as these are accessible on all the pages. They will be available as soon as you include the header include file, and you can use them in your custom scripts. For more details see Chapter 8.
- `http://www.phpbb.com/phpBB/viewtopic.php?t=135383`
  This provides a discussion of tweaks for large boards. The owner of the huge `go-gaia.com` board shares his optimization tweaks.

Other Sites of Interest

A few non-technical links concentrating more on the human side of building and managing an online community are:

- `http://www.big-boards.com/`
  This is a list of the largest boards on the Internet. It contains all kinds of boards: not only phpBB-powered ones. Note that the largest board on the Internet (`go-gaia.com`) is phpBB-powered!

- `http://www.theadminzone.com/`
  This provides the Admin Zone forums—discussion forums and resources for online community administrators.
- `http://www.webmasterworld.com/forum103/274.htm`
  This features an article listing best practices regarding phpBB security. In general, WebmasterWorld is a very good community site; you might find the section for community building especially interesting. It is accessible from: `http://www.webmasterworld.com/forum103/`.
- `http://www.sitepoint.com/article/james-atkinson-founder-phpbb`
  This features an interview with James "The Finn" Atkinson, the founder of phpBB. Sitepoint (`http://www.sitepoint.com/subcat/community-strategy`) is another great place to visit, read community-building articles, or hang out at the community-related section of the forums.

C

phpBB Code and Permission Cheatsheets

In this appendix you'll find both a quick reference for the BBCodes used while posting, and tables that describe the phpBB privileges system. You will find more information about the BBCodes in Chapter 3 and about the permissions in Chapter 5.

BBCode Cheatsheet

The available BB Code tags are divided into four categories based on their purpose—tags used for formatting, for creating lists, for quotes and code snippets, and finally for adding images and links.

Formatting

Code	Results and Comments
`This is [b]bold[/b]`	This is **bold**
`...and this is [i]italics [/i].`	...and this is *italics*.
`Now - [u]underline [/u].`	Now - underline.
`[u][i][b]Nesting...[/b][/i][/u]`	***Nesting...*** For nesting tags, close the last tag you opened first, and keep going in the reverse order until the first tag is closed.
`[color=darkred]Dark red color using color name[/color]`	Dark red color using color name
`[color=#000099]Blue, using HTML color code[/color]`	Blue, using HTML color code

Code	Results and Comments
`[size=1]Hardly visible text[/size]`	'1' is the smallest possible value for text size, which results in almost invisible text.
`[size=12]Normal text[/size]`	Normal text
`[size=29]The largest[/size]`	The largest '29' is the largest font size.

Lists

Code	Results and Comments

`[list]`
`[*]Apples`
`[*]Pears`
`[*]Bananas`
`[*]Oranges`
`[/list]`
	• Apples
	• Pears
	• Bananas
	• Oranges
	This is an example of an unordered list. Every item in the list starts with `[*]` and ends with a new line.

`[list=1]`
`[*]Apples`
`[*]Pears`
`[*]Bananas`
`[*]Oranges`
`[/list]`
	1. Apples
	2. Pears
	3. Bananas
	4. Oranges
	Ordered lists are created just like the unordered ones—by adding an `=1` parameter to the list tag. Lists always start from 1, so typing `=5` will not make the list start from 5, but will cause the entire list to be displayed as it is, exposing the BB tags.

`[list=a]`
`[*]Apples`
`[*]Pears`
`[*]Bananas`
`[*]Oranges`
`[/list]`
	a. Apples
	b. Pears
	c. Bananas
	d. Oranges
	Ordered lists can also use letters instead of numbers.

Code	Results and Comments
[list] [*]Apples [*]Pears [*]Bananas [*]Oranges [list=1][*]Apples [*]Pears [*]Bananas [*]Oranges [list=a][*]Apples [*]Pears [*]Bananas [*]Oranges [/list] [/list] [/list]	• Apples • Pears • Bananas • Oranges 1. Apples 2. Pears 3. Bananas 4. Oranges a. Apples b. Pears c. Bananas d. Oranges You can nest lists.

Quotes and Code Snippets

Code	Results and Comments
[quote]Just a quote[/quote]	**Quote:** Just a quote
[quote="The dude"]Quoting another user[/quote]	**The dude wrote:** Quoting another user
[quote=" http://mail.yahoo.com "]Free web mail[/quote]	**http://mail.yahoo.com wrote:** Free web mail This shows an undocumented behavior in the BBCode parser that allows you to quote a site and at the same time create a link to the site. Notice the spaces surrounding the URL.
[quote=" test@example.com "]I'm a test[/quote]	**test@example.com wrote:** I'm a test The same undocumented behavior in phpBB's BBCode parser allows the creation of an e-mail link.

<table>
<tr><th>Code</th><th>Results and Comments</th></tr>
<tr><td>[code]
  if (!$sleeping)
  {
    keepPosting();
  }
[/code]</td><td>Code:
  if (!$sleeping)
  {
    keepPosting();
  }
The code tag is designed to display code snippets, using a fixed-width font.</td></tr>
<tr><td>[code]

| Sad | Glad |

| Mad | Bad |

[/code]</td><td>Code:

| Sad | Glad |

| Mad | Bad |

The fixed-width font of the code tag allows posting of indented programming code, but can also be used for posting tabular data and ASCII art.</td></tr>
</table>

Inserting Images and Links

<table>
<tr><th>Code</th><th>Results and Comments</th></tr>
<tr><td>[img]http://www.packtpub.com/images/
Packt.png[/img]</td><td>[PACKT PUBLISHING]
The img tag allows you to include images in your posts, provided the image is available on the Internet and you know its URL.</td></tr>
<tr><td>http://www.packtpub.com/
www.packtpub.com</td><td>http://www.packtpub.com/
www.packtpub.com
phpBB will convert any string that looks like a URL into a link.</td></tr>
</table>

Code	Results and Comments
`[url]http://www.packtpub.com/[/url]`	http://www.packtpub.com/ When using `[url]` explicitly, the link is not underlined. It uses a CSS style (`postlink`) that the automatic link conversion does not.
`[url=http://www.packtpub.com/]Packt Book Store[/url]`	Packt Book Store This is the best way to add a link. The text of the link is different from the URL.

`[url=http://www.packtpub.com/]`
`[img]http://www.packtpub.com/images/Packt.png[/img]`
`[/url]`
	This is an example of creating a clickable, linked image.

Permissions Cheatsheet

Permissions are discussed a bit in Chapter 3 and then in detail in Chapter 5. The table that follows provides a quick reference to such permissions.

Permission Types

Permission type	Description
View	Users can see that a forum exists on the board's front page.
Read	Users can list forum topics, read the postings, and view the profiles and contact information of members.
Reply	Users can post their opinions about existing topics.
Post	Users can start new topics.
Edit	Users can edit their own postings.
Delete	Users can delete their own postings, as long as no one has replied to them.
Sticky	Users can start sticky topics.
Announce	Users can post announcements.
Vote	Users can vote in polls.
Poll create	Users can create polls for others to vote in.

Permission Levels

Permission level	Description
ALL	Everybody who accesses the board, including members currently not logged in.
REG	A registered member of the board who has logged in.
PRIVATE	A special permission level that is assigned individually. (Refer to Chapter 5.)
MOD	A moderator who can do everything to a forum.
ADMIN	A board administrator—someone who can access the Administration Panel.

Simple Mode Permissions

	Public	Registered	Registered [Hidden]	Private	Private [Hidden]	Moderators	Moderators [Hidden]
View	ALL	ALL	REG	ALL	PRIVATE	ALL	MOD
Read	ALL	ALL	REG	PRIVATE	PRIVATE	MOD	MOD
Post	ALL	REG	REG	PRIVATE	PRIVATE	MOD	MOD
Reply	ALL	REG	REG	PRIVATE	PRIVATE	MOD	MOD
Edit	REG	REG	REG	PRIVATE	PRIVATE	MOD	MOD
Delete	REG	REG	REG	PRIVATE	PRIVATE	MOD	MOD
Sticky	MOD	MOD	MOD	PRIVATE	PRIVATE	MOD	MOD
Announcement	MOD	MOD	MOD	MOD	MOD	MOD	MOD
Vote	REG	REG	REG	PRIVATE	PRIVATE	MOD	MOD
Poll create	REG	REG	REG	PRIVATE	PRIVATE	MOD	MOD

D

phpBB Database Structure

This appendix describes all the phpBB database tables, listed with their fields, relationships, and brief comments describing each table field. As you know phpBB database tables can have a prefix, specified by you when installing. In this appendix, the default phpbb_ prefix is used. This appendix was created with the help of phpMyAdmin (http://www.phpmyadmin.net).

phpbb_auth_access

This table defines group (and user) privileges.

Field	Type	Null	Default	Comments
group_id	mediumint(8)	No	0	Group ID from the groups table. Every user is part of a group, even if the user is the only member of the group. In this sense only group privileges are set in this table. **Links to: phpbb_groups -> group_id**
forum_id	smallint(5)	No	0	Forum ID from the forums table. **Links to: phpbb_forums -> forum_id**
auth_view	tinyint(1)	No	0	Is this group allowed to view the forum with the forum ID specified? "View" means see that this forum exists. Values are 0 for 'No' and 1 for 'Yes'. The same values are used for the rest of the fields.
auth_read	tinyint(1)	No	0	Is this group allowed to read the forum?
auth_post	tinyint(1)	No	0	Is the group allowed to create topics in the forum?

Field	Type	Null	Default	Comments
auth_reply	tinyint(1)	No	0	Is this group allowed to reply to existing topics?
auth_edit	tinyint(1)	No	0	Is this group allowed to edit own postings?
auth_delete	tinyint(1)	No	0	Is this group allowed to delete own postings?
auth_sticky	tinyint(1)	No	0	Is this group allowed to create sticky topics?
auth_announce	tinyint(1)	No	0	Is this group allowed to post announcements?
auth_vote	tinyint(1)	No	0	Is this group allowed to vote in existing polls?
auth_pollcreate	tinyint(1)	No	0	Is this group allowed to create new polls?
auth_attachments	tinyint(1)	No	0	Is this group allowed to attach files to postings (not used in the stock phpBB version).
auth_mod	tinyint(1)	No	0	Is this group allowed to moderate the forum?

phpbb_banlist

This table contains banned IP addresses, user IDs, or e-mail addresses.

Field	Type	Null	Default	Comments
ban_id	mediumint(8)	No	-	Autoincrement.
ban_userid	mediumint(8)	No	0	ID of the user to ban as defined in the users table. `Links to: phpbb_users -> user_id`
ban_ip	varchar(8)	No	-	Banned IP address (encrypted).
ban_email	varchar(255)	Yes	NULL	Banned e-mail address.

phpbb_categories

This table stores forum categories.

Field	Type	Null	Default	Comments
cat_id	mediumint(8)	No	-	Autoincrement.
cat_title	varchar(100)	Yes	NULL	Title of the category.

Field	Type	Null	Default	Comments
cat_order	mediumint(8)	No	0	Display order of the category.

phpbb_config

This table stores board configuration.

Field	Type	Null	Default	Comments
config_name	varchar(255)	No	-	Name of the configuration variable.
config_value	varchar(255)	No	-	Value of the configuration variable.

phpbb_confirm

Not used in this phpBB version.

Field	Type	Null	Default	Comments
confirm_id	char(32)	No	-	-
session_id	char(32)	No	-	-
code	char(6)	No	-	-

phpbb_disallow

Usernames defined in this table are not allowed when registering.

Field	Type	Null	Default	Comments
disallow_id	mediumint(8)	No		Autoincrement.
disallow_username	varchar(25)	No		String that is not allowed as a usernames.

phpbb_forum_prune

This table defines the rules for pruning forums.

Field	Type	Null	Default	Comments
prune_id	mediumint(8)	No		Autoincrement.

Field	Type	Null	Default	Comments
forum_id	smallint(5)	No	0	ID from the forums table. **Links to: phpbb_forums -> forum_id**
prune_days	smallint(5)	No	0	How old a topic should be in order to be deleted.
prune_freq	smallint(5)	No	0	How often phpBB should check for topics to delete. A value of 1 means "every day".

phpbb_forums

This table contains information about the forums.

Field	Type	Null	Default	Comments
forum_id	smallint(5)	No	0	Autoincrement.
cat_id	mediumint(8)	No	0	ID from the categories table. Category to which this forum belongs. **Links to: phpbb_categories -> cat_id**
forum_name	varchar(150)	Yes	NULL	Title of the forum.
forum_desc	text	Yes	NULL	Description of the forum.
forum_status	tinyint(4)	No	0	Status of the forum (0 is enabled, 1 means disabled).
forum_order	mediumint(8)	No	1	Display order relative to other forums in the same category.
forum_posts	mediumint(8)	No	0	Number of posts so far in this forum.
forum_topics	mediumint(8)	No	0	Total number of topics in this forum.
forum_last_post_id	mediumint(8)	No	0	ID of the last post from the posts table. **Links to: phpbb_posts -> post_id**
prune_next	int(11)	Yes	NULL	Date (Unix timestamp) for which the next forum pruning is scheduled.
prune_enable	tinyint(1)	No	0	Is pruning enabled for this forum?

Field	Type	Null	Default	Comments
auth_view	tinyint(2)	No	0	Permission level (who is) allowed to view. `0` is ALL, `1` is REG, `2` is PRIVATE, `3` is MOD. The same values apply for the rest of the columns in this table.
auth_read	tinyint(2)	No	0	Who can read the forum? See `auth_view` for the allowed values.
auth_post	tinyint(2)	No	0	Who can create topics in the forum? See `auth_view` for the allowed values.
auth_reply	tinyint(2)	No	0	Who can reply to the existing topics in the forum? See `auth_view` for the allowed values.
auth_edit	tinyint(2)	No	0	Who can edit postings in the forum? See `auth_view` for the allowed values.
auth_delete	tinyint(2)	No	0	Who can delete postings from the forum? See `auth_view` for the allowed values.
auth_sticky	tinyint(2)	No	0	Who can create sticky topics in the forum? See `auth_view` for the allowed values.
auth_announce	tinyint(2)	No	0	Who can create announcement topics in the forum? See `auth_view` for the allowed values.
auth_vote	tinyint(2)	No	0	Who can vote in polls in the forum? See `auth_view` for the allowed values.
auth_pollcreate	tinyint(2)	No	0	Who can create new polls in the forum? See `auth_view` for the allowed values.
auth_attachments	tinyint(2)	No	0	Who can attach files to the postings in the forum? Not used in this stock phpBB version.

phpbb_groups

This table contains usergroup information.

Field	Type	Null	Default	Comments
group_id	mediumint(8)	No	-	Autoincrement.
group_type	tinyint(4)	No	1	Group type. 0 is an open group, 1 is a closed group, and 2 is a hidden group.
group_name	varchar(40)	No	-	Name of the group.
group_description	varchar(255)	No	-	Group description.
group_moderator	mediumint(8)	No	0	ID of the moderator of the group. 0 for personal user groups. `Links to: phpbb_users -> user_id`
group_single_user	tinyint(1)	No	1	1 if this group is a single-user personal group, and 0 if it's a normal group with more members.

phpbb_posts

This table contains information about the postings.

Field	Type	Null	Default	Comments
post_id	mediumint(8)	No	-	Autoincrement.
topic_id	mediumint(8)	No	0	Topic ID from the topics table. `Links to: phpbb_topics -> topic_id`
forum_id	smallint(5)	No	0	Forum ID from the forums table. `Links to: phpbb_forums -> forum_id`
poster_id	mediumint(8)	No	0	User ID from the users table. `Links to: phpbb_users -> user_id`
post_time	int(11)	No	0	Time of the posting as a Unix timestamp.
poster_ip	varchar(8)	No	-	Encoded IP address of the user who posted.

Field	Type	Null	Default	Comments
post_username	varchar(25)	Yes	NULL	Username of the poster. Applies to anonymous posters only. The value is NULL if the poster was logged in. Also, when you delete a user, all his/her postings start showing as posted by anonymous and phpBB populates this field for all user postings at the time of the user deletion.
enable_bbcode	tinyint(1)	No	1	The option set by the poster to determine whether any BBcode should be processed and replaced as HTML.
enable_html	tinyint(1)	No	0	Same as above except for the enable/disable HTML option.
enable_smilies	tinyint(1)	No	1	Same as above, but related to whether the smilies should be parsed or be left as smilie codes only.
enable_sig	tinyint(1)	No	1	Whether the poster's signature should be appended to the posting.
post_edit_time	int(11)	Yes	NULL	The last time (Unix timestamp) that the posting was edited.
post_edit_count	smallint(5)	No	0	How many times this posting has been edited.

phpbb_posts_text

This table contains the actual texts of the postings.

Field	Type	Null	Default	Comments
post_id	mediumint(8)	No	0	Posting ID from the postings table. `Links to: phpbb_posts -> post_id`
bbcode_uid	varchar(10)	No	-	Identifier string used by the BBCode processor.
post_subject	varchar(60)	Yes	NULL	Subject of the posting.
post_text	text	Yes	NULL	The text of the posting.

phpbb_privmsgs

This table contains data about the private messages.

Field	Type	Null	Default	Comments
privmsgs_id	mediumint(8)	No	-	Autoincrement.
privmsgs_type	tinyint(4)	No	0	Type of the message. Integer value from 0 to 5, where 0 is read message, 1 is new message, 2 is sent message, 3 is saved, 4 is saved outgoing, and 5 is unread.
privmsgs_subject	varchar(255)	No	0	Subject of the message.
privmsgs_from_userid	mediumint(8)	No	0	User ID of the sender. `Links to: phpbb_users -> user_id`
privmsgs_to_userid	mediumint(8)	No	0	User ID of the recipient. `Links to: phpbb_users -> user_id`
privmsgs_date	int(11)	No	0	Unix timestamp when the message was sent.
privmsgs_ip	varchar(8)	No	-	Encoded IP address of the sender.
privmsgs_enable_bbcode	tinyint(1)	No	1	Did the sender enable BBCode for this message?
privmsgs_enable_html	tinyint(1)	No	0	Did the sender enable HTML code for this message?
privmsgs_enable_smilies	tinyint(1)	No	1	Did the sender enable smilies for this message?
privmsgs_attach_sig	tinyint(1)	No	1	Did the sender check the field to append his/her signature to the message?

phpbb_privmsgs_text

This table contains the texts of the private messages.

Field	Type	Null	Default	Comments
privmsgs_text_id	mediumint(8)	No	0	ID from the private messages table. `Links to: phpbb_privmsgs -> privmsgs_id`
privmsgs_bbcode_uid	varchar(10)	No	0	Identifier string required by the BBCode parser.
privmsgs_text	text	Yes	NULL	Text of the private message.

phpbb_ranks

This table contains definitions of the user ranks.

Field	Type	Null	Default	Comments
rank_id	smallint(5)	No	-	Autoincrement.
rank_title	varchar(50)	No	-	Title for the rank.
rank_min	mediumint(8)	No	0	Minimum number of postings required by the rank.
rank_special	tinyint(1)	Yes	0	1 for special ranks, 0 otherwise.
rank_image	varchar(255)	Yes	NULL	Rank image filename and path, relative to the where phpBB is installed.

phpbb_search_results

This table contains search results data.

Field	Type	Null	Default	Comments
search_id	int(11)	No	0	Search identifier.
session_id	varchar(32)	No	-	Session identifier from the sessions table. `Links to: phpbb_sessions -> session_id`
search_array	text	No	-	Serialized array of search results data.

phpbb_search_wordlist

This table contains the words used in the forums.

Field	Type	Null	Default	Comments
word_text	varchar(50)	No	-	The actual word.
word_id	mediumint(8)	No	-	Autoincrement.
word_common	tinyint(1)	No	0	1 for common words, 0 otherwise.

phpbb_search_wordmatch

This table stores information about where a word is used.

Field	Type	Null	Default	Comments
post_id	mediumint(8)	No	0	Posting ID from the postings table. **Links to: phpbb_posts -> post_id**
word_id	mediumint(8)	No	0	Word ID from the search wordlist table. **Links to: phpbb_search_wordslist -> word_id**
title_match	tinyint(1)	No	0	1 if the word is found in the title of the posting, 0 otherwise.

phpbb_sessions

This table stores data about the current sessions.

Field	Type	Null	Default	Comments
session_id	char(32)	No	-	Unique session ID.
session_user_id	mediumint(8)	No	0	User ID from the users table, or `-1` if the session belongs to a non-logged user. **Links to: phpbb_users -> user_id**
session_start	int(11)	No	0	Unix timestamp of the session's start.
session_time	int(11)	No	0	Unix timestamp of the last page hit.
session_ip	char(8)	No	0	Encoded IP address of the user.
session_page	int(11)	No	0	Identifier of the page that the user is currently viewing. Pages are defined with minus sign as constants in the `includes/constants.php` file. Pages with non-negative integer values are actually forum IDs.

Field	Type	Null	Default	Comments
session_logged_in	tinyint(1)	No	0	1 if the session belongs to a logged in user, 0 otherwise.

phpbb_smilies

Smilies repository.

Field	Type	Null	Default	Comments
smilies_id	smallint(5)	No	-	Autoincrement.
code	varchar(50)	Yes	NULL	Smilie code (like ":)").
smile_url	varchar(100)	Yes	NULL	Filename of the smilie image.
emoticon	varchar(75)	Yes	NULL	What type of emotion the smilie represents, e.g. Happy, Grumpy, etc.

phpbb_themes

This table contains theme settings.

Field	Type	Null	Default	Comments
themes_id	mediumint(8)	No	-	Autoincrement.
template_name	varchar(30)	No	-	Name of the template.
style_name	varchar(30)	No	-	Name of the style.
head_stylesheet	varchar(100)	Yes	NULL	Filename of the stylesheet (the `.css`).
body_background	varchar(100)	Yes	NULL	Filename of any image used as a page background.
body_bgcolor	varchar(6)	Yes	NULL	Hexadecimal (Hex) color code of the page background, for example '`ff00ff`'. Note that there is no sharp sign (#) before the color code.
body_text	varchar(6)	Yes	NULL	Hex code of the color used for texts on the page.
body_link	varchar(6)	Yes	NULL	Color of the links.
body_vlink	varchar(6)	Yes	NULL	Color of the visited links.

Field	Type	Null	Default	Comments
body_alink	varchar(6)	Yes	NULL	Color of the active links.
body_hlink	varchar(6)	Yes	NULL	Color of the hover links (when the mouse is over a link).
tr_color1	varchar(6)	Yes	NULL	The description of these fields is in the `phpbb_themes_name` table.
tr_color2	varchar(6)	Yes	NULL	
tr_color3	varchar(6)	Yes	NULL	
tr_class1	varchar(25)	Yes	NULL	
tr_class2	varchar(25)	Yes	NULL	
tr_class3	varchar(25)	Yes	NULL	
th_color1	varchar(6)	Yes	NULL	
th_color2	varchar(6)	Yes	NULL	
th_color3	varchar(6)	Yes	NULL	
th_class1	varchar(25)	Yes	NULL	
th_class2	varchar(25)	Yes	NULL	
th_class3	varchar(25)	Yes	NULL	
td_color1	varchar(6)	Yes	NULL	
td_color2	varchar(6)	Yes	NULL	
td_color3	varchar(6)	Yes	NULL	
td_class1	varchar(25)	Yes	NULL	
td_class2	varchar(25)	Yes	NULL	
td_class3	varchar(25)	Yes	NULL	
fontface1	varchar(50)	Yes	NULL	
fontface2	varchar(50)	Yes	NULL	
fontface3	varchar(50)	Yes	NULL	
fontsize1	tinyint(4)	Yes	NULL	
fontsize2	tinyint(4)	Yes	NULL	
fontsize3	tinyint(4)	Yes	NULL	

Field	Type	Null	Default	Comments
fontcolor1	varchar(6)	Yes	NULL	The description of these fields is in the `phpbb_themes_name` table.
fontcolor2	varchar(6)	Yes	NULL	
fontcolor3	varchar(6)	Yes	NULL	
span_class1	varchar(25)	Yes	NULL	
span_class2	varchar(25)	Yes	NULL	
span_class3	varchar(25)	Yes	NULL	
img_size_poll	smallint(5)	Yes	NULL	Not used.
img_size_privmsg	smallint(5)	Yes	NULL	Not used.

phpbb_themes_name

Names of the elements that are set up in the themes table.

Field	Type	Null	Default	Comments
themes_id	smallint(5)	No	0	-
tr_color1_name	char(50)	Yes	NULL	-
tr_color2_name	char(50)	Yes	NULL	-
tr_color3_name	char(50)	Yes	NULL	-
tr_class1_name	char(50)	Yes	NULL	-
tr_class2_name	char(50)	Yes	NULL	-
tr_class3_name	char(50)	Yes	NULL	-
th_color1_name	char(50)	Yes	NULL	-
th_color2_name	char(50)	Yes	NULL	-
th_color3_name	char(50)	Yes	NULL	-
th_class1_name	char(50)	Yes	NULL	-
th_class2_name	char(50)	Yes	NULL	-
th_class3_name	char(50)	Yes	NULL	-
td_color1_name	char(50)	Yes	NULL	-

Field	Type	Null	Default	Comments
td_color2_name	char(50)	Yes	NULL	-
td_color3_name	char(50)	Yes	NULL	-
td_class1_name	char(50)	Yes	NULL	-
td_class2_name	char(50)	Yes	NULL	-
td_class3_name	char(50)	Yes	NULL	-
fontface1_name	char(50)	Yes	NULL	-
fontface2_name	char(50)	Yes	NULL	-
fontface3_name	char(50)	Yes	NULL	-
fontsize1_name	char(50)	Yes	NULL	-
fontsize2_name	char(50)	Yes	NULL	-
fontsize3_name	char(50)	Yes	NULL	-
fontcolor1_name	char(50)	Yes	NULL	-
fontcolor2_name	char(50)	Yes	NULL	-
fontcolor3_name	char(50)	Yes	NULL	-
span_class1_name	char(50)	Yes	NULL	-
span_class2_name	char(50)	Yes	NULL	-
span_class3_name	char(50)	Yes	NULL	-

phpbb_topics

This table contains data about the topics.

Field	Type	Null	Default	Comments
topic_id	mediumint(8)	No	-	Autoincrement.
forum_id	smallint(8)	No	0	Forum ID from the forums table. `Links to: phpbb_forums -> forum_id`
topic_title	char(60)	No	-	Title of the topic.
topic_poster	mediumint(8)	No	0	ID of the user who started the topic. `Links to: phpbb_users -> user_id`

Field	Type	Null	Default	Comments
topic_time	int(11)	No	0	Unix timestamp when the topic was started.
topic_views	mediumint(8)	No	0	How many times the topic was viewed.
topic_replies	mediumint(8)	No	0	How many replies there are in the topic.
topic_status	tinyint(3)	No	0	Status of the topic. 0 is normal, 1 is locked, and 2 is moved.
topic_vote	tinyint(1)	No	0	1 if there is a poll attached to the topic, 0 otherwise.
topic_type	tinyint(3)	No	0	0 is a normal topic, 1 is a sticky one, 2 is an announcement.
topic_first_post_id	mediumint(8)	No	0	ID of the first posting in this topic. `Links to: phpbb_posts -> post_id`
topic_last_post_id	mediumint(8)	No	0	ID of the last posting in this topic. `Links to: phpbb_posts -> post_id`
topic_moved_id	mediumint(8)	No	0	If this is a service topic just to remain as a placeholder in the forum where the topic was moved from, then this field contains the ID of the moved topic. `Links to: phpbb_topics -> topic_id`

phpbb_topics_watch

This table contains a list of users watching specific topics. "Watching" means that the users have requested to be notified when a reply is posted to the watched topic.

Field	Type	Null	Default	Comments
topic_id	mediumint(8)	No	0	ID of the topic being watched (as defined in the topics table). `Links to: phpbb_topics -> topic_id`
user_id	mediumint(8)	No	0	User ID from the users table, the watcher. `Links to: phpbb_users -> user_id`
notify_status	tinyint(1)	No	0	1 if the user was notified, 0 otherwise.

phpbb_user_group

Switchboard table containing the groups and the group users.

Field	Type	Null	Default	Comments
group_id	mediumint(8)	No	0	ID of the group from the groups table. `Links to: phpbb_groups -> group_id`
user_id	mediumint(8)	No	0	ID of the user from the users table. `Links to: phpbb_users -> user_id`
user_pending	tinyint(1)	Yes	NULL	1 if the user is pending, 0 otherwise.

phpbb_users

Users repository.

Field	Type	Null	Default	Comments
user_id	mediumint(8)	No	0	Autoincrement.
user_active	tinyint(1)	Yes	1	Is the user active? 1 is yes, 0 is no.
username	varchar(25)	No	-	Username.
user_password	varchar(32)	No		Password.
user_session_time	int(11)	No	0	Unix timestamp of the last page hit by the user.
user_session_page	smallint(5)	No	0	The last page this user has viewed.
user_lastvisit	int(11)	No	0	Last login timestamp.
user_regdate	int(11)	No	0	Unix timestamp of the registration date.
user_level	tinyint(4)	Yes	0	0 is a regular user, 1 is an administrator, and 2 is a moderator.
user_posts	mediumint(8)	No	0	Total number of posts by this user.
user_timezone	decimal(5,2)	No	0.00	Time zone of the user.
user_style	tinyint(4)	Yes	NULL	Selected style ID from the themes table. `Links to: phpbb_themes -> themes_id`

Field	Type	Null	Default	Comments
user_lang	varchar(255)	Yes	NULL	User's selected language.
user_dateformat	varchar(14)	No	d M Y H:i	Format for all the dates displayed on the board.
user_new_privmsg	smallint(5)	No	0	Total number of new private messages.
user_unread_privmsg	smallint(5)	No	0	Total number of unread private messages.
user_last_privmsg	int(11)	No	0	Unix timestamp when the most recent private message was received.
user_emailtime	int(11)	Yes	NULL	Unix timestamp, the last time an e-mail was sent to the user, using the phpBB e-mail feature.
user_viewemail	tinyint(1)	Yes	NULL	1 if this user has decided to make the e-mail public, 0 otherwise.
user_attachsig	tinyint(1)	Yes	NULL	1 if the user's signature is to be attached by default, 0 otherwise.
user_allowhtml	tinyint(1)	Yes	1	1 if the user has decided to have HTML enabled in postings by default, 0 otherwise.
user_allowbbcode	tinyint(1)	Yes	1	1 if the user has decided to have BBCode enabled in postings by default, 0 otherwise.
user_allowsmile	tinyint(1)	Yes	1	1 if the user has decided to have smilies enabled in postings by default, 0 otherwise.
user_allowavatar	tinyint(1)	No	1	1 if this user is allowed to have an avatar.
user_allow_pm	tinyint(1)	No	1	1 if this user is allowed to use the private-messaging system.
user_allow_viewonline	tinyint(1)	No	1	1 if the user agrees to make his/her status (online/offline) public.

Field	Type	Null	Default	Comments
user_notify	tinyint(1)	No	1	1 if the user has selected to be notified by e-mail on replies, 0 otherwise.
user_notify_pm	tinyint(1)	No	0	1 if the user has selected to be notified by e-mail on any new private messages, 0 otherwise.
user_popup_pm	tinyint(1)	No	0	1 if a new pop-up window should inform the user of a new private message, 0 otherwise.
user_rank	int(11)	Yes	0	ID of the rank assigned to the user. **Links to: phpbb_ranks -> rank_id**
user_avatar	varchar(100)	Yes	NULL	User's avatar. URL or server path and filename of the user's avatar image.
user_avatar_type	tinyint(4)	No	0	Avatar type. 0 for none, 1 for uploaded, 2 for remote, and 3 for gallery.
user_email	varchar(255)	Yes	NULL	E-mail address of the user.
user_icq	varchar(15)	Yes	NULL	ICQ number of the user.
user_website	varchar(100)	Yes	NULL	URL of the user's website.
user_from	varchar(100)	Yes	NULL	User's location.
user_sig	text	Yes	NULL	User's signature.
user_sig_bbcode_uid	varchar(10)	Yes	NULL	BBCode identifier for the signature.
user_aim	varchar(255)	Yes	NULL	User's AOL messenger ID.
user_yim	varchar(255)	Yes	NULL	User's Yahoo! messenger ID.
user_msnm	varchar(255)	Yes	NULL	User's MSN messenger ID.
user_occ	varchar(100)	Yes	NULL	User's occupation.
user_interests	varchar(255)	Yes	NULL	User's interests.
user_actkey	varchar(32)	Yes	NULL	Activation key.
user_newpasswd	varchar(32)	Yes	NULL	New temporary password.

phpbb_vote_desc

This table contains polls-related data.

Field	Type	Null	Default	Comments
vote_id	mediumint(8)	No	-	Autoincrement.
topic_id	mediumint(8)	No	0	Topic ID from the topics table. **`Links to: phpbb_topics -> topic_id`**
vote_text	text	No		Poll question.
vote_start	int(11)	No	0	Unix timestamp when the poll was started.
vote_length	int(11)	No	0	Time (in milliseconds) this poll is to be active.

phpbb_vote_results

Poll option answers and vote results.

Field	Type	Null	Default	Comments
vote_id	mediumint(8)	No	0	Vote ID from the `vote_desc` table. **`Links to: phpbb_vote_desc -> vote_id`**
vote_option_id	tinyint(4)	No	0	Consecutive number of the possible answer to the poll.
vote_option_text	varchar(255)	No	-	Poll answer text.
vote_result	int(11)	No	0	Number of votes for this poll answer.

phpbb_vote_voters

Data about who has voted in which poll.

Field	Type	Null	Default	Comments
vote_id	mediumint(8)	No	0	Poll ID from the `vote_desc` table. **`Links to: phpbb_vote_desc -> vote_id`**
vote_user_id	mediumint(8)	No	0	User ID from the users table. **`Links to: phpbb_users -> user_id`**
vote_user_ip	char(8)	No	-	Encoded IP address of the voter at the time of the vote.

phpbb_words

List of censored words.

Field	Type	Null	Default	Comments
word_id	mediumint(8)	No	-	Autoincrement.
word	char(100)	No	-	Naughty word.
replacement	char(100)	No	-	Replacement word.

Index

A

B

C

D

E

F

G

H

I

R

S

T

U

V

W

Thank you for buying Building Online Communities with phpBB 2

Packt Open Source Project Royalties

When we sell a book written on an Open Source project, we pay a royalty directly to that project. Therefore by purchasing *Building Online Communities with phpBB 2*, Packt will have given some of the money received to the phpBB project.

In the long term, we see ourselves and you—customers and readers of our books—as part of the Open Source ecosystem, providing sustainable revenue for the projects we publish on. Our aim at Packt is to establish publishing royalties as an essential part of the service and support a business model that sustains Open Source.

If you're working with an Open Source project that you would like us to publish on, and subsequently pay royalties to, please get in touch with us.

Writing for Packt

We welcome all inquiries from people who are interested in authoring. Book proposals should be sent to `authors@packtpub.com`. If your book idea is still at an early stage and you would like to discuss it first before writing a formal book proposal, contact us: one of our commissioning editors will get in touch with you.

> **NOTE** We're not just looking for published authors; if you have strong technical skills but no writing experience, our experienced editors can help you develop a writing career, or simply get some additional reward for your expertise.

About Packt Publishing

Packt, pronounced 'packed,' published its first book, *Mastering phpMyAdmin for Effective MySQL Management*, in April 2004 and subsequently continued to specialize in publishing highly focused books on specific technologies and solutions.

Our books and publications share the experiences of your fellow IT professionals in adapting and customizing today's systems, applications, and frameworks. Our solution-based books give you the knowledge and power to customize the software and technologies you're using to get the job done. Packt books are more specific and less general than the IT books you have seen in the past. Our unique business model allows us to bring you more focused information, giving you more of what you need to know, and less of what you don't.

Packt is a modern, yet unique publishing company, which focuses on producing quality, cutting-edge books for communities of developers, administrators, and newbies alike. For more information, please visit our website: `www.PacktPub.com`.

Printed in the United Kingdom
by Lightning Source UK Ltd.
104541UKS00002B/179-206

9 781904 811138